To Shaylene.
    on her 14th
  birthday
With Love & Prayers
  your Friend & Sister
In Christ
      Helen D Howe.

1988.

SEVENTY-FIVE YEARS ALONG THE RED DEER RIVER

EDITED BY HELEN D. HOWE

Standard Book No. 0-919212-07-7

ACKNOWLEDGEMENT

With sincere appreciation I wish to acknowledge the magazines and periodicals from which I obtained useful information: Cattleman's Magazine; Farm and Ranch Review; Star Weekly and the Brooks Bulletin.

The Alberta Wheat Board, Calgary, Alberta; The Post Office Department Edmonton, Alberta; Special Areas of the Municipal District, Hanna, Alberta for maps and to the Water Resources Division, Province of Alberta.

To Kathyrn Krause for her Art work; Robin Krause for Publicity and Promotions; Bryon Callaghan on Public Relations; James L. Nesbitt, Editor of the Brooks Bulletin for moral support, encouragement and advertising.

Last but not least to John R. Gordon for his generous contribution of material and to all those who assisted in any way.

First Printing 1971
Second Printing 1977

Printed By
Friesen Printers
Calgary, Alberta
Head Office, Altona, Manitoba

ii

FOREWORD

It is unusual, to say the least, for an easterner to be writing a localized history of the Canadian West, particularly a comparative newcomer — but that's the way it is.

Helen D. Howe is a native of New Brunswick and proud of it but her "adopted land" of the prairie west is her true love.

The broad rolling prairie country with the cuts and valleys sloping into the muddy Red Deer River — the broad expanse of azure blue sky — the multi-colored sunsets splashed across western sky — the rolling thunderheads and winds of cyclonic proportions — the abandoned homesteads, grey and colorless as its memories ebb into nothingness — the lively branding bees and get-togethers afterwards — the dull grey winter's day with biting winds edging knife-like through to the bone — the comforting lowing of beef cattle as they bed down for the night — the jostling, dusty, gravel-throwing journey to the nearest paved highway — the community picnics and parties and the quiet gatherings at the local church — the christenings, birthdays and deaths that make their marks on members of the community — these, yes, these are things that concern Helen Howe and about which she must write.

Perhaps more than anything, however, Helen Howe is interested in the pioneer days of the prairie west, particularly while there still are a handful of men and women who took part in the early settlement and many whom she knows. There is a certain amount of glamour to these pioneers but more than that there is revealed in them the sense of accomplishment, the stoicness under adversity when they were subjected to the whims and vagaries of both weather and market, and the fact they "stuck to it" to bring a raw country under the cloak of social progress. These people and what they represent are the sparks that ignite the fervor and interest of Helen Howe.

An open-handed and open-hearted person, Mrs. Howe is a friendly conversationalist with quick perception and ready wit. Things must be spelled out for her, however, because she recognizes only colors of black and white — no greys. Perhaps this could be attributed to her having eight brothers and two sisters where co-operation and competition are meaningful things.

Some people believe she has a stubborn streak but we call it tenacity of purpose and we refer to her single-minded objective in writing this history in the face of discouragement and laissez-faire attitude from several people. This also was reflected in her first marriage when she raised five children, took in boarders and made it on her own. This was when she spent some 17 years in Ontario which involved an unusual occupation for a woman, particularly at that time, in selling automobiles.

In the late 1950's Mrs. Howe came west to Calgary and the country captured her heart; she felt this was where she belonged. Still determined to better her lot in life she enrolled on an eighteen-month course at the Henderson Business College, where after only six months she emerged with a diploma in her hand and went forth into another field of the business world, that of a Steno bookkeeper. In 1964, she met and married rancher Chester C. Howe of Buffalo, so pulling up city roots she came to live in the shortgrass country, 200 miles east of Calgary, along the Red Deer. She was simply fascinated!

In the course of time she submitted a weekly news budget to The Brooks Bulletin, the community newspaper serving the area as a weekly, and her first column was published June 23, 1966. We cannot speak warmly enough of the conscientious part she has played in recording the news and happenings in her home area. This small newspaper has twenty-two correspondents and Mrs. Howe easily ranks among the top. She's painstaking and sensitive when it comes to writing and thus we are confident that "Seventy-five Years Along the Red Deer River" will contain the type of interesting material for which she has become well known through The Bulletin.

Earlier in her ranch life Helen Howe learned from Chester (to her dismay) that she had unwittingly set out eggs under broody chickens that were unfertilized. You don't have to tell Helen anything more than once! She readily adapted to ranch routine and the life in the prairie country is where she finds fulfillment. Where else could one find a mother of five, grandmother of ten, with meals to prepare, help to supervise, brandings to assist at, a garden to raise plus the general housework and community activities — and still write a book! As a friend she has our respect and admiration; as a budding author she has our confidence. We too are ready to tread the path back through the years in "Seventy-five Years Along the Red Deer River."

James L. Nesbitt,
Editor, The Brooks Bulletin,
July 1, 1971

EDITOR'S NOTE

Shortly after coming to this district in 1964, I stood on a hill overlooking the valley of the Red Deer River and gazed at the surrounding country of short prairie grass, cactus and Russian Thistle, dotted here and there with rocks of every shape and size; and with gophers of uncalculated number running about. I could also see the impression of a well-beaten path, grassed over with time, leading directly to the river where years ago the large herds of buffalo went to drink. Close by, rocks formed circles, indicating the spot where Indians had camped while they hunted these animals which roamed the prairies in large numbers and grazed as peacefully as the herds of Hereford cattle do today. While I stood there I had a burning desire to turn back the hands of time and share the joys, excitement and the hardships of our early pioneering settlers. I was particularly interested in the lives of those who came to the Red Deer River settlement, now known as Buffalo. This feeling stayed with me and in 1967, Canada's Centennial Year, I attempted to record a history of Buffalo and its people, but due to lack of interest and co-operation on the part of some of the present generation, and realizing that history must have dates, name and actual facts, which I knew would be impossible to obtain under the circumstances I tried to become immune to my feelings, but as the years passed and my love for this country increased, as did the encouragement of some of the former residents, I felt I would have no peace until I finished what I wanted to do. So once again I took up the challenge.

This being the seventy-fifth year since the first white man established a ranch on the Red Deer in this particular district, I thought it only fitting and appropriate that some record be written. This I have endeavored to do, realizing full well that not everyone is represented in this book, but thankful to those that have submitted stories, pictures, documents and other interesting material to make up the pages of this book.

It is hoped that all who read this book will find it not only interesting, but will be filled with respect for our early settlers who braved the elements of this rugged country, giving up the comforts of the homes they left to endure hardships in a land where it is not uncommon for the temperature to drop to sixty below in winter and soar to a high of over a hundred in summer; where blizzards can rage for days at a time; where weeks can pass without rain and where prairie fires can spread for miles destroying the grazing and farming land so necessary for their very existence.

But come they did! From every State in the Union and from every province in the Dominion, as well as from many of the countries across the seas, each bringing with them the customs and traditions of their native land, which over the years have been blended together to make this part of the country the unique district as we know it today. Living side by side as they did with their neighbor, each speaking his own language, they still were able to communicate and work together in harmony.

Now I don't presume to lead you to believe that these people never had any disagreement with each other, but I would compare them with the Irish family, which my grandfather a typical Irishman, used to tell this story about. It seems one day a very aggressive tax collector called at the home of a financially-embarrassed family. The family consisted of mostly boys, all big men, standing about six-foot and weighing anywhere from 190 to 225 pounds and when the tax collector arrived they were "going right to it" in the yard; fists were flying; eyes were turning black and blue and lips were cut and bleeding. He watched horrified, then asked the father why he allowed the boys to fight in such a manner, "Doesn't that cause hard feelings amongst them?", he asked. "Oh no," said the father, "just keeps them in trim and ready to handle any outsider should they try to interfere." Grandfather said the tax collector soon lost some of his aggressiveness and was very polite when he reminded the Irishman that his taxes were overdue. So it is in this community when the chips are down, or any misfortune overtakes one family, all petty grievances are forgotten and everyone joins forces to aid in any way they can.

TABLE OF CONTENTS

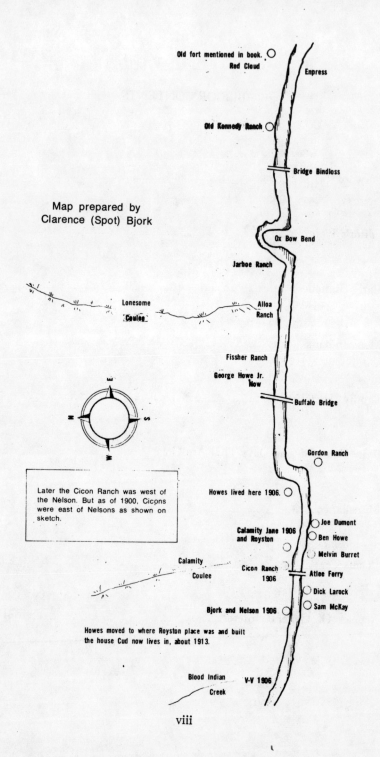

Map prepared by
Clarence (Spot) Bjork

Old fort mentioned in book. ○
Red Cloud

Enpress

Old Kennedy Ranch ○

Bridge Bindloss

Ox Bow Bend

Jarboe Ranch

Lonesome
Coulee

Alloa
Ranch

Fissher Ranch

George Howe Jr.
Now

Buffalo Bridge

Gordon Ranch
○

Later the Cicon Ranch was west of
the Nelson. But as of 1900, Cicons
were east of Nelsons as shown on
sketch.

Howes lived here 1906. ○

Joe Dumont ○

Calamity Jane 1906
and Royston

Ben Howe ○

Melvin Burret ○

Calamity

Coulee

Cicon Ranch
1906

Atlee Ferry

Dick Larock ○

Bjork and Nelson 1906 ○

Sam McKay ○

Howes moved to where Royston place was and built
the house Cud now lives in, about 1913.

Blood Indian

Creek

V-V 1906

viii

EARLY RANCHES

The first ranch on the Red Deer River, in this district, was located by two cousins, Andrew and Alex Gordon in 1896. This ranch was the largest in the district, for several years and in 1905 carried 12,000 head of cattle. Tom Mossop was foreman for about 20 years, Allen Robinson was wagon boss, other men who worked or were closely associated with the Gordon ranch included such names as Bill Jenkins, Billy Henry, Percy Stimson, Jeff Barber, Bill Hunt and Bill Rae. While Tom Mossop worked for Andy Gordon he built a blacksmith shop of logs, which is still standing and the method he used to dovetail the logs is a work of art.

Lincoln and Bob Howe also worked on the Gordon ranch. These boys came to this district in 1906 with their parents and five other brothers, Cud, Ben, Alfred (Kid), Charlie and Grant. Their father, George Howe, was a horse rancher and moved here from Fort Macleod. Farther west ranches owned by Fred Nelson and Magnus Bjork were established the same year. At the mouth of the Blood Indian Creek the V Bar V was originally built by Len Sparrow and purchased by J. R. Hallam, in 1905. Mr. Hallam came to this country with the Northwest Mounted Police, who had a detachment where the Blood Indian Creek empties in the Red Deer. After Mr. Hallam resigned he took up ranching right there. He build a dam on the Blood Indian to irrigate the river flats. This is now the headquarters of the V Bar V, which continued to grow over the years and now controls close to three townships. Tom Owen had a ranch near this place in the early days, he kept cattle and sheep as well as horses, this later became part of the V Bar V. W. H. McKay helped build the first shack, barn and cattle shed for Mr. Owens in 1900, while he, McKay was working for the P. K. Ranch. A log building built while Mr. Hallam was there is still standing but the old ranch house was burned down some years ago.

The Quail Ranch was located by William Rae before 1900, was acquired by John Quail and afterwards owned by M. J. Stapleton where he resided until his death in 1936.

The Mexico Ranch U Bar C, was owned by Lord Delaval J. Beresford and established by him about 1900, after he moved his entire outfit from Old Mexico, (he brought the first Mexican cattle to the Red Deer River) along the Chisholm Trail which ran through Texas, Oklahoma, north to Montana and into Alberta and it took two years to make the trip with a herd of steers. Lord Delaval was a brother to the late Lord Charles Beresford of the British Admiralty. He was killed in a train wreck in North Dakota in the winter of 1906. His original range boss was a Mr. Jackson (Happy

1

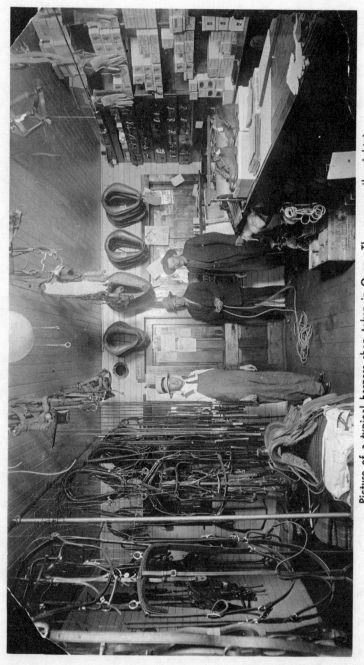

Picture of a typical harness shop taken in Oyen. The man on the right is Judson, centre Howard McCullough, the man on the left it is not certain, although it may be Tom Lees the owner of an early era harness shop.

Jack) who lived a very colorful life and died in the early sixties, near Wardlow.

The P. K. (Prince & Kerr) Ranch was located about 1896 at the mouth of the Berry Creek and was operated by John and Chester Eide. During the cold, hard winter of 1906 and '07 an estimated loss of 2,000 head of stock was suffered by this ranch. There was two feet of snow on the level and cattle which normally would be grazing on the winter lease had to be fed and the rancher found that seven hundred tons of hay wasn't enough to feed them from the 14th of November to the last of April.

Other ranches south from the Red Deer River include those established by Kerr & Finlay, Harold and Matthew Keay and the Orangevill previously owned by Alex Gordon and later owned by Joe Hewitt.

Before 1905 most of the cattle in their district were shipped from Medicine Hat and Suffield where stockyards were available and where the local Brand Inspector J. H. G. Bray would inspect the brands. Between 1900 and 1905 thousands of Mexican longhorn cattle were brought into Alberta and with each herd one or two or perhaps more southern cowboys would arrive. Such names as Jim Spratt, Jim McGarry, Hank Smith, Nate Schofield, George Bell, Dick Laswell, Jeff Barber (who later worked for the Gordon outfit) Billy Kendall and many others, most of whom have long since departed.

At this time most of the beef from these ranches was sold for export the demand being for heavy steers, four and five years old. Most of the fat cows were purchased for home consumption by local butchers, P. Burns & Co., Calgary or for shipment to Winnipeg, Toronto or Montreal. The Gordon, Ironside & Fares Company was the principal exporter, most the buying being done by Mr. H. W. Fares. The roundup wagons during this period were maneuvering everywhere. The buckboard or democrat usually preceded the roundup and such people as George Lane, George Emerson, Jim Pierce and Howell Harris were often in the district.

Alex Gordon was a cousin of Andrew Gordon, and it was Alex Gordon who was associated with the Ironside and Fares Company.

In 1897 the Shannons located on the Red Deer River and at the same time a young Frenchman by the name of Hector Prince located very close to where Bindloss stands today. In August of 1899 he was helping Fergus Kennedy cross the river with his cattle when he was drowned.

Fergus Kennedy came from Ontario in 1899, and located on the north side of the Red Deer River, Clint Jarboe also located in that neighborhood soon after. A few of the ranchers that located

3

west of the Gordon ranch, near Majestic, were Fred Nelson, (uncle to Magnus Bjork 2nd) Magnus Bjork 1st located about seven miles above the Gordon ranch on the north side of the river in 1906. A horse rancher named George Howe located a couple miles east of Bjorks, also on the north side. He had seven fine sons.

AN INDIAN PRAYER TO THE GREAT SPIRIT

O, Great Spirit, whose voice I hear in the wind,
And whose breath gives life to all the world — hear me.
I am a man before You, one of Your many children.
I am small and weak, I need Your strength and wisdom.
Let me walk in beauty, and let my eyes ever behold
The red and purple sunsets.
Make my hands respect the things You have made,
My ears sharp to hear Your voice.
Make me wise so that I may know
The things You have taught my people.
The lessons You have hidden in every leaf and rock.
I seek strength, O, my Creator not to be superior to my brothers,
But to be able to fight my greatest enemy — myself.
Make me ever ready to come to You, with clean hands and straight
    eye,
So when life fades as the setting sunset,
My spirit may come to You without shame.

METIS INDIANS

Having mentioned most of the ranches operating at this time and having recorded the names of a few of those employed, I cannot pass without recording the names of some of the earlier Metis families, who were so closely linked with the very life of the ranches. There were the Tanners, La Ronde, Cayen, Boyer, Dumont, Ward Cunningham, Lawrence, Munro, Quesnelle, Hanson, La Fromboise, La Roche and the MacKays, (pronounced Mac Eye) especially Neill, Colin and William Henry, all of whom are very well known to the present generation. Colin and Neill still live in Brooks, while Wm. Henry MacKay passed away in November 1967. These boys were the sons of Samuel MacKay and Catherine La Fromboise. William Henry was born December 4th, 1882 in Medicine Hat and was the first child to be born there after the railroad and townsite were surveyed. It might be interesting to note that Sam MacKay's oldest sister, Maria married Sergeant Major J. H. G. Bray of the original Northwest Mounted Police and was later a Brand Inspector at Medicine Hat and Suffield. Many readers will remember some of the articles written by Wm. Henry MacKay and published in the Cattleman Magazine in the late forties and early fifties.

4

In June 1888, W. H. MacKay's father and a man named Alex Gardipie hunted buffalo north of the Red Deer River, they saw a small herd of eleven head a few miles south of Cereal. Mr. MacKay killed two bull buffalo.

Metis is a French word derived from the Latin, miscere — to mix. The name was given to the offsprings of the white fur traders and the native women of Canada — it was natural for these men, living among the Indians and far from their own traditional society, to unite with the Indian women. The Metis developed as a separate culture. They were proud of their mixed blood, and being remote from white settlements for more than a century, they evolved an independent way of life that was neither Indian nor European. Physically they combined the best characteristics of these two races. According to Southesk, they were "tall, straight and well proportioned, lightly formed but strong and extremely active and enduring." They are a merry, light-hearted obliging race, recklessly generous, hospitable and extravagant.

The Metis were as free as the wilderness they were born in. They loved the excitement of the hunt. Many of them depended on the buffalo for their livelihood, while others would leave their small farms to join in the chase. On occasion they would use the original Indian method of hunting down a herd and stampeding it off a cliff or creek bank. They would dry the meat and grind it with crushed berries to make pemmican for the winter. The buffalo also provided skins for warmth and leather, and the dung was used as fuel. Full-grown male buffaloes were up to six feet high and weighed a ton or more. The Metis gradually had to abandon their farms to follow the dwindling buffalo herds farther and farther west. These hunting expeditions were well organized.

They used buffalo carts, travelled in bands under chosen leaders, and hunted according to a code of rules and restrictions. Often they were accompanied by priests who celebrated mass every day, taught the children and visited the sick. In winter, many of them camped out. As the buffalo grew scarcer, these camps became permanent villages and eventually the villagers had to fall back on farming and fishing to make a living.

THE BEN ANDERSON STORY by Mrs. Pauline (Hefferman) Anderson

Ben Anderson came from Minnesota in 1912. His brother Ole came with him. Their father, Burtal (Burt) came in 1917. Burt ran the ferry across the Red Deer River in 1919-'20. Ole returned to the States and got married, came to Canada and lived one year

5

Mrs. Ben Anderson and her sister "Sister Mary Frances", 1968.

Ted Anderson, World War II.

then went back to the United States and raised a family. He homesteaded on the land where Chester C. Howe now lives.

Prior to coming to the Red Deer River District, Ben and Ole worked near Outlook, Saskatchewan at carpentry and farm work.

Ben arrived here on a bicycle which he rode from Alsask, a distance of over one hundred miles.

After selecting a homestead site, he continued his trip to Medicine Hat and filed on the land, then back to the Red Deer. The round trip would be another hundred miles or more, still riding his bike.

My parents lived a few miles north of the Anderson homestead. I recall that our first home was a granary about 12 by 14, in which I had a wood-burning stove. Water had to be hauled and stored in a cistern. When I arrived here by horse and buggy a few of the people I recall living here were: Mr. and Mrs. John Bailey; Henry Edgar; Mrs. Hartwell, (this would be Clyde Hartwell's mother); Carl Cunningham, who later married Maggie Lavik, they had two children after leaving this district in 1921; Alex Kavanaugh, a bachelor, but his sister married Ole Kjarland; Findlay and Reg Judson; Tom McCarthy, who was married later to Grace Callaghan; Mr. and Mrs. Dan Callaghan; Mr. and Mrs. Burt Daniels; Mr. and Mrs. Coltman, they had two grown sons, Rex was one, they moved to Vancouver; Mrs. Warnham; Mr. and Mrs. Hugh Brown; Joe O'Brien, bachelor; George Miller and a Mr. and Mrs. Ralph Burr, they had two sons and when they left here they went up north some place.

I finished grade school in Ontario. Went to high school in Oyen. Ben and I had seven children, three sons and four daughters. Our oldest daughter, Alice, was born at the home of my parents, after I lost the race with the stork. We had started for the hospital at Oyen but only got about fifteen miles from home near where my

6

parents lived, when we realized we were not going to make it. The doctor came from Empress, the next day or so after Alice was born. Doctors were usually summoned by the message being relayed from one ranch to the other. Alice is now married to Ed Fischbuck and lives near Oyen. They have five children. Another daughter, Sheila, is married to S. Talarico and lives in Medicine Hat and they have three children. Joan married Charles Standish, they live in Burstall, Saskatchewan, and have one child.

Gene Anderson married Violet Harrison, who came to this country from Ontario, as a private tutor for Magnus Bjork's children, Magnus Jr., and Linda. Gene and Violet live just north of the Red Deer River and have three children, Burt, Pam and Bonnie.

Bill Anderson married Frances Gay, they live at Hanna. They had two sons, Bill and David. Bill lost his life in a highway accident in June, 1971. Ted and Iris both live at home on the original homestead. In later years Ted acquired the homestead of R. S. Gravette and John Bailey which adjoined our place. Ted served in the Armed Forces 1943-'46, with the Calgary Highlanders and spent 1944-'46 overseas, mostly in Holland.

Ben passed away in December, 1962.

SCOTTY BAIN STORY by Edgar Stone

A fellow who was known for his easy, amusing manner and broad Scottish accent. He held an important spot in the Buffalo Community as its "Village Blacksmith". He was a real artist at the job of forge welding, which of course, was the order of the day before the widespread use of the acetylene and electric welders.

Scotty Bain in the centre, Edgar Nelson teacher, Harry Halowka section man.

He shared the blacksmithing ability with another — Archy MacKinnon, and the two became notorious rivals for more reasons than one. As a lark, some of the "local yokels" on a Hallowe'en night bout hoisted Archy's buggy up on Scotty's endless chain.

7

Much to the prankster's disappointment before dawn, Mr. Gordon — always a peacemaker and fearing the consequences, carefully removed the buggy and put things to right again.

Scotty had got his start on the Prairies by taking a job as a common labourer for the famous Dr. P. C. West, of the West toothbrushes. His gift as a blacksmith became quite evident when making repairs on machinery and Dr. West kept him on in the capacity of blacksmith. He ran a big breaking outfit for this man and broke many acres of new sod in the Kindersley area.

Later on coming to Buffalo, he worked with such old-timers as Ole Kjarland, Howard McCullough and Ben Anderson, as sod buster as well as separator man on the old threshing machines. In the early days, Scotty and others did custom breaking for the busy settlers. Thus many of our farm acres had their first sods turned by the young Scot.

Scotty enjoyed many activities of the Community and spent his last years at Woo Sam's, keeping the Delco running so Woo could enjoy the luxury of electric lights and coolers for his dairy products and pop, before the power finally came to our community in 1958. He was an ardent bridge player and spent many happy hours with the other fans of the day. Although to the "outsider" Scotty was jokingly known as the "town drunk" and a real character, to those who knew him well, he was highly regarded and we all knew that under that rough exterior, lay a heart of gold.

Olaf Skjenna Jr., used to accompany Scotty on hunting trips, a sport which Scotty took very serious. He was a crack shot with his 250 rifle as he was with his 12-gauge shotgun. He was a bachelor and this might account for the fact that he would be scantily clad on these early morning goose-hunts. Olaf says that it certainly wasn't the clothes that kept him warm, so it must have been "goose fever" coupled with the essence of sugar cane, imported from Jamaica. Scotty died on June 23, 1951.

THEDORE (TED) BARNEKO

Ted Barneko was born on August 22, 1907, he was an only child. He lived the first part of his life in the British Block and came to the Buffalo district in 1941. He lived in Cavendish during the school term and his first teacher was a Mrs. Emery. He had to leave school when he was in the fourth grade to "scratch" for a living.

In 1918 he suffered a bout with the flu. He went eleven days without food and seven of those he was delirious. Dr. Dan McCharles was the doctor who tried to look after the folks that were sick, but there were so many and with roads the way they

8

Wm. Barneko and team, 1913.

were in those days, even with his Model "T", the doctor couldn't possibly get around to them all. Ted said the hardest work he ever did in his life was to breathe beneath the weight of the blankets when he was so sick. Ted remembers when the railroad tracks were being laid in 1914, most of the work was done with mules, but there were a few teams of horses.

ARNOLD AND HELEN BEGLAW STORY

Many things could be said regarding Arnold, Helen and their family, as they have been of service to each of us in one way or another since coming to Buffalo in 1954, at which time they took over the post office and the telephone switchboard for this district. It would take a book of considerable size to cover their many acts of service to the community, to say nothing of the many things which they did for the individual at one time or another.

When Arnold and Helen attended the same school at Atlee, Arnold was very shy, so he would serenade Helen from a distance, he walking down the railroad, while she walked along the road with the other girls. Arnold was known as the local "Wilf Carter" in those days. During summer holidays Arnold would work on the local farms from early morning until late at night, doing everything from milking cows to cooking meals, even to washing wool blankets in an attempt to make them softer to sleep in. All this he did for the big sum of $9.00 per month.

This romance between Arnold and Helen was interrupted when Arnold's family moved to Retlaw. Later Arnold joined the armed forces and served overseas. In the meantime Helen worked in Calgary. After the war the young couple were married in March, 1947. As the wedding was to take place at her parents' home, the wedding party along with the minister and several members of Arnold's family,

9

as well as other guests travelled from Calgary to Atlee by train. The engineer agreed to let them off at the railroad crossing near Helen's home as there were too many people to travel in the buggy. The roads were very muddy at this time of year and George Brassard, Helen's Dad made several trips from the house to the Atlee hall taking the bride and groom and all the guests to and from the dance which followed the wedding.

Arnold and Helen lived in Calgary for a while after their marriage, later they moved to Indus. This union was blessed with four children, Dianne and Duane were born in Calgary, Douglas was born in Indus and Donnie was born after they came to Buffalo. It was at Indus, one day, Dianne was spoiling for a beating, when her mother attempted to oblige her. Helen found that the child could run faster than she could, but much to Dianne's amazement and indignation, Uncle Del Brassard was able to outrun her, so he administered the punishment. This, Dianne never forgot over the years, she abided her time and so on her wedding day, she hid Uncle Del's pants, thus preventing him from attending her wedding.

Duane was only about five years old when they came to Buffalo and bought out Bill and Boo Thompson. One day it was thought that Bill's team was running away, while Jack, his son was driving them. Bill got very upset and threw his hat on the ground and jumped on it. Young Duane witnessed all this and for a long time after whenever he saw Bill he would do the same thing. Helen said he ruined more hats that way.

After Arnold came to Buffalo he worked at several different jobs, beside the post office and telephone, he served as school janitor for a while, drove the school bus, was the Insurance Agent for hail insurance and various farm jobs. Helen served for several years as president of the Ladies Club and was always ready and willing to assist with any social event.

Arnold gave up his career as a yodeller and took up Bingo at which he proved very lucky, winning a car, chesterfield, camera and a set of golf clubs. Luck was his in yet another form one night while travelling to Cappon, about twenty some miles north of Buffalo, with Jack Thompson and some others, the truck got stuck in the snow and in their attempt to dig themselves out Arnold accidently got run over. The truck passed over his head, but he was not seriously injured.

Dianne married Brian John Johnston in September, 1966 and they have two children.

Arnold and Helen left this community in September, 1968, to live in Burnaby, B.C.

10

THE BJORK FAMILY by Clarence (Spot) Bjork

We came from Montana to the Red Deer River in the summer of 1906. We came by train as far as Dunmore. Father met us with a lumber wagon. Dunmore is six miles east of Medicine Hat, and is as far as the train came from Lethbridge at that time. We crossed the South Saskatchewan River at Medicine Hat by ferry, there was only the railroad bridge across the river at that time. We came north to what was known as the Andy Gordon ranch then. In low water we used to ford the river up by Lincoln Howe's place, otherwise we used to cross in front of Bruce Dawson's place (now known as the Crooked Tree Ranch) by boat. We would take the wagons apart and take them over piece by piece and then swim the horses over. It would take a day just to get the outfit across the river. It was a two-day trip to Medicine Hat, where now it is just a couple of hours. In those days whoever went to the "Hat" used to bring the mail for everyone living up and down the river and leave it at the Gordon ranch. The first winter we didn't get any mail all winter and the folks were taking a daily paper, the Great Falls Tribune so we had a real load of papers in the spring. When we moved to the Red Deer in 1906, we had four hundred head of

Original Bjork log shack in 1910 still occupied by the present Bjork family.

cattle, but in the spring of 1907, after one of the worst winters this district has ever seen, before or since, we had only forty head left. Everyone along the river had about the same percentage of loss.

People who lived along the river, at that time, starting at Empress, were: the Kennedy Brothers; Clint Jarboe; the Fisher Brothers, they lived where George Howe lives now; the Howes lived about a mile west and south of where C. B. Howe lives now; Henry Edgar lives just north of where the bridge is; "Deadwood" Dick Royston; "Calamity Jane" Jane Rudd; Steve Cicon lived down where my brother Magnus holds the "Old-timer's Picnic" every five years; west of our place was the Vee Bar Vee, I don't remember who was

11

living there then; and just six miles from the Vee Bar Vee Sundail Williams lived. He left in 1907 and of course the Gordons were here also. Most of the early settlers lived on the north side of the river, why I don't know. Perhaps it was because that is where the springs were. Just west of where the Jenner is and later known as the Stapleton ranch, was the Lord Beresford ranch. Later Tom Owens moved in, then the Gravettes and the McCulloughs. Until the railroad came in 1914, we used to have to drive the cattle we had to sell (which weren't many after the first winter) to Suffield or Brooks and sometimes to Kindersley, Saskatchewan. In later years we shipped from Halsbury, west of Atlee. This was where the first stockyards were. Later we shipped from both Atlee and Buffalo. The Atlee ferry was put in, in 1916 about four miles west of our place, but you could not cross most of the time. The other ferry was at Pancrus now known as Cavendish and later one at Buffalo, just west of where C. B. Howe lives, and still later the Buffalo ferry was down where the bridge is now. Then a ferry was put in at Steveville and after that was put in we used to trade in Brooks, until George Brassard opened the first store at Atlee. In 1911 the R.C.M.P. had a post at the Vee Bar Vee, then known as Parvella. There was also a post office open there, we used to bring all the mail to our place and someone would pick it up on Sunday. The first police at Parvella were Hutchins and Bob White, followed by Elliot and Casey Oliver and others.

The first school I went to was in Medicine Hat in 1909 and '10. The next year we had a teacher at the ranch. Our first teacher was a Miss Imes, who later married Bill Conrad, she stayed for two years. Then a Miss Carter, followed by a man named Mitchell, then a Miss Austin, who later married the famous "Blue Beard" who drowned her in a lake near Spokane, Washington. Our next teacher was a Miss Christie, who married Leland Pound, then a Miss McKay, who married Clyde Hartwell, that is where I stopped school. After she left we had teachers for a few more years and then Mother moved to Chinook where Eileen and Norwood finished school.

There were eight children in our family. Margaret, who married W. C. (Scotty) McKee. They live at Trout Creek, Summerland, B.C. Grace married Dave Sneddon, a former resident of Atlee. They now live at Nampa, just south of Peace River. Eileen, the only one of us who was born in Canada, married Alvin (Otto) Haugen. They live in Spokane, Washington.

Evelyn, died in 1910 in Medicine Hat. Edna passed away in Empress in 1923. Norwood married Phylis Marr, from Chinook. They live at Kelowna, B.C. Magnus, who still lives on the ranch married Natalka (Tiny) Dziatkewich. They have three children, Magnus III

12

and Linda, both at home and Billy at Red Deer. Linda married Keith Love from Oyen on July 9, 1971.

I married Dorrell Anderson in 1956. I left the Red Deer River in 1935 and went to Reno in the Peace River district. The only difference between that Reno and the famous one in the U.S.A., is that in Reno, Nevada people get divorces but in Reno, Alberta, they didn't bother. In fact I know of one case where a husband traded his wife with a clear Bill of Sale and the household furnishings for a team of horses and got a wagon to boot. I was very much in "the know" as I ran the General Store in that area from 1940 to 1950. From there I went to Valleyview and then to Bassano and we now live in Calgary.

In 1956 Magnus and Tiny hosted the first "Old-timer's Picnic" in commemoration of the establishment of the Bjork ranch by Magnus Bjork Sr., fifty years before. Father passed away in 1939. My brother is now the Senior Magnus Bjork and his son is Magnus Jr.

The following is the write-up which appeared in the Brooks Bulletin covering the picnic held in 1956.

Mr. and Mrs. Magnus Bjork, well-known ranchers on the Red Deer River, entertained several hundred of their friends at a picnic last Sunday, July 22, in commemoration of the establishment of the Bjork ranch by Magnus Bjork Sr., fifty years ago.

The ranch is located 40 miles south of Chinook and the holdings extend to the river. Early in the afternoon cars commenced to arrive at the river bottom, an ideal spot to hold a picnic among the native cottonwood trees. Estimates varied as to how many people assembled for the occasion. Some placed the number at around 1000 while others estimated the crowd to have reached the 1500 mark. Later in the afternoon a ball game was arranged, children participated in running races and other games were enjoyed. The event provided an excellent opportunity for a get-together of old-timers and many memories of the pioneer days were recalled by the groups of people during the afternoon and evening. The feeding of the multitude posed no problem for the Bjork family, the only request being that each family provide a frying pan. Meat was specially prepared in Medicine Hat and when the call came to "come and get it" 650 pounds of well-seasoned hamburger meat was served to the crowd. It was not long before fires were lit and sizzling hot hamburgers and buns were most thoroughly enjoyed. Over 45 gallons of coffee were also served.

Much could be written concerning the early days of ranching in this section of the province and the pioneering spirit possessed by the few who located here some fifty or more years ago, and those whose rugged individualism eventually built this country to what it is today.

It was in July, 1906 that the late Magnus Bjork with his wife and young family drove a herd of 500 cattle from Montana to the present site of the Bjork ranch. History records that the winter that followed was the most severe that this province has ever experienced and like all ranchers who were here at the time, Mr. Bjork lost most of his stock.

Despite the misfortune experienced the first year, the family decided to remain where they were. In later years the ranch was operated by members of the family and during the past several years Magnus Bjork Jr., has had the responsibility of looking after operations. Mr. Bjork Sr., passed away in 1939 and Mrs. Bjork in 1942.

Fred Nelson and Juel Schier in 1912 or 1914.

Sunday also marked the occasion for a happy reunion as all members were home for the day. They include, Clarence and Norwood now making their home at Reno in the Peace River district, Mrs. Grace Sneddon also of Reno, Mrs. Eileen Haugen, Spokane, Washington, and Mrs. Margaret McKee, resident of Medicine Hat.

A guest book was passed around for everybody to sign and some of the old-timers names that appeared were: F. Bushling, R. S. Gravette, Jim Hannaford, C. B. Howe, G. Brassard, J. Smith, Ben Anderson, D. Lush, Mrs. McLennan, Vic Lawrence, Len Gray, O. Skjenna and Albert Smuhl, just to mention a few. Albert Smuhl was the ferryman right near the ranch for 26 years. There were friends from Stettler, Spokane, Reno, Empress, Athabasca, Fleet, Coronation, Black Diamond, Manyberries, Indus, Calgary, Medicine Hat and of course from every one of the smaller centres within 50 miles.

As darkness fell many left for their homes at distant points, while some remained to enjoy the music of a string orchestra playing under the stars, bringing to a close a most happy day and memorable occasion, thoroughly enjoyed by young and old alike.

14

The second picnic was held five years later in 1961. E. F. (Shorty) Brown gave the following account of the day's events, which was published in the Brooks Bulletin in three parts, under the heading of "Man with a Notebook".

Editor's Note:
Mr. E. F. Brown has given a very good coverage of the Atlee district and the people who used to live there. Atlee is directly across the Red Deer River from the Bjork ranch. All three articles, written by Mr. Brown, are not available in their entirety.

(See old times at Atlee picnic, page 338)

STORIES BY MAGNUS BJORK as told to Robin Krause

Much of the land now held as grazing lease by the ranchers along the Red Deer was broken up by homesteaders at one time, for cultivation. These people, many of them immigrants, invested everything they had in their homesteads, and spent many back-breaking and sometimes heart-breaking hours breaking and working the land. Mere elequent than words in describing the labor invested, are the huge rock piles, picked by hand, still standing beside what once were plowed fields. For most of these pioneers, tragedy struck with the drought and depression of the thirties, and the farms were abandoned as many of the farmers moved on, seeking a living for their families, while their land reverted to the Crown. Others, more hardy or more fortunate, were able to stay on until their deaths or retirement, when their land was purchased and added to nearby ranches.

On the Crooked Tree ranch, as on most others, the designations given to the various fields read like a litany, calling off the history of these earlier days; John's east and John's west, for John Petrock, whose big barn is still a landmark; the Frenchman's field; the Boeschling field; the Lovedale field, which once contained the Lovedale school; the Kelse place; and on the south side Sam McKay's and the Sam Hyde place. It is not until one listens to the "old-timers" reminiscing, however, that these people come alive, and the rock piles, basement holes and broken wagon wheels are again owned by real people. Here are a few anecdotes of these people, as told to me by Magnus Bjork. In most cases, names and dates have been omitted; these who were there will recognize the characters anyway; those who weren't will enjoy the stories just as well this way.

At one time in the district north of Bjork and Crooked Tree ranches, there were two bachelors who lived and farmed together. They were hard-working and honest, but liked a good business deal as well as anyone.

Amongst their ivestock, they had a milk cow called Spot, because of a large white spot on one flank. Spot had been a good cow,

15

Threshing wheat at Bjork's ranch in 1928.

but for an exasperating habit — she couldn't be kept out of the garden. She was also rather past her prime, as one day one of the bachelors decided to sell her at a nearby farm auction. Nothing was said about her deficiencies, and she fetched a fair price, and the owner came home feeling quite satisfied with his deal.

It was a few months later that another neighbor had an auction, and feeling a need to replace old Spot, our friend decided to attend. It was spring, and the livestock, having spent the winter in the barn, were well covered with mud and manure. However, our friend was a good judge of cattle, and picked out and bought a milk cow, at which he considered a good price. He came home with his prize, and announced to his partner, "Well, I got a good buy today. Come and see the milk cow I bought." His partner went to the window to view the remarkable animal, and exploded with rage. "Do you know what you've done? You've bought back old Spot!"

"The hell I did!" was the retort, "I bought a damn good milk cow." "Well come and see then," his partner returned, and our friend looked out the window in time to see a cow's flank, from which enough mud had fallen to reveal an unmistakeable spot, just disappearing into the garden.

There was, at one time in the Lovedale district a couple who personified Jack Spratt and his wife. The husband tall, thin and consumptive, so that everyone said "Poor old Dave, he won't last long, you know." His wife, on the other hand, was less than five feet tall, and was almost as broad as she was tall. It was said that they couldn't sit side by side on the buggy seat, because she weighed her side down so badly her husband kept sliding toward her; so when they went anywhere, she rode the buggy, in the middle of the seat, while her husband rode alongside on the saddle horse. The lady on occasion rode horseback too, and had a trench dug in the manure pile at stirrup height, to help her get mounted. Thus it was

16

Fred Nelson's homestead shack, Magnus, Margaret and Clarence Bjork in 1907.

Mr. and Mrs. Magnus Bjork (the first).

that she mounted up one day and rode over to the post office for the mail. The postmaster, a hefty fellow, helped her dismount, and she was able to do her business, have tea with the postmaster's wife, and visit with the other patrons. When she was ready to go, the postmaster improvised a mounting block by placing an oil drum upright, with a box beside it for a step. The horse, however, was having none of this, and tried to shy away, so the postmaster held him by the bridle and cinch, and tried to pull him close enough for the lady to mount. She, from the top of the barrel, could just reach the saddle, so she grasped the horn and cantle, and dived onto the horse's back, lost her balance, and went right on over. The postmaster, appalled, managed to grab her ankle, and there he was, holding her with one hand and the horse with the other. The lady was too heavy for him to pull up, and he dared not let her fall on her head. The women in the house, meanwhile, were watching this spectacle, and their merriment can be imagined. The lady was finally lowered to the ground, with no injury to anything but her pride, but the story was the main piece of gossip in the district for weeks. As for old Dave, he lived to a good old age, outliving his wife by fifteen years.

There are always bad eggs among the good, and the homesteaders were no exception. There was one fellow who was especially well known to his neighbors for his crooked dealings, and he had one trick which he often used to hoodwink newcomers. At that time the rail terminal for the district was at Chinook, and almost every train brought in homesteaders who would wait in town until they could catch a ride with someone going their way. Our hero seemed to get frequent shipments of freight, and when he came to town to collect them, there would usually be someone wanting a ride. Of course, our friend was more than glad to offer one, but "Doggone it, here's this shipment of freight I wasn't expecting yet, and I've left my wallet at home. 'Fraid I'm going to have to go all the way back and get it." Of course the grateful passenger would offer to loan the money, and our friend would accept with great relief, promising to pay at the earliest opportunity — and that would be the last the passenger would see of his money. Inevitably though, our friend finally met a persistent debt collector. The amount of the loan was considerable, and after several unsuccessful attempts to collect, the creditor decided to go to our crooked friend's home and stay until he got his money. He arrived early in the morning, but his host had already left for the day. The lady of the house invited him in for coffee, and he settled in to stay. Hours went by, and he showed no sign of intending to leave. The lady, who was about as treacherous as her husband tried several devices to persuade her unwelcome guest to leave, but in vain. Finally, in desperation, the 'lady' went behind the curtain separating the sleeping area from the rest of the house; picked up the chamber pot, and, coming up behind her stubborn guest, emptied it on his head. He fled, never to return. Even in the old West, virtue didn't always triumph!

These stories are about only a few of the many people whose homes once dotted the countryside. What of the others, the Andersons, McDuffys, Powers, and Finks, Macdonalds, Campbells, and Jonases, the Beaufort Watkins, the Wilson brothers, Dave Cochrane, who kept donkeys, and all the others? Well, if you sit with the old-timers around a crock of rye whiskey on a winter's night, or at a branding on a hot summer day after the keg goes dry, you may hear stories even better than these.

SAUL BOYER

Saul Boyer was born at Eastend, Saskatchewan in 1882. His father was a Metis from Fort Garry. Saul was born while his family, with a large band of Metis were on a buffalo hunt. It was one of the last annual buffalo hunts on the Canadian plains. His family and several others were, rather roughly, loaded into railway cars and taken to Regina in 1885, where they were kept until the hostilities of the Northwest Rebellion ceased. His people were hunting in southern Alberta or Saskatchewan at the time, despite the fact his father had no intentions of joining the rebellion they were still put under guard.

Saul was only 11 years old when he started riding yearling colts, but it didn't take long for him to graduate to bigger and tougher broncs. In his early teens he began to ride and break horses for a living. At the same time he was regularly using a rope. He and his family were living in Medicine Hat, when he was 15 or 16 years old Saul made a journey which has never been equalled. Old-timers still talk about it whenever they get together. For more than 300 miles by saddle horse and then 60 to 70 miles on foot, went Saul, driving nine head of 5-year-old Texas Longhorn steers half the way. Saul had been offered $20 to deliver a telegram to a cow camp far out on the Red Deer River. He had worked the country the summer before and knew just where he was supposed to go. Saul struck out on the journey with his saddle pony. A day or so out on the long trail, he stopped at the ranch of the late James Mitchell, a pioneer rancher of southern Alberta. Mr. Mitchell inquired where the young cowboy was going. When Saul told him, Mr. Mitchell said he had nine head of Longhorn steers in the same locality and would give Saul $20 to bring them back when he came. Mitchell had tried to bring the steers back himself several times without success.

"Forty dollars for the trip, that was big money. Times were tough then, the 1890's were a lot tougher than the dirty '30's, late one night Saul found the camp by riding for the lamp light in a window. The men were up late playing cards or he might not have had a beacon to direct him in. He was almost exhausted when he reached food and warmth, he spent the night there and delivered the telegram the next day and rode on in search for the steers, when he located them they were in a corral with another bunch at the ranch of "Horseshoe" Smith, near Leader, Saskatchewan. The Smith cattle were turned out but the Mitchell cattle were kept in and Saul let them go without food and water for a few days to tone them down a bit, then he let them out. Those steers took off and ran for about fifteen miles before they settled down to graze, Saul found it quite a job to keep up to them and keep them headed in the right direction, by the time Saul had the steers trail-broken, he was weary and decided to have a little sleep. He unsaddled his horse, tied one end of his lariat to the hackamore shank on his horse and the other to the horn of his saddle. He stretched out across the saddle, figuring that if the horse moved too far away he would feel the pull and be awakened. When Saul did wake up he saw that the rope had become untied from the hackamore shank and the horse, unaware it was free, was peacefully grazing near at hand. Telling the story later, Saul said, "I knew what I was up against, it was a case of catching the horse or walking the rest of the way to Medicine Hat. I was a pretty good roper, even in those days, but figured it would be better to walk slowly up and catch the horse if I could. Just in case, I built a loop and then started to ease up to the horse. My rope must have swished on some brush because, just as I was about to put my hand on him, the horse spooked and took off. I swung my rope and caught him. But he kicked and jumped just as the loop went over his head, and got a hind leg through the loop. He really went to it then. I hung onto my rope and the horse took out running, kicking and dragging me. I wasn't worried about the dragging at first, figured he's choke down after a while. Then I got to thinking about the rough country I was being dragged through. Sooner or later I was going to hit a stone and get crippled before the horse choked down. I didn't want to be crippled up away out there all alone, so I let go of the rope."

With the horse gone, there was nothing for Saul to do but start walking. He was determined still to take the steers back for Mitchell, so he put his saddle in a safe place and then started after the steers. Not used to seeing a person on foot the Longhorns came circling around Saul, bawling, snuffing and digging in the ground. Some almost tossed the young cowboy on their horns. But he just kept on walking and after a while those steers got used to him and settled down. He was able to herd them in the direction he wanted them to go. It was coming spring; creeks and sloughs were high. As Saul followed the steers he was sometimes belt deep in icy-cold water. The ground was rough and travel was difficult. Saul and his Longhorns finally reached the border fence of the Drowning Ford Ranch, about 25 to 30 miles northeast of Medicine Hat. He opened the gate and drove the steers through. Determined to finish the job, Saul drove the cattle another 5 to 10 miles to the home corral of the ranch. There was food and rest there, but not for long. Saul was in rough shape; when he pulled the wet boots from his feet, his toes ballooned out until it looked like they would pop off his feet. No later than the next day, he was back on a saddle horse and drove the steers on into Medicine Hat where they were slaughtered. The distance the tough young cowboy travelled by foot was somewhere between 60 and 70 miles. Mitchell said afterwards there never was another man who could have done the job.

By the time Saul was 17 years of age he was riding the rough string for several ranches in southeastern Alberta and Saskatchewan. During the South African War he went down into Montana to break horses which were being sold to the British Army. But most of the time he broke horses, rode on roundups and did regular cowboy work in Alberta and Saskatchewan. Men who had rode hundreds of miles with Saul were two old-time cowboys and well-known ranchers by the name of Crockett, were top hands themselves, said there never was quite the equal of "Old Saul." Saul could gather a band of horses out of several different herds on the prairie and start off with them. Most times like that it would take about six good riders to keep a band together, let alone keep them going in the same direction. After a few miles, Saul would be riding peacefully along behind his horses. Generally he'd be riding a horse that he had saddled for the first time only a few days before. Saul always rode a bronc in preference to a well-broken horse. When he was night-hawk with a herd he preferred a bronc to a horse which had done the job before. Saul did most of his roping with a rawhide rope which was 65 feet long. He could throw a rope as far as anyone around at that time. He never bothered with big time rodeoing, but preferred to clown at a rodeo, still he won several bucking contests. In 1908 he was clowning at a bucking contest in Medicine Hat. Saul drew a tough bronc and swung aboard backwards, looking out over the animal's tail instead of its head. Saul just wanted to give the spectators a little more for their money. He was wearing a beautiful big black hat and as the blindfold was jerked from the horse's head, Saul began doffing the big hat and bowing to the spectators. He rode the bronc for several jolting jumps and then sailed gracefully through the air. He lit in a sitting position in the arena, facing the grandstand and still doffing his hat and bowing graciously. One time in Medicine Hat Saul bet someone he could ride his horse over the railway bridge across the Saskatchewan River. The bridge is a long narrow one; the beams which carry the railway tracks are 6 inches to a foot apart; there isn't any floor between the beams, just the South Saskatchewan — 'way down below. The horse had to step from one cross member to another, and do so very carefully. Saul rode the horse over the bridge and turned it around and rode back. A policeman was waiting for him and Saul was taken away and locked up. His friends said that someone should have been waiting to give him a medal. The next day Saul was advised to leave town for a while. Saul told them that was what he had in mind.

Saul was never known to abuse a horse and any horse he broke and trained could be ridden by anyone. Whenever he rode into

21

town he always saw that his horse was well cared for before he did anything for himself and he would check occasionally while there to make sure the horse was alright.

Saul was a fine-looking man and always dressed extremely neat, he was very particular about his appearance and always kept his shoes highly polished. There are two things Saul Boyer is best remembered for; first his outstanding ability as a roper and rider and he is equally recalled as a man of unusual good humor. A few years ago he retired and spent his last days in Medicine Hat. He passed away in November, 1967, at the age of 85.

DANIEL CALLAGHAN AND HIS FAMILY by Mrs. Grace (Callaghan) McCarthy

Daniel Callaghan was born in Arthur, Ontario in 1862 on his Dad's farm. His grandfather, a school teacher, had come out from Ireland and acquired the farm. Originally, the family name was O'Callaghan, but his grandfather dropped the 'O' when he arrived in Ontario. Mr. Callaghan ran away from home at the age of sixteen to work as a teamster in the woods in Michigan. He later farmed in the Dakotas where he met and married Margaret Emma Reynolds, a teacher. Later they moved to Chicago where he drove a horse-streetcar for many years.

They had five living children. The first, a son, Maxwell Andrew who lived to be eighty-one years old, he was a retired Major

Mr. and Mrs. Leroy Callaghan, Bryon, Greg, Gary, Donna and Bev.

22

in the U.S., Army at the time of his death in 1969. Their second child Irene died at the age of seven with either croup or diptheria. They also lost a baby just a few weeks old. Then they had a set of twins, Joseph Leroy and John Leo.

Mr. and Mrs. Callaghan, Maxwell and the twins moved to Carrington, North Dakota, where Mr. Callaghan farmed and had the dray business with a couple of men driving drays. Elizabeth Iris was born in 1900 and Grace Genevieve was born in 1904.

Mrs. Callaghan's health was poor and doctors said she would have to get away from the cold winters. They sold out everything with the exception of a few Jersey milk cows and moved to California. There he planned to run a dairy, but it didn't work out, as he developed asthma so badly. Again he sold out.

He came to Alberta in 1912 and took out a homestead north of the Red Deer River in 1914. Joe, one of the twins also came out and took a homestead north and east of his father. They built a good sod shack with two glass windows in it.

Mr. Callaghan had some land ploughed by walking plow ready for a crop in 1915. The wheat averaged fifty bushels to the acre and No. 1 Northern brought a good price of well over $2.00, I think nearer three.

Joe joined the Army and went through World War I, was slightly wounded once. He farmed for many years after returning. His choice of a homestead was poor, so he gave it up and bought Purl Moor's homestead, another returned soldier and later bought Joe O'Brien's.

The family home in Los Angeles, California burned in November of 1915. Mother was hurt in the fire and was a semi-invalid the rest of her life. She, with the other twin, Leo and Iris and I came to the Buffalo district in April 1916.

Leo helped on the farm for less than a year, then joined the U.S. Navy, returning each spring to visit and help.

Mother died in 1924.

My father kept on farming but never had another good crop after 1916, the same year he built a good house. He died in the Empress hospital in 1933. That district is a "next year" country and he kept thinking next year we will have a good crop.

He was a fine living man, never known to criticize anyone. He never smoked, drank nor swore in the presence of his family. He was missed intensely by his close knit family.

Joseph Leroy Callaghan was born in Carrington, North Dakota in June 1896. He was one of a set of twin boys, the other being John Leo.

23

Byron Nelson, Leo Callaghan, Jim Findlay, unknown, 1924.

Joe finished school in California and in the spring of 1915 he came up to Alberta to help his father Daniel. He also took out a homestead north and east of his father's, but it proved to be a poor choice and he gave it up. In the meantime, he helped his father build a sod shack. Joe enlisted in the Army in the First World War and left shortly for overseas. While there he was badly gassed and wounded in the waist and his hand was left partly paralyzed. He was fortunate. He was made a Corporal of Supplies and stayed a year or two after the war to help clear up details.

When he returned he helped his father and worked with the CPR in the winter in Moose Jaw. In 1926 he married Thelma Gravette. They lived in California where he worked with his brother Max for two years. On returning to Alberta he rented Purl Moor's homestead. Purl was also a returned soldier with a homestead, but he couldn't stand the loneliness.

Joe later bought Purl's place along with the O'Brien place. Both these places are now owned by Joe's son, Leroy.

Joe and Thelma had one daughter, Maxine Audrey in California and Leroy Daniel after they returned to Buffalo. Farming being as it was, Joe continued to work winters as boiler maker's helper for CPR shops in Moose Jaw.

About 1937, Joe decided that the beautiful lush irrigated farms in the Brooks district would be for him. However, being a cautious soul he went for one summer and worked on an irrigated farm for experience. After a summer of 4:00 A.M.' s'til midnight, he found that the beautiful lush country still had no money than the "dried out district" and you worked twice as long and hard with absolutely nothing to show for it except being much wiser. He decided to stay in Buffalo and continue to struggle with the elements.

Maxine and Leroy finished school at Emslie and then went to high school in Buffalo. When they went the ten miles to Buffalo high school, they drove the old Model "A" Ford with the Howe girls, fall and spring but "batched" in Buffalo in the winter. Leroy would work after school for Woo Sam who run the general store. Maxine went to Medicine Hat to finish high school when the school was discontinued in Buffalo, and later attended the University in Edmonton to become a teacher.

Sometime in the forties Joe started to work with the Department of Highways, at first with the special areas and later in the Hat for the Department.

People will remember the years he worked at Atlee and later near Empress running the ferries.

Being diabetic his health was deteriorating and he retired in Medicine Hat and did part-time commissioner work. His health failed completely and he stayed with his sister Grace and then his daughter Maxine in Edmonton. For less than two years he lived in the New Veterans Home in Edmonton where he passed away in July 1969.

Leroy married Racheal Skjenna of Buffalo in 1950. They had six children: Bryon, Beverly, Terry, Garry, Greg and Donna.

Maxine married Leo W. Nugent of Bow Island in 1951. They lived in Medicine Hat, Calgary, Edmonton and now back in Calgary. They have seven children: three boys and four girls.

Editor's Note:
Bryon Callaghan and his sister Bev, both live in Calgary. Bryon is with MacLeod Bros., a men's clothing store and he has a contract with Paramount Studios and has been making a film with Lee Marvin. Bev is employed at a Medical Clinic in that city. Terry lost her life in a highway accident in 1965, Gary goes to Medicine Hat this fall to attend high school while Greg and Donna will still be attending our local school.

MRS. GRACE (CALLAGHAN) McCARTHY
Mother, Leo, Iris and I came to Buffalo in April 1916. Dad had left the team of horses tied to the lumber wagon on the north side of the river. There was no ferry and the ice-floes were still running in the river. Dad met us at the train with a homesteader from south of Buffalo. He took us down to the river and we crossed in a small row boat. The river was running high and the ice floes were knocking at the small boat. It was a most unpleasant trip. Dad had pulled a granary along side of the sod shack, fastened

two boards the length of the granary with leather hinges to use as windows. The house was a bit of a shock to say the least.

The country was full of sloughs and the mosquitoes were terrible, I don't believe they have ever been so bad since. We spent many nights that summer sitting outside around a smudge fire made of buffalo chips and sage brush. It was a dreadful summer and the winter was worse. Dad had a marvelous crop of wheat the fall before (1915). He had a good crop again in 1916 and so with the help of good neighbors got a storey and a half wood frame house built in place of the granary. A homesteader by the name of Pat Doyle was going to plaster the house but winter set in before he got there and it was too cold for the job. It was a cold winter, sixty below at times. Dad hauled wood from the river, approximately seven miles, and coal from Atlee. The round trip would be over thirty miles. The house was so cold, water froze in the pails. Even the food froze at times. Mother had several bad spells with her heart.

Joe was in the army overseas and Leo joined the U.S. navy to train as an oil-burning fireman.

Tom McCarthy at 7 Bar 7 Ranch, 1922.

Flight Officer Patrick McCarthy in 1945.

Iris had married Jim Findlay in February, 1917. Their daughter, Lucille was born a year later in Los Angeles, where Mother, Iris and I had gone a couple of months before the baby was expected. I got in a few months of school while there. We all came back to Buffalo in the spring. Mother stayed until winter set in, then Dad sent her back to Los Angeles, where we still owned a small cottage. She never spent another winter on the homestead. I became chief cook and bottle washer. I learned to ride and drove a four horse outfit on the

26

land. Still no school, but I went to Atlee a few months to school that winter. The teacher was not much older than myself and some of the other pupils. The school was so cold we spent most of the time huddled around the furnace in the small basement.

Our diet those first years consisted mostly of home cured pork, and potatoes. There was no such thing as fresh fruit and vegetables being shipped in then as there was in the later years.

We tried to raise a garden but the gophers got anything that did grow. Most years it was too dry and then there were the grasshoppers. Dad always managed to raise potatoes by planting in low laying areas where the snow runoff laid late in the spring.

Our neighbor to the south, Clyde Hartwell and his mother (who was also Clint Jarboe's mother — she was married twice) had a nice little house, nice dishes and bookcases full of books. I loved going there as a girl of 12 or 13 years. I read all their books and looked for more. Most homesteaders just had the bare necessities and we had as little or less than most for everything had been lost when our home in Los Angeles burned in November 1915 — someone pulled the sewing machine out and Mother's piano was saved but otherwise, we just had the clothes on our backs.

In June of 1916, Dad, Jim Findlay and my brother Leo were doing some road work around the north side of the river breaks to get to the Cavendish Ferry. Mom, Iris and I decided to go visit Mr. and Mrs. Lavick and their daughter Maggie. They were homesteaders who lived south of Cud Howe's on the west side of the road. Iris and I had quite a time harnessing and hitching a quiet team of horses to the buggy, but finally we were away. We were made very welcome had a visit over a cup of tea, when suddenly about 4:00 P.M. a storm came up, wind, rain and hail. It was a good thing the horses were tied in a shelter. After the hail had stopped and the rain eased up we decided we had better start for home. When we got to Cud's place we found a rushing torrent of water down the coulee we had to cross. Cud's dam had gone out so we went back to Lavick's. Things had got worse there — the hail had broken and torn off the tarpaper roof and it was raining inside almost as much as outside. We all got in the buggy and drove back to Cud's, he had a big well-built log house. We spent the night there. He had an old-fashioned gramophone, everyone danced on until a couple of the records were completely worn out. Then we decided to try and get some sleep. There was just one bed. It was decided that Mrs. Lavick, Mom, Iris and I would have the bed, lying crosswise. Mr. Lavick and Cud settled down in a couple of big chairs. Maggie insisted she was going to sleep on the floor. She wrapped herself in a blanket, took a pillow and eventually everyone settled down and

27

slept. Suddenly about 4:00 A.M. we were awakened by a terrible screech — a mouse had run over Maggie's face. That put an end to any more sleep that night. When morning came Leo came with a team looking for us. Even then, where the road crossed the draw below the dam the water was still running as high as the horses' breasts.

The men had come home from the road job due to the storm, found no one home and the roof of the granary, which we had been using as sleeping quarters was torn off. The wind had blown some of our clothing away when the roof went. What was left of the bedding and other things were a sodden mess. Just a little incident to add to the discomfort of our homesteading days.

One summer, school was held in Costello's shack, a homesteader just west of Ole Kjarland, this would be about 1920, I think there were about six or seven children attending, myself included.

Thelma Gravett, Tommie and Anne Lupin, they lived just east of Ole Kjarland's. Helen and Hughie Brown, can't remember if there was another one from that family. Our teacher was Miss Gwen Taylor from Medicine Hat. I went to school in Empress in 1921 and '22. I started late but stayed till the end of the term in June.

In 1923, I married Tom McCarthy, while he was foreman at the 7-7 ranch before the McLennan family moved to the ranch.

Our first child was born in Los Angeles, California, where I had gone to be with my mother. Also the ranch was too far away from any change of medical care.

When Mother had a slight stroke, Dad and Joe had come and were there when she passed away in March, just a month before our son Patrick was born.

In 1925, Tom and I left the ranch and he farmed for Ole Kjarland from April that year until the fall. Then he decided to move on to his homestead just east of where the bridge is now, on the north side of the river. Mr. and Mrs. Dick Elliott, parents of Mrs. Cud Howe, had been living on the place for about seven years, so Tom built an addition to the house and the Elliotts stayed with us for a year and a half, as I was expecting another child. Nora Kathleen was born in January 1927.

In 1927 the crops were good. Tom worked hard enough for two men. He got 100 acres in wheat and it averaged thirty bushels to the acre. The next year we had a very promising crop at the end of June, but in July a three-day-hot wind shrivelled it to nothing. Tom also had a marvelous garden. Mrs. Elliott and I canned eighty quarts of green peas.

Mrs. Elliott was a grand person, loved and respected by all who knew her. Years later after Mr. Elliott died she came to Medicine

Hat and lived with us for 18 months. She passed away in the 1940's at her daughter's home in Buffalo.

In 1927 and '28 whooping cough swept through the country and we lost our baby girl. She developed pneumonia. We sent word to Dr. McNeil, via a barbed wire telephone, there were no roads and no train running that day, but Dr. McNeil got a man with a speeder from Leader to bring him to our home, it was over 30 miles on an open speeder and the temperature was 35 below. Tom met him with a sleigh. The doctor said she had a slim chance and gave us our orders — a steam tent and mustard plaster every two hours. We worked very hard but two days later her heart gave out and six days less than a year our beautiful little girl was gone. Pat coughed for many months and there were times we were afraid we would lose him too.

We only had the one good crop. After that there were no crops and very little garden. Tom, Pat and I went to Vancouver lived there for three years and in 1932 came back to the homestead, that fall our second daughter, Barbara Ann, was born, ten months later Michael Dennis arrived.

One of those dry years, 1935, I think, Tom had planted potatoes along the north side of the homestead. They were doing well considering the conditions. We also had a garden on the south side of the house near the river. We had ditch water for the garden and even carried water by the pail when the river was low. Well, in July, we had a nice garden. One hot day when I needed some vegetables from the garden, I took my butcher knife and headed for the garden and to my horror there were 15 or 20 razor-back pigs. (I later found out they had completely razed our potato patch.) They were having a marvelous time. Frantically rushing to save our precious vegetables I tore after the pigs and to my dismay they split in two bunches, one group went east and the other went west. The east bunch I drove a quarter to a mile away and then got rid of the west group. To my horror the east group were back and so the merry chase went on. As I chased them they rooted up the row in their greedy snouts. Completely exhausted and frustrated I threw the knife in exasperation and to my shocked surprise I saw a curly pig tail fly through the air!

Tom sold his homestead to George Campbell and we moved to an irrigated farm at Duchess. We grew tons of everything, but nothing was worth much. We had to give the garden stuff away, and eggs were a mere 7 cents a dozen, butter was only 15 to 25 cents a pound.

Pat joined the Air Force after finishing high school. He went overseas a year later as a bomber pilot. Tom went to work for the

29

Department of Highways. We moved to Medicine Hat where Barbara and Michael finished high school. Barbara Ann went on to become a nurse, Michael took a job with Mannix Co. Ltd. Pat came back a Second Lieutenant from the War in the spring of 1946. He married about a year later and has four sons. He lives in Calgary. Barbara Ann and Michael both married in 1960. They each have two children.

Tom and I sold our home in Medicine Hat in 1968 and are now living in Calgary.

Adoph Wozeske, better known as "Fisher", his father having died and left four children in Germany, the mother remarried a man by the name of Fisher, who with his two brothers, Fred and Otto and their sister, Anne immigrated to Minnesota, U.S.A. Anne later married Dennis McCarthy, a Minnesota farmer and had eight children while her brothers came to Alberta. The Fisher family came the same year (1903), as did Clint Jarboe, both families travelled by covered wagon. The two ranchers were among the first on the Red Deer River — the originally Fisher ranch has changed hands many times over the years, but is still often referred to as the Fisher place.

Their sister's two oldest children, Mary and Tom came to their uncles' ranch in 1913. Mary married Jack Horne, whose father was a homesteader from Ontario and lived near Cappon. Mary and Jack had four children, but lost their first little girl in the flu epidemic in 1918. Later two boys and another girl were born. These two boys, Jack and Jimmie served in World War II. Mary Horne died in 1961. Jack remarried and is now a great-grandfather.

Tom McCarthy stayed on the ranch with his uncles till the ranch was sold. Both Fisher and Jarboe sold at the same time to Jack Foster. Fisher stayed on and ran the ranch for a year and Saul Boyer ran the Jarboe ranch. Then when Fisher left, Fosters ran their south place and sold the Jarboe place to W. D. McLennan and Tom acted as foreman for a couple of years.

Tom married Grace Callaghan in February 1923. Otto and Fred Fisher died while still fairly young, but Adoph lived to be eighty-six, making his home with his nephew Tom and family in the later years of his life.

Adoph Fisher was known for his stoic ability to ignore pain. One particular time he was driving a four horse team from Medicine Hat with a load of supplies. Somehow he broke his wrist on the way home, but he managed to drive to the south side of the Red Deer River. He still had to get across to his ranch on the north side. He managed to get help and only after arriving home safely with his team attended to did he go to Empress and have his arm cared for.

30

The following article appeared in the Medicine Hat News a few years ago.

MRS. E. FINDLAY, SISTER OF LOCAL WOMAN WINS TRIP TO ITALY

Mrs. Elizabeth Iris Findlay, 53, of Vancouver, only sister of Mrs. Thomas McCarthy, won a trip to Italy when she followed a "foolish impulse" after reading of the essay contest in a newspaper.

Mrs. Findlay searched her soldier son's letter for the background for an essay entitled, "Why I would Like to visit Italy" which won her second prize.

Trooper James D. Findlay of The Lord Strathcona Horse, is buried at Cassino, where he died May 25, 1944, during the march on Rome.

"I would like to see his grave and some of the things he saw. He wrote me so enthusiastically after he landed in Southern Italy, that it wasn't hard for me to write my essay," said Mrs. Findlay.

Mrs. Findlay will leave New York on November 25th on her trip which also includes England, Ireland and Scotland.

E. IRIS (CALLAGHAN) FINDLAY

My father, Daniel Callaghan homesteaded in the Buffalo district on land located five miles north of the Red Deer River and two miles east. There were four children in our family, two boys, Joe and Leo, my sister Grace and I. Joe married Thelma Gravette, they had two children, Maxine and Leroy. Maxine is married and lives near Edmonton, Leroy married Racheal Skjenna. They still live on the homestead.

Grace married Tom McCarthy and now lives in Calgary. Leo married late in life and worked for years on the C.P.R., both brothers have passed away. I have lived in B.C., for several years. I have three daughters, my son James Daniel was killed in action in Italy in 1944, while serving in the Canadian Army Forces. My brother

Joe Callaghan when he joined the army.

1941, Iris Findlay and daughters, Grace, Lucille and Betty.

31

Joe served in World War I. Our first post office in those days was Gold Springs. The first school was Emslie school, named for Jack Emslie. He and Jim Findlay were boyhood friends in Scotland and came to this country and took up adjoining homesteads in 1910. My father's homestead joined Jim Findlay's. Kid Howe located their land and brought them down from Oyen.

Some of the people that lived in the district at that time were: R. S. Gravette, George Howe Sr., and his sons, Howard McCullough, the Wozeske (Fisher) Brothers and of course the Gordons.

CALAMITY JANE (MRS. JANE RUDD)

Although this woman did not stay on the Red Deer very long, approximately four years in all, she is well remembered by many of the old-timers. A coulee on the shore of the Red Deer has been named for her. Someone said it was so named that it was so unpredictable, especially in the spring during the run-off. When it is filled with flood waters it is very deceiving and treacherous to cross. Dick Imes tells of the trip Calamity Jane and Dead-Wood (Dick Royston) made with his father, J. W. Imes, in 1905.

"A widow, Mrs. Jane Rudd and her helper Dick Royston came up from Big Timber, Montana to Gold Butte in 1903 with 500 head of stock. They were held up there along with J. W. Imes and son, Montana, and Steve Cicon of the Big Hole Basin, Montana, for one year. They were unable to cross the boundary line due to regulations to clean up the mange in Alberta and Montana. When they moved again, they put their outfits together, about 1000 head, with Calamity Jane as the captain. She would start the herd out at daylight and was on hand if trouble developed. Loose stock along the way was troublesome, but one of Jane's wild yells would soon clear the way. She was the first out in the morning and the last to eat supper. It was 180 miles to the Red Deer where Steve Cicon had his homestead on the Blood Indian Creek. Calamity Jane and Dead-Wood Dick built a two-room log cabin on the north side of the river. Dick also built the largest hayrack on the river and the loads he hauled were talked about for years."

Kid Howe tells a story of Calamity Jane which happened during the hard winter of 1906-'07. He went to help Calamity Jane and Dead-Wood Dick skin the dead animals. They put the hides on the live ones, as they thought it would help keep them warm, but she lost all but 24 head, which she later sold to J. W. Imes.

THE BILLY CAMPBELL FAMILY by Alfred Campbell

My father Billy Campbell came to the Dorothy district in 1909 and to the Buffalo district in 1930. There were four children, George who married May McLennan, Elizabeth (Boo) who married

William Thompson in 1937, they have two sons, Jack and Bob. Jack married Sammy Brassard and they have three children and live at Cavendish where Jack is employed on the Alberta Trunk Line. I married Jean Moore, Empress, in 1942, we have two sons, Clayton who is married and has two sons, they live in Saskatoon. He has his Masters in animal science and is presently working for his Ph.D. Allison is not married, he lives in Vancouver. He served with the R.C.M.P. for a few years but is now working as Public Relations for a Photo Finishing Firm. My other sister, Molly never married and she lives in Red Deer. Our mother passed away in the fifties and father died in 1935.

Some of things I recall that happened while we lived on the Red Deer River, was the river itself, especially when it would go on the rampage and overflow its banks as it did in 1940 when the water covered the flats on our place (George Howe lives there now), and in 1951 the flood waters came up and took out our corral fence after the ice had jammed as high as a house. This was the same year that the water came up in Cud Howe's house. The fall before when they had been doing some excavating preparing the foundation for the house they had moved in, the cold weather came before all the job was finished which left piles of mud all around the entrance, so in the spring things were quite muddy. To prevent too much of the mud being tracked into the house, Cud had a "catwalk" erected which entered the house through the bathroom window. He was down inspecting the river one day and when he turned to walk back to the house he saw that the water from the river had reached the house and Mrs. Howe was calling to him to come rescue her. In all the excitement and accustomed to entering the house over the catwalk, Cud again used the bathroom window to go in, but somehow as he went over the window sill he slipped and landed in the bath tub on all fours. Mrs. Howe said later, it wouldn't have made any difference had he came in through the door as the water would have cleaned his feet before he got very far, as it was about four feet deep then.

In 1938, a blizzard struck the district and lasted for three days, my brother, George had a ranch at Leader and I was still on the home place. We had cattle on both places and the storm killed approximately 100 head between the two ranches, while C. B. Howe lost all of his cattle. 1937 was a very dry year and on May 24 we had one of the worst dust storms I have ever seen.

Harry Muzyka said he was working for George Campbell, who in 1936 was living where Jack Thompson used to live, just north of the river by the bridge. George had about 1000 head of cattle, feed was scarce and four men couldn't haul feed fast enough to feed them. Harry recalls that they had to haul the hay from Buffalo which had been shipped in. In 1960 Alfred sold out to Ray Eggar and moved to Medicine Hat.

The Campbell's brand on the cattle was ☐ S on left rib, and on the horses **BY** left hip and $\underset{C}{O}$ also left hip.

THE DONALD McKENZIE (HAPPY) CAMPBELL FAMILY

The Campbell ranch is part of the old Andrew Gordon ranch. By hard work and initiative, Happy and his wife Mary, have built this ranch into a thriving horse and cattle unit. From the spring-fed (watered) hay meadow, they put up enough feed for winter.

They have three sons, Jim, Johnny and Billy as well as six daughters, Patricia (Mrs. Harold Fieldburg), Mary Jane (Mrs. Ben Hern), Peggy (Mrs. Billy Herman), Kay (Mrs. George Lapp), Kathy (Mrs. Don Southerland) and Judy.

The family are all very fond of horses and very good at helping out on the ranch. Kathy and Don, for instant train quarter horses and back in 1961 Reg Kesler sent them a bunch of colts to school and gentle for the annual Calgary horse sale. Reg said of them, "Anything that Kathy and Don can't put under a usin' saddle will generally qualify for the Dallas Finals. I just turn them in with the 'Bucking' String."

Happy recalls one day at the Medicine Hat Stampede. "I had signed up in the calf roping event, but the day of the show I couldn't make it, but Mary went along with Kathy as she was entered in the girls' barrel race. When they called my name for the calf roping event, Kathy rode in there on her pet barrel racer, and told the calf-chute judge that she would take Happy Campbell's calf.

Despite the fact calf roping, as far as the chute-judge was concerned, was still a man's game, Kathy did take the event, after she'd explained to him that our family works as a team, if one couldn't do it, then another member of the family steps in and does all they can to get it done. Plus the fact our family never likes to see anything go to waste and as the entry fee had already been paid, so Kathy, with her little quarter horse in the calf-barrier, ropes ready gave a nod of the head and the calf was released and they were off in a cloud of dust, three whirls of the rope and the girl made her cast, looping the calf neatly about the throat. The arena dirt flew high as the horse, feeling the slight touch of the bridle rein broke to a sliding stop. Kathy's slight figure was a poor match for the fighting calf, but somehow, she managed to throw it. Three quick wraps and the half-hitch, her hands went up. While her time was not good enough for that day's events, it was good enough for most arenas, but the important thing was our ranch was represented."

34

Before coming to the Red Deer, Happy worked for such outfits as the Pat Burns and the Streetcar ranches.

It was while he was at the Streeters — Harry, Allie and Jack, who were great ropers, Happy began roping calves at Canadian rodeos. Happy is of slight build, and has always been interested in all types of athletic sports, not only roping, but he is quite handy with a pair of boxing gloves. This past winter he has been teaching the students of the Buffalo school the fine art of boxing.

TRIBUTE TO MRS. MAMIE CICON — ON HER 80th BIRTHDAY, IN 1969 by Robin (Baker) Krause

Mr. C. B. Howe and Mrs. M. Cicon on June 14, 1969.

There's a famous storyteller, who lives down Buffalo way,
A chronicler of good times and events of yesterday.
At brandings and reunions, where'er folks gather around
They hark to Mamie Cicon, for they know her tales abound.
If you ask her about the early days when she was just a lass,
She'll tell you how her parents, from the province of Alsace,
Came sailing o'er the ocean (it was a daring thing)
And settled in Eureka, beside the famous springs.
Now Mr. Schier was anxious to make the good crop grow,
So he hitched the horse and buckboard and trekked to Idaho.
And then, 'twas some time later, the year of 1910,
They gathered house and children up and started north again.
This time they reached Alberta, tho' some weeks it did take
And filed upon a homestead right near to Cabin Lake;
But a young man seeking horses Steve Cicon was his name,
Spied the pert young Mamie, and made Schiers move their claim.

35

So they moved into our district (brother Juel lives there still)
And built a homestead cabin tight up against the hill;
But about a year later, Mamie left her family there,
And moved next door to Cicons' her life with Steve to share.
They built a fine log cabin, a half-mile over west,
And there raised six fine children, four boys, two girls, the best.
And all were very happy, 'til in a storm one day,
The hired man said calmly, "Steve, the roof just blew away."
Yes, the cabin was quite topless, and underground they flew,
Mamie, Steve, the children and the dauntless hired man too;
But floors within log cabins are not made waterproof,
And rain poured down and drenched them from the air-conditioned
    roof.
When the cyclone left them, for so the storm had been,
They cautiously crept upward to view the ravaged scene,
And found the roof, in leaving, had smashed the windmill too,
And one and all decided 'twas time to start anew.
When the new house was completed, the one you see today,
The family settled in again to work, and oft' to play,
And there are many stories that you will want to hear,
The happy will bring laughter, the sad may bring a tear.
There's the one about the milk cow, who the granary did spy,
The afternoon that Mamie entertained the W.I.
And up and down the roadway the ladies tell with glee,
She chased the cow so they could have some ice cream with their tea
The Cicons had a democrat to drive into the town,
"We're going to lose the children," said Mother with a frown,
And kept on counting noses, to see that all were there,
For the bottom of the buggy was in great need of repair.
And so they bought a Buick, a beautiful machine,
A shiny big MacLaughlin — the neighbors all were green!
And tho' through the depression it had built-in setting hens,
With gasoline, it sallied forth to run about again.
As the years moved to the thirties, the times for all were tough,
And often it is hardship that makes folks show their stuff.
And Mamie's ingenuity is talked about today,
As she fed and clothed her family in a multitude of ways.
It seemed throughout the decade fortune shunned them constantly,
For in 1937 Steve was stricken suddenly.
And though they struggled bravely, the next spring it was found
That during a flash blizzard, their cattle herd was drowned.
But through all this misfortune, Mamie's spirit still was strong,
For like a supple willow, she could not bend for long.

36

And now she started over, the family carried on,
They knew that naught could daunt them with Mom to lean upon.
So onward through the forties, the years throughout the war,
They carried on, though soldier Bill would come home never more.
And tho' I can't forever tell stories at this rate,
There's one more tale I've heard of which I feel I must relate.
It seems inventor Rusty had built a balance scale
To weigh the pigs for market, to ship upon the rail,
And asked his Mom to test it: she exclaimed with glee,
"If I'm supposed to be a pig, why then a pig I'll be!"
She jumped and squealed quite spryly — the effect it was so real
The old sow, resting nearby, knew she heard her piglet squeal,
And up and after Rusty, who was heard to roar with rage
As he ran into the sunset — "Ma, can't you act your age?"
Well, I am but a novice at the storytelling task
If you want to hear them better, may I suggest you ask
The famous storyteller, who lives down Buffalo way,
The one whose eightieth birthday we honor here today.
Whose keen determination, well mixed with hard work too,
And endless sense of humor has brought the family through,
And if you look about you, I'm sure that you would say,
That not a one among us could call them poor today.
And now for all we gathered, I'd like a toast to pose,
To Mrs. Mamie Cicon, whose fame and fortune grows,
Our wishes for you, Granny, we offer with great cheer—
For now and ever after — God Bless, Good Health, Long Years.

   Editor's Note: Our good friend and trusted neighbor passed away
in May of this year. (1971)

MR. AND MRS. ALBERT COOK by Etta (Cook) Rubbelke

   My parents, Albert and Marie, and I, came from Clifford,
Ontario in July, 1912. My father worked on the irrigation ditches
at Suffield and we lived in a tent until we moved to the homestead,
seven miles south of Cavendish in late August.

   In 1933 or '34 my parents moved to the Frank Hughes place,
now occupied by Arnold Rubbelke and family. In about 1949 they
moved into the town of Buffalo. My father passed away in April,
1951, my mother continued to live at Buffalo until 1965 when she
went to live at the Newbrook Lodge at Brooks, Alberta.

   I recall my school days at Cornland and Cavendish. I used to
ride a horse and once a week while returning from school I would
pick up our groceries. One day the weather was quite warm and so
was the horse, the worst happened. Can you picture a white horse
with melted butter running down its sides?

I have many recollections of the happy fun times we used to have at picnics both at Cavendish and Buffalo. One thing that is very vivid in my memory about a picnic in Cavendish was back in 1921 or '22 when Andy Ulrick and Slim Tillier took part in the entertainment for the day. Andy was the stagecoach driver and Slim rode shotgun for him. The stage was hauling passengers and the mail along with the customary money box, there were others who wore masks and took the part of the outlaws, led by a fellow by the name of Rotter.

When Andy got his passengers and money box on board and Slim was seated up with the driver and the four-horse team stood waiting for the starting gun to sound, a large crowd had gathered to watch the excitement. Suddenly the shot from the starter was sounded and away went the stagecoach travelling first west and then south, towards where Howard Jones now lives. Close on their heels came a bunch of outlaws, guns ablazing and soon Slim hits the dust, the stagecoach was robbed and the passengers were scattered and the outlaws made a "clean get-away." It was all very real and very entertaining. Andy said afterwards if he'd had a team of mules they would never have caught him. I think he had a special team of mules in mind, one that was noted for being "runaways".

MR. AND MRS. ARTHUR (SLIM) DAVIDSON ON THEIR 25TH WEDDING ANNIVERSARY
by Violet (Bicknell) Stone

At home on the range a rough and roguish guy,
A Saskatchewan lad gone west under the big blue sky.
The going was tough and the wages small,
And at times it was rough to even live at all.
But he was young and brave of heart,
And determined to make a roaring start,
    That Guy named Slim.

At the Gilchrist ranch he started his great career,
As an animal lover he would make it never fear.
As a bold cowpuncher he rode the range,
At times he felt lonely and sad and strange.
But he kept real busy and as time went by,
He made many friends to help it fly.
    That Guy named Slim.

Now it happened a gal who was named Irene,
At the Gilchrist ranch had just made the scene.
Her big blue eyes and curly hair,
Caused many a fellow to stop and stare.

Now all these chaps she just passed right by,
But one had caught her with the wink of an eye.
  'Twas a Guy called Slim.

Now Slim was lucky both at cards and at love,
But at Anti-I over with no moon above,
Made a dash for the catch of the season to make
When a clothes-line got in the road of his take,
It cut his lips but he still could smoke,
But the kissing he missed sure did provoke,
  Her Guy named Slim.

Now another time when his luck was down,
He purchased a brand new hat in town.
He was happy and proud as he rode back out,
But the wind took his hat and he gave a shout.
Rushed into the river where it had blown,
While his sweetheart waited afraid and alone.
  For a Guy named Slim.

They had many meetings on the ranch and off,
But the place they love best was the old hayloft.
The question was popped and the day was set,
And they both gave thanks that they had met.
At Milk River October eleventh Rev. Karpoff tied the knot,
And the Twin River school saw a dance so hot.
  For the Guy named Slim.

Now this young couple settled right down to work,
And 'tis said that neither was prone to shirk.
They worked for Gilchrist and Alton the same,
Even tried their hand at the gold rush game.
When Slim joined his father in northern B.C.,
To share in the wealth of the family tree.
  Of a Guy named Slim.

They ran the Twin River post office and store,
Gave a hand to brother Earl and many more.
During fifty-two and fifty-three,
They became acquainted with you and me.
As they took up residence at the new Jones place
Where we learned to know Irene's happy face.
  And a Guy named Slim.

They finished work there in fifty-three,
Spent the winter at Beck's, it seems to me.
Now tired of working and wandering about,
Decided to buy Percy Taylor out.

Spent winter down on the Ferguson spread,
That he was lazy could truly never be said,
     Of a Guy named Slim.

Though multiplication was not part of their lot,
To their family they've added full many a lot.
They've divided their time and their love and their joys,
When kind neighbors doubled with both girls and boys.
Now to us all it's easily seen,
To most kids they've become our Aunty Rene.
     And a Guy named Slim.

We are glad they reached this twenty-fifth year,
With a home of their own and a farm all clear.
And that we have them here with us as neighbors and friends,
For their kindness and goodwill knows no ends.
As their Silver Anniversary we help celebrate,
To Irene give our blessings and congratulate.
     That Guy named Slim.

THE WILLIAM DEARING FAMILY by Mrs. Lauretta Dearing (1967)

The Dearing family came to this district in 1916 from Sault Ste. Marie, Ontario. They homesteaded on the S.W. 16-21-5-4. They had four children: Lila (Mrs. Elias Schlaht) died in 1970, Hazel (Mrs. Wm. Paisch) Grande Prairie, Daisy (Mrs. Denzel Bunny) lives at Duchess, Alma (Mrs. Charlie Wambeke) lives at High River. Gilbert (Bob) Dearing and Orville live at Okotoks, Clifford lives in British Columbia, Roy lives at Bowden and Vernon lives at Buffalo. Orville and Clifford served in the armed forces from 1941 to '46.

Other people living in this district when the Dearings came were: A. McKay, Darts, Dillworth, Mayhew, J. Scanes, Mode, Salzwedel, Earl Thompson, Edington, Taylors, Edgerton, Allan Gatenbow and Baptiste.

The post office was at Pancras, (Cavendish) when the Dearings arrived by horse and buggy. Their first home was a converted granary. Mrs. Dearing's father, Henry Smythe was the first superintendent for the Sunday school which was held in his house, with older boys and all adults attending. For entertainment there was hockey, parties at Mrs. Dearing's parents' home, who also had a lawn croquet set which was used a great deal, and of course, there was also a ball game. The Dearings lived here until 1954. Mrs. Dearing passed away in 1968.

Mr. and Mrs. Fred Dewald. (No story submitted but the following was written by Mrs. Violet Stone for their 25th Wedding Anniversary.)
Fred and Vera DeWald

He was a bashful country boy,
His father's pride, his mother's joy.
Girls as a rule did him annoy

For Fred they had no part
Until a Scottish lass he found
A right sweet lassie, I'll be bound.
And with her started running around.

For Vera won his heart.
So teacher chose a wedding gown
In '41 they settled down.
Soon made their home near Buffalo-town

On the river flats.
For honeymooners, just the place
But there was lots of bush and space
On their pump-house flat.

They made a home so nice and neat
With paint and plumbing all complete.
Their hospitality hard to beat

Bade you come inside.
Both were so clever in their way
Fred's hands knew not an idle day
As Vera used her head they say

For teaching on the side.
They were a busy pair indeed
Spring made them realize the need
Of hoe and rake and lots of seed

A garden they must grow.
As weeds and bugs and drought they fought
They turned a lonely barren lot
Into a regular beauty spot

A place we loved to go.
With all the things they had to do
They still had time for me and you.
For building halls and meetings too
This busy, busy pair.

Now they live out Ralston way
Still both are busy every day
And it behooves us now to say
Such folks as these are rare.

41

Years have a way of passing by
These twenty-five did really fly.
No matter now had hard we try
We can't believe it's true.

Forgive us if we couldn't wait
For the proper day to celebrate
Our wish sincere at any rate
We now extend to you.

THE JOHN FOSTER STORY by Stacey Foster

My father and mother were born 40 miles from Ottawa on the Quebec side of the Gatineau River. My father was born May 1, 1864. Their parents came from the north of Ireland along with a group that settled there. My father came to Melfort, Saskatchewan, first in 1896 before the railroad came in. He worked at Melfort for the summer and took up a homestead and then went back East in the fall. He was married in 1899. They lived at Cawood, Quebec, until

Stacey Foster 17 years. Clinton Jarboe. John Foster 56, born in 1864 — died 1953. Adolph Fisher and MacGuckin.

Carl Hoag, cook and Garner Foster 1925.

1904 when they came back to Melfort, with three boys and two girls. The two girls died shortly after coming to Melfort. The oldest boy died with the flu in 1918. Three more girls were born in Melfort and another son in 1916.

We run about a thousand head of cattle and 650 head of horses in Alberta, although we cut down on our horses as soon as we could. I went to Alberta in 1920 when I was only 17 years old and ran the ranch until 1930 when we sold it. My father and brother stayed in Melfort to look after the farm and cattle. We had a larger operation in the cattle business in Melfort than we had in Alberta, but the land in Melfort got broke up as they started farming on a larger scale when World War I broke out. By 1920 there was no

42

more room for cattle so we moved to Alberta. In the fall of 1917 we sold 850 head of cattle to Pat Burns to be shipped overseas.

My father and I went to Alberta in the summer of 1919, where he bought the McFarland ranch and horses. On April 23, 1920, I brought 250 head of cattle from Melfort. I was holding them south of Oyen at Appleby's place on May 6, when a storm came up from the east and drifted the cattle west to Alkali Creek. I rode to the ranch to get help to gather them up and take them to the ranch. Adolph Fisher, Clinton Jarboe and Mac McGuckin rode out to help me. I went back to Saskatchewan and stayed until October. In the meantime my father had bought the Jarboe and Fisher ranch from W. D. McLennan, the cattle and horses were included in this sale. He also bought 144 head of horses from John Wilson. McGuckin was working for Wilson at this time. Saul Boyer was working for us and we lived on the Jarboe ranch until we sold it back to W. D. McLennan in the fall 1922. We then moved to the Fisher ranch. Father sold the Fisher and McFarland ranch to Thomas Campbell from Kamloops on March 23, 1930, including the cattle and the saddle and work horses. That fall Thomas Campbell sold the ranches to William Campbell, from the Dorothy district. Wm. Campbell had two sons, Alfred and George.

George bought a ranch at Leader, Saskatchewan and Alfred took over the ranch on the Red Deer for a few years and in 1960 Ray Egar took up residence on this ranch and in 1962 the ranch was bought by George Howe and he and his family still live there.

In 1929 I married Ethel Olds, her parents were homesteaders just north of our ranch. We have two daughters and one son. One daughter Margaret is married to Bob Lowe and lives in Lethbridge. Gladys is married to a druggist and lives in Regina and George, our only son, is married and lives in Melfort where he owns a Men's Wear Shop.

JOHN R. GORDON by Mrs. Jennie (Stewart) Hausness

John came to this district as a very young lad, with his parents, Mr. and Mrs. Andrew Gordon, the first white family to settle here. (See "True Tales of days that are gone.")

He was an ordained minister and worked tirelessly to spread the Gospel in the district. He always had a student minister come during the summer months and even supplied them with a horse and buggy or saddle horse to make their calls.

During the "dirty thirties" he had a general store and he never saw anyone go hungry. Later he gave up the store but kept the post office and the Esso bulk tank.

I worked for the Gordons from 1922 to 1935, cooking for 25 to 35 men. No one ever came to the ranch that wasn't made to feel welcome. The Gordons ran both horses and cattle and it would take four or five days to do the branding. SC left rib, > G right rib, horse brand was + right jaw. John married Fay Sparks in Medicine Hat in 1916, they moved to Oliver, B.C., where they had a mixed fruit orchard. In a few years they came back to the Buffalo district and took over his father's ranch, where the Majestic ranch is now located.

They had one daughter, Biddie, (Mrs. George Burchell) to bless their union.

It is my opinion that if ever a Saint walked on this earth, John R. Gordon was one.

They left the Buffalo district in 1946 and have lived in Calgary ever since.

HERCHELL P. GRAVETTE

I came to this district in 1907 with my mother and sister, Thelma, from Missouri, to join my father, Rudolph S. Gravette who took up homesteading on Section 22-18-13 in 1906. Our first home was a dugout in the side of a hill. The front was made of poles and logs, and it had a dirt roof. In 1911, logs were retrieved from the Red Deer River to add more to the house. It was thought these logs had broken loose from a sawmill far up the river, no doubt around Rocky Mountain House, the only habitation, and this was an early trading post founded long before a road was found to the Pacific Ocean. Most every house built by the early settlers had some of these logs in them, obtained in the same manner. For years a pile of these logs could be found on the ranch where Fisher, later Alfred Campbell lived, and now George Howe lives.

The first post office was Gold Springs, so named because of the yellow sand found in the spring, and situated just east of the McCullough ranch buildings.

A few of the people already living here when we arrived, were Kennedys, Van Cleves, Clinton Jarboe, Herb Gallup, Howard McCullough, the Gordons, George Howes, Bjorks, Nelsons, Hallam, Tom Owen, Wozesky and Fishers. Some of the Metis living here when we came were: Sam McKays, Dick Laroche, Joe Dumont (Joe and his father were killed at Duck Lake) and Alex LaFromboise.

There was no church until much later, but services were held in the various homes whenever there was anyone to preach. My sister and I received our schooling at home from our mother, who taught us history, geography, reading, physiology and geometry, all from books she had brought with her from the U.S.A. She was a very good

Grace McCarthy, Audrey Gravette, Thelma Gravette, Mrs. Ben Anderson, Mrs. C. B. Howe, with children in 1926.

teacher too because by the time I was 10 years old I could do cube roots in mathematics and name every bone in the human skeleton. When I was 11 or 12 my father hired a fellow by the name of Carl Cottingham, commonly known as "Bronc." He was a college graduate from the States. It was about this time the country was beginning to settle up and father was able to get a real teacher, a Miss Luella Arnold from Alsask, who later married Lincoln Howe. Not only was she my teacher, but she was also my first love. Why the very thought of her name would fill me with goose pimples all over. I was only a boy of 13 at the time, while she would be in her late twenties. Our entertainment in those days would be whatever we could invent: dances, card games and bucking horses. My mother cooked on a cast iron wood and coal stove. There was no coal available, the wood was gathered along the river banks. For a quick fire we often used "buffalo chips" which were quite plentiful. They produced a very intense heat and one got used to the heady aroma from the flames. Coffee was in beans and had to be ground by hand.

The nearest doctor was at Alsask, so whenever a child was born in this country the doctor usually didn't get here until a day or so later. Neighbor women would be midwife for each other.

We ran horses and cattle. Our horse brand $\underset{U}{\mathrm{I}}$ (left jaw)

Our cattle brands $\overline{5\,M}$ (right side) $\underset{V}{ZM}$ (left hip)

It was quite a few years later before grain was raised for commercial purposes. Our first plow was the walking plow or the "old foot burner" as it was called. The cattle drives in my time

45

were just from the lease to the siding where we loaded them, a distant from 10 to 30 miles.

All I can recall about the Royal Northwest Mounted Police was that they were stationed for years at what is now known as the V Bar V. They would patrol the river front for miles. It was unlawful to shoot antelope, but I never heard of anyone being arrested. The RNWMP were quite awesome to us kids. All mother would have to say was, "The Mounties will take you away," and we would sure try to be good.

As I have mentioned it was unlawful to shoot antelope. This is a true story about some people, it was so long ago I don't remember their name. These people had antelope steak cooking on the stove when the Mountie stopped at their home for the night. Come supper time, the Mountie ate as much or even more than anyone else. After supper the rancher and the policeman were coming from the barn after doing the chores for the night. It was very cold and the smoke from the stovepipe on the house was quite dense, someone had probably put a chunk of wood in the old tin heater; the Mountie stopped, sniffed the air and casually remarked, "That smells like antelope hair." Just a nice way to let the rancher know that he wasn't fooled one little bit by the nice supper steaks.

Meat was always frozen in winter. It was too hard to cut and very few people had meat saws. I remember one day visiting at the home of C. B. Howe and as mealtime drew near, his wife, Eileen said, "Cud go cut some steaks." Cud went out to the old log house, which was formerly lived in but now was being used for storage, storing anything from "soup to nuts" as the saying goes. He takes this hind quarter of frozen beef from a big spike nailed in the wall and takes it outside in 40 degree below weather, lays it down in the snow, puts one big overshoe (with foot inside, of course) on the meat and with a big double-bitted axe began to swing. Well, steaks began to fly, all sizes from slivers to two inches thick. When he got out of breath us kids began to pick them up out of the snow. We even found steaks fifty yards from the scene of combat.

When I was about 14 or 15 years of age, I had an old Ivor Johnston six-shooter which I had won from Ole Kjarland in a cribbage game. Well, I carried this shooting' iron for sometime, concealed of course. When I was riding the lease and the commons I don't know how many Indians I killed; shot heads off imaginary rattlesnakes; silver dollars, in the air, went spinning and there never was a draw which equalled that of "Old H.P.J." Well, after a while, after I had become a "seasoned veteran of the plains," I was quite daring one evening, while sitting around the old tin heater after supper, I produced my shootin' iron and began to clean it up, drew an oiled

Kid Howe and Pals.

rag through the barrel, oiled all the working parts and was really beginning to have it shining like a silver dollar. Well, about this time, my dad, who was sitting at the radio, earphones clamped to his ears, looking like something from outer space, looked around and saw what I was doing. Well, after the doors quit rattling, the roof settled back down and the brimstone cleared away, I was not so dense but what I gathered he was very much against this "wild-west" life that I had been enjoying. I was supposed to give the gun back to Ole, but that I wouldn't do. But knowing my father, I knew I had to get rid of the gun, but before I "departed" with it, I wanted to hear it "bang". I had no shells but I knew where I might get some, so up to the "Old Howe" ranch I went. Kid had some 45 automatics which fit but, being more powerful than ordinary 45's I was afraid to shoot it out of my hand, so we put it in a vise there in the shop, tied a string to the trigger and to further complicate things, Grant put a wagon rod down the barrel, well, we played the binder twine out around the corner of the building; got down on our hands and knees, so we wouldn't be hit by flying timbers and pulled the string. The results were quite disappointing: "no big boom," just an ordinary gunshot and a slight thump when the wagon rod hit the ceiling. We went inside to view the results. The handle of the six-shooter was still in the vise, the barrel was over in a corner and the cylinder, with five unfired shells lay alongside the wagon rod. Well, there were yet five unfired shells **that had** to be used up. Someone suggested putting the cylinder on a post and shooting it off with a shotgun. No one seemed anxious to do the shooting, but it seemed

47

alright if I would do it, after all it was my party. Well, I banged the old shotgun at these five shells in the cylinder sitting on the post and the results were most gratifying, quite a large "boom", all the shells went off, the cylinder exploded into a thousand pieces, one which hit me in the shin, I was afraid to look because I just knew that I was mortally wounded, but shucks there wasn't even any gore, just a red spot where I was hit. Well that was the last of my six-gun days.

In the early days, before we had any schools in this part of the country, different ranchers would engage the services of young teachers who would live with the family. I recall one teacher who was teaching at the Bjork ranch, a Miss Imes. A fellow from Medicine Hat, Bill Conrad (they later married) came sparking Miss Imes. For privacy they used to walk up the coulee (ravine) away from everyone and sit on a big white rock (it's still there) and make "woo". One day when we were up at Bjorks this took place, only us kids were not very far behind and when they got seated, we rolled rocks down the hill towards them: rocks as big as a stove, it took all us kids to get them started. Once they gained momentum they would bounce 100 feet into the air and crash, sparks would fly and we would have another one on its way. We never thought of them being hit, they were supposed to get out of the way. They did or they wouldn't have been with us anymore. I suppose it could have been called "attempted homicide," but goodness sakes, we never thought once that anyone could have been injured, to say nothing of probably been blasted off the face of the earth. It was just nice clean fun.

Then there was Magnus Bjork's last day in school. "Skinny" he was always called, even to this day he is Skinny to all his boyhood friends. Their school was a private governess at home, as I mentioned before. One cold day in January the boys at the Howe ranch see this horseback rider riding into the yard. He had a big sheepskin overcoat on with earflaps down, it was around 45 below. He put his horse in the barn and came on into the house. "Why, it's Skinny," Lincoln says. "What is the matter, Skinny? Why are you not at home in school?" "Well," says Skinny, "when a person gets to know more than his teacher, there is no use going to school any longer." It seems as though Skinny and his teacher had an argument about something and Skinny being more informed on the subject under discussion than the teacher proved his point and she had to admit that he could be right. So terminated Skinny's educational program. Those were the happy days.

Then there was the time that I decided to sow my "wild oats". What a forlorn hope for the young fellows those days. When there was practically no "summerfallow," (no girls). My center of interest was a war nurse. I can't remember her name, she came back from overseas after World War I, with a fellow by the name of Jack Robinson, "Big Jack" he was called. Well after a lot of planning I managed to get an extra horse and saddle for her and we rode down to the hills on the south side of the Red Deer River, got off our ponies, found a nice place to sit down in the shade of a big rock on a hot Sunday afternoon. We held hands and I was allowed to kiss her once or twice. (She was nearly old enough to be my mother.) After some time of this innocent fun, things reached an impasse. I was wondering what to do now and I was completely "stumped". Then I remembered some of the books that Mother had hidden from us kids, but which I had managed to find and read. It seemed in the books that the girl who was "wronged" could blame it on the villain who would promise her marriage. That was the secret then. Hadn't I wronged her? Hadn't I kissed her? Then I was the villain. So I proposed to her and after talking it over I was to join the army and turn my pay over to her. Soon it was time to go home. I was still wondering just what went haywire. She told Ed Pound all about it and I was the victim of very bad jokes for some time. I decided never to trust another woman and vowed I would remain pure all the rest of my life.

Editor's Note: H. P. Gravette had three wives, one son, three daughters, three stepdaughters and two stepsons, six grandchildren.

There was this green Englishman by the name of Ronald Hurd. (He died some years back with cancer.) Back in the early twenties, I was running a separator on a big steam threshing outfit, owned by the McKay Bros. at Helmsdale, about 27 miles north of Buffalo. Labor was scarce and immigrants were being shipped over to Canada from the "Old Country" to help with the harvest on the prairies. So one day the Boss brought back from town a young lad around 18 or 19 years of age, a lad from England, fresh from the old sod. This was Ron Hurd. They gave him a job hauling water for the steam engine. After he had been with us for about a week, we were threshing for a person by the name of Charlie Algreen. Now Charlie was alleged to be the countryside bootlegger.

In the granary, we were threshing into, was a 40-ounce bottle of this home brew. I believe the main object was to soften me up so that I would probably give him 90 lbs. of wheat to the bushel, I couldn't drink the stuff, so I didn't give him much over 60 lbs. Well, Ron came up to where I was at the granary door and he saw this bottle standing up in the wheat alongside the door. He wanted to know what it was so I told him and he managed to get down two or three drinks of this powerful stuff. After the next tank of water he hauled he came around again. His eyes were

49

shining and as big as an owl's. I asked him if he felt anything and he assured me that he didn't feel a thing so I told him that we could fix that and he was all for it. He took a big drink until he lost his breath so I insisted he have one more. "Take a big one, Ron," I said and he lowered it about three inches then away he went for another tank of water. After a long time, water in the steamer was getting low so they began to blow the whistle "which meant water is low, come with what you have". Meanwhile, about a mile or two away Ron had driven up to this slough which he was getting water from, threw out the big long hose, and began pumping, but the hose was not in the water so old Ron was pumping nothing but air for about an hour. When he heard the whistle blowing he checked the water level in the tank and found it was nil, he then noticed the hose laying out on dry land, he put it in the slough pumping a few gallons and headed back to the rig. I'll never forget the scene: across the dusty summerfallow came Ron on his tank wagon; behind him the sun was just going down; the long hose dragging behind the wagon. He hadn't even coiled it up and put it on top of the tank where it belonged. His head was bowed in his hands and only had one line, the other one was dragging on the ground. By this time the engine had quit blowing its whistle, no steam left and Ron didn't even have enough water in the tank to fill a tub. As I mentioned labor was scarce so he wasn't fired. After threshing was finished I persuaded him to come home with me and help do chores for the winter. He did, and stayed and worked for my father for a number of years.

Later before freeze-up we were crossing cattle over the river to Buffalo, to ship from there. One old steer was quite troublesome, he didn't want to swim the river with the rest and with him heading for the brush and being chased out again, he became overheated and laid down and died. The next morning I had Ron come with me to help skin and cut-up this steer for coyote bait. When we arrived to where the dead steer was, we had company, the ferryman, "Bronc" the same person who used to be my schoolteacher, was there. I believe he had a notion to use the animal for coyote bait himself. Well, I was standing alongside the steer and I happened to lean my knees against the side of the dead animal and bubbles came out of the steer's nose. Ron cried out, "It's alive! We can't skin it!" Bronc told him to go across the river and get his axe to kill it with. Well, Ron got the axe and he got the job of killing the dead steer. Everytime he would hit it I would make some more bubbles come and Bronc would say, "Hit it again, hit it until it bawls and when it bawls it is dead." Well, Old Ron wound up and delivered a heck of a blow, broke the axe handle. I quit pushing and making

Ron Hurd, World War I.

bubbles and declared the animal sufficiently dead. Bronc was mad because his axe handle was broken and things weren't nearly as funny to him then. That winter at our Christmas Concert, Francis (Buster) McCullough, who was on the entertainment committee made up a song consisting of things that had happened to several of the neighbors around. Buster, who was quite clever this way, arranged the incident to a humorous song sung to the tune of "Howdy Do you Do", which was the rage that year. Of course, this incident of Ron Hurd with the dead steer was included, which went something like this: "As a butcher you're a bird, hits them twice, sometimes a third."

Ron was quite a boisterous sort of a fellow and enjoyed a joke even at his own expense. He threw his head back with a great, "Haw Haw". A neighbor who was sitting on the bench just behind him leaning forward to hear and see better, was struck between the horns by the back of Ron's head and knocked kicking. After we rubbed him with snow he was able to enjoy the concert. Ron didn't even have a headache.

Later that winter, a fellow by the name of Clyde Jarboe came to the ranch one day riding a horse which he had just recently broken to the saddle. Well, Ron wanted to be a rider so Clyde Hartwell, who was also staying with us that winter, and I would get Ron on Clyde's saddle pony and put the spurs to him. This was a morning ritual when we went out to do the chores, of course Clyde Jarboe wouldn't be with us. One didn't wake the company up to help do the chores. Well by the end of a week, Ron could stay on sometimes by squeezing the jug handle with both hands (pulling leather). So when Clyde Jarboe got ready to leave he never could understand why his well-broke pony bucked him off four times in a row before he got him tamed down. To this day I don't believe he ever found out we caused his pony to buck Ron off three or four times before breakfast.

Ron Hurd wanted to learn the American game of poker. We taught him a little bit to get him started like the relative power of

51

different hands, etc. Whenever there was a dance at Buffalo or anywhere there was always an accompanying poker game. In Buffalo it was held in the backroom behind Woo Sam's store. This one night Ron was playing in the game with all the seasoned poker players of the time. I was not taking part as I was one of the orchestra, but whenever there was an intermission I would go out to see how my pupil was making out. When you watch a poker game for a while you get the lay of the land pretty plain. My father had been losing all night and his arch-enemy and near neighbor,

Called in the reserves. Party lasted over a week on the Red Deer.

As it was.

Too big a task for one man.

Joe O'Brien was the big winner, then this one hand came up. The betting was very brisk and soon one of the biggest pots of the evening came. If Dad won this one he would recoup all his losses. They were playing "stud poker" and by the time all the cards were out, there were only three players contesting the pot. O'Brien, Ron Hurd and Dad, in that rotation. O'Brien had a pair of threes early in the game and was betting them high, on the last card he caught the third three and he pushed all into the pot. Dad had tens back to back and caught a third ten on last card and here is what the three hands looked like then.

52

O'Brien — hole card nothing — 3-3-8-3
Ron — hole card nothing — 10-J-Q-K
Dad — hole card ten — 10-6-5-10

Well Ron with his big possible straight on top called, well, with the possible straight just called, Dad's three tens were no good, so he tossed them in. Ron turned over his hole card which was nothing and O'Brien pulled in the pot. Ron thought that he had a straight as long as the ones on top was a straight. Well Dad was fit to be tied. There was fire and brimstone with a lot of descriptive adjectives regarding "green Englishmen".

The next day Clyde Hartwell and myself were going hunting and asked Ron to come along. He had a horse but no saddle, so we told him to borrow Dad's. He said that he was scared to ask him and Clyde asked him why and he said, "I run a whizzer on him last night." You see he was learning the poker phrases if not the game.

One night Herchell Gravette and Ron Hurd were coming home from a dance. It was very late and they were travelling by team and wagon, with Ron as teamster. When they reached the south side of the river the horses didn't want to go any farther. Herchell got down from the wagon, tied the bridles to the hames and when he got back on the wagon he let a "war-whooper" out at the horses and they took off. Ron still with the reins in his hands was unaware of what Herchell had done, so when he thought the horses were going too fast he tried to rein them in, thinking they still had the bit in their mouth. Turning to Herchell he told him he couldn't hold them. "You want to get home don't you?" Herchell asked him. "Yes," said the frightened Englishman, "but all in one piece." The horses never slowed down until they reached the home corral.

Old-timers will talk until this day about some of Herchell P. Gravette's "run-aways".

The following is a story about a "run-away" when I was about 18 years old. Even at that age I had to ask my father's permission to go to a dance. There was a dance at Atlee one Friday night. I had Dad's permission to go, with the understanding that I'd be home in the morning to haul in the four loads of rye. I'd borrow a horse and buggy from Ole Kjarland, I picked up my date and away we went.

It was nearly daylight when we left the dance and during the drive to the young lady's home, we decided I should stay over and we'd go to another party on Saturday. After all, I could haul that rye another day. So after the party on Saturday night, we thought it would be nice if I'd stay and we would visit some friends on Sunday, so by the time I finally got home it was around ten o'clock

Monday morning. Mother told me that Dad was very cross because I hadn't got back to haul that rye in. Father was out on the lease checking the cattle, so I decided to harness the team and get the rye in before he got back.

Everything went fine until I went to climb up on to the big hayrack. As I pulled myself up over the side of the rack, it tipped, frightening the horses and they took off with the rack dragging behind the wagon, leaving me sitting on the ground with pieces of the rack wrapped around my neck. They went through a gate which was too narrow, the rack was completely torn from the wagon, but they now had part of the garden fence to rattle behind them, frightening them more. In some manner they got turned around and came back the way they'd gone. Getting to my feet I tried to flag them down, but as they turned out around me, they got too close to the well pump, a horse went on each side of the well, breaking the wagon tongue and pulling the pump and about twenty feet of the pipe out of the well.

The pipe was bent so bad it was literally twisted like a pretzel, with the crooked pipe bouncing along behind them, they destroyed everything that lay in their wake. As they went passed the corner of the house the team and wagon were still connected by the traces, the wagon wheel caught the corner board, ripping it off and as they made another hole in the garden fence, they lost the wagon and one horse fell down and the last I saw of them, they were still going, one horse dragging the other.

It was sometime around supper time before I, with the help of a neighbor, retrieved the team and it was a few days later, before the rack and harness were repaired sufficiently to haul in the rye. In the meantime the pump and pipe were repaired and replaced. But it was a great deal later and I was quite a few years older before I had nerve enough to ask permission to go to another dance.

When Bob Howe and I were youngsters growing up together, we believed in "drinking Canada Dry". Now Bob was a very good friend of a neighbor, who couldn't see the use of going without "refreshments" when it was so easy to make. This brew could be made by putting potato peelings and grain or anything along these lines in a pail, this would ferment into mash, then the pail of mash, with a stool sitting in the middle of the pail and a basin of cold water sitting on the stool would be placed over heat and boiled two or three times, then the drippings from the heat hitting the bottom of the basin of cold water would be drained off. This mixture would be aged for a few days. One day when the neighbor had a batch ready to be tapped, he'd asked Bob to come help him sample it. I went along with Bob, even though I was underage. This was

54

one time that the mixture was not allowed to age, so we spent the night "sampling" and eating dill pickles. Of course, this "refreshment making" had to be done without the Mounties knowing about it, but sometimes they would get "wind" of such activities and in many cases they spent days trying to locate a "still". One of the favorite places for concealing these were in the cellars. Sometimes the pipe from these stills would be connected in with the stovepipe and in another case the man of the house installed a chemical toilet, vented it up through the roof, but instead of it being used for his wife's comfort it was just another way to pipe the fumes from the still. The most ingenious concealment was by a man who had a full cellar and built a false cellar, which was hidden behind a wall complete with hooks for hanging work clothes on, but a couple of these hooks served a double purpose. One could turn a button on the inner wall by just a twist of the hook another hook served as a signal to anyone in the false cellar that the Mounties were in the regular cellar and that they were to stay "put" until the Mounties left. After home brew was ready to be bottled a safe hiding place had to be found. One man used to hide his in the carcass of a dead horse, while another fellow used to hide his in a badger hole.

One time Arnold Peterson, Mike Kulyk, Bob Howe and I were going to Dick Steele's place to play poker. Arnold had a Model "T" with a little box behind where the rear seat used to be, so before the game we drove to a place up near Cappon for some "moonshine". On our way back through Dowker's lease, over rocks and washouts, the road never was any good, Arnold and Mike were in the front seat, Bob and I each had an apple box a piece to sit on in the back. Mike had his arm along the back of the front seat and that gave me an inspiration. If I pushed Arnold's cap forward he would think Mike did it. No sooner thought of then put into execution. The result was admirable. Arnold glared sidewise at Mike but said nothing, probably he thought it could have been an accident. I repeated the performance a few more times and the last time I massaged Arnold's scalp with my knuckles. That did it! Arnold stopped the old Ford, got out pulling Mike with him and they crossed swords right there on a moonlight night. Mike was dancing around, he still had on his big white wooley schapps. After honor had been upheld, they got back into the car, Arnold with a big black eye, but no signs of conflict on Mike. Arnold doesn't know to this day that it was me who was the instigator.

Years ago during prohibition the only beer sold was what was known as two percent. One could drink a washtub full and never feel a thing. Well, Old Woo Sam managed to get the real stuff once in a while, where I'll never know. Anyhow he would sell it to us young

55

fellers for seventy-five cents a pint. Well, we didn't mind that as long as our money and the beer held out. One day Bob Howe and I were in town and he had some real beer. Well sometime after we had enough even though we hadn't called a halt to the drinking, we discovered that we were drinking the two percent and paying seventy-five cents for it. Whether Woo Sam had run out of the real stuff or whether he thought we wouldn't know the difference, I'll never know. Anyhow, Bob and I figured that anyone who would swindle anyone like that, was not a very good citizen so we decided to put him in a barrel and ship him back to China. Well, we got him into an empty barrel but were having quite a time getting a board nailed across the top. We could get a nail through one end but Woo Sam kept pushing his head up against the board that we were trying to get the other end nailed down. Well, we had struggled with this kind of business until patience finally run out so the next time he pushed up on the board with his head, Bob brought the hammer down on the board with great force. The blow would have felled an ox so the effect on Woo Sam's head was quite successful, no trouble getting the lid nailed down after that. He might have been killed, but who would think of a gruesome thing like that. So we put the barrel with him in into a wheelbarrow and pushed it over to the depot and told the station agent to ship him C.O.D. back to China. Woo Sam was going to get the Mounties, but I believe Wallace King, who used to own the poolroom and livery stable, talked him out of it.

Mother didn't believe in drinking and hated the stuff. I don't know as I can blame her when I think back of the things my father and I would do when we were "tanked up". Not that we drank together, but I recall one time my father was in Buffalo, Joe O'Brien was also there. Now these two men didn't like each other but would always drink together and then argue about who raised the most wheat, so this day things got rather hot between them and the fist started flying. Later when Dad came home he was mumbling something about, "I sure chased that feller out of town." Mother said, "Rudolph, I think by that black eye, he must have turned on you." Another time, Clinton Jarboe and my father went to Medicine Hat. In those days a trip like this was only made twice a year, one in the fall for supplies for winter and again in the spring. Well this trip, the men took their wives along and as usual besides the groceries there were a few bottles of whiskey, gin or whatever suited their taste. On their return trip, when they reached the south side of the river and while the men were figuring the best way to get the wagon and supplies across, this being in the days before either ferry or bridge, Mrs. Jarboe suggested to mother that they

56

hide the men's liquor. But mother thought it would be a better idea to pretend they had broken the bottle, so they proceeded to pour the liquor into a half-gallon jug, then filled the liquor bottle up with water, so the bottle would appear full, then waited until they were sure the men would see the accident that was about to happen. Knowing the men would soon be looking for a drink, they waited and when the men came looking for the bottle one of the women would be helpful and pass it to them. As they did so, you guessed it, they let it slip and it smashed into several pieces right there on the river bank.

Why some of us young fellers didn't kill ourselves or at the best get badly injured when we got "tanked up" I'll never know. One night, a feller by the name of Briggs (I can't remember his first name) and I were coming home from Buffalo, we'd been drinking as usual, when we got to Dick Elliott's place, just north of the Red Deer River, near where the bridge is now, we spied three horses in his pasture, so we decided we should rope ourselves a couple of fresh mounts. We didn't stop for bridle or saddle and when we got on their backs they took off through the bushes. It was so dark we couldn't see where we were going and the thought of whether these horses had ever been ridden before, never entered our minds. We soon found out they could run and there was nothing for us to do but to hold on for our lives. With only the horses' manes to cling to, this was no easy task, but stay on we did until the horses ran under a wire clothesline. It was then we parted company with our mounts and the only injuries we received were a few welts across the stomach.

There is no end to the stories I could relate about the things us young lads did. But I don't recall ever hearing such words as "juvenile delinquency." I guess perhaps it was the actions of us youngsters that help to keep the phrase "The wild and woolly west" alive. I have mentioned before that I was only about 11 or 12 years old when Miss Arnold was my teacher and that she later married Lincoln Howe. I was always curious to know what people did when they were courting, so I decided that I would spy on Lincoln and Luella one night. There was just one problem, how to get downstairs where they were without my father hearing me. The window was my only means, so I would need a ladder. So I took two cottonwood posts and nailed a few crossbars on them and then hid it until after dark. Bedtime came and everyone went to bed, but Lincoln and Luella. So outside I went, something that was not uncommon as there was no indoor plumbing in those days. I carried the ladder and placed it under the window. Now I was all set. All I had to do was wait until the hired man, who shared my room, went to sleep. It wasn't very long until his snoring told me that it was safe to make my move. Very quietly I got out of bed, crossed over to the window and down the ladder I went. It was a very disappointing trip for me. I don't know what I expected to see, but all they were doing was holding hands. I waited for a while, but nothing interesting happened. I was getting sleepy, so I went back up the ladder and crawled into bed. I was nearly asleep when I heard the hired man getting up and he went down the ladder, now whether he was too heavy for the crossbars, or whether I was not a very good carpenter, anyway he never stopped until he hit the ground. The noise was enough to wake the dead, even if it hadn't been, the "beller" out of my father would have. Well, that hired man came up those cottonwood posts, minus the crossbars, just like a squirrel. Everyone blamed him for the ladder bit, and any connections with me was never mentioned.

One Sunday things were rather quiet, so Bob Howe, Clarence Bjork and I went down to the river to see if there was anything doing down there. It was not uncommon for folks to gather at the river and have a picnic. Usually they would have a swim before lunch time. We were riding along and sure enough there was a bunch of young people in swimming and nearby was this nice white cloth spread out and loaded down with all the niceties that make up a picnic. We didn't think it very nice of someone having a picnic and we weren't invited, so we reined our horses in close to where the lunch was. Reaching down we each took a corner of the cloth and tied it all up in a nice neat bundle, put it back on the ground and leisurely rode away.

Another Sunday, Bob Howe and his friend Jesse Robart were riding their horses up near Cappon and they came to where the folks around there were holding a church service. They had both been drinking and Bob was on the outs with his "lady love" because of this, and she wasn't speaking to him, but she was inside where the meeting was going on. Bob turned to Jesse and said, "Don't you think we should go to church? And in case there aren't any more seats, I guess I'll take my own along." With this Bob proceeded to rein his horse through the door right in where the minister was preaching. Everyone turned to see what all the commotion was about and gasped with surprise to see a horse and rider standing there. The minister interrupted his sermon and calmly asked the cowboy to please remove his hat. Bob said afterwards the minister's attitude sure had a sobering effect on him.

When I think back on those early days I can't help but feel a little sorry for the womenfolk. The handicapped conditions they had to contend with and the struggles they had trying to make a home for their menfolk. I remember one time, my wife and I were living in this shack, as it would be classed by today's standards. I had this holstein cow, she was so tame that she actually was a nuisance at times. This particular day, we had gone with Clarence and Skinny Bjork to look at a truck, that some of us had a notion of buying. While we were away from the house the cow got into the kitchen. It was the spring of the year. She had been on green grass, which didn't help the situation any, and she left her "calling card" all over the place including the ceiling. How she managed that I never could figure out. But what a mess! Before we could even think of spending the night in the house water had to be hauled and the kitchen completely washed down. Then it was days before the dampness was gone. Of course, it was not only the animals that could make a mess of things. One day two of the Howe boys, Bob would be one, and no doubt Alfred, or Kid, as he was known would be the other, anyway they went over across the river to Atlee where a couple of Hebrew boys ran the store. Something one of the storekeepers said or did rubbed the Howe boys the wrong way. Grabbing a bag of flour and a tin of syrup they littered the entire store and left remarking as they went out the door, "That should take some of the nastiness out of you boys." Speaking of flour reminds me of a Club Meeting which was held at the home of Lincoln and Luella Howe. Luella was very good at Club work. They had this club called the Mavis Club, where every member had to take turns at writing the "Weekly News". This one particular evening a fellow by the name of Walter Greenwood was to be initiated into the Club.

Two of the Howe boys, Bob and Lincoln, put a flour sack over the "new victim's" head and then stood him head first in a pail of cold water, as Walter gasped for breath he inhaled the flour dust into his lungs, which nearly killed him. A milder form of initiation was locking a new member in a room, and if they could get out, they qualified. This was not too bad, when the new member was a woman, but when it was a man, especially one that weighed around 200 pounds, they would take frame and all off. The Howe's new house was left in shambles one night. But we still thought it was all "just good fun."

When my sister Thelma grew up, she had many admirers, two that I remember were Mark Bunn and Joe Callaghan. (Joe was the one she finally chose.) They were bitter rivals and things used to get very interesting when both boys happened to come calling at the same time. Mark had a malady, which could show up whenever he got upset, and anyone witnessing his actions when this occurred would think he had a stroke. Many will remember seeing him "under these spells" when he would be acting as Umpire at ball games, and when someone disagreed with him on some point in the game,

59

he would immediately have "an attack." Such was the case one Sunday afternoon when both young men arrived at our home to see my sister. Mark, thinking that Joe was getting more attention than he, conveniently took "a stroke". This in turn made Joe mad because now Mark was getting all the attention. Mark had been carried to a cot and as he lay there staring into nothingness, Joe stood beside him muttering, "I'll kill him, I'll kill him." It was some time later, when Joe and Thelma were married at Bassano, that my father, mother and I were returning from the wedding. The roads were very rough coming across the irrigation. My father was driving and everytime he hit a bump we would leave our seat and hit the roof. Mother was complaining and told him to slow down, but as usual, whenever Dad was in the "sauce", he didn't listen to anyone, just told us to watch those jugs that they didn't get broken. After all they contained what he had left from the wedding and as we were going to stop for the night at Mark Bunn's place he wanted some refreshments for his friend. In the morning when Dad had trouble getting his car started Mark decided he would accompany us home with his car, just in case we had more trouble. Dad was still feeling pretty good from the previous day's activities and he kept trying to pass Mark, but Mark would speed up and this would make Dad swear. Soon they met a car and in the dust Dad managed to get past Mark. When we reached the ferry on the south side of the river our car had stopped again, and in the process of trying to get it started, both cars landed in the bull bushes. Dad's got so tangled up in the bushes and they couldn't get it started anyway, so Mark drove us the rest of the way home. When he reached our garage, he drove in and went right through and came out the back. Whether his brakes were not very good or whether he had taken one too many "nips" from Dad's jug, I really can't say. Or perhaps he was still brooding about Thelma's choice.

Life was hard back in those early days, but we survived because we had the willpower and a good sense of humor. We sure didn't depend on doctors whenever anyone suffered an injury received from working with the wild broncs. I remember the time Clyde Hartwell was kicked by a horse in the mouth. The blow drove his tooth up into his jaw and Clint Jarboe sharpened a pair of clinchers and pulled the tooth out. Another time a fellow by the name of Ed Holloway was working for C. B. Howe and he broke his collarbone when he dived in shallow water, but he never stopped work and with his arm in a sling he drove a six-horse team.

I left the Red Deer River district in 1936 and lived a while in the irrigation district near Brooks and from there I went to live in Calgary, where I worked for the C.P.R. Later when I tired of working

I spent my time playing bridge and visiting my boyhood friends on the Red Deer. One thing to be said about that part of the country, one who has ever lived in it will feel himself being drawn back time and again.

One might even say "an old-timer would break his neck to get there" as was nearly the case in May 1969, when Clarence Bjork, Clyde Jarboe and I were travelling by a car from Calgary, with Clarence at the wheel losing control when the right rear tire blew. The three of us rolled around inside the car like marbles before the car plunged into a twelve foot V-shaped ditch. The car was a total wreck, with both the windshield and back window broken as well as three of the side windows. Clyde who crawled out the back window said he never thought we'd come out of it alive. We were all able to get out of the car on our own, and about two hours later a passing motorist found us sitting on the side of the road having lunch. Traffic was not very heavy on the road, so we made the best of what could have been a very bad situation. C. B. Howe and Clarence's brother Magnus came and took us the rest of the way to Buffalo and later returned us to Calgary.

In my earlier life I married Audrey Bunn, Mark Bunn's sister. We had one son and three daughters. Faye married Art Kidner and lives near Edmonton, they have one girl and one boy. The boy is married and lives near Stoney Plain, where he is a boss on construction work.

Doreen married Ken Epps, a heavy duty mechanic, they have two boys in their teens and live near Huston, B.C.

Our son Armond married Margaret Burgee, from Bassano. They have two children. One girl is married and lives at Brooks. Armond lived for a couple of years on the Red Deer when Ray Eggar lived on the Alfred Campbell place. Frances is not married and she makes her home in Tulsa, Oklahoma.

MR. AND MRS. J. R. HANNAFORD — HOWIE by Mrs. Sena (Stennes) Hannaford

Why were so many of our old-timers labelled as colorful characters, or dynamic personalities? Was it because of their many varied expeiences, and the education they received in the school of hard knocks; or was it because only the adventurous and non-conformists had the spirit required to leave family and homeland to make their way in a strange environment?

James Hannaford was born on a farm in Devon, where he learned about machinery and engines. This early experience was to prove helpful in various circumstances. His mother passed away when he was a small boy, and when his father remarried and four more

Mr. and Mrs. Jim Hannaford in garden at Howie.

James Hannaford home at Howie.

Jim Hannaford at Howie in 1941.

Mr. and Mrs. Alfred Stennes on 45th Wedding Anniversary, 1956.

children were added to the family, James and his brother John ran away to seek their fortunes in London. John remained there to become a city policeman, but James emigrated to the United States, where he worked as a farmhand. Later he operated a sawmill in Manitoba, ran a private launch on Lake of the Woods, then took up a homestead at Fairlight, Saskatchewan. During the winter he worked as an electrician in Winnipeg.

Emma Bromage was born in a factory town in Northamptonshire. Her father was a supervisor and they lived in a comfortable suburban home. Emma began part-time work in the shoe factory at the age of eleven, and learned to be an expert seamstress. She wished to become a nurse, but this was not considered to be a suitable occupation for a nice girl, so she decided to go to Western Canada. There she did housework for ten dollars a month till she met and married James Hannaford in 1906.

Frost and rust took their toll of the crops on their homestead at Fairlight so early in 1912 they emigrated to Brooks, where Mrs. Hannaford and the two little boys, Edmund and Robert, took up residence in a shack, while James and a friend, Eric Tuckett went out to the homestead sixty miles to the northeast where they broke fifteen acres of virgin soil, and constructed a barn and shack, complete with dirt floor.

Here the family arrived late in October after a five-day trek by covered wagon. Mrs. Hannaford and Robert had contracted typhoid fever while in Brooks and were both very ill. Dr. Anderson was called — and he made one of his many long trips on errands of mercy. Later Jim too, fell ill with the fever, and he was still weak and pale in the spring when he went to Brooks for supplies and to negotiate for the purchase of a tractor. Weeks passed, and Jim had not returned so Mrs. Hannaford and the two boys set off to look for him. At Steveville they found his coat hanging on a tree near the river, but their fears were soon allayed when they were told that Jim had been there, but had returned to do some plowing on the other side of the river with his newly acquired Big-4 tractor, and ten-bottom plow. This huge machine represented a monstrous gamble to the little family, as it first took their entire savings of eight hundred dollars, and was to be paid for in three annual one thousand dollar installments with interest at eight percent, or ten percent after due. It therefore was necessary to keep it going from daylight till dark six days a week, but never on Sunday. Homesteaders were glad to hire breaking done, but as the Big-4 could travel only two miles per hour, organization was required to map a route. Five acres were broken up near the homesite, and the following year a large shelter belt and the beginning of an extensive perennial garden were planted. Later these peonies, lilies and roses were subdivided to be planted in many neighboring gardens as well as in later homes in Calgary and at Botha.

Stories about friction between ranches and homesteaders are not all fiction. Fuel was a major problem on the prairies, so long trips were undertaken to gather firewood in the coulees and along the river bottom. Mr. Hallam of the Vee Bar Vee made a complaint to the Mounted Police who were stationed at his ranch. They visited nearby homesteaders, ordering them to return the firewood to the ranch, and appear before the J.P. (guess who?) Jim Hannaford appeared in court and paid a five dollar fine, but insisted that he was only obligated to return the wood to the spot where he found it. Later he found that this was Hudson Bay land so he procured a permit to gather wood there, and returned for one particular large log which was used from that time forward as a chopping block. Later they became friends and Mr. and Mrs. Hallam were very happy to have the Hannafords call on them at the coast.

THE LATE JAMES R. HANNAFORD FAMILY by Mrs. Sena (Stennes) Hannaford

James R. Hannaford (1884-1961) and Emma Bromage (1884-1962) married in 1906. They had four sons and one daughter — Edmund born 1909, and Robert born 1911, both in Fairlight, Saskatchewan, Dora born 1914, Tommy born in 1915 and Harry 1919, all in Howie, Alberta.

TOMMY passed away while attending Olds Agricultural College in 1934.

EDMUND married Isobel Flanagan in 1936 and resided on a farm at Howie. They had two children, Shirley and Donald — moved to a farm near Botha in 1948 where they still reside.

ROBERT H. married Sena Stennes in 1939 resided in a small house on the home farm at Howie. They had three children, Ronald, Joan and Glen. In 1946 they moved to a farm in the Botha district where they still reside.

DORA MAY married George Dawson in 1941. They had two children, Richard and Susan. They live in Toronto.

HARRY married Marvel Jacobs in 1946. They had three children, Dale, Lee and Kim. In 1949, Harry and his Dad bought lots on the same street in Calgary, and built new homes there. Marvel and Harry still reside there.

James R. Hannaford had boundless energy and an enthusiasm for all community activities. He worked with parents in neighboring school districts to open a school in 1920. His interest continued — and eventually he became the first chairman of Berry Creek School Division No. 1.

He was also interested in organizing the Alberta Wheat Pool and served as a delegate for many years. District meetings during that time took on the air of a community picnic with whole families for miles around attending.

Another annual event which many neighbors looked forward to was a picnic held on the farm the first Saturday in July each year. For several weeks prior to this, the men were busy clipping hedges and getting the flower beds and garden into top condition. Mr. and Mrs. Hannaford would make a trip to Calgary to buy small prizes for races and other sports events which culminated in the rolling pins throwing contest. The target at first bore a strong resemblance to Jiggs from the famous comic strip, Maggie and Jiggs, but during the wartime years his appearance changed, and became an image of Adolph Hitler. At the final picnic the neighbors made a presentation of a chime clock which was given a place of honor in the Hannaford's new home.

JENNIE (STEWART) HAUSNESS

I was born in Ireland and came to the United States with my parents, Mr. and Mrs. Hugh Stewart. I came to the Buffalo district in 1922 via Nebraska and Atlee. I attended school in Atlee. I have two brothers, Bob and John and one sister, Georgina. I worked for Mrs. John Gordon for quite a few years. When I married John Hausness I went to live just east of Buffalo. We left there in 1948 and since his passing in 1954 I have lived in Kelowna with my two brothers. It is always a great pleasure to return to Buffalo for a visit and see all my friends and former neighbors.

Jennie Hausness and Rena Mercer making hot cakes at a parade in Buffalo.

John Hausness with his 17 pounder.

65

JOHN HAUSNESS by E. Stone

Homesteaded east of Buffalo. He was a bachelor for many years and the boys of the neighborhood interested in mechanics used to love to spend hours in his shop. He was a very clever machinist and had many firsts to his credit for this area. He built the first super heterodyne radio set which brought people from all around to see (hear) its wonders. He also built one of the first collapsible trailers which he used to take on fishing trips to B.C. He was practically self-sufficient by keeping everything in running order around the farm with the help of his well-equipped shop. One of his favorite answers to those who would ask what he was making was, "I started to make a shovel, but it split and I'll just call it a fork."

He later married Jennie Stewart and they had a very interesting home full of things John had made for it and kept spic and span by his wife.

John's homestead was where Clarence Rinker now has a lease. He broke land with oxen and a walking plow, his brand for his livestock was Ⅎ

John Hausness left this district in 1948 and lived in Kelowna, B.C., until his death in 1954.

THE WALTER HEILAND STORY

My father, Robert Heiland came to Canada from the States and filed a homestead in 1915 and my mother, who was born in Switzerland and had met and married my Dad, while they both still lived in the United States, came with my brothers and sisters in 1916.

I was born in one of the many small homestead hamlets that sprung up during the wave of settlement that swept into Western Canada during the first fifteen years of this century, namely Cravath Corners, located at the junction of the roads east from Steveville nine miles, and on to the Red Deer River, and from the north, south seven miles to the same river, between Howard Sandgate and Dr. Anderson's place.

My mother is still living with my sister, Ruth, near Stettler and my Dad died in 1936.

As a young man I rode the Rodeo circuits. Among the horses I came up against were two very well known ones; Captain Kid and That's All, the latter, was and still is a top bucking horse. Both these horses were from the Jack Longmier stock at Empress. But in 1957, I had the tables turned on me when a young filly looped her rope around me and led me to the altar. On the other end of that rope, I found a dark-eyed, dark-haired young lass from Patricia, Dorothy Groves. Dorothy was born in Champion, daughter of Mr.

Mr. and Mrs. Walter Heiland, and sons, Rob and Wade, 1970.

Walter Heiland's mother and father's wedding picture, 1905.

Mr. and Mrs. J. L. Groves, 1968.

and Mrs. Jim Groves. The family moved to the Patricia district in 1937, later Jim sold his holdings there and bought the News and Tobacco Store in Brooks. Following our marriage, Dorothy and I worked for Jack Coates at Wardlow, then in 1960 we hired on with Bruce Dawson, who had taken over the original Nelson spread and when Bruce sold out to the Krause Brothers in 1968, Dorothy, our two boys, Robbie and Wade, and I went to work for Howard Jones near Cavendish. It was while we were still there, the doctor advised me to take life a little easier, so much to our disappointment we had to give up the life of "cowboying" and it was then we purchased the Buffalo General Store, this was in 1969.

67

When we took over the store it meant that we had to dispose of what livestock we had, with the exception of our four horses, the boys, two Shetlands and our other two saddle horses, which we were fortunate enough to be able to run with Chester Howe's stock down on the north bank of the Red Deer. Where we are free to visit and ride our animals at our own leisure, and thus giving me the opportunity to teach our sons the skill of riding, roping and herding, so necessary to life in this part of the country, especially if our sons wish to follow in "Dad's footsteps". They are both very fond of the ranching and riding life and due to lack of help on several of the local ranches we spend many hours together riding for these ranchers. We feel that we have the best part of two worlds.

Dorothy is very active in the community as well as spending her days in the store.

SWEN (SAM) HILLSTED STORY

I was born in Norway in 1879. I was six years old when my parents, my four sisters, my three brothers and myself moved from Norway to the United States. We settled in Hillsboro, North Dakota. I went to school in Hillsboro and even attended a Norwegian school there. I filed on land northwest of Williston, North Dakota, and "proved up" in 1911 and then I came to Canada. I worked in Edmonton until the fall of 1912 and on my way back to the United States I filed on land north of Medicine Hat. I had the N.½ of Section 2-20-5-4. I stayed in Hillsboro with friends and relatives that winter but came back to Canada in 1913. I hired out to a rancher, Mr. Tom Beel of Medicine Hat and worked for him part of two years but quit in the fall of 1914 and went back to Williston as I had a crop to look after on my land there.

I returned to Canada in the spring 1915 and hired out to W. McLennen on the Red Deer River, just nine miles west of my homestead. I looked after nineteen head of stock and the stallion that was imported from Scotland. I did the farming for him that summer, including a crop on the sheep ranch at Atlee, besides a crop for myself, using his outfit. I had broke 20 acres on my own place and rented the 20 acres which Louis Wilhelmson had broke on his place. These were all very good crops. In 1916 my own wheat made better than 60 bushels to the acre, so I bought an outfit that fall for myself and started farming for myself in the spring of 1917. In 1918 I bought another half section from Bill Allport, the west half of Section 12-20-5-4 and I also leased the east half of Section 11 for pasture. My brand was ŜH on right thigh.

In 1942 when the British took over for the bombing field I bought a place five miles south of Bindloss from Harry Tucker and

The first homestead house built in 1913, S. Hillstead.

Sam Hillstead taken later years on the old homestead. I had 7,000 trees on this place, there are caraganas on the south.

took off two crops and then sold to Bill Barnes in 1944. Moved to Canoe, B.C., where I lived for sixteen years, then I sold out and retired to the Scenic Valley Lodge at Penticton, B.C. I expect this will be my last move. "My get up and go, has got up and went, but I really don't mind when I think with a grin, of all the grand places my get up has been."

Now this happened in the thirties. I can't remember the year. I had to go to town to fill up with gas in the old Model "T" Ford. I drove past Conrad Danielson's place on the way to Buffalo, as he was going to Medicine Hat with me the next morning. When I got to the railroad crossing, the engine of the train with two boxcars came along, but it was just crawling along slowly, after it passed I drove to the store and was getting the gas when two men came running with their hands up in the air and asked if I would run that engine down. You see they had been switching so the train would be on the side track, but they got the main line and backed up to the caboose to have supper and they both left the engine and it started off and they never heard it. Well they got in the car and I took them to Empress. The section man there took his "speeder" and caught it on the grade west of Empress and had it on the side track when we got there.

Now for a little excitement when I worked on the ranch. I was doing the summer-fallowing. The horses were getting good feed and I guess they were all green, had only drove them a few days. The horse next to the pole leaned on it and it broke off so they started to run and finally the broken stub stuck in the ground and clevis broke and I was pulled over the levers of the disk. At this time they were going pretty fast, but I was still hanging on, but flat on the ground. I had on a "bib" overall which filled up with dust and dirt and I looked like a stuffed sausage, but I slowed them down so I could get on my feet and stop them. I didn't get hurt, just marked some on the back of my legs, that's all.

69

I never married and all my family is gone, my last sister passed away in 1966.

THE GEORGE HOWE FAMILY by Mrs. Mildred (Stewart) Howe

George Howe was born in Derbyshire, England in 1850, son of Alexander Howe and Mary Fox Howe, and came to Long Island, New York, with his parents in 1858, where his father bought sixty acres of land. The family lived here for five years, then they moved to Fairplay, Wisconsin, where the father, Alexander died in 1874. In 1879, George married Olive Bradwell in Galina, Illinois. The next year, George and his only brother, William, went by train to Deerlodge, Montana, where he was joined by his wife, Olive, in 1881, just after the death of their infant daughter. In 1882, a son,

Mrs. George Howe Sr.

, The youngest Howe, taken in 1971 at Louis Cicon's branding, C. B. Howe's great-grandson, Neil.

Benjamin was born. By this time, George had acquired a homestead in a beautiful valley about two miles north of Flathead and began raising cattle. Soon he needed more grazing land, so he took the cattle farther north to a section which is now Kalispell and Marion, Montana.

George's brother, William, returned to Wisconsin and brought their widowed mother to Kalispell in 1884. They travelled by train to Missoula and from there travelled by wagon and on horseback to Kalispell where she died in 1901.

In 1891 the railroad was built to Kalispell and ran through the cattle country. Many more settlers came into the Valley and again George needed more grazing land. By now George and Olive had three more sons, Charles born in 1884, Cuthbert Bradwell, in later years known as Cud, was born in 1887 and Alfred, later known as Kid, was born in 1889, so George and his family left Montana to go eastward, but his cattle had strayed across the border into Canada.

Alexander Howe's (C. B. Howe's grandfather) baptismal certificate, February 7, 1819.

Mr. and Mrs. Alexander Howe's (C. B. grandparents) marriage certificate, January 22, 1849.

Ben Howe, George Howe Sr., Adolph Fisher, Howard McCullough, Mr. Gallop, R. S. Gravette, and Clint Jarboe taken at Oyen Hotel in 1912.

71

There wasn't any border patrol in those days but George would have to pay a tax to bring his cattle back into the United States, so instead he moved his family to Canada. They made their home near Fort McLeod where in October 1892 another son, George was born but died a year later. In 1894, Lincoln was born and in 1897 Grant was born and finally in 1901 Robert was came along. In 1906 George moved his family by wagon and herded his cattle to the Red Deer River Valley, near what is now known as Buffalo.

The first year the family lived in a dugout in the side of a hill near where Magnus Bjork lives. The following spring they built a log house and in 1910 built a frame house, which was later moved down river to where it now stands. Cud still lives in it.

George Howe passed away in 1914.

According to many tales by the old-timers of this district, one would have to search far to find men who could equal the ability of the seven sons of George Howe, when it came to riding, roping, breaking of wild horses, and when it came to drinking, gambling and raising just "plain hellery" they were usually a way a head in that also. But despite all their wild antics they were always considered to be gentlemen and their descendants are proud of the name of "Howe".

BENJAMIN married Margaret Maidment of Cappon, Alberta in 1922, for a few years following their marriage they lived along the south side of the Red Deer River but in the early twenties moved to British Columbia. They had five children Susie, Georgina, Jean, Margaret and Charles.

Benjamin died in 1966 and his wife Margaret died in 1971.

CHARLIE was killed by lightning in the spring of 1913.

CUTHBERT BRADWELL see the C. B. Howe story.

ALFRED (Kid) married Susie Maidment of Cappon, Alberta in 1918. They had one son John, who married Evelyn Coleman and they have four sons, Stephen, Norman, Gary and Ronald. They all live in British Columbia.

LINCOLN married Luella Arnold of Campbellford, Ontario in 1921, who came to this district as a school teacher. They had two children, Georgie and Olive. Lincoln passed away in 1970. Luella still makes her home in B.C.

GRANT married Mildred Stewart of Pitt Meadows in 1929. They had two children Allan and Edith. Allan married Freda Jensen of Victoria and they have one daughter Patricia. Edith married Charles Lasser and they have three children Sheri, Bob and Don. They all live in Pitt Meadows and have visited this district many times.

Grant Howe passed away in 1970, just one month after Lincoln.

Mildred still resides in Pitt Meadows.

ROBERT married Susie Maidment Howe in 1939. They live in New Westminster, B.C. They have no family.

In the early twenties the Howe boys, with the exception of Cud, left this district and moved to B.C., their mother went with them where she lived until her death in 1938.

C. B. HOWE STORY

I was born in the State of Montana in 1887 and was given the name Cuthbert Bradwell, but since early manhood everyone has known me as Cud. I was a lad of three or four years old when my father, George Howe, moved the family to Fort McLeod, Alberta, in 1891. We moved to the Red Deer River district in 1906. This country was wide open when we arrived and cattle were allowed to roam and graze over a radius of many miles, thus everybody became "saddle broke" nearly as young as did the broncs of which there were many in those early days. R. H. (Dick) Imes wrote one time regarding the "Old-time broncs and bronc riders"; "All old-time bronc riders were judged in competition, on absolute finish rides, unless some skull duggery was indulged in. How many times have the top rodeo riders of today been bucked off at the horn, or after, and received a qualified ride, and then gone on to win the ride? Not that they are not good riders. They are, but they are ten-second riders. Another thing, they never had the experience that the old-time rider had of riding broncs on icy footing, frozen ground, rocks, badger holes, and rough country where a horse might buck over a cut bank into swimming water. Most boys riding today in rodeos never saw a roundup wagon or the open range. All the old-timer bronc riders who contested were actually range cowboys, and they rode more bucking horses, as a general rule, than any rodeo rider of today ever does. They all broke horses and rode from five to ten hours a day".

In those early days a man was as useless without his horse as the horse was without a man. One's very life often depended on his ability to ride.

The winter of 1906 and '07 was one of the worst winters this country has ever experienced in the cattle business and many ranchers, including myself, turned to raising horses, as these animals are more able to forage for feed in the deep snow and can go longer without water than cattle. After the country was settled by homesteaders and the cattle had to be confined, I turned to wheat farming and for many years used horses for this work.

In 1916, I married a young English girl, Eileen Elliott, who had come from Toronto to this country with her parents, Mr. and Mrs. Richard Elliott. We had three sons and three daughters. Chester, Laurence, Edna, George, Dorothy and Shirley. Despite the years of

73

Mrs. George Howe Sr., and Lincoln on the original Howe ranch, 1914.

C. B. Howe on horse, Mike Katzen on wagon.

Howe Brothers picking out a "Bad One". Note: House in background before moved to present site and occupied by C. B. Howe.

Elmina Mitton, Abitz and Charlie Howe, 1905.

74

drought and blowing dust, as well as the low prices for cattle and wheat, we managed to struggle through and on the whole we had a very good life.

For a few years we lived in a log house about five miles north of the Red Deer River and in 1928 when we found we required a bigger house I bought one which had been abandoned by some settler who had left this district after suffering many hardships in an attempt to make a living at farming in this dry belt district. The house was moved a distance of about 30 miles, with the help of my neighbors with horses and tractors, and placed on a foundation close to the log house. A short distance from this house I built a dam to hold the water from the spring run-off and during the summer I would use this water to irrigate my farm land.

Because we lived north of the river and our nearest point for buying supplies was Medicine Hat, we often experienced great difficulty in crossing the river.

Cud B. Howe, 1913.

Sod shack built by George Howe Sr., and his brother at Kalispell in 1884 (still standing there in 1967).

In the spring of 1907, my father and two of my brothers, Ben and Kid, and I with a four horse team and a saddle horse, went to Medicine Hat for a load of supplies. It took a week to make the trip and it was customary for travellers to stay overnight at the Halfway House (halfway between the Red Deer and Medicine Hat).

When we left, the ice in the river was solid, but when we returned, a week later, the ice had broken clear from the banks and was floating in a solid junk. We unhooked the horses, unloaded the groceries, took the wheels off the wagon and transported everything across the ice. The horses we led across in single file and when we reached the north bank we re-assembled and loaded the wagon, hitched the horses to it and continued our trip home. Less than an hour from the time we crossed the river, the ice broke up and went out. We had timed it just right that time.

As the years passed by our family received their education at the Emslie school, despite the fact it was very difficult to obtain teachers that would stay any length of time as the district was considered an isolated area. I served on the school board for several years and when a young lad named Bill Thompson applied for the position as teacher, I couldn't help but have some misgivings, as he was only a year or so older than my oldest son, Chester. But as it turned out Bill stayed with us for seven years and proved to be a very wise choice by the school board.

In the twenties my five brothers, Ben, Kid, Lincoln, Grant and Bob left this district to make their home in British Columbia. Our mother went with them.

In the forties our children started to leave the nest to make homes of their own. EDNA was the first to go when she married Mac Meyer, a young man who had come to this district as the Wheat Pool Elevator operator. They have four children. George who is now married and have two children, lives at Kindersley where he has his own business in oil. Don who is also married and has spent the last year in Algeria with an oil company. Bruce and Bev, the twins, are still at home with their parents on a farm in Okotoks, Alberta.

In 1943, GEORGE married Loretta Brassard, whose parents homesteaded in the Atlee district, just south of the Red Deer River. They have five children. Jock (George) who is presently working in Medicine Hat at a meat processing plant.

Ron and Reg (twins) who still carry on the business of ranching with their father. Reg is married and has one son, Neil.

Mona is at present attending high school in Medicine Hat and Susan who is in her last year at the Buffalo school.

DOROTHY married a neighbor boy, Rusty Cicon. They have four children. Valerie who married George Sinclair. They have one son. William, Sandra and Guy, all living with their parents at Calgary.

SHIRLEY married Quinton Donovan. They live in Brooks and have three children. Carol, Joyce and Patrick.

CHESTER married late in life. He married Mrs. Helen Ferris, in 1964. (See Chester Helen Howe).

LAURENCE has never married and still lives at home.

In 1949, I obtained more land, this time on the north bank of the Red Deer, and moved the house, which my father built in 1910, on to the site. We were living here in the spring of 1951 when the Red Deer went on the rampage. The ice jammed and caused the flood waters to spread over the flat and it came into our house to the depth of about two feet. And in the spring of 1965 it repeated the performance, but this time it was only about six to eight inches. i recall we had this fellow working for us and when it came time to mop up the water and silt, after the ice jam broke and the water

76

was going down, I was sweeping the water down the furnace opening in the floor, when this fellow became very excited and said, "Hey
Cud, don't put that water down there, you'll ruin the furnace." I
stopped sweeping and looked at him as I asked, "How in h--- do
you think the water got in here, if it didn't come up through the
floor from the basement?" Sometimes I figured this chap wasn't
overly-bright.

Regardless what we might be working at, this same chap would
have to stop every morning at ten o'clock and have his coffee. So
it was one morning, he had gone to the house to have his coffee.
Well this particular morning, Helen, Chester's wife, was there having
coffee with the Mrs., now whether the wife had ever told Helen of
the very annoying habit that this fellow had, of licking off his spoon
and then put it in the sugar bowl I don't know, but the trio were
sitting at the table and just as he reached with his spoon for the
sugar bowl, Helen moved the bowl and the fellow nearly fell face-
down on to the table, while Helen suggested it would be more sanitary
if he used the spoon already in the bowl. The wife said afterwards
she had often felt like saying something to him about this habit,
but she was rather timid and would never hurt anyone feelings,
whereas, our daughter-in-law was more out-spoken.

After the hardships we had suffered over the years raising our
family through the drought and winter blizzards which took their
toil of our livelihood, and with the coming of the hydro power to the
district, life was just beginning to be easier for Eily and I. We had
taken a few trips to Florida and was just starting to enjoy our
sunset years, when she took sick very suddenly and without warning she passed away in 1965, leaving me alone. Laurence and I
have carried on with the help of several housekeepers, which for one
reason or another always seemed to be coming or going, until Mrs.
Martin came in 1967 and who is still with us.

One might say I have lived my entire life on the Red Deer
River and now as I go into my 85th year it appears that this is
where my life will end. The Irish sing a song that Ireland is a
"little bit of Heaven" (or it was before all the uprisings there over
the past few years) but I feel that this district along the Red Deer
would run it a photo-finish.

STORIES by the late Lincoln Howe

A fellow by the name of Henry Edgar sold a team of horses to a
Belgian woman. She took the team home but in a day or two she
took a dislike for the horses, so she went back and tried to get her
money back. Henry would not give it to her. She so hung around
all day hoping he would change his mind, but by night time he

Charlie Howe and Alexander Mitton
before 1913.

Lincoln Howe, 1914.

hadn't given her the money so she went to bed in his bed. Henry went to a neighbor, and wanted to know what he should do. Later when he returned to his home she was gone. He was very glad because he was sure she was crazy and he didn't know what she might do next. Afterall she was the same woman who'd tried to trade her daughter for a team of horses with another man, but the district had stopped her.

Lincoln recalled one time advertising for a girl to do housework. A girl by the name of Mary was on her way by train to fill the position when she inquired of her fellow passengers for directions to reach her destination, a fellow who stuttered, by the name of Ed Hubble gave her the required information, ending with, "Yes, by God (stuttering away) by God thems the folks what wakes their help up by firing a six shooter." Mary was so frightened she never got off the train.

One very mild day, Mark Bunn, Hershel Gravette, my brother Kid and I went to Atlee in an open touring car to pick up some liquor which had been shipped in by train. There had been a chinook that day and water was laying around. Kid who was driving the car got stuck in about four feet of water. Mark, who was just a short fellow and was sitting in the back seat said, "How am I going to get to dry land?" Kid said he'd carry him on his shoulders. So with Mark perched on his shoulder Kid had only gone about three feet when he purposely fell head first into the water.

78

STORIES by Alfred (Kid) Howe

When I first came to the Red Deer River district with my parents and brothers, there were several Metis living along the river. Early one morning I saw one of these fellows, Alex LaFrombois, about three miles from his home and fearing that something might be amiss

Mr. and Mrs. Alfred (Kid) Howe.

I asked him, "What are you doing away out here?" Alex said, "No porcupine, no breakfast." That was one time I was glad I hadn't been invited to breakfast.

Dick LaRoche, another Metis, had a large family of ten or twelve children. One day with his wife and children in a wagon his team of broncs started to run away. The woman started throwing the children one by one, out of the wagon and by the time Dick got the team stopped the children were strewn all over the prairie. They retraced their steps and picked the children all up.

In 1906 Melvin Burritt and I were living in a dugout just east of where Chester Howe lives now. One night there was something moving in a bunch of tin cans on the garbage heap. In the early morning I took the gun and shot into the cans and rubbish, scaring poor Burritt, who was still sleeping, near to death. As it turned out my shot had hit the mark killing a badger. Next night the same noise started up again, so the next morning I gave Burritt the gun and he also shot into the junk; another badger. We skinned the father and mother badger and hung their hides outside the dugout. I knew that it was either us or the badgers who had to go, being winter I figured it was best to eliminate the beasts.

There used to be a man by the name of Miller living in the district. He lived alone and one day when my brother Cud was going past Miller's house he saw this freshly butchered pig hanging and

79

knowing that Miller was not there, Cud left his horse and walking in the footsteps made by Miller earlier, he reached the house, took the carcass inside and placed it in Miller's bed. That night when Miller returned he couldn't find his pig any place, he went to the neighbors to inquire if they had seen anyone around his place during his absences. When his neighbors couldn't enlighten him he felt very discouraged and returning to his house went to bed in the dark. It was then he found his pig, but I don't think he ever knew who the culprit was.

STORIES by Robert (Bob) Howe

Back in the early thirties while working on the Buffalo bridge, I got in "dutch" with the law when I kinda roughed up the merchandise in the local general store, while under the influence of drink. The next day I was still drunk and as sick as a dog, when the Mountie from Empress arrived to arrest me. There was another fellow, Ron Hurd, who got mixed up in this with me, and he also was arrested. On our way to the court hearing in Empress, the Mountie, a big Scotsman said, referring to the previous day's activities, "If I'd have been there I'd have kicked the H--- out of you kids." I said, "You get out here now and try 'er." But he didn't take me up on the invitation. When we get down to Empress and they takes us into court and there was this police dog there. I said to Ron, "You know I never did like policemen." This guy says, "What did you say?" I says, "I never did like police dogs." Anyhow it cost me $30, Ron didn't have any money. It was $15 a piece.

So we wanted to get some whiskey, there was no place around Empress to get it, we'd have to go to the Hat. (Medicine Hat). So we takes a notion to go across the bridge, the railroad bridge, (this was before the highway bridge was built,) so we went to the lumberyard and got two or three 16 or 20 foot boards and we were going across the railroad track with the car, well that's a helavuh hard thing to do, especially when the train comes, it's not so bad when you get on the track, but when you get over to the other side and you try to get out of it, Ron had left me and I'm alone with this old Ford and it was a borrowed car too. Well, we ended up in Medicine Hat and got locked up in "the can."

Now I had another fine to pay, but I didn't have enough money so went to the bank but they refused me until I phoned Johnnie Gordon, a man for whom I had worked for several years, he told them to give me the money. I would like to point out something here about Johnnie Gordon, a mighty fine man. He lived by the Word of God, but never once have I even known him to refuse to help his fellowman, nor condemn him for his actions. Many

Left to right — front: Ben Howe, Linc Howe, Cud Howe, Kid Howe, Bob Howe. Back Row — Luella Howe, Mildred Howe, Grant Howe, Susie Howe.

times, though, he was like the proverbial oil on the troubled waters, while he lived along the Red Deer, always trying to "put to right" some of the mischief us young fellows would get into.

Editor's Note: I have heard others say the same thing. Edgar (Ted) Stone says he can recall seeing Johnnie Gordon standing in the doorway of the Community Hall watching the young people dancing, although he never took part in the dancing he would say how much he liked watching them enjoying themselves. Despite the fact he was also their Sunday School teacher, he never condemned them for dancing. Ted also recalls that Mr. Gordon would loan the baseball players his car or truck to travel 25 or 30 miles to play a game. One must remember that a car or truck in those days was considered more of a luxury, whereas, today it is a necessity.

I remember one time I had a sore shoulder, dislocated or something, anyway my brother Kid, took me to Oyen to the Vet, there wasn't any other doctor there, just the animal doctor, and he wasn't allowed to give me any anesthetic or anything so he says to me, "Go down and get yourself a 'mickie' and down the whole of it." I did as he said, then he takes a yank on this arm of mine, the only good it done was to sober me up in a hurry. So Kid had to take me to Calgary to see a medical doctor. There they tied my arm up. We were staying in a hotel and Kid, he'd celebrated and he was drunk but I was sober, this arm was hurting so much — — so I go down town. I was walking along Ninth Avenue when this big old colored woman spotted me, she says, "Come in here, Mister, I want to see yah."

So I thought maybe she wants a horse broke or something — so I goes in there. Well! She had different ways, this one, she about scared me to death. It sure weren't horses she had on her mind. I got out of there; forgetting the pain in my arm — got out on the street and I go to beat h--- back to Kid, but he was drunk, he wasn't much help to me. Boy! I sure thought I'd had it, as that was about the first nigger woman I'd ever seen in my life and I'd say she was an axe handle or two across. I thought, boy! if that one had've gotten a hold of me, I would've had more pains that what I've got. You know something? My arm never hurt again until I got home.

One day when I was just a youngster I had to take a team of horses to a widow woman who had some bad luck — fire or something, I can't remember now what had happened. Anyway I drove this team to her home about 25 miles away. I got there just at noontime. She asked me to have a meal with them. I was very bashful in those days, besides there were two young girls there, so I told her I'd just finished eating. She knew this wasn't true because it would take a while to drive a team that distance. Anyway, I finally sat down, I looked around and I spies this cornbread and something I thought was corn syrup, but it was vinegar, so I poured some of this on my cornbread. The girls they giggled to each other, so I thought to myself there's something wrong here. If they hadn't gone through all this fuss I might have gotten a surprise, but I knew there was something amiss. I ate the cornbread and vinegar and reached for more cornbread and I put more vinegar on the next ones, I smacked my lips and said, "That's pretty nice stuff." The girls never cracked a smile. About a month later I heard about it. They'd said, "That Kid Howe might be tough, but that young Howe has got them all beat.

A couple of months or so later I go back to see them and I take Jesse Robart with me. The family was very religious and I knew from before that they would be asking a blessing at mealtime, so when the woman and the girls bowed their heads, I grabs the dish of mashed potatoes and passed them to Jesse and then quickly folded my hands and looked very pious. When the blessing was finished and heads were raised here was poor Jesse sitting there with the potatoes in his hands and no place to put 'em. Boy! he was just as red — and mad, oh! he was going to shoot me.

That country along the Red Deer River around the turn of the century was what one might call "wide open" and one had to be able to ride and handle a horse, else he might find himself walking, consequently we all learned to ride at a very young age. Many times we would have to ride miles and eat and sleep in the wide-open spaces for weeks at a time, while on a roundup. But it was a good life and some of my fondest memories are those days spent on the prairie. Since leaving there in the twenties I had worked as a longshore man on the British Columbia coast, until I retired a couple of years ago. Each year my wife, Susie, and I motor down and spend a week or so on the prairies, visiting my brother Cud and many of our old friends.

When the rancher, his wife and six-year-old son paid one of their rare visits to town, they stopped in at the local tavern. They all walked up to the bar where the rancher drawled, "two whiskies."

The six-year-old looked at his father in surprise and said: "What's the matter, Paw? Ain't Maw drinking?"

Magnus Bjork (the second), Lincoln Howe, George Howe Jr., Laurance Howe, Ron Howe, Chester Howe, Reg Howe, Johnnie Smith, 1967.

Mr. and Mrs. C. B. Howe, New Year's Day, 1965.

To C. B. Howe — on his 80th birthday — by Violet (Bicknell) Stone

How fitting that in this Centennial Year
We should take time to honor this true pioneer
1887 was the year of his birth,
And in the eighty that followed he's proven his worth.
As a young lad he use to be careless and free
A handful for mother, six brothers and he,
They were all full of mischief and energy too
And at times they could create quite a hulaboloo.
They made many moves, and in 1906
Found them homesteading out here in the sticks.
They found them a coulee on the lovely Red Deer
Where they dug themselves in for that first hectic year.
Although to us moderns, 'twould seem like pure grief
Those boys came out thriving on Bannock and Beef.
They rode a bronc better than any proud dude,
And they all knew the joys, of a swim in the nude.
Now as Cud grew to be a fine looking young chap
He could not quell the urge, for a girl on his lap.
He took Eileen out in a fine horse and cart,
And while closing the gate, he near lost his Sweetheart.
But though pranks were the by-word in this happy home
The competition was high when Cud he did roam.
The ending was happy in nineteen-sixteen
And Cud won the hand of his charming Eileen.
There life was a mixture of troubles and joys
As they raised a nice family, of three girls and three boys.
Now times were quite hard, but the years how they flew,
In the best home by a "Dam Site" that they ever knew.
Although Cud was married and loaded with care,
He still liked to go on the odd little tear,
He enjoyed playing pranks, both little and big,
And it's said that he put Miller to bed with a pig.
The family all grown and flown from the nest,
Cud returns to the homestead and there did invest
In modern facilities, comfort galore
With travel and bridge games, what could he ask more.
Now we all owe Cud plenty for daring to come
Where no man had trod, nor called it his home.
Now on this birthday, let's all give three cheers
For a man who saw Buffalo, in its formative years.

In Memory of Mrs. C. B. (Eileen) Howe — by Violet (Bicknell) Stone who passed away in July, 1965.

She measured high among the chosen few.
Whom I deemed friend she was true blue.
She spent no time in idle gossip's clutch
But made each waking hour account for much.
Her nimble fingers with her needle flew;
She knew a busy mind is happy all day through.
She gave her all to family and friend,
A selfless soul who never failed to lend
A helping hand to those she held most dear.
Her active mind so full of wit, would cheer
A passing stranger on his merry way,
Or add a happy moment to a mirthless day.
Her character above reproach in every way,
A lady through and through, as all will say,
So patient, understanding, full of grit,
It's true that she'll be missed no little bit.
To be like her, would be one's fondest dream,
Held in such great respect and high esteem.

MR. AND MRS. GEORGE (LORETTA BRASSARD) HOWE
ON THEIR 25TH WEDDING ANNIVERSARY
written by Violet (Bicknell) Stone

'Twas two nights before New Year's back in '43
With the world full of romance on the old prairie;
And George was all happy and full of the same,
That he convinced Lorry to please take his name.
A real quiet wedding sure enough it must be
And Helen and Rusty both did agree.
To do all the honors for this happy two
As they nervously uttered a faint "yes I do."
They were happy and snug and seldom did roam
From the Elliot place which became their first home.
In the spring they moved west to the ranch Vee Bar Vee.
And George he punched cattle for young Happy C.
Lorry was radiant out on the ranch
And the family tree sprouted another Howe branch.
As she bore her first chip from the famous old block
A bouncing big fellow we all know as Jock.
A couple more moves made from Campbell to Bruce
George and Lorry were tired of wandering loose;
So they bought out Pa Brassard and settled them down
On the old family estate near old Atlee town.

Reg and Ron Howe, twin sons of Mr. and Mrs. George Howe Jr., in 1951.

Jock who had reached the ripe age of five
Awaited with pleasure a playmate to arrive.
For two weeks he waited with good Aunty Frank
For the old stork must be up to some sort of prank.
Now George became lonesome and Jock he was blue
Aunty Frank was wondering what she could do.
'Twas a hot Sunday morning that fifth day of June
And the birds were all singing their happiest tune.
A great day for a picnic it then was agreed
So they packed up a lunch and to Empress did speed.
They must take advantage of this lovely weather
And a picnic would bring Mother, Father and Sonny together.
At Empress George jumped from the car with a shout
Ran up the steps to fetch Lorry out.
Returned in a moment, two fingers held high.
Like the sign Churchill made with Victory nigh.
Some would feel double trouble had sure come their way
But to George it seemed a Victory he'd won that day.
It's twins he called out with a grin and a shrug
And proceeded to give his first born a big hug.
The three boys were dandys you all will agree
But a mother needs help, and a family tree
Is slightly unbalanced with a nary a girl
So Mona arrived and her dark hair did curl.
To her mother a helper and her father's delight
Mona brought them much pleasure by day and by night.
Her eyes were so dark they seemed to just snap
She was quiet and gentle but took no time to nap.
Now again in September of fifty-seven
The good stork arrived with his bundle from heaven.
Now Susan as blonde as sister was dark
Added warmth to the family and a certain spark.
Her dancing blue eyes were chuck full of fun
And a place in their hearts she surely had won.

86

So now the family seemed all complete
And back to the river the Howes did retreat.
On the Alf Campbell place they have a fine home.
We hope that from it they never will roam.
They now have been married for twenty-five years.
And still going strong or so it appears.
So congratulations on the first five and a score
And may you with God's help see twenty-five more.
It's been a nice evening all merry and bright
So Lorry and George we now wish you a "Good-night."

OUR LIFE IN ATLEE by Loretta M. (Brassard) Howe

My father, George Brassard, was born in Ste. Anee de Prescott, Ontario, in the year of 1891. He had four brothers and one sister. He came west to Rolla, North Dakota in 1907, at the age of 16 years. There he worked in a store for his uncle for a year and a half. Then he came to Saskatchewan and homesteaded. He didn't like it there so went back to Rolla, North Dakota.

In the year of 1911 he came out to Medicine Hat with friends who were coming out with carloads of settlers' effects. They landed in Alderson in those days it was known as Carlstad, sometime in March. He homesteaded and pre-empted the W½ of Section 4, Township 22, Range 7.

They came from Alderson to the homestead in a team and wagon and built his house of shiplap and tar paper. He found it very cold.

John Pound Sr., came out about the same time and homesteaded five miles east of Dad. He was followed out by his wife and family of eleven children a year or so later. The first winter out was not so cold and very little snow. They went to Alderson for all their coal and groceries with a wagon or democrat. Never used a sleigh. There was a coal mine south of Jenner on the Wise homestead. The coal was very poor.

There was very little sickness and those that were sick went to Medicine Hat. The first teacher in the Atlee district was a missionary but Mom or Dad don't remember his name. The first church was held in homes in the district. There were many ministers to come but don't know the name of the first one. He came all the way from Alderson which was 65 miles and those days there were no cars to travel the distance in an hour or better. It used to take a couple of days.

The first store was built in 1914 by Lawrey's Ltd. He had a store at Tilley, Denhart, Jenner and now at Atlee. The store opened April 24, 1914 and Dad managed it for him until the winter of

87

Mrs. Matt Sneddon and Mrs. George Brassard on their way to a W.I. Meeting.

1915. He then bought it and a fellow by the name of Tom Wilton bought the one at Jenner. Magnus Bjork (the first) was one of the first customers. He rode "Old Brownie" over and after searching for sometime found the store. His comment was "Why the hell did you build the store in a hole where nobody can find it?"

At this time the track was laid one rod past the public crossing just east of the Atlee townsite. The first school was built in Atlee in 1916 on land that was given them by the late R. C. McKee though there had been school in the district held in homestead shacks before this.

The post office at that time was in the store and Mr. Websdale from Jenner hauled the mail from Alderson to Jenner and Dad hauled from Jenner to Atlee. J. R. Hallam then hauled the mail from Atlee to Parvella and Howie. J. R. Hallam had been a former Mounted Policeman and also Justice of Peace for the district. Though everyone thought him a very stern man he did have a sense of humor. Tom Wilton had been fined for buying hides and he and Dad had a phone on the telegraph line at eleven o'clock every morning they talked to each other. This one day Tom told Dad he was going to be pinched for buying hides without a licence. So Dad thought he had better go the Mountie at Parvella and see about it and the Mountie pulled a summons out of his pocket and said, "Here is a summons I was just going to serve you". He asked Dad if he wanted to go to court or go home and he would serve him the summons. Dad decided he would go to court then and save the three dollars it would cost to have him serve it. Dad appeared in court and Hallam told Dad it was $800.00 or a month in jail. Dad said he would take the month in jail. But after a little discussion between Hallam and the Mountie they decided to let Dad off for $8.00.

88

On August 18, 1916, Dad married Eva Pound, the oldest girl in the Pound family. Dad did all his courting with a buggy and team of mules, of course there were many comments from the boys of the Pound family about this.

Adelbert, their son, the first white baby born in the Atlee community, arrived on July 2, 1917. They had a Russian midwife and though they tried to get a doctor, it was impossible to get one. They phoned Empress and the doctor couldn't come, so they tried Medicine Hat. He arrived about 4 p.m., eleven hours after they had phoned for him.

Collin McKay still remembers this and often reminisces about the old times and remembers many events of those days. Collin was the only one who ever came to the store for his mail and groceries with a dog team and Dad remembers him as a handsome young man.

Stan LaRoche was also one of the original young men of the Atlee district who Dad remembers very well.

The elevator was built in 1915 and was first in operation in 1916, operated by Charlie Lloyd who married Gladyce Bunn. It wasn't unusual to see wagon loads of grain strung out for a half mile waiting to go through the elevator. One incident of note is Mr. Buschling hauling his first load of grain to Atlee in 1916 with a team of oxen. Grain used to come into Atlee from as far north as Chinook fording the river down near the Hallam place, now known as the Vee Bar Vee ranch.

R. C. McKee hauled groceries for about four months from Tilley before the train began hauling. W. C. (Scottie) McKee was helping Dad in the store at this time. Dad broke ten acres of land the first year on the homestead and ten acres in the second year. Mr. Bunn harvested the crop as a renter.

The John Pounds left for North Dakota again on October 7, 1919. Granddad Pound had gone ahead and Dad went down to get the rest of the family to catch the train out in a real October blizzard. Three of the boys stayed, Willmar, Edwin and Leland and

Grain hauling at Atlee 1913.

1913 at Pounds on a Sunday afternoon.

two girls Clara and Eva (Mom). Fred came back and worked in the district for a few years only to return to North Dakota. Hattie came back and married an old neighbor, Rex Bunn. They remained in Alberta. Olive and Alma came back in 1929. Olive remained in Alberta and married R. C. Thomson, but Alma returned to North Dakota where she has remained.

In 1917 Dad sold the store and went farming. "What a deal that was," he commented, "Ha".

M. L. Tuve and Prairie Lumber Company had come in and built stores so Dad sold to Louise Epstein and Abe Rabinovitch. By 1918 the other stores had gone broke and these two bought them out. Atlee consisted at that time of three stores, a lumberyard, poolroom, a livery stable, a school and a restaurant. There are many stories that could be told of these times. Many humorous and many tragic.

Dad and Mom stayed on the old homestead until 1948. They had increased their holdings but the purse strings were still tight as they had emerged from the dirty thirties, still happy but with footing that was hard to stand on. All through the hard years, their door was always open for anyone passing by. Rich or poor, were always welcome, and many a bed was prepared for wanderers in the thirties for men passing through on foot looking for work and no hope of finding any. It was heartbreaking to see some, they were hungry and bedraggled with no hope for the future at that time.

Many a Sunday the doors were bursting with young and old who had gathered to play ball for the afternoon and ended up at Brassards for supper. There was always something to eat, the big treat being a large freezer of ice cream which was prepared every Sunday morning. Mom mixing it and putting it in the freezer then the job of turning the ice cream freezer usually fell on some of us kids, of which there were five of us plus one.

Joe Allard had come to our household in 1932 and stayed until he was married in 1946 or 1947. His dad, Louis Allard, had herded sheep for us and when he became aware of the fact that he was sick and probably wouldn't be here long he brought Joe to us, something we were never sorry for, as a brother Joe was one of the best.

In about 1926 Johnny Gordon proposed a community lease and in 1932 it was organized. The first meeting consisted of about 30 signed members but by the time it was organized there were only seven left: L. L. Pound, George White, Dick Ripley, Bill Lawler, Andrew Ness, H. W. Bunn and Dad. Bill Lawler became President and Dad was Secretary. Bill Hewitt and P. C. Hepburn and one other (I don't recall his name) came down and it got going. They found they didn't have enough cattle to stock the lease so Buffalo community was asked to join. Atlee had the lease south of Majestic and Buffalo had the lease they still have. Later the lease south of Atlee, which at that time belonged to Stapleton was added to it. Some of the riders were: Jim Spratt an old Texas cowboy, known by all as a sort of a rough old character but with a soft spot too. I remember one time he came to our place with Murray Stapleton and Colette who was only five at the time, was writing on the blackboard, taught by Bill Carson, who was an old family friend, she wrote for a while with her right hand and when she got tired she wrote with her left hand. Jim noticed this and thought it was the greatest. For sometime later he never passed by without stopping and leaving a dozen oranges for the little girl.

Jim Brodie who is still in the country and is a cowboy of long standing. Ralph Rathburr, the happy little cowboy, Gordon Hughes, Archie Garroick, Jim Andrus, Jim Campbell and Win Vanderloh. The lease now includes members from Jenner and Iddesleigh.

Dad farmed in Atlee until 1948, when he moved to Indus and went back into the store business. He stayed there until 1968 when he moved to Medicine Hat. We, George and Lorry Howe, bought Dad out and we lived there until 1962, when we sold out to Pete Kornelson and Albert Johnson of Brooks, who at the time owned the old Gordon ranch adjoining us to the east. We moved to Buffalo, to the Campbell ranch which we bought from Ray Eggar, who had bought the place from Alfred Campbell approximately three years before.

George and I were married in December 1943 and have five children, Jock (George Jr.), Ron and Reg, the twins and two girls, Mona and Susan. Our son Reg, married Linda Bale in 1969 and they have one son, Neil William, and live in a separate house at the ranch.

91

The Pound boys — John, Edwin, Willmar (Pat), Fred John and Leland.

Pound Girls — Alma, Hattie, Clara, Eva.

Adelbert lives in Calgary where he has worked on the C.P.R., practically ever since leaving Atlee except for a couple of years he served in the Army. He married Dib McManus, a Calgary school teacher who came out as a young girl and taught at the Vee Bar Vee ranch, which was formerly the H. R. Hallam ranch. Del and Dib have nine children: Karen; Elizabeth (Sammy), who married Jack Thompson and now lives in Cavendish; Rocky; Dan; Michelle; Therese; Mary-Kate; Shane and Renée.

Francis (Frankie) married Don Thompson the adopted son of Mr. and Mrs. Emile Sandgate in January 1940. They had two sons, Dick and Bud. She divorced Don and married George Arden in August 1952, they have two children, Dale and Lynn and presently live in Brooks, Alberta.

Helen married Arnold Beglaw, whose father had been section foreman at Majestic some years before, in March 1947 and have four children, Diane, Dwayne, Douglas and Donald. They live in North Vancouver, B.C. (See Arnold and Helen Beglaw Story).

Colette, who was the only one left at home when Mom and Dad moved to Indus, went with them. She married Ken Olson from Iddesleigh in March 1950. They have four children, Bill, Denise, Wendy and Bob. They live on the farm south of Jenner. Now as I write this in July 1971, Mom and Dad have 26 grandchildren and 15 great-grandchildren. Mom and Dad have always remained young and even now as Dad goes into his 81st year and Mom into her 75th, they still enjoy good health and are happiest when their door is bulging with company young and old. They celebrated their 50th wedding anniversary in 1966 at the Jenner picnic grounds with a large number of friends and relatives.

The greatest joy being the arrival of Dad's two brothers, Joe and Jake, their wives and members of their families, his sister Mamie and the arrival of her daughter, Therese and granddaughter Michelline,

92

who flew to Calgary from Montreal and even surprised Mamie by their arrival.

Now as we pass by the old townsite of Atlee and see only the schoolhouse left to mark the passing of many good years, it makes one feel a little lonely. There were so many old friends, neighbors and school chums. It is always a great pleasure to meet again and reminisce about old times.

The Sneddons, who were our closest and dearest neighbors, our Uncles and Aunts and cousins with whom we spent many a Merry Christmas, New Year, Thanksgiving and many special occasions, or old school chums who it is always a great joy to meet again. Though I have not mentioned many of you in this article, you will always be remembered and God bless you all.

CHESTER AND HELEN HOWE by Mrs. Kenneth (Sharon-Ann) Gray

When mother first mentioned her desire to have such a book compiled, I know she had no idea how much work it would involve, but as always when she got the notion something should be done she would take the bit in her teeth and go ahead and do her best. Over the past five years she had gained great interest in the area and its people through her column in the Brooks Bulletin.

I recall many obstacles she overcame during the years we five children, of whom I am the youngest, we were growing up. I remember Mother announcing she was going to enroll in a business course. We all had our misgivings about this, as she had been out of school for about twenty-five years, and that was only grade school, but she surprised us all when she completed an eighteen-month course in only six months and received two diplomas showing in excess of 97 per cent in both.

Valentine's Day 1964, was the first time we, Ken and I, knew anything of a rancher in mother's life. We were very surprised when she announced in June that she was going to leave her office job to marry Chester Howe. Before long our respect for him increased immensely and all five of us were very pleased and happy with her choice. We took great joy in teasing Chester, for he went from a bachelor to a husband, stepfather of five, and grandfather of the then eight grandchildren. This sudden intrusion on life was taken with unbelievable calm, and all of us still wonder at his ability to adapt to his new way of life.

The change from city to ranch life was quite an adjustment for mother. Her love of the outdoors, gardening and the so-called slower pace of the country has proven beneficial. Working together, they

93

Chester Howe with bale picker, Don Woodcock on wagon.

Chester C. Howe's house, 1970.

Chester Howe on Buck — 1964.

Chester C. Howe, as "the proud father of the Bride", Ken and Sharon-Ann Gray.

C. C. Howe and youngest grandson, Douglas Gray.

Chester C. Howe at Niagara Falls, 1964 "Man what I couldn't do with that water".

94

have expanded Chester's somewhat small house and dry land into an attractive home and garden.

We know very little of Chester in his bachelorhood days, but he has told us about his land being the Old Dick Elliot place and about having worked and lived here himself since the early forties. We enjoy coming to Buffalo, helping when we can, or just being with Chester checking his livestock.

Chester and mother travelled to New Brunswick in 1964 by car, and flew back there again in 1970, visiting her relatives in New Brunswick and his Mother's people in Toronto, and showing Chester the eastern part of Canada. He was interested in the eastern methods of farming and ranching, and took a great deal of pleasure in the trips. But I kind of think Air Canada gave him the best thrill. My grandmother Calhoun ventured west to spend two summers in Buffalo and Chester, as always, opened his home welcomely.

I recall one weekend in 1965 their home was filled with everyone of his "instant" children and all the grandchildren. I often wonder if the "City Dudes" really did help harvest that weekend. But Chester made all eighteen of us feel welcome and needed.

In recent years, to aid his harvest, Chester constructed a machine from old scrap iron that picks up eight bales at a time, loads them onto a wagon, and then to the stack. My husband, Ken, agrees that Chester's ingenuity in making this machine has turned hard work into almost play.

We found it interesting to learn how Chester obtains the much needed water for his alfalfa crop. He is able to flood approximately 100 acres by pumping 120,000 gallons of water per hour up an 18 foot rise through a 12 inch intake pipe into the four to six foot ditches. As mother's garden also needed water, he didn't stop at just that. By connecting hydrants to the well he was able to make water available in abundance for both flowers and vegetables.

We consider ourselves most fortunate indeed. Not only have we a safe and healthy place for our two year old son and us to visit, but mother is in her own element. We have learned many interesting facets of ranching, and met a lot of wonderful people in the area. All of this we accredit to Chester. Their home is open to company all year round to share with them the unpolluted beauty of Buffalo and the Red Deer River. This we truly appreciate.

STANLEY HURL by Edgar (Ted) Stone

The Hurls were homesteaders of the Cavendish area and moved to the Mode place in about 1927 and later took over the Salzwedel place. Besides farming, Stanley worked as Pool agent at Sharron, Cavendish and Buffalo, and finally gave up the farm and spent the

Mr. and Mrs. Stanley Hurl at family reunion, 1958.

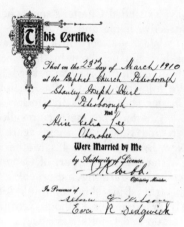

Marriage certificate, Mr. and Mrs. Stanley Hurl.

last few years before retirement in the Swenson house which was purchased by the Alberta Wheat Pool in the forties and moved to Buffalo from the British Block.

Stanley was an ardent baseball enthusiast and kept a boys' baseball team going for many years. This was probably sparked by the fact that he had four boys of his own, Willie, Del, Norman and Clarence. Sports days were the order of the day and although few cars were in evidence in the late twenties, the few model "T"s and others which made their appearance were loaded to the "hilt" with these merry gay clad youths and as many fans as could be squeezed in. The boys remember many exciting incidents which took place as they wended their way down prairie trails to points ten to twenty miles away in all four directions. The mothers of the boys also have their fond memories of bolts of grey flannel, which they fashioned into the "bloomery" uniform of the day as well as the bulging picnic baskets packed to sustain the healthy appetites of these eager young fellows after the games.

Mrs. Hurl, too, was an active member of the W.I. and later the Buffalo Women's Club which was started to do wartime duties in the early forties and later took an active part in raising funds to remodel the old hall in 1946. The Hurls were always in attendance at community functions from church services to the country dances, which they loved so well. While Mrs. Hurl took her place on the kitchen committee, Mr. Hurl acted as "square dance" caller and a very capable floor manager to keep the dances rolling smoothly. We have yet to find another with the built-in enthusiasm and energy

96

to take his place in this capacity. The Hurls were sorely missed when they retired and moved to Calgary to live, in 1955.

THE STANLEY HURL FAMILY by Clarence Hurl

Homesteaders in the Cavendish area were all young families with small children, and all were scarce of funds. To make life bearable and enjoyable they had to take an active part in the events of the community and create their own amusement. Life now found the Hurls participating along with their neighbors.

January 1st, 1926 — back row: Willie Hurl, Archie Ferguson, Slim Tiller, Stan Hurl, Mrs. Gilham, Mrs. Johnson and Mary, Len Johnson, unknown, Jack Gilham and Bill Parker. Front row: Norman Hurl, Mrs. Hawkins, Dan Hawkins, Mrs. Hurl, Mrs. Hames, Bill Hurl and Ernie Hames. In front: Clarence Hurl, Lucille Hawkins and Harold Gilham.

Saturday afternoon found all the people at the hamlet of Cavendish enjoying a sports day. The men in a game of football or baseball, the women swapping recipes, discussing families and in deep conversation, and cheering on the game. A dance followed the strenuous afternoon, the music being supplied by capable local musicians who could really give out with real toe-tapping tunes. Stan was one of the many who contributed to the gayety by playing the violin, calling square dances, and managing the evening.

No babysitting in those days, so children of all ages came along with their parents, and when they became tired they would be placed along the side benches and in bunks to rest, while the parents danced away the wee hours of the morning.

Sunday would usually find a large group of neighbors gathered at one neighbor's place or another for an afternoon of rodeo events; riding bucking horses and cattle, and saddle horse racing. These culminated in a supper prepared by the women after which all went home happy and satisfied.

As the years went by, Hurls became members of the Buffalo community, and as in Cavendish, they continued helping to organize

97

and work with their pioneer neighbors. The local school and Hall Boards, Sports and Entertainment Committee, U.F.A. — you name it — found Hurls aggressive members, often Stan acted as veterinarian when neighbors had problems with their stock.

His interest in sports and entertainment brought Stan to the foreground. Managing the hardball teams provided him and the young people much satisfaction and produced many good ball players, who journeyed to distant towns during the dirty thirties and often came home the victors. Stan became involved managing the local girls' softball team, a team which became well known in those parts at the local picnics for miles around.

Train service was one train a week — east on Wednesday evening and west on Saturday morning. The people congregated in the hamlet these evenings for mail, groceries and friendship sessions.

When water was located in Buffalo — Stan undertook to keep the pump in service, and to obtain and help to build a shed to house it.

Allie Hurl doing spring work, the year a horse fell on Stan.

Allie was as active in her role as Stan in his. Gatherings at the Hurls long remembered her festive meals; her willing co-operation with other wives made possible the many community gatherings. More than once Allie acted as a "nervous midwife" — and brought babies into the world. She served too in sadder occasions, as an undertaker.

A lasting tribute to the Hurls might aptly be:
There are hermit souls that live withdrawn
In the place of their self-content;
There are souls like stars, that dwell apart,
In a fellowless firmament;

There are pioneer souls that blaze their paths
Where highways never ran —
But let me live by the side of the road
And be a friend to man.
Let me live in a house by the side of the road
Where the race of men go by —
The men who are good and the men who are bad
As good and as bad as I.
I would not sit in the scorner's seat
Or hurl the cynic's ban —
Let me live in a house by the side of the road
And be a friend to man.
I see from my house by the side of the road,
By the side of the highway of life,
The men who press with the ardor of hope,
The men who are faint with the strife,
But I turn not away from their smiles nor their tears,
Both parts of an infinite plan —
Let me live in a house by the side of the road
And be a friend to man.
I know there are brook-gladdened meadows ahead,
And mountains of wearisome height;
That the road passed on through the long afternoon
And stretches away to the night.
And still I rejoice when the travellers rejoice
And weep with the strangers that moan,
Nor live in my house by the side of the road
Like a man who dwells alone.
Let me live in my house by the side of the road,
It's here the race of men go by —
They are good, they are bad, they are weak, they are strong,
Wise, foolish — so am I.
Then why should I sit in the scorner's seat,
Or hurl the cynic's ban?
Let me live in my house by the side of the road
And be a friend to man.

Sam Walter Foss (1858-1911)

Joseph Stanley Hurl, one of fourteen children of Mr. and Mrs. Wm. James Hurl of Harvey Township, Lakefield, Ontario — Born April 1890; Alice Celia Lee, one of nine children of Mr. and Mrs. Wm. James Lee of Otonobee Township, Peterborough, Ontario — born 1888; were married on the 23rd day of March, 1910 in Ontario. On March 18th, 1911 their firstborn, a son made his appearance, and was appropriately named — Wm. James.

Allie Hurl out for a ride, a horse lover all her life, she spent many days training horses to jump and race and at all Old-Time picnics she would participate in the saddle horse races.

Mr. and Mrs. Stanley Hurl.

The call of the West was answered and Stan, as he was known to all — left Peterborough in 1911 to begin his search for a new life and home for his family. Allie and son came West in 1912, after Stan had a steady job at the Claresholm Experimental Farm. Here Allie operated a boardinghouse where she housed and fed six high school students. Two sons were born in Claresholm, Delmer in February 1914 and Norman in December 1915. The ambition to own their own farm won over the local doctor's offer to rent his farm, so in 1916 Hurls started their life on a prairie homestead five miles south of Cavendish. During later years Stan was heard to say the deal may have been a mistake, though many years in Cavendish area were gratifying ones. A fourth son, Clarence, was born in September, 1920.

One day in 1926 while summer-fallowing, Stan was unable to find the furrow because of the drifting sand, he became determined to look for a farm with heavier land. So 1927 saw the Hurl family, bag and baggage, moving to the Mode farm in Buffalo which they farmed for eleven years. In 1938 they moved to the Salzwedel farm, two miles closer to the hamlet of Buffalo. The older boys attended Cornland school until the dwindling population made it necessary for them to attend the Cavendish school. In the Buffalo district the young people attended the Lila school. During the "dirty thirties" William went to Innisfail to work on a farm, Delmer to Rainier to

100

clerk in a store and Norman to work as an attendant at the Ponoka Mental Hospital, where he became a trained nurse.

In 1943, Stan accepted the local Pool elevator agency, and by the fall of 1944 they moved into the hamlet of Buffalo, thus retiring from the farm. Clarence left Buffalo in search of a new life.

At age 65 — Stan retired from the Pool elevator and bought a home in northwest Calgary. For the next three years he kept busy doing odd jobs around his neighborhood. In December, 1957 he took ill and passed away in August, 1958.

Three sons, William, Delmer and Clarence reside in Calgary, Norman in Edmonton. William, married to Lillian Krause of Innisfail, and have one daughter, Judy; Delmer married to Etta Hatch of Oyen, have four daughters — Donna, Darlene, Marlene and Lorna; Norman married to Marguerite Morrissette of Morrinville and have a family of three — Maxine, Dennis and Wesley; Clarence married to Ruth Skjenna of Buffalo, have six children, Deryl, Carol, Myna, Gayleen, Kelly and Shelley.

HURL ANTIDOTES:

As Allie entered the Cavendish store one day, she was greeted by the proprietor with, "Hello Mrs. Hurl, the Mounted Police were in a short while ago looking for you." Wondering what created their interest, she questioned as to why? Apparently the family in Peterborough had asked the assistance of the Mounties in locating Allie, as they had not heard from her for over two years, they were wondering if she was still alive. Needless, to say, Allie wrote a letter to her distant family that night explaining the circumstances.

When Clarence was a couple of months old Allie and her helping hand, Mabel Morrison, decided to drive with team and sleigh to the hamlet of Cavendish, five miles distant. Allie bundled her baby up very carefully, and Mabel was to hold him for the journey. Carefully wrapping the blankets around themselves in the sleigh they headed for town. On arrival at the Cavendish store, the horses were tied up, and both women went into the store with Mabel still carrying the baby. Allie immediately exclaimed, "My baby, you have got him upside down." A few anxious moments were spent as hands speedily unwrapped the infant, and a sigh of relief was given when he was found well and happy.

P.S. FROM THE BALCONY. It's tough to live with such an inferiority complex of both ends looking alike.

Stan was always the floor manager at the local dances. Occasionally, when he had a dance going full swing, he would disappear for a short time. His favorite movement on entering the hall as the dance was finishing was to wipe his mouth with his handkerchief, and carry on. Oddly enough, the calling seemed to have developed a slightly louder tone and a little more zest. HMM — wonder why?

During the dirty thirties twice as many potatoes were planted to ensure the families of an adequate supply for winter. It was one of these years when the following incident occurred.

Thunderclouds formed many times but passed on leaving the scorched prairie wool and crops to suffer. One day, however, they formed and produced a heavy downpour of moisture to the parched land below. When this proved to be more than a mere shower, Stan went out in his shirt sleeves and was heard to shout, "send her down David! send her down!" With this he retired to the Winnipeg couch to relax.

Someone, somewhere answered the plea and produced a lengthy rain. After his rest, Stan found it still raining heavily with the runoff starting to build up in the sloughs. When the storm subsided, the language developed a different tone as half the potato crop was under water. However, if memories are correct, there was an adequate potato supply for the winter.

The year Mrs. Lovell Stone had reached her half century, the neighbors decided to have a surprise party at the Stone home. This was during the spring thaw when the running water was under-cutting the large snow banks. Peter and Laura Dickrow and baby son Lance and Mr. and Mrs. Albert Cook had driven to Hurls, and with a fresh team from Hurls all continued on towards the destination. Stan had chosen his favorite team for this trip, and stopped to pick up Mr. and Mrs. Dearing, Vern and Daisey a short distance away.

Vern and Mr. Cook were standing in the back end of the sleigh box while Pete was in front with Stan. Daisey, Allie, Laura, Mrs. Cook — holding Lance, and Mrs. Dearing were sitting on a bench along the inside and Clarence was standing in the middle of the other side. As the team were winding along trying to keep the sleigh on snow, the lower side gave way and over went everything; Vern on his back in mid-stream along with the bridge table, Mr. Cook on his feet in the stream, Daisey and Allie holding themselves up with their hands submersed in water up to their elbows, and unable to do anything for laughing at their predicament. Laura had somehow jumped clear of all blankets to catch her baby, as Mrs. Cook tossed him. As the sleigh upset Clarence caught the baby and held Mrs. Cook and Mrs. Dearing up with his hands until Laura had rescued her baby out of the mess.

Stan immediately called for Clarence to come to help him hold the team as they were known to run away, but this was impossible. As well as being held down by two women his feet were all tangled

102

in blankets. Pete Dickrow went to Stan's aid, thus preventing any further catastrophe.

Vern finally decided that he was getting wet and had best move, so crawled out of the puddle. When all sorted out and reloaded in the sleigh box, they continued on to the Stone home where the wet clothes and shoes were replaced with dry ones. The delightful party carried on without any further mishaps to the wee hours of the morning.

Stan's grandson Deryl, at the age of two or three years, took a fancy to his grandfather's watch, and one day asked him for it. Stan's answer was "Someday when I'm an old old man, I'll give it to you." A couple of years went by with nothing more said on the subject.

One day as this same pair were heading home from the town well Deryl wanted his grandfather to race him home. "No," said Stan, "I can't run, grandpa's an old old man." "Give me the watch," was the immediate demand.

Hurls never had to worry about the oat bundles twines not being cut, as Allie had the odd habit of finding them at the most inopportune times. It never failed that when she had both hands full, she would get both feet tangled in uncut twine. Most times she was able to save herself from falling, but occasionally when in a hurry, she would go flat on her face. Sometimes on the bare ground and sometimes in the not too clean puddles at the barn door.

Hurls had a part hackney team that were very balky, which at times wouldn't pull the hat off your head. During harvest time Allie drove to Cavendish once a week to sell her homemade butter. The team would be hitched to the democrat and tied to a post near the house before the men went to the field after dinner.

Around one-thirty Allie could be seen going to the team, untie them, and be in the driver's seat ready to go. The team would back up a bit, but would refuse to go ahead. Patience won out and in a few minutes Allie would be going down the road hell bent for leather for about one-half mile applying the whip. The team, warmed up in more ways than one, now settled down to an ordinary gait for the balance of the journey, and Allie being a horse lover was in her glory.

Boxing Day 1934 saw Allie and Clarence in Ontario visiting relatives. Stan was now the chief cook and bottle washer at the Hurl household, as well as keeping check on the outside winter chores. One morning Norman went on the sick list and remained in bed while the morning chores were being done. As the family — including Oscar Skjenna — sat down to a breakfast of Stan's special pancakes, Oscar turned and threw one at Norman. Norman ate

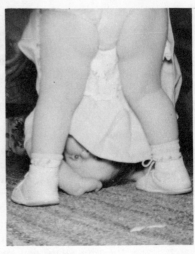

Hurl twins, Kelly and Shelly.

that one, climbed out of bed, dressed and came to the table to complete his breakfast of 20 more pancakes. Oscar made the remark that he would sure hate to feed Norman when he was well.

Allie was teased many times about hanging out her shingle after having to deliver two babies in the Buffalo area.

The summer of 1949 was very wet with rain nearly every day. Clarence's wife Ruth was expecting as was Mrs. Emile (Shorty) Brown of the district. The Canadian Mother and Child Book was lying on the table at Clarence's home one day, and Allie asked if she could take it and read it. So that evening she read through it just as a precaution.

Luckily for her she did, as she was called out that night to help in a delivery at the Brown household. Away she went with the book clutched under her arm. As the baby was being born, the father sat at the foot of the bed and read aloud step by step the procedure recommended, then he was asked to go outside as she cleaned up and took care of the new baby and mother.

FOOTNOTE:
To Allie's relief Clarence was able to get his wife to the Empress Hospital for the birth of their child.

About five years later when living in the hamlet of Buffalo Allie was again called upon. At three A.M. one morning a knock came on their door, a neighboring rancher, Magnus Bjork about to become a father, informed Allie that he was bringing Tiny in. They had been stuck on the Red Deer River hill which prevented them

104

from being able to reach the hospital in time. Being winter time, the water reservoir and kettle were hot. Stan was sent to get Boo Thompson to help with the delivery. This was a bit out of Boo's line but she came down about 3:30. However, by this time Tiny had delivered her baby with no complications and all was well. The doctor was phoned for verification, and Tiny remained at the Hurl household for the normal required time.

MR. AND MRS. CLARENCE (RUTH SKJENNA) HURL ON THEIR 25TH WEDDING ANNIVERSARY

by Violet (Bicknell) Stone

You started out a pair of kids, childhood sweethearts true.
Time was when we were sore afraid, something would part you two.
Needless to say, we mind the day
You stopped by first to let us know
Your plans were made and you would go
Through life together.

A soldier and his candy kid, a happy pair were you
For nothing ever could break up, a love that was so true.
The mood was gay, you set the day
You choose the festive Christmastide
To take your vows as groom and bride
And stay together.

The war was soon to end and now to find a job was tough
Attempting many different tasks the going sure was rough.
So now which way? It's hard to say
Should you milk cows or maybe teach?
For you were bound a goal to reach
Pulling together.

With children coming one two three, the doghouse had its place
It seemed at times that old man stork would surely win the race.
Dad made it pay, both night and day,
It took Ruth all her time to bake
And clean and sew, for they must make
A home together.

It seemed that now your house was full, for now you numbered eight
You'd have no time — there'd be no room for friends to congregate.
But night or day, the same old way
Your hearts had room for still one more,
While both, at your ever-opened door
Welcomed together.

A message we'd like now to send, to friends we hold so dear
Congratulations to you both, you've reached the silver year.
May I relay, a golden ray
Of sunshine and of happiness
Wished from our family and God Bless
Your day together.

R. H. (DICK) IMES

My father, J. W. Imes, was a farm-raised boy and was familiar with driving cattle to market in Chicago. He moved from Monticello, Indiana, to Bozeman, Montana, in 1877 the year after Custer's Battle on the Little Big Horn. Although he was a schoolteacher and principal in different pioneer schools, his greatest interests were in cattle. My mother came from Bloomington, Indiana, the same year, to teach school near Helena, where she met my father and they were married in 1888 and continued teaching together for several years. Their first child, born in 1889, was a boy and they named him after the state — Montana. Montana learned to be a cowboy in the Big Belt Mountains around Chestnut, Montana. Chestnut was nine miles up Rocky Canyon from Bozeman and was a coal mining town. My parents had a store and the post office there for several years and had cattle in the mountain range. Montana's first saddle came from Chicago. Shortly afterwards he roped a wild mountain yearling and partly amputated three fingers of his right hand, caught in the dally around the saddle horn.

By 1900 the range in the Big-Belts was restricted and started my father on the hunt for open range. North of Great Falls was open clear to the Canadian Border. So in 1901 my father started to gather his cattle for a drive to the Sweet Grass Hills. But a fall in some loose rock on a steep mountain side in Rocky Canyon crippled one leg, so the drive was called off for a year. In 1902 plans for the drive were completed and six inches of snow was on the ground when their first camp was made near Belgrade, about ten miles west of Bozeman. Montana who was only 14, was riding a white mare named Pet, one of the best horses ever to reach the Red Deer from Montana. Mother bade him a tearful good-bye, as everyone we knew said he would freeze to death in Canada, providing he survived the hardships of the trail. Mother had been against the move and made desperate efforts to change my father's mind. My father and Montana moved their cattle — 70 head — down the Gallatin valley on their way north towards Helena. Near Helena a heifer broke her leg and Dad had a butcher dress her and sent three quarters of the meat back to us.

This was the only animal they lost on the trip that I know of. They crossed the Big-Belts at Neibart, the snow being very deep.

106

They were still in the Big-Belts when an accident occurred which shows some of the difficulties which they had to contend with. Gathering the cattle one snowy morning they found a bunch had eased themselves into a field of alfalfa stubble. After driving them out my father rode over to the owner's house to see what he owed him for the damage. The man, a small rancher flew into a terrible rage and made for my Dad to give him a beating. Unable to get his coat off my father took the only course open to him. He laid the man's face open with a lash of a bull-whip which stopped him in his tracks. After making a settlement for the haystack which the cattle had damaged, Dad was thankful to get away as he was certain the man was mentally unreliable. They bought feed when it was available and as a rule the stock were well fed. They had a team and other equipment on the north fringe of the Sweet Grass hills just north of the Canadian border on a ranch my father had rented from a widow. On the trail, Dad and Montana lived on fried cornmeal mush, bacon and beef, lots of Arbuckle coffee and dried apples. Their bedding and spare clothes were packed in an 18 oz. tarpaulin 14 feet long and 54 inches wide slung over a horse's back. The grub was also packed on a horse as they couldn't use wheeled vehicles in the snow of the mountains and on the plains they couldn't use a sleigh for lack of snow in many places. They rolled their bed in makeshift shelter except when they were invited to stay at a ranch which was usually extended to them if their plans fitted the occasion. One time, Montana told me, there was six inches of snow on their bedding when he woke up. He said it was the warmest he ever slept in his life. They cooked on open fires. I don't know how long they were on the trail, but they were safely in the Sweet Grass Hills on New Year's Day 1903.

In 1904, Dad and Montana were joined by Steve Cicon, Dick Roysdon, later known as "Dead-Wood Dick" and Jane Rudd, a widow woman, who was also known as "Calamity Jane", all from Big Timber, Montana. They all moved north to the Red Deer from the Sweet Grass hills.

Dad and Montana were home the winter of 1906-07 and Montana was going to college. Steve Cicon was wintering our cattle with his own and had lots of good range and considerable feed but conditions were so bad he was unable to haul enough hay and he lost heavily. Steve had more hay than anyone else except Nelson and Bjork and could stand more cold than a dozen ordinary men. When only eight of our cattle out of a herd of 108 head survived the hard winter of 1906-07, the blow was too much for my mother and she passed away shortly after. Calamity Jane and Dead-Wood Dick had a cabin on the north side of the river and they wintered their cattle with Cicon. Dick was a tremendous hay hauler and had the largest rack on the Red Deer which he built himself. In 1908 Dad bought what cattle Jane had left after the hard winter, only 24 cows and calves, at $24.00 a head, calves thrown in. Then she and Dick went back to Big Timber where they went into sheep — her pet hate.

In 1940 Montana made his way back to the Red Deer after an absence of 21 years. When Montana reached the Red Deer it seemed to put new life in him and healed him, though he had been given only a short time to live after a brain tumor operation several years before in Benton-Harbor, Michigan. He was in good health again out on that old river he loved so well when an accident terminated in his death on December 6, 1952. The stamina required on the Montana and Alberta ranges pulled him through until he got back to the Red Deer. There is pull to that old river that draws people back, some for over a thousand miles, for one last visit. This is a poem I wrote in 1917 after being down in southern Arizona.

R. H. (Dick) Imes and his wife now live at Forest Lawn, Alberta.

THE LURE OF THE RED DEER

There's a land far south of winter,
Where it's summer all the time;
Where the Spanish Senoritas blossom in that gentle clime;
Where the hot red chili pepper stings a northerner's nose.
Where the gilded Gila Monster and the giant cactus grows,
Where a softly gleaming southern moon,
Seems to turn all things to gold.
Yet I'm ever drifting back here,
To a land of storm and cold.
I don't know the reason,
That I come back every time
To a land that's so far northward
Of the Mason-Dixon line.
I guess there must be magic
In that ancient Red Deer stream
That halter-breaks a cowboy
And brings him back again.
When I feel my days are numbered
I'll drift again once more,
To the valley of the Red Deer
To die beside its shore.

CLYDE JARBOE

My parents, Clinton and Lola Jarboe came to the Red Deer River district in 1903 from Casper, Wyoming. We made the trip by team and covered wagon. This was the same year that Adoph Fisher and family, as well as his two brothers, Fred and Otto came. Our ranches were adjoining and our lives were very much connected.

Our first home was a dugout and life was very rugged in those early days. I recall some of the stories of things that happened even before we came. In the late 1800's the place which Fergus Kennedy later owned, was owned by a man and his wife whose name I don't recall. They came along and settled with about 15 or 20 head of cattle. They had a dugout and a place for a couple of cows and they cut their hay for the year. This dugout was near the present irrigation dam of Jack Longmier. One morning the man set out up the coulee looking for a little meat on the hoof. His destination was the bend in the coulee where a ridge was formed of large rocks and animal paths. Up on the side of the coulee there were bushes in which to hide to wait for game. It was there the Indians shot and killed the man. The fellow's hired hand had moved with the widow and the stock down on the fork of the Red Deer River away from the fated place. Later the Shannon's took over this first homestead area and to this day an old rock chimney and rock oven can be seen still standing.

In 1904 or '05 a man blew into this area from Wyoming called Karl Snellrod. He came from a good family, was well-educated, but was the owner of itchy feet and had wandered all over the world. He called himself the "Walking Man". He came to rest at the Jarboe place temporarily. About six weeks later my father, Clint, and Karl were working in the fields cutting hay, but this soon proved to be a very dissatisfying team, an especially annoying day ended with my Dad coming in very peeved. It seems Karl couldn't understand

Picture of an early Jarboe home with Mrs. Jarboe in the doorway. Clint with young Clyde at his side and Fisher on the horse.

Mrs. Jarboe at the back of a covered wagon box that has been set off the wagon. It is probably the same one they used when they came into Alberta from Montana.

why they couldn't take the cookstove to the fields instead of them having to come to the house.

Jim McGarry and Jim Spratt decided one summer they wouldn't work that season so headed off to Moccasin Flats purchasing food-stuff and putting up a little hay for the horses. Soon after they were joined by Tom Mossop who decided to join the group. The trio didn't last long and the falling out culminated with the division of the frying pan, tea kettle and food being divided into three portions. Although they really didn't part company, the morning ritual went like this for each — for instance, Jim McGarry would arise, cook his breakfast, wash his dishes, pour the dirty water on the fire in the stove, then leave. Then Jim would do the same and this would continue until each had their breakfast and go on his way. Each one to his own so that none of the others would have any benefit from the living arrangements.

One time Jim Spratt was working for my Dad and Fisher. Dad sent him into town (Medicine Hat) for a couple of quarts of whiskey and when Jim didn't return when expected Dad got suspicious. Jim and the whiskey had arrived at a nearby neighbor, where quite a bit of the whiskey was consumed, before Jim decided to start for his camp. However, before leaving, Jim wanted to fortify his journey so he stashed what was left in his coat pocket, the coat was brand new, he had just purchased it. When Jim reached his camp he felt it was time for a little refreshment and reached into his coat pocket to find the liquor no longer there. Grabbing his hunting knife he started cutting the new coat into thin ragged strips and muttered, "You S.O.B. of a coat, you'll never lose another bottle of whiskey for anyone else."

110

Cecil Barber (now of MacDonald and Barber — commissioned buyers at the Calgary Stockyards) was the ferry man on the first ferry across the Red Deer at Bar House and since things were slow that day, Cecil was quietly fishing when Jim Spratt appeared and starting shooting at the fishing float bobbing in the water. Spratt was quite drunk and said, "Now take me across this — river." Cecil though he might as well as Jim wouldn't let him fish.

Jim Spratt, as one of the last real westerners, many a story can be told about him. One I recall hearing is the time he got his first Model "T" Ford car. He drove into Buffalo one day in this old Ford, he wasn't wearing any boots. As you may remember the old Model "T" had pedals. Old Jim says, "I just can't feel how to trigger her with my boots on." He was quite a fellow to chew tobacco. He was coming from Medicine Hat one day, liquored up as was the custom when a trip to the Hat was made. I forgot now who was with him, but anyway when Jim wanted to spit, he would just spit straight ahead. Well it wasn't many miles before the windshield was so covered with tobacco juice that it was impossible to see through it, so he up with his foot and put his boot (must have worn them that day) through the glass and all was clear again.

JIM AND PEARL KELLINGTON by Pearl (Dobb) Kellington

We have not lived in this area too long, but when we moved here in 1965, it was the fulfillment of a dream we had had ever since we were married in 1942, but financially were unable to get land enough to make a living. We had one quarter near Eston, Saskatchewan, but this was not enough to live on so Jim bought grain a few years, also worked in a garage. Then in 1951 he went in business with his brother in garage in Glidden, Saskatchewan. Glidden began to fade so we moved back to Eston, and went in partners with the John Deere dealer there for eight years.

Jim was born and raised at Eston, his Dad was one of the old-timers of that district and lives in the Senior Citizen Home there. Jim's mother passed away in 1967, just four months before their fifty-fifth wedding anniversary.

We have three girls, two married at Eston, Sandra at home when she isn't attending school in Medicine Hat. We have one son, Trevor, and it was for him that we were anxious to have a farm for him to grow up on. My sister married Roy Hern of Empress, Alberta. Roy was with the railroad but they too, wanted the freer life so bought Mrs. John Fowlie's farm south of Bindloss in the Social Plain district. One time while we were visiting them we heard the rumor that Mr. and Mrs. Ray Vaughn might be selling their farm, so we got up our courage and came to see them. It

111

took nearly two years before things were finalized and we moved here. We knew a few of the people but not very well. We moved on the 16th of March. It was twenty below and the roads were terrible. I had the car, with my plants and our wee dog, and I high-centered twice and had to be pulled out by the truck.

Dog trained as a babysitter for Pearl (Dobb) Kellington in 1919.

Mr. Vaughn had passed away in Calgary the first of March, but Mrs. Vaughn was still in the house, so we moved in to a vacant house of Ben Hern's. Dean Moore had told us to let him know when we went by his place and he would give us a hand to unload, so we blew the horn as we passed. Someone had plowed the yard out for us and by the time we drove in there, there were lights coming from all directions, our new neighbors coming to give us a hand to unload. This was about eight in the evening and my sister had a delicious supper prepared for us hungry travellers.

This incident alone made a deep impression of the kind of people we were going to be living amongst. We were so grateful as we were "all in" from loading in Eston and the hard trip over.

Our son-in-law and daughter who had accompanied us returned to their home two days later. Jim was going to go with them to bring back another load, but as it was storming so bad he only went part way to see that Ken and Faye got home alright. It was six whole weeks before we got the rest of our things.

We moved into our own place the following November, situated ten miles southeast of Bindloss. Whenever we go to Bindloss we can see the hills of the Red Deer River beyond Bindloss and they never look the same; the sun hits them one way or another or they look greener or the snow shows up a little more one time than another. And we head southeast, towards the 41 highway, we see the hills of the old Saskatchewan River and they are the same, always looking different and one often sees deer or antelope or the cattle grazing in our Beautyland community pasture, which is owned by eleven rancher farmers.

Some people think the hills look terrible and desolate, but I love the things of nature and they are so beautiful, if one would only take the time to look for them.

I would like to go back to some of the earlier days as my Dad, Henry Dobb, of Eatonia, Saskatchewan, is one of the "getting fewer" old-timers. He will be eighty-five in November and has seen many good times and many hardships. He filed on his homestead about forty-five miles northeast of Empress in 1910. He arrived in Kindersley with his brother and proceeded to find their homestead, but had to travel on foot forty miles. There had been a prairie fire and they walked in the charred grass looking for the corner stakes of the sections. It was getting late and they saw a shack so they headed for it. There was no one home, but they went in anyway. They were very tired and when it got dark they lit the lamp and a little later there was a knock on the door, so they figured they'd better let on they owned the place, so invited the man in. They all had a good laugh when later it was made known that he was the rightful owner. The three became very good friends and this place was only about five miles from where their own sections were.

In 1918 my father's brother, Theodore Dobb and Jack McGregor built a house in Bindloss. I haven't been able to find out if this house is still standing.

When my Dad and Mother were married in 1916 they drove to Empress, with horse and buggy, then drove back the next day.

In November of 1918 I was about to make my arrival in to this world. Dad took Mother to Kindersley ahead of time, again by horse and buggy. He would come every other day to visit her, finally I arrived but my Mother got the flu and passed away four days later.

When I was two weeks old my Dad took me home and looked after me. My aunt helped sometimes. I must have been left alone quite a bit. One day he had to go some place so he got me ready then went out to get the team hitched up and came back for me, but while he was in the house the team ran away, so he had to unwrap me and go get his saddle horse to go after the runaways.

He did have one faithful helper, old Nellie, our dog. He was very good at training dogs and when I fussed he had her trained to push me in the carriage, she would push the carriage one way as far as it would go, then go around and push it back again. She would also go to the neighbors with a note or go get the horses or cows whichever he told her. One night she woke him up and fretted until he followed her to the barn where he found his saddle horse down in the stall and would have been dead by morning if he hadn't released her.

In 1920 Dad remarried. Mom was a schoolteacher. Their first child, a boy died, then they had five girls, and we are all living within a two-hour drive of home and have many happy "get-togethers". In 1930 our house burned down but in a few days the neighbors had moved a vacant house to our place and had it pretty well furnished.

My Dad and Mom lived in this house until 1963 when they retired to a new house in Eatonia. My youngest sister lives on the home place.

In the six years we have been living here in Bindloss things have changed quite a lot. Students used to get Grade Eleven here but now they have to go to Medicine Hat for Grade Ten, which means that the young people, including our daughter, have to be boarded out when only fifteen, since the paving of Highway No. 41, the trip to the Hat has been made easier.

The church was real active, but now it is a struggle to keep it going. Some families have retired, others have moved away, but maybe if we hold tight the powers that be will realize they need the farmers and the farmers need the kind of life there is in a community like this.

I can still remember the dirty thirties and still have no use for the wind or the dirt blowing, but do love the open spaces, the hills, the flowers and the animals of the prairies. So as long as we are able I imagine we will be found, "Home on the Range". In our little grey home in the West", two of my favorite songs.

WILLIAM KINNIBURGH

I was born in Tennessee and came to the Buffalo district in 1920 and lived there for eight years. Before moving to the Red Deer River we lived at Purple Springs, returning there, via Lethbridge, where we still live. I married Zelda Boddy and we had three sons, all three served in Canada's Armed Forces during World War II. Later years our sons have operated a crop spraying service out of Purple Springs. Our son Jack now flies commercial planes for Time Air.

Mrs. Wm. Kinniburgh, Mrs. C. B. Howe, Wm. Kinniburgh, Frieda and Jack Kinniburgh with one of natures loveliest in 1958.

THE DELMERE KITT STORY

My wife Ann and I perhaps are not what one might call "Pioneer of the Good Old Days", but our coming to Canada in 1966 from England was, I feel, just as much a change and daring adventure for us as it was for the earlier settlers who left their homes in different parts of Canada and the United States to settle in this part of the country. We **certainly** were looking for a better opportunity and we **did** find our lives and our way of living drastically changed.

I was born in Tondu, Wales in 1936, a son of a railroad engineer. When I was two years old my parents moved to Newton Abbot in Davenport, where I grew up and received my education at various Primary and the local Grammar school. In fact, from the age of eleven I attended the same school as Ann, so we have known one another since younger than eleven as we only lived a city block apart.

We both completed thirteen grades, Ann went on to Lincoln Training College for two years training to be a teacher; and while she was teaching in Bas Stoke, I attended Reading University until 1958 and when I failed in my grade to meet the University standards I did my National Service and became a nursing orderly. I spent nearly three years at that. By 1960, Ann had taught at various schools and she was teaching at Ashburton Primary when we were married on August 4th that year.

The first two years after we were married we lived in the country of Newton Abbot, in a little farm cottage without any electricity or gas, but there was a tap, so we knew what country living could be like without the amenities and we found we made our way. We gradually improved the cottage and we stayed there for two years. Then we moved into a little terraced cottage in the town of Newton Abbot and I went back into education. I attended St. Lukes College where I completed three years training in two years. Then I was a Certified teacher.

115

Buffalo School under the supervision of Mr. and Mrs. Delmere Kitt, 1969 - 70.

I had done some teaching back in 1958. I had started the regular professional career as a teacher at Ashburton Secondary school. I had taught biology as a subject. In fact, it was while I was at Ashburton, that I had hoped the situation in the teaching profession in England would improve and I tried all ways to increase my salary which was less than $200 per month. There was such little hope of promotion and the costs were so high that we could see no sort of hope of owning a house of our own or this kind of thing. This is why I feel we were in the same kind of mind as the early pioneers, who came here seventy-five years ago — sort of moved to desperation — not being able to make a go of it within your chosen field in the country you were reared in.

So we looked across the sea to Canada, to see, in fact, if we could advance our profession and enjoy a reasonable standard of life.

Some friends of ours had come over to Canada in 1965 and they had been teaching in the north of Alberta — they found that the children were just like country children anywhere else and the conditions were very amendable and although they were isolated they found they could make a good living and they were enjoying it. And, of course, they had all the kinds of situations for advancements, which exist here and which just don't exist in England. Once you have finished your training course over there it's virtually impossible to get back in it again and improve your qualifications. Once you become a teacher, that's it, you can't advance a Course at a time and become a better teacher, hopefully.

So we burned our boats in 1966. We sold our furniture in order to get the money for our passage to Canada. We were employed by Northland School Division No. 61, at Grouard Vocational school. Grouard is about twenty miles north of High Prairie, right on No. 2 Highway. It's on the shores of Lesser Slave Lake and in Grouard we overlooked Buffalo Bay, so we've had more contact with Buffalo.

I taught Math and Science at Senior and Junior High School there, the first year.

This was our introduction to Canada — getting used to the winter and the isolation and all the problems associated with moving into a different culture — the kind of adjustments you have to make and although it was a hard year — it was a year full of opportunities — we worked out our plan of attack, if you want to call it that, for improving our qualifications and advancing our position and this sort of thing and it was really refreshing. I suppose it was like the sod busters seeing their first crop. Here we were, coming out from England in desperation — very sad to leave our friends and all our relations and the familiar places behind us — and coming into a

117

completely new situation, but we were able to "map" out the land and plan what we were going to do.

I found I had good recognition for the courses I'd done in England and that I was acknowledged with two and two-fifths years of education so that, if I did three summer schools and a year at University this would get me my degree. So I worked on this plan.

The second year, in order to finance me in University, Ann went back to teaching, which again was an unprecedented thing — the accepted custom in England, of course, is for the wife and mother to stay at home. One of the chief reason being, to employ a babysitter it would cost as much as the teacher would earn. Well we did employer a babysitter, an Indian girl, Rose McGilvery, from St. Brides. Ann had been out of teaching for seven years and she was looking forward to getting back into it.

We were in the situation where our children received the attention of a full-time babysitter and of course, we were only a couple of hundred yards from the school and were home at lunch time, so we were never away from the children very long. We have three children: Philip, Joan and Abigail.

We completed our second year there, Ann teaching the Grade One and I continued teaching Math and Science at the Junior High School level, and the summer of '67 I took two courses in Anthropology and Linguistics, studying Indian cultures.

When we finished in Grouard in 1968, we came down to Edmonton. I took a Summer School Course in philosophy and I signed up for a full year 1968 and '69. I studied philosophy, educational psychology and plant anatomy and classification — botany subjects.

I was very fortunate, I achieved a Bachelor of Education Degree with distinction. This gave me a great feeling of pleasure and success as I had failed at Reading University in 1958. Perhaps it points up to the children we teach now — you can fail at certain periods and then you can make a comeback as long as you put your back into it.

After our year at Edmonton, during which time Ann taught Kindergarten — our children were either in Kindergarten or being looked after by our friends — all very complicated but it all worked out very nicely — we decided to move a bit farther south. We wanted to move into a rural area. We'd been travelling light; we were lucky enough to get furnished accommodations in the north and again at Edmonton, so we thought we'd like to continue that, rather than to settle down and find ourselves a home. We wanted to stay clear of that until we were clear of the University costs.

So we looked around, in fact, we applied to over thirty places and Buffalo was the place, on paper, which presented the most inter-

118

esting situation to us. We visited Buffalo in May 1969, we liked what we saw, we liked the school, we liked the people we met and we liked the Divisional Superintendent, the Chairman of the School Board. We found everyone very pleasant and amicable and we liked the countryside, so we decided to come here. All I can say is that we liked everything we saw so we decided to give it a try and we haven't been disappointed. In fact, our respect for the people of Buffalo and the area has grown considerable. We enjoyed being here in the beginning and we still enjoy it.

I must say though we were spoiled the first year here with that short winter of 1969 and we weren't quite so happy with the winter this year (1971), but we'll get used to it. We understand that 1969 is more like the winters here.

What we especially like about Buffalo; we like the rolling country side, we like trees too, but we didn't like the bush forest of the northern part of the province. They were thick and dense, yet short-standing and it gave much more feeling of desolation than the area around Buffalo does. I've heard the word desolation used in Buffalo, but I can't go along with this at all. Of course, people say, "What about the trees?" Well we're only three miles from that beautiful Red Deer River and anytime we want we can go down there and be amongst some of the finest trees I've seen, in Alberta any-way — those fine trembling aspens (poplar) down there. So it offers us the river and we like boating. It's a place for the children to play on a sandy beach, when we need it. It offers us the trees when we want them, it offers the great beautiful vista, this in terms of the geography of the area and much more important is the friendliness of the people — can't be beat, that's all I can say. We've been accepted completely and we sincerely appreciate this. We got more invitations than we can cope with and we try to reciprocate fairly successfully, I hope.

The school itself, being sort of a family concern, as we run the school as a family concern — perhaps it could be compared with the local people; with the farmers and ranchers — who run a family concern, being very keenly concerned with what you do on your own place and we are equally concerned with what we do in our own school and I think this helps our liking the place. The fact it is our own show and we get nothing but encouragement from the Divisional Officers and the people of Buffalo, so that we enjoy working in the school and giving all we can to the school and of course, the children feed it right back to us as much as we put in to help them. Their enthusiasm develops and encourages us by the work they hand back.

119

I think I can be sure in saying the children certainly like coming to the school if the attendance figures are any indication. We like them being in school — we like the whole set-up — the individual approach we can make to the children — we can get to know them extremely well; we get to know their successes and their failures and how we can assist them. Of course, having known failure and success myself, this makes me appreciate that some experience difficult, where others don't and that everyone has something that they're particularly good at.

My job in the school as a teacher, is to assist those children in those things they're not so good at. We find the children appreciate this and we are quite happy with the programs of instructions and the way they are going.

The basement has been converted into a useful classroom and we have received some very valuable pieces of equipment in the Science Laboratory and various things of this type, so that we can give the children a program at least as good as they'd get in the city, with the exception of Industrial Art and Home Economics — they do suffer there.

Chiefly they all work together and they do get the individual attention. The great complaint of the younger generation right now is that schools are like machines — the students are pushed in one end and turn the handle and the finished product comes out the other end. Of course, the country school can be the direct opposite and we hope the Buffalo school is.

The chief concern of the school is the humanity factor — it's people dealing with people, achievement is important too, but you won't get good achievement from the child if he is unhappy and dissatisfied in the situation — if they feel they're just being put through like sausages in a sausage machine, then they miss the pleasures that the country school can offer.

THE JOE KULYK STORY

I was nine years old in 1916, when my father, Steve and my mother, my three brothers, Tony, John and Mike, my three sisters, Mary, Sophia and Kattie came to Alberta from Manitoba. We lived a year in the Cappon district before moving to the N.E.¼ of 35-23-6-4 where my father homesteaded. My brother Mike still lives there. I remember we came to Oyen by train and some friends met us with a team and farm wagon to transport us to Cappon. It was in March, the snow was all gone and the crocus was in bloom.

I was only ten years old when my father got a load of flax straw from Dave Cole which we hauled by oxen to the site where we were to build our house. It was very late in the evening and as

Joe and Russel Kulyk residence farm, Buffalo.

it was a six or seven mile walk back to where we were living at the time, Dad considered it too far for me to walk, so he left me to sleep in the straw pile. There was a slough close by where he hobbled the team of oxen. During the night stray range horses came to the slough to drink. I was so frightened to be left alone that I had buried myself in the straw and it was just coming dawn, when I felt something tugging at my pant leg. Happy at the thought that it must be my father, I quickly threw back the straw, only to find it was one of these range horses. It had been eating the straw and had got my pant leg in its mouth. It was hard to determine which was the more frightened, me or the mangy looking animal with its long shaggy mane, as it took for the hills. It was shortly after this that my father built our house. Wood for building houses was very scarce, some were fortunate enough to retrieve logs and poles from the Red Deer River. My father built a frame house and used rye straw for the roof. In some cases slough grass was used, but the rye straw was best for keeping out the rain and snow. The interior of our house was plastered with mud and straw. Ordinarily mud wouldn't do, one had to dig down and get a special kind of mud. This was mixed with short straw and water. This mixture was packed between the two by fours, which had lathe strippings across, and when the clay or mud dried a trowel was used to remove the roughspots. To this surface a mixture of finer clay was applied giving a very smooth finish. Then whitewash was applied twice a year.

This house is still standing and my brother Mike lived in it with his family until after 1964.

The art of mixing the clay and mud was quite a feat in those days. Often several of the neighbors would gather and help out. The mixing was done similar to that of treading grapes (for making wine) with the bare feet. Horses and/or oxen were used when there was a large amount to be mixed.

121

To be considered a "homesteader" one was required to break approximately twenty acres of land over a three-year period. In 1917 I broke land with a team of four oxen and a sulky plow. This was also known as a breaker plough which made a fourteen inch furrow. Later I used a gang plough, which would make a twenty-eight inch furrow.

My schooling consisted only of what I received in Manitoba before I came to Alberta. In later years I took advantage of the different courses offered in welding, machinery, etc. My younger brother, Mike and my sisters attended the Lovedale School, which was two miles west of where Paul Dziatkewich now lives.

Joe Kulyk's separator at harvesting.

Dziatkewich family harvesting, 1941. Mrs. Dziatkewich, the mother, on the stack, the girls on the rack and Stanley Dziatkewich in front.

I remember there were lots of buffalo bones and skulls laying around in the fields in the early days, but later these were all gathered and shipped away. In the early days, cattle were not so wild and we trailed our cattle to Buffalo, crossing the Red Deer River by ferry, at shipping time. Before the grain elevator was built in

Buffalo, we hauled our grain to Atlee. There were no churches in the district, sometimes a minister would arrive on horseback and hold services in the various homes. We had to make our own entertainment. Maynard Orpan would play the organ and I would play the fiddle for dances and social gatherings.

In 1930 and '31 I helped to build the bridge across the Red Deer. It was a very mild and open winter, many times we worked in our shirt sleeves. In 1946 when the river flooded and the ice chunks took out the bridge at Empress, there was some talk of moving our bridge to replace theirs, but two carloads of the farmers and ranchers in the district went to Edmonton to protest against such a move, the results being that we still have our bridge.

In 1934 I obtained a place of my own from Frank Osland, who still lives in Kelowna. I also obtained his cattle brand   F̃O   on right hip.

In 1941 I married Annie Muzyka. In 1946 we obtained more land, this time from Ole Kjarland --- N½ 12-23-6-4, where I still live with my wife and our only child, a son, Russel.

Our post office was Gold Spring in 1917.

My parents are both gone now, but my brothers and sisters are all still living. My sister Mary married Mike Vowk and lives at Drayton Valley. Sophia married Joe Semenciew and lives in Oshawa, Ontario. They have the Clover Leaf Motel there. Kattie married William Muzyka and they live in Cereal. John married Martha Malyx and they live in Vegreville. Mike married Florence McKee and they live on the old homestead and Anton (Tony) married a Miss Podolsky and lives near Cereal.

In the early days any land that wasn't leased was known as "open lease" or "the commons", and ranchers would pay one dollar per head to run their animals there. One year Stacey Foster, Roy

Wedding, 1917, Joe Kulyk's sister, Sophie and Joe Semenciew.

123

Whaley and a brother of Roy, Mike Hasson, Stan Tomkins and myself among others had 1500 to 2000 head on the commons, north of where George Howe's ranch buildings now stand, when a disease broke out among these animals and a Government Inspector made us dip the animals in a special solution of warm water with sulphur and some other ingredient, I can't recall what it was. This dipping required a special setup, a cement trench nine feet deep and six feet wide with a chute leading into it. Grappling hooks were also required to assist the animals, especially the young calves as they would be in well over their heads. The nearest dipping trench was overy twenty-five miles west at Hallams who lived where the Vee Bar Vee is now situated. After trailing our animals to the dipping pens Mr. Hallam demanded a fee of fifty cents for each head in advance. This wasn't too bad for the farmer or ranchers who only had eight of ten head, but the animals were all together and would require a great deal of cutting out and sorting to put through those owned by the men who could pay. So it was decided to run them all through together, but the Whaley brothers and their partner, Stan Tomkins who had around 1000 head had no money. Roy Whaley said he could get the money so he jumped in the saddle and took off. For three days we waited, our cattle were corraled with no food and as we hadn't expected to be gone from our homes more than a day we had no food with us. Those working for Mr. Hallam were called to their meals by a "dinner bell" and as soon as Mike Hasson heard that bell he would go in the cook house, help himself to a plate of food and go outside to eat it, and when the crew arrived the cook would always be short one plate. At last Stan Tomkins cut out about forty head to pay Mr. Hallam for the rest of the animals. It didn't take long to run them through and we started back home. We hadn't gone very far when we met Roy coming. He was unable to get the money, so we continued on leaving the forty head with Hallam. We were all nearly starved, after three days without food, so we sent Roy to get us something to eat. Later he came back with a can of jam and some bread. Mike Hasson had a team and wagon to carry the calves in when they got too tired to walk. To keep the calves from jumping out their feet would be tied. When we stopped that night we found some of the calves had bounced out of the wagon, these were later found back on the trail with their feet still tied, and would have starved to death if we hadn't found them.

Trees and water have always been scarce here on the prairies. Before wells were dug, water was hauled from the Red Deer River, often as far as ten miles or more. And in winter when there would be no snow, ice from the river would be hauled or carried to melt

Four Generations — Mrs. Steve Kulyk (Joe's mother), Mrs. Sophie Semenciew (Joe's sister), Mrs. Helen Broion (Joe's niece), Mrs. Broion's daughters.

Katie (Kulyk) Muzyka and Annie (Muzyka) Kulyk, cook car for early harvesting, 1931.

Joe Kulyk and Russel ready for rounding up cattle for branding.

50th Anniversary of Mr. and Mrs. Steve Kulyk, their family — John and Martha, Tony and Pearl, Bill and Katie Muzyka, Mike and Florence, Joe and Annie: (Joe and Sophie Semenciew, Mike and Mary Vowk not in picture).

Russel Kulyk agricultural classmates.

down for water. If one didn't have a team to haul water it would be carried in buckets on the ends of a pole across the shoulders for a distance of four or five miles.

One year before 1917, three men, one was Guy Romain's father, each with a team of horses were hauling wood from the river. When they stopped at the Howe ranch, they were advised to stay as a storm was coming. They disregarded the warning and proceeded on

125

their way only to be lost in a blizzard. Where the teams were found later, it was evident from the marks in the snow, that the men had left the wagons in an attempt to find the road. Later the body of one man was found hanging on a fence north of the McLennan ranch, where Dooley Allen lives now. Only the foot of another one was found, it was still in the boot, the coyotes had eaten the rest. There is no record of the third man ever being found.

The prairies have long been known for sudden blizzards and bad storms. One day in March, years ago, the late Ed Splinder and two other men from Brooks came to this part of the country with a team of oxen. The weather was very pleasant when they started out, but a blizzard came up without warning. The men said later they waited until their oxen laid down and then they laid down between to keep warm.

ANNIE (MUYZKA) KULYK

I was only two years old when my father, Steve Muzyka died leaving my mother with three small children, my two brothers, Bill and Harry and myself. Our parents had come from Manitoba to Alberta in June 1925. Later my mother married Carl Dziatkewich and they had three boys, Joe, Mike and Stanley and two girls, Lily and Mary. I went to school at Lovedale and later at Arethusa. Lily and Mary completed their high schooling in Buffalo and went to Calgary to further their education to become teachers. Mary, who married Harry Diakiow now teaches at Cereal and Lily who married Elmer Ertmoed teaches at Bindloss. I married Joe Kulyk in 1941. We have one son, Russel. Russel attended school in Buffalo and later took his high schooling at Cereal. After he finished high school he went to Alberta College in Edmonton for one year, and took his Agricultural Technology in Vermilion. Our nearest neighbors when I was growing up were the Burt Danielses, who homesteaded where Stanley Dziatkewich lives now. There were five children in the Daniels' family, Bill, Dorothy, Marjorie, Lloyd and one other girl I can't recall her name. They are all married and have families. Dorothy and I were inseparable when we were girls, we regarded each other's home as our own. Dorothy lives near Innisfail. Mr. Daniels didn't have a team to haul water with so he had to carry it from down near the river, approximately thirteen miles. He also carried groceries from store in Buffalo another four miles. The Danielses were very good neighbors, and proved that when Carl Dziatkewich (my step-father) was kicked in the stomach by a horse and died within twelve hours, leaving Mother, then only about thirty-eight with eight children to raise. Mr. and Mrs. Daniels took over all arrangements,

Joe and Annie Kulyk 25th wedding anniversary, 1966.

including buying groceries and later when Mother wanted to pay them for their kindness, especially for the groceries, they told her that if she wished them to remain friends that she would never mention it again. Some years later Mother who was very handy with a needle, embroidered a tablecloth and gave it to Mrs. Daniels, who said she would treasure it forever and would use it when each of her children got married. The Danielses moved from this district during "the dirty thirties." Mrs. Daniels still lives in Lethbridge. My mother passed away in 1952. One stepbrother, Mike died in 1966 leaving a wife, the former Nena Martin and one son Carl. A few years later Joe married Nena, and a son was born to them in June 1971. Harry Muzyka married Madeline Kelly from Hamilton, Ontario, who had come to this country as a teacher for Magnus Bjork's children, Magnus the third and his sister Linda. They live near Cereal.

Editor's Note: The following was written in honor of Joe and Annie Kulyk on the occasion of their Twenty-fifth Wedding Anniversary.

ANNIE AND JOE KULYK by Violet (Bicknell) Stone.

> She's my Annie, I'm her Joe,
> Sounds like a couple we all know.
> She was so petite and dainty,
> With a heart so big and true,
> And he so big and bashful
> He confided in a few.
> Their courtship was so quiet
> A secret guarded well.
> And even when they married
> Were reluctant still to tell.
> But he knew she was his Annie,
> And she knew he was her Joe,
> So they've had a happy marriage
> And their love did swell and grow.

They made their wedded bliss last out
About eight years or more
And then a baby filled their nest
What could they ask for more?

He was so cute in every way
As pretty as a girl.
It was indeed a saddened day
When they cut off his last curl.

He grew into a handsome lad
His parent's pride and joy.
And through twelve years of school, has proved
He's every inch a boy.

And so the years have come and gone.
They've managed to survive.
Some good, some bad, but either way
They number Twenty-five.

Although the day itself we missed,
Our greetings are still true.
So may I say from everyone
Happy Anniversary to you!

My sisters and I have always kept several of our ancestors' traditions alive in our homes and families. Besides the regular Christmas we always celebrate January 7 in true Ukrainian custom. We enjoy very much going out caroling on the previous evening. Sometimes we entertain our friends and neighbors by dressing in our native dress and doing the native dances, with my husband, Joe, supplying the music on his fiddle. It is wonderful to live in a country where our customs are enjoyed by our neighbors, without the feeling of prejudice. I remember when I was still a very young girl and my mother couldn't speak English, she always managed to convey her thoughts to her neighbors. We always felt that language wasn't necessary among friends, they always had their own way of understanding, and being understood. Even with the barrier of different languages, there was Norwegian, Swedish, Russian, Polish, German as well as English spoken in this country when my parents arrived, but I can never recall that our family ever felt that they were "outsiders". I remember hearing the Honorable John Diefenbaker speaking in Winnipeg, a few years ago when Joe, Russel and I were on a holiday in that city. He said that a flower garden wouldn't be very interesting if it only contained one flower, such as roses, or daisies, or Iris or any one of the many flowers one sees in a garden, but it took several different flowers to make a garden beautiful, so it is with a nation or country, it is made more interesting when different nations are represented.

DICK LASWELL by R. H. (Dick) Imes

One can never think about bronc riders of open-range days without thinking of Dick Laswell, better known as "Bone-Head" Dick, or "Cannibal Dick" in cow camps from the Red Deer River to the Musselshell in Montana. Dick was never known to be bucked off unless he was drunk, and got the name of "Bone-Head" Dick because he would mount the meanest of horses any place, whether it was on the rim of a cut-bank with a 20-foot drop, or on slick ice with not a chance of the horse keeping his feet, and yell, "Tunt 'em loose."

Dick was a cracking good pick-up man, too; and if he ever got hold of a hackamore rope, no horse could ever jerk away. Dick showed me a hackamore hitch requiring only an eight-inch piece of strong leather string, which, used correctly, would keep a mean horse from bucking or stampeding and with which a horse could be reined very quickly. Dick showed it to me after I had made a wild ride on "Bar U Fox" at our Bar U round-up camp just north of Cassils and about six miles west of Brooks, in the fall of 1918.

Dick and Renie Lane (the latter on "Two Bits," a well-known Mexican roping pony, later killed when Roy Lane roped a big Mexican steer on him at the '19 Calgary Stampede) were all set to pick me up, but neither got close to my horse until he quit bucking and was winded. Then it was Laswell who got there first with the mostest. The first thing Dick did was to hand me his shot-loaded quirt with minute instructions on how "to whip it out of him." With "Bone-Head" holding him with his horse and yelling, "you're doing swell, you homely so and so," I plied the quirt and thought about my right spur, tangled hard and fast in the end of my hackamore rope. From then on, though, that sorrel three-quarter thoroughbred was a gentleman compared with what he had been and never bucked again while I rode him. I always used Dick's hitch on him, though after that I had no trouble keeping from bucking or running any horse I ever used it on. Laswell is the only rider I ever knew who knew this hitch.

Many years ago, I read an article by a western writer, Frederick R. Beechdolt, in which he speculated on how the outlaws of the Old West would change to fresh and often unbroken horses and ride them away. That they could not do it with a bridle or an ordinary hackamore was certain. Dick Laswell went to California in 1923, where I heard he got a job at a big golf course.

129

THE HOWARD McCULLOUGH FAMILY by Francis (Buster) McCullough

My father, Howard McCullough was born in Indiana, at Gary, near Chicago, in 1880 I believe. He grew up in and around Chicago and as a young man he was employed with The Chicago Spring Balance Company and F. A. Hardy and Company, wholesale opticians. His father was a conductor on the Monon Railroad and didn't retire from active service until he was eighty-three years old.

Right after the turn of the century, Howard headed west to grow up with the country. He herded sheep for a ranching outfit for a year or two along the Little Big Horn River near Cody, Wyoming.

Sometime during this period he became acquainted with Clint Jarboe and in 1901 they made an excursion across the northern boundary of Montana into what was then known as Assiniboia. They liked what they saw and returned to Montana to accumulate some livestock and belongings to return in 1903 to embark in the ranching business. I have "Bills of Sale" for horses bought by Howard in 1903. One is for a four-year old mare, dated March 25, 1903, at Garland,

F. N. McCullough, Howard's father on a saw horse in front of the two room homestead. Note the old tin heating stove sitting between the doors.

Wyoming and another is for seven mares purchased April 22nd, 1903 at Rockford, Montana. As a point of interest the total cost of these eight mares was $460.00. Howard along with Clint Jarboe and his wife Lola, arrived in Medicine Hat in June, 1903. Certificates signed by I. C. Hargrave, Official Veterinary Inspector, show they had horses inspected on June 12, 1903.

Helen McCullough, Olaf Skjenna, Mr. and Mrs. Buster McCullough.

My father had eleven and Jarboe had eight which I assume was the total of their herd. The trip was made across country in a covered wagon with what few belongings they had, besides the horses, stored in it. A custom stamp on one of the documents, associated with their arrival in Medicine Hat, is oval shaped with a crown and Customs Canada across the top and Medicine Hat, N.W.T., across the bottom. On October 8, 1903 an application was filed by my father for a homestead on the north side of the Red Deer River and the fee was ten dollars.

The first years were spent in a dug-out-type dwelling dug in the bank just a few hundred feet west of Gold Springs. Gold Springs is about four miles north of the bridge.

One of the first tasks they undertook was to gather limestones from surrounding hillsides and kiln them for lime. They built a kiln in the bank and brought in a lot of wood, piled the limestones in on it and kept it fired for several days until they were slakened into lime. The lime, of course, was used to make mortar for chinking the logs of the building they were to build. The remains of that project are still visible in a little coulee about one hundred yards west of where Gold Springs comes out of the ground.

The Wozeske brothers arrived about the same time and established a ranch about three miles farther down the river. They were three bachelors who were never married and their spread was where George Howe now ranches. They were named Otto, Fred and Adolph. Adolph was never known by most people by any other name than Fisher and I would assume many of his acquaintances never knew his real name. A story relating about Fred Wozeske who,

131

2,000-11-'01.

MEMORANDUM.

[Customs stamp: CUSTOMS CANADA / JUN 29 1903 / MEDICINE HAT, N.W.T.]

To _____

CUSTOMS, CANADA,

_____ 190___

Rec'd of C. A. Jarboe the sum of thirty Dollars, duty on 3 mares & left leg —

S. W. Walton

Collector.

Custom receipt for Jarboe — note the Custom stamp designating Medicine Hat as North West Territories.

Department of Agriculture.

Medicine Hat 12 June 1903

I certify that I have this day examined the following animals:—

Horses 11
Mules —
Cattle —
Sheep —
Swine —

the property of   H. McCullough
and I find the same free from any contagious disease.

Inoculating Free disp.

J. C. Hargrave
Official Veterinary Inspector.

Department of Agriculture.

Med Hat. 13 June 1903

I certify that I have this day examined the following animals:—

Horses 8
Mules —
Cattle —
Sheep —
Swine —

the property of   McCa Jarboe
and I find the same free from any contagious disease.

Free disp.

J. C. Hargrave
Official Veterinary Inspector.

Two documents signed by J. C. Hargrave, whom some of the old-timers may recall, acknowledging horses brought into the country by McCullough and Jarboe.

Medicine Hat, Oct. 8 /03

Received from F. H. McCullough for Homestead application Ten _____ 00 Dollars

G. A. Cochran.

Note the unofficial look of this receipt for a homestead application.

Medicine Hat, Assa. *Oct 15* 190 4

M *Howard McCullough*

% *C Jarboe, Red Deer.*

BOUGHT OF # JAMES RAE, *Steveford*

HARDWARE MERCHANT
✠

E. & O. E.   Accounts due when rendered. Interest at 10% charged on all overdue accounts.

DATE	ARTICLES	FOLIO	CREDIT AMOUNT	DEBIT AMOUNT	TOTAL
Oct 13	To 21 ⅔ lbs shoes ³²⁵ 3 lbs shoe nails ⁷⁵			4 00	
"	" 20 + ¾ lb calks, ⁵⁵ 33 lbs + ½ calks ¹⁰⁵			1 60	
"	" 25 + 9/16 calks 9⁰			90	
	By Cash		5 00		
			5 00	6 50	
				5 00	
				1 50	✓

Howard and Vanetta McCullough with Buster in his mother's arms in doorway of their first home.

133

coming upon some families of berry-picking picnickers swimming in the Red Deer River, decided that was a pretty good place to be on such a fine day. He said, "I tot I schust as vel choin in the fun, so I sloffed off my clothes, let out a yell and into the river chumped." Needless to say this idea was not accepted in the true spirit of fellowship and Fred soon found he had the whole river to himself. It's kind of too bad the idea didn't go over, it could have advanced the mixed nude bathing program in Alberta by many years.

Some time during this early period R. S. Gravette arrived to establish a homestead about a mile and a half west of the Mc-Cullough place. I don't know what year he arrived, but from a letter written by Jarboe in February 1910, he was building a house at that time as Clint mentions going up to give "Arkansas" (pronounced Arkensaw) a lift with it. His house and most of the ranch houses along the Red Deer were made with logs and there is an interesting story in connection with that.

It seems that a whole winter's cut of logs got away from a lumber company working in the foothills at the upper end of the Red Deer River. The river ran full of logs for several days and everyone along the river fished out logs and used them later to construct their buildings. At first they were pulling them out by hand, by tieing onto the ones that lodged on the bank or snagging the ones floating close to shore. They also used a rowboat, rowing out into the stream, hooking onto a log and rowing back to shore. However, this proved to be a "man-killer", rowing against the current during the high water period, so they mechanized. By using horses on the bank they would row a line out from shore and hook onto some logs and the horses would pull the logs and boat back to shore, thus speeding up the operation tremendously as well as eliminating a lot of back-breaking rowing.

These logs that they fished out of the river were all stamped with the brand of the logging firm that had cut them. The company sent their agents down the river in an effort to collect for the logs that had been retrieved, explaining that as the logs had their markings they were their property, unless paid for. The river residents agreed that this was no doubt true, but as they were not prepared to pay for them, the company should take them back. This, of course, was impossible and explains the reason for so many log buildings along the Red Deer, many of which are still in use and in good condition.

The early ranchers were getting into the cattle business as quickly as they could and some had quite sizable herds, when the hard winter of 1906 and 1907 struck. There were heavy losses in the cattle business and some ranchers were reluctant to continue with them and switched their operations to horses. Horses being more capable of foraging for themselves through the winter without having to be provided with feed and water, as long as there was snow on the ground, seemed to appear advantageous over cattle.

Howard was one who went into the horse business and over the years developed a fairly sizable herd of Percheron horses. Horses were comparatively of good price in the early years and kept the Mc-Culloughs in bread and butter for quite a few years. With the advent of motorized equipment, which really came into its own after the First World War, horses were replaced by tractors and trucks, and the horse market went to pieces.

Around about 1910 or there abouts, the Gold Spring post office was established and was located at my father's place. Mail was brought in from Lanfine, on the C.N.R. line to the north. One of the early carriers to bring the mail in was Alex Moore and I believe he brought the mail every two weeks. In later years after the Canadian Pacific Railroad was completed, mail was picked up at Cavendish (first called Pancrus) for distribution from Gold Spring. There were many times, due to seasons or weather, that mail pickup was quite a challenge. Winter blizzards, freeze up of the river in the fall and the breakup in the spring, were some of the more serious problems to contend with. The Gold Spring post office distributed mail to residents within a fifteen to twenty mile radius on both sides of the river. Generally the trip to the post office was made on horseback and almost always included a meal for the person as well as the horse, and many times they would stay overnight before returning home. This was all part of the service provided by the Gold Spring post office, and for a remuneration of probably one or two hundred dollars a year, however, this was the way of life that was enjoyed by everyone and it was an unthinkable thing to arrive at anyone's place without staying for a meal or two or spending the night. I might also add that postage rates in those days was only one cent for postcards and two cents for letters, with comparable low rates for parcels. On the twentieth day of October 1910, my father and mother, Vanetta Headley, were married and set up housekeeping in a two-room log shack. In September of 1912, I was born and as was the custom, almost immediately given the nickname of Buster. Adolph Wozeske, nicknamed "Fisher" is credited with bestowing the name on me. Nicknames were quite prevalent and some of the names to be recalled are "Arkensaw" for R. S. Gravette, "Cud" for C. B. Howe, "Spot" for Clarence Bjork, "Skinny" for Magnus Bjork and "Big Jack" and "Little Jack" for Jack Robinson and Jack Dyer. There were three "Oles" that used to get their mail at Gold Springs, one was Olaf Skjenna and to further complicate things, two were Kjarlands, there was "Black Ole" because of his dark complexion and the other being fair was "White Ole". Olaf Skjenna was also nicknamed "Midnight Ole" because he always arrived late in the day for his mail.

An ex-circus trapeze performer, named Carl Cottingham, who was only about the height of a short broom handle and weighed about a hundred and ten pounds, with a rock in his hand, always bouncing around like a jack rabbit and quick as a cat was nicknamed "Bronc."

Some of the tales related about Bronc tell of his shenanigans while helping my father build the big log house, which replaced the original two-room shack. Scaling walls without the use of a ladder, running pell-mell across open ceiling joist or swinging from rafter to rafter in true "Tarzan" style was part of his daily entertainment. He liked to stand atop the wall and pretend to be falling only to turn a flip and land on his feet beside some one looking on in awe. His wife, Maggie, was at least a foot taller than he and when he was asked how he managed to kiss her, he would demonstrate by jumping up and wrapping his legs around her waist, which would put his face well within kissing distance and kiss her. (In order to adhere to the modern trend of writing, I have to bring sex into it.)

One day during a lull in a branding party, a wager was arranged between Cud Howe and Tom McCarthy and the bet was that Cud couldn't wrestle Bronc and put him on his back, no mention was made of Bronc putting Cud on his back. Cud, of course, was big enough to make two or three of Bronc. The story I have heard says that Bronc was about as hard to hang on to as a "greased pig" and was all over Cud like a tent. About the time Cud figured he had him on his back under him, Bronc would wind up sitting on Cud's back, fanning him with his hat in true cowboy fashion.

There were four children in the McCullough family and they were raised without the aid of vitamin pills, polio shots, television or narcotics. They were Buster, Helen, Irene and Jack and all grew up to take their places in society, with the exception of Jack who was killed in a mishap with horses when he was ten. Schooling was also accomplished without the aid of school vans or carpeted schoolhouses, in fact not even a school as school was held in a community hall, known as the Emslie Hall. It was a seven mile jaunt every morning and night for the McCullough kids with their horse and buggy, and one or two dozen buggy wheels wound up in the scrap heap before schooling was over. A couple of those buggy horses also seemed to get an education and learned how to pace themselves so that they could endure the daily grind, however, they would often put on an extra spurt of speed when a storm was brewing in an effort to get home before it struck.

136

Medicine Hat, Assa. 1804 190 7

M *Howard, McCullough*

LEDGER FOLIO 9

BOUGHT OF STEWART & TWEED LIMITED
GENERAL MERCHANTS
WHOLESALE AND RETAIL

Terms..

Ten per cent. interest charged on overdue accounts

DATE	ARTICLES	FOLIO	CREDIT AMOUNT	DEBIT AMOUNT	TOTAL
Sept 27	1000 # Oats 1900 / 2 Pk Sugar 625			25 25	
	15 # Coffee 600 / Tin B Powder 225			8 25	
	20 # Lard 325 11# Bacon 242			5 67	
	11½ OS Bacon 205 / Tin Tea 100			3 05	
	5 # Y+B 450 2# Bull Durham 400			8 50	
	2 # Pay Roll 100 Cig Paper 50			1 50	
	2 Pk Matches 50 10 # Butter 350			4 00	
	50 # W Beans 350 / Gal Pickles 110			4 60	
	2 Sks Flour 600 15 # Pears 300			9 00	
	1 Coffee Pot 125 Plum 100			2 25	
	1 Tin Coil 225 Biscuits 50			2 75	
	2 Salmon 35 2 Sardine 25			60	
	O Bef 20 Apples 50 Candy 25			95	
	6 Bottles Catsup 240 Overalls 125			3 65	
	Mitts 185 Sweater 300 Hose 50			6 35	
	Hose 90 Overshoes 210 Underwear 75			7 75	
				94 12	
	a/c Rendered			52 65	
					146 77

Store bills of 1904. The earlier bill has the work "Steerford" which was the name of a ferry crossing the Red Deer River a few miles upstream from the present Bindloss Bridge location.

The McCullough's with their 1918 McLaughlin Buick. One of the early cars that travelled the country when there was only wagon ruts for roads.

137

In the early years of Emslie school was closed from around Christmas until March because the distance that most of the children had to travel was too great to be out during the severest part of the winter.

My father continued in the ranching and farming business until 1941 when the ranch site was sold to Johnnie Smith. During that time they persevered many lean years and also enjoyed the good years of 1915-16 and 1927-28. In the early years trips were made to Medicine Hat about twice a year with four horses hitched to a wagon to procure the needed supplies for the next six months, an excursion which took about a week, however, during the next few years all this changed. In 1914 the railroad was built, towns sprung up, ferries and bridges spanned the river, automobiles replaced the horses, so that a trip for groceries and supplies could be completed in hours rather than a week. Settlers moved in to take up homesteads on every available plot of land so that what was once wide open spaces became a close knit community, complete with picnics, schoolhouse dances and party line telephones, hooked to the barbed wire fences.

The early settlers of this great province of ours deserve a big salute for their courage and fortitude in establishing a home in what was virtually an undeveloped wilderness. The pioneer spirit of brotherly love and fellowship with a true desire for progress and equality was surely exemplified in the contribution the early homesteaders bestowed on this rapidly developing province and nation.

I would like to think that on the great scroll that records the names of those who helped develop this great province, of which we are so proud, that the name of McCullough will be written down.

EDITOR's NOTE:

Buster McCullough married Ragna Skjenna in 1943, they have five children, Vanetta, Frank, Myron, Myrna and James, they live in Edmonton, where Buster is employed by the Alberta Trunk Line.

Irene McCullough married Harold McFadgen and they have three boys, and live in Calgary. Helen married Nick Maley, they have no family, and live in Calgary.

WILBER McGUCKIN by Mrs. Helen (Nellie) Wilson McGuckin

Wilber (Mack) was born in Stonington, Illinois in 1879, he moved to Kansas in 1886 and to Oklahoma in 1894, the year following the opening of the Cherokee Strip.

He came to Alberta in 1916 and the Empress area in 1917. For the next several years he spent most of his time breaking and selling horses for the Wilson ranch.

We were married in 1922 and farmed in Social Plains from 1924 to 1931, then we moved south of Cavendish where we ranched until retiring in Calgary in 1951.

I was born in Manitoba and came to Medicine Hat in 1903. My father's name was John Wilson and my mother's maiden name was Helen McDonald. We had two daughters, Helen and Joyce (Mrs. J. M. McElroy) both of Calgary, and one son, L. C. McGuckin of Boulder, Colorado.

We lived in the hamlet of Buffalo from the fall of 1944 until July 1945, in a house we rented from John R. Gordon. Our daughters went to school there for one term. Helen's teacher was Mr. Klink and Joyce's teacher was Mrs. Fred DeWald.

Howard Jones now lives on the ranch where we used to live.

RENA MONKMAN

It was on Easter Sunday in 1916 when I arrived in Buffalo, by train, with my mother, Mrs. Olaf Skjenna and my brother Oscar. My father had filed a homestead in 1913 on the land where my brother Olaf Jr., still lives. When my father first came to Canada from Minnesota he worked at Medicine Hat, helping to build a Roman Catholic Church. He was doing spring plowing for Pete Hesson the day we arrived. I attended school in the original Lila school which was first started in 1921 and located on the northeast

Ross Monkman.

Bill Mercer

corner of the southeast quarter of Section 17, Township 21, Range 5, west of the fourth meridian. The first teacher was Mrs. Mary Allen. This was near where Vern Dearing still lives. His father Wm. Dearing was the school board chairman, my father was also on the school board and served there for several years.

On Friday, November 18, 1932 I married William Hanna Mercer in the Buffalo Memorial Hall. Rev. George A. Shields performed the ceremony. I had met William Mercer when we both worked on the Monarch ranch, owned by Horne and Pitfield. Harold Moon was the manager. In 1932 there were 2,700 sheep on this ranch. William and I had two children, George, who still lives at home and Doris, now Mrs. Ed. Kornelson. They have four children and live at Rocky Mountain House.

In 1937 while William and Conrad Danielson were out antelope hunting, they had wounded an antelope and William was driving a car to follow the wounded animal and as he shifted the gears he accidently caught his sleeve on the trigger of his gun and shot himself through the stomach, the bullet came out through his spine. He drove the car to the nearest ranch and Harold Moon came to Buffalo, eighteen miles away, to get me. William passed away four hours later.

In 1939 I opened a restaurant in the hamlet of Buffalo, in the house owned by Rex Bunn for which I paid him a monthly rent of five dollars. This house was later occupied by Mrs. Cook and still later moved to where Arnold Rubbelke lives; his parents Mr. and Mrs. Frank Rubbelke now live in it. The house was big enough to seat as many as ten people at a time and I've had as many as 34 for one meal. I had the place for approximately seven years.

In the early forties I married Ross Monkman and we had two sons, Robert and Jack. We made our home on the original McKay homestead, where I still live. Robert married Lorraine Oslon July 31, 1971. They live in the house once occupied by Stanley Hurl, and later owned by Alberta Wheat Pool. Robert carried on farming after his father passed away in 1963, and Jack is in the oil business.

Aerial view of Rena Monkman and sons place taken in the fall of 1970.

In 1957 both my parents passed away, a brother Oscar Skjenna died at the age of 24 in 1936.

The following is a poem composed by Mrs. Edgar (Violet Bicknell) Stone in honor of Ross Monkman on his 70th birthday.

To a fine old-timer
Honest and true.
We are meeting tonight to honor you.

So on this milestone of time
We would wish you well
With a homey rhyme.

As a young adventurer
Strong and bold.
With a pack, your worldly possessions to hold

You came and you conquered
All those you met
And settled at Cavendish homestead bet.

With horse and oxen
You tilled the soil
A dashing young bachelor
Whom none could foil.

The twenties brought you
To Buffalo's land,
Where you've known hard times
As well as grand.

A few more years in bachelor state
And you found the one who has made a true mate.
So you settled down on the old McKay farm
To add two fine sons, both full of charm.

So we wish you now on this special night
Many happy returns, 'cause we think you're just right.

141

TO RENA MONKMAN ON HER SIXTIETH BIRTHDAY.
by Violet (Bicknell) Stone

Born of a strong Norwegian strain
Many Scandinavian traits remain.
To make her a woman of high renown
Who's spent most of her days in our little town.
Though her life has known sadness and losses too,
We've seen her courageously smiling through
With her glib sense of humor and cheery smile
She's helped many a friend over the last half mile.
When church or community makes a demand
She's always ready with a helping hand.
To give of her talents, her money or time,
To keep things running, with rhythm and rhyme.
She plants a great garden year after year,
Much more than she needs it would appear,
Know the surplus that happens to grow,
To relatives and friends she'll gladly bestow.
We think of her fondly just making her calls,
To neighbor and friends whatever befalls.
Loaded down with gifts from her bag of tricks,
With a smile of good cheer for a friend in a fix.
A pretty cake or a pie, some jam or a tart,
A small gift to cheer a lonely heart.
Some milk, some eggs, a jar of cream
Her bag is near bursting at the seams.
She remembers birthdays, not a few,
Must buy a gift for me and you,
At Christmas her list is a mile long
Cards, gifts and treats for all the throng.
That's generosity, warmth and hospitality too
The latter's well-known to me and you.
Invited or not the welcome mat's out,
And the coffee pot on without a doubt.
So tonight it's her turn on her special day,
We would like to show in some small way.
Though she gives 'til it hurts, it's not in vain,
For friends to the end we'll all remain.
To choose a gift was no easy task,
For Rena, you've everything you could ask.
So we hope that our choice not so glamorous, true.
Will help give some joy and some warmth to you.

Editor's Note: The gift was a base heater.

142

Wm. H. Mercer who died at the Monarch ranch, accidently shot while hunting. September 28th, 1937.

How still he lies, his eager spirit fled,
He who yesterday was full of life and glee,
How can we think of him as dead?
And ne'er again his genial face to see.
He laughed at life, and seemed endowed,
With all the swift abandon of his race.
He was so young to go, this Irish lad,
And to his little family hoped to fill a Father's place.
His hand so swift to help, he always led
Where help was needed most,
Remember this, oh Lord, and grant him grace,
To find both peace, and happiness amid the Heavenly Host.
But now he rests, no pen or voice,
His slumbering heart or ear can thrill,
For God and time have made their choice,
And only memory left his place to fill.

Mrs. Helen Sanford
Monarch ranch, Buffalo, Alberta.

MRS. FRANK (MINNIE) MORRISON

I was born in Ontario and came West in 1917, homesteaded near Cavendish in 1918. Around 1925 when Cavendish was abandoned we moved to Buffalo. We first lived on Franciso and then in 1932 we moved to Armstrong's.

My maiden name was Cook and I married Frank Morrison, we had one daughter, Mable (Mrs. R. Plowman) of Port Moody, B.C.

During the thirties we took our wheat to the mill in Medicine Hat. In 1930 and '31 the men went down to the river and mined their own coal.

The bridge was built across the Red Deer River in 1931.

In 1924 Jimmy Schanes was a storekeeper in Buffalo.

We had always had a good time while we lived here, for entertainment there were dances, concerts, bridge games, and various suppers, as well as hockey and baseball tournaments. Crops were very poor, but we raised horses and cattle.

We left the district in 1939 and after the death of my husband, I lived for a few years in different places and now make my home at the Newbrooke Lodge and spend as much time as possible with my niece, Mrs. Frank Rubbelke at Buffalo.

HELEN AND MABEL NASH by Violet (Bicknell) Stone

When Mabel Nash, now Mrs. Bill Spicer of Chatham, Ontario called on us on Sunday, July 11, 1971 she said she could remember Alan Gatenby who homesteaded just east of our place. He had one of the first cars in the district and took her and her sister, Helen for a ride. The two girls were living in the teacherage at the time as Helen was teaching school here in 1926-'27. Mabel also remembers going to a dance at Atlee, in a closed-in cutter with a heater in it, with Claude and Louis Brace. A blizzard came up and she and her sister were asked to stay at the Brace home at Atlee. The two girls slept three in a bed with Viola Brace. She also remembers Charles Louis of Wallacburg, Ontario who was the student minister here in 1927.

FRANK RUBBELKE FAMILY by Etta (Cook) Rubbelke

Frank was born in Cologne, Minnesota in 1882. He started homesteading in North Dakota at the early age of 19 and in 1913 came to Canada, shipping his stock and equipment by rail to the district then known as "Little Sweden" living there until 1941, when he along with his neighbors were forced to relocate elsewhere, due to the take-over by the Department of National Defence of the huge 1,000 square mile British Block.

Frank besides being a good farmer was also known for his skill in masonry. While he lived in North Dakota, he would take turnabout with his brother, Louis each year, one working the farm while the other would carry on their trade in masonry. Another brother, Hank, also a mason, lived in "Little Sweden" but around 1923 he left farming and devoted his full time to his trade.

One of Frank's first love was baseball, at which he was very good. He had very large hands and could run like an antelope, very few balls could get past him. Frank was also a wonderful dancer, very light on his feet. In 1925 Frank married Etta Cook, seven children blessed this union, three sons, Arnold who is married and has four children and farms just south of Buffalo; Norman, who is also married, has three children and lives in Burstall, Saskatchewan. The youngest son, Blayne is not married and works for a ultility company in High Level; four daughters, Mrs. Elain Franklin who has six children; Helen, Mrs. Gibb Gilham, who has nine children and lives at Oyen; Bernice, Mrs. Mike Richter, who has five children and lives in Medicine Hat and Gail, Mrs. Jim Andrus. They have one adopted son, and live in the Buffalo district.

When the Rubbelke's farmed in Little Sweden they hauled their wheat to the Alberta Pacific Elevator at Cavendish until the Alberta Wheat Pool took over, then they hauled their wheat to Buffalo. This

144

was when Buffalo was quite a busy place. Woo Sam had a cafe, Jimmy Scane had the general store and post office, Wallace King had a livery stable. It was later that McKinnon had a blacksmith shop.

In January, 1931, we suffered the loss of our home in a fire, following which we bought two houses and joined together and built on extra rooms to accommodate the growing family. Later the house was moved to Buffalo and we lived there until the fall of 1970 at which time we moved south of Buffalo, close by Arnold's home.

In the thirties, Frank owned some hounds and he and his friends used to spend many exciting hours hunting coyotes. Gasoline as well as money was scarce in those days, so a team and sled was their means of transportation. On these hunts one could be nearly freezing when suddenly a coyote would be spotted and soon the excitement of the chase would generate plenty of heat. Frank always enjoys a good joke, whether on himself or others. One time while Frank was still a bachelor, he went to visit a friend, another bachelor, who was sick. He told Frank he would like some homemade bread, so Frank who could make wonderful bread, set about to comply with his friend's wishes. He had no more than got started when another bachelor stopped by for a visit. During the course of the visit they were teasing Frank about his bread making. Frank took their joking all in good humor and proceeded to give his tormentors a few pointers in the art of bread making by trying to convince them that the "rising" of the bread, was induced by tossing it towards the ceiling.

Frank and Louis Wilhelmson walked fifty miles to Medicine Hat in one day and their only complaint was that their feet were sore. Not many men, young or old, could perform that feat today.

THE SALZWEDEL FAMILY by Clarence Hurl

Mr. Martin Salzwedel, his wife Elizabeth and son Frank home-steaded in the Buffalo area approximately 1910. After being a

Mr. and Mrs. Salzwedel at their home in Medicine Hat.

Customs Officer at Gretna, Manitoba, during the time of Sir Wilfred Laurier. They had spent some time in Winnipeg after coming from Germany.

During their farming years, Martin was noted for his runaway horse outfits, while Mrs. Salzwedel was noted for her excellent cooking — especially German dishes in "De big white house on de hill vith two front doors in de backside." Martin was also the source of amusement on the local barbed wire telephone of the district. His favorite saying was, "I vill cut de vire in de morning" when he could become annoyed with the local young people.

Their foster child, Ethel, on growing up left the farm and at present she and her husband, Reg. Richards are living at Hammond, British Columbia.

In 1938 Mr. and Mrs. Salzwedel retired to Medicine Hat.

OLAF SKJENNA SR

The following was found among the effects of the late Olaf Skjenna, who passed away in the spring of 1957. Article is dated February 24, 1955.

"I have for several years been asked to put my experiences in Western Canada, into a book form. I have been reluctant to do such a thing for several reasons; one is that I might be misquoted or

Olaf Skjenna Sr., homestead shack built in 1913.

Olaf Skjenna Sr.

perhaps misunderstood and secondly somebody might find themselves insulted. When I write down what I have gone through in the past forty years, it is going to be nothing but the truth, with no extra color added.

All beginning is hard in all new countries, it has always been that way. A great pioneer James Hill one time said, 'Pioneering does not pay'. There has never been said a truer word.

I have always said, in spite of everything, that Canada is the greatest country of all, to start pioneering in and I still maintain that this statement is true. We have now gone through two world wars

146

and ten years of depression and came through it all with a sane mind, but owing to my age, just about worn out, as far as my body is concerned.

I have kept a diary in all these years and marked down anything of note. However, I will have to boil all this material down a lot, otherwise the book would be far too big, and perhaps of little interest.

When I lived in my homeland in Europe, I sometimes seen posted ads like this: Come to Sunny Alberta and get rich. I did not pay much attention to these posters at the time, but in my school days I very often studied a very large map of North America, in which the Dominion of Canada showed up magnificent and naturally interested all school children in my class. Very much so on account of the great size.

I almost forgot about this great country until years later. After farming our old home in Norway for some years, I finally decided to rent out the old farm and immigrate to U.S.A. I had lived there eight and one-half years from the time I was three years old until I was eleven and a half years. My parents suddenly decided to go on a visit to my homeland, from which they never returned. I was

Olaf Skjenna Sr., and his horses.

reluctant to go with them when they left but had no choice. I was doing very well in the American school and my teacher advised my parents that I could learn everything I tried to do. However, at the ripe age of thirty I finally came back to the state of Minnesota to start anew.

After farming my auntie's farm for a year I decided to have a look at Canada. Some of my friends advised me urgently not to settle down in Canada. It seems that several of their friends had started to farm in Canada and met with a lot of bad luck. Some crops froze, while others were ruined by drought. Other handicaps were the long way to market their produce, which brought a lower price than in U.S.A. All manufactured goods were generally a lot higher than in the States, on account of unreasonable high tariff walls. With all these things in mind things certainly looked very black.

However, I found plenty of work in a city with the queer name of Medicine Hat and the wages were better than in the U.S.A. I had looked over most of the Western States even the great state of California, which at that time was dominated to a great extent by people from the orient, either yellow or black, it does not make much difference.

While I worked in and around Medicine Hat, I got acquainted with a young "Yanky" who had taken up ½ section of land north of this city and advised me to do the same thing as he had done. We arranged a trip with some others and I did find a piece of land on which I did enter on the 26th of August, 1913. All beginning is small and hard and I soon found it was rather tough going. I soon found out that Jim Hill's words were absolutely true when he said these words, "Pioneering does not pay".

In the fall of 1913 I made a trip to my hometown in Minnesota in order to raise the necessary funds to start farming this land, a ½ section looked very big to me, I was used to these 40 and 80 acre patches, which are very common in other parts of the world. After squeezing one of my old relations very hard he finally lent me some money, but far from the amount I really needed. I had made an agreement with one of the boys, which had filed on land close to me, that we should bring a team of horses each, we realized that we needed at least a four-horse team to do any breaking. I arrived on the land at the time agreed, but my friend had not arrived. He lived in Iowa and I thought he had got a bit delayed. Soon I found out he had arrived with a carload of equipment, including horses, in Medicine Hat, but he had then got a message from his father in Iowa, offering him to take over the home farm, on very good terms. Being the only son he accepted and shipped his carload back. This was a hard blow to me. I had the same offer in Minnesota from my great uncle, but I spurned the offer, I would not go back on an agreement and break my word. I had bought a team of horses on the market in Medicine Hat and found that one of the horses was unfit to drive double. He was one of these horses that cannot be legally sold on an auction. I could have beaten the rancher in the courts, but I had no time and money to waste on a crook. I finally traded with a man that had use for a horse for single driving. I got back a smaller horse but I got a horse that was really good in double. I thought at the time that I had landed in a land of crooked

148

people. The result was that I got very little broke that year. It was a very dry year anyway so I thought it did not matter much.

In the fall of 1914 I drove out 150 miles northeast to Druid and got in all the threshing I could get. The crops were small up there too, so all I could get in was thirteen days at five dollars a day. Before I left there I traded my team for four good oxen. Driving home one hundred and fifty miles with oxen required a lot of patience as I could advance only about thirteen miles a day. It took me twelve days to get home. I slept on the trail most of the time. The weather was good so I did not mind the trip, even if I was alone. On the whole trip I seen very few people as it was new country at that time. When I got home I found that the prairie fire had swept the country and burned up my stack of hay. This was a bad drawback. I had stacked my hay on a piece of breaking so naturally I thought I was safe from fire, but a strong wind had blown some of the hay of the stack just enough to make a way to get at my hay. The neighbors had stopped the fire just as it had cleaned up the pasture on my land. I had enough grass on a section that was owned by a big land company, so I was not short of pasture. However, I sure missed that good stack of hay. My oxen got restless and tried to start for home, finally they got over to a wild man from the U.S.A., and managed to get into his feed stack. He misused them very bad, so one oxen died, another got sick and died later in the fall. I could have brought action against him but it would have helped me very little. He was broke and did not own his land yet. So I took my loss and said nothing. The evidence was good enough, the dead animal was laying close to the stack and by careful look I could see he had managed to kick him right on the spleen, which is sure death, even to a big ox.

I put in a pretty cold winter in my shack which was only one ply of lumber with paper and sod around. Being a crop failure year the Federal Government shipped in enough coal for everybody and also feed for both man and beast. It no doubt was a sizable burden for them especially when they had a World War on their hands. World War I started that summer and cost plenty. Our Allies across the seas needed a lot of grub and help in manpower. The cry from our friends across the seas was this, 'For God's sake raise wheat.' The people of the prairies answered that call and broke up every available acre possible. The summer of 1916 was the banner year of the drought areas. They had nearly 130 million bushels of No. 1 wheat to market. In the better districts of the U.S.A. and Canada the wheat crop was so badly damaged by rust, that it yielded only three or four bushels to the acre, poor grade at that. There was far too much rain, very much like 1954, regarding excessive moisture.

149

Laurence Howe, Shirley and Mrs. C. B. Howe, Mrs. Iris Findlay, Dorothy Howe, Chester Howe, and Jack Findlay.

Olaf and Art Skjenna, World War II.

One of our leading statesmen said these words, "Even if the drought area had never raised another bushel of wheat, the breaking up of this land was justified, they have done their duty." A commission sent over from Britain and France in 1917 said this, 'We might have lost the war if we had not got that wheat, we were terrible short anyway'.

It certainly is a different story now, our young smart aleck who was hardly in kindergarten at that time, puts up their damn nose and try to tell us that this land should never been broken up. Some even go farther and tell us it should have been given back to the Indians. What a mockery! The Indians with their squaw corn scarcely raised enough for their own use.

In the fall of 1914 the railroad from Swift Current to Bassano was ready and a train was run once a week over this new line and though very slow took good care of our shipping in, coal and other supplies. A black spot in this affair might be mentioned. I do not think it was the fault of the company, but rather the fault of some stupid and head strong official. There was a very large supply of wooden material left over when the line was finished, such as fence posts slabs and many other kinds of wooden material, it was said 123 carloads of wood too much. The settlers were willing to buy this stuff but were refused to get near this material. They had gangs of men working all fall burning it all up. It costs them thousands of dollars to destroy this material. A number of settlers went in and stole quite a large supply and were all pulled into court and fined for stealing. Any employee of the company who gave anything away was fired. It is needless to say that the railroad company did not get very popular with the people that someday should be their customers. However, most of us lived through it

150

all and prosperity started to make its appearance on the prairie. We had two very good years, 1915 and 1916, with crops from 40 to 50 bushels per acre. The government established the wheat board in 1917 and took gambling out of the farming. The price was first set at $1.98 cents a bushel right at our loading platform (not Fort William). Later it was raised by an agreement between our Federal government and our allies across the seas to $2.48. This price was "Universal" over Western Canada and it lasted until the fall of 1920. The grain gamblers were itching to get into the game again and Premier Meighen was not strong enough to hold the reins. After the wheat board was taken off, the racket started and it ended up in

Olaf Skjenna Sr., on the cultivator and Art Skjenna on the tractor.

The Skjenna family.

disaster for many farmers in the West. They had bought lot more land and machinery, horses, etc., and gone deeply into debt with their markets ruined it could only end in misery. Needless to say it effected the economy of all the West.

When I was working in Druid in the fall of 1914 I saw there was lots of vacant land in this district almost every other section was not taken possession by anybody. I found out that this land was

151

bought up by a large company in the U.S.A., and some in Eastern Canada. They were holding this land for a very high price, from forty to fifty dollars an acre. Consequently nobody could afford to buy it. I was told that these companies had bought this land from the Federal Government for a very small price. It is quite understandable that this condition created a lot of hardships for the people which had started to farm. They had difficulty in starting schools and municipalities under these conditions, because most of these people were not paying taxes or doing anything to build a community. I asked several people why such conditions could really have started. They just did not understand it themselves. One fellow remarked sort of dryly, 'Just another stupid neglect from some stupid government official'. These vested interests made some easy millions.

Here in our district there was a lot of very stony land opened up, while some of the finest land was allotted to small ranchers who never broke up an acre. However, these millionaires did not want to buy land in this part of the drought area.

In the summer of 1916 we had a very large cloudburst, it looked like a very big giant pouring water over the land with millions of big buckets. All birdlife was dead over a very large area, even gophers drowned after they crawled out of their holes. We sure missed our friends, the prairie birds who hold the control over the mosquitoes. I never have seen so many mosquitoes in all my life. There were several sizes of which the horse-mosquitoes was by far the largest. They tortured almost the life out of man and beast. I had to quit breaking.

That spring I had bought a four-horse outfit from the Gordons and I took on a job of breaking a few miles of twelve-furrow fireguards along the south side of their lease. The land was very stony, driving horses and fighting mosquitoes. It got on the nerve of the horses so bad they almost turned crazy. Once I got off the plow and walked behind for a little while. Some way or other one of the horses got one of his hind legs up in the spreader lines and pulled the whole outfit back, upset the plow broke the pole and got tangled up so bad I had to cut one of the lines to save the horses from getting choked to death. If I had been riding on the plow I would never have had a chance to escape, it happened so fast, I just barely got a chance to jump aside. I would have been pinned under the whole outfit.

I had to keep the horses tethered at night. One morning I got up at daybreak and found that all the horses had broken their chains and were gone, except one gray mare who could not break loose. While I was standing there and swatting mosquitoes, I heard something like thunder to the west of me. There was no cloud so I

152

could not make out what it could be. I soon found out! To the south of me in the S S lease were mostly horses that summer and soon I saw them coming on the gallop, chased by millions of big mosquitoes. Lucky for me there was a good fence between me and these 400 horses. They stopped for a few minutes and thousand of mosquitoes came and settled down on my mare, believe it or not, they were so thick I could not see her color. I stood there for two hours swatting mosquitoes in order to save her life. I must have killed millions, because they finally became fewer and fewer, I had won the battle. It took two days before I found my other horses. It was a big pasture and very hilly, over 26 sections of land in one enclosure. I had to give it up the horses became nearly played out in fighting these pests and I had enough of it myself. It had taken me most of two weeks to clear and break four and one half miles.

We got a good crop in 1916. I had rented a farm between me and Buffalo, where I had thirty acres of very good crop. It had been hailed very early in the spring shortly after the crop was up, but it came back and ripened very good.

I had no binder so I hired my closest neighbor to do the cutting. It was cheaper than investing money into a binder, when I needed the money for other things. I had in less than 60 acres that year so that was not enough to expect any large amount for buying machinery.

These machine companies generally had a hellish nerve to charge for their machines. An eight foot binder cost $276.00 cash. In a lawsuit between a railroad company and a machine company, it was proved that it cost them only $37.50 to make a binder, another result of these high tariff walls, which desperately tried to squeeze the living daylights out of the farming population in this great God given country.

Olaf Skjenna Sr., sod homestead shack, 1917. Mrs. Olaf Skjenna Sr., Oscar, Rena and Oliver sitting on the ground.

I got out and put in a few days threshing in the district east of us. I made good wages, but I would have done better if I had stayed home and stacked my wheat and flax. A neighbor who had a bad bunch of cattle and perhaps was bad himself, got the habit of not looking after his stock, so they got into my stooks and did a big damage. However, as usual in them days — "

Editor's note: It is very regrettable that one of Mr. Skjenna's descendants did not attempt to finish this article. But to give the reader a clearer picture of the character and personality of this early pioneer, the following was a portion of Mr. Skjenna's last Will and Testament, dated May 31, 1957.

Oliver Skjenna

Hugo Gilham, Olaf Skjenna Sr., Charlie Johnson standing at back. Mrs. Gilham and son Bertle, Mrs. Johnson and Edna, Mrs. Skjenna with son Art. Rena, Oscar and Willie Sandercock in front row.

"I, the undersigned, Olaf Skjenna at the full age of 77 feel the full weight of age bearing down on me, and my heart and the rest of the body are getting gradually weaker, want to give my children and grandchildren a farewell and advice.

Be forever kind and helpful toward each other as you have always been. Rather than practice anything like sinful and hateful doings, be always kind and forgiving towards each other. Help each other if possible and you shall withstand in the day of evil which might come over this earth anytime now. Pray for each other and stand united with God for your own salvation and others. Remember, above all else, that our Lord and Savior "paid" for all of us a restful place in Heaven, when He shed His blood on the Cross. All we need is faith in His great work. "Seek ye first the Kingdom of Heaven and all the other things shall be given unto you." This has been my great standby. Let it also be yours. I am delivering my soul in my Savior's hands. I am fully assured that He has saved my soul and cleansed it in His precious blood. He will place it entirely faultless in my Heavenly Father's hands at my Heavenly Father's throne in Heaven. I am always expecting my children, under all circumstances whatever it shall cost of personal sacrifices, offering, to defend the teachings and doctrines about complete forgiveness for sin with and by the blood which Jesus shed for us on the Cross and by that alone."

OLAF SKJENNA JR.

I entered this world in October, 1920 and have spent my entire life in the Buffalo district with the exception of the four years I served in the Royal Canadian Air Force, 1942 to 1946. I went overseas in 1944 and spent most of the time in England, Belgium and Holland. I visited Aberdeen, Scotland, on furloughs. I married Mary Dziatkewich. We have three sons, Robert attending high school in Calgary, Melvin and Dennis at home. I have resided on the original Skjenna homestead, which my father Olaf Sr., filed on in 1913, three and a half miles south of Buffalo. I had four sisters and three brothers. Mrs. Rena Monkman, Ruth (Mrs. Clarence Hurl) lives in Calgary, Ragna (Mrs. Francis, "Buster" McCullough) lives in Edmonton, Racheal (Mrs. Leroy Callaghan), Oliver is married and lives in Calgary, Arthur is married and lives in Medicine Hat, who incidently has a son, Olaf, who is a medical doctor, a very honorable profession to carry on under the name of "Olaf". Our brother Oscar, passed away in the early twenties. I have been a member of the Masonic Lodge and am a Past Master.

I attended the Lila school and have served on the school board as well as taking an active part on the church board.

With three active boys one finds it necessary to take time out from farming and go fishing. One day while fishing in the Red Deer River, I caught three Goldeyes on one line. That's about the best I can do for a "fish story".

JOHN W. SMITH FAMILY'S LIFE ON THE RED DEER

In 1941 the government of Canada expropriated, for defense research, the area known as the British Block, where we had lived for 25 years. Others who shared this experience will no doubt recall the terms, which can be described as an order to vacate on very short notice, with a minimal cash settlement for patent land and lease land was simply cancelled.

We moved to the Red Deer River, we ranched for a period of 28 years. In these past years we have known all the old-time ranchers in the district. We brought with us 150 head of horses and around 180 head of cattle, however, on account of smaller holdings here we were forced to sell some of our livestock. We sold our horses to a

Great Falls cannery for 1½ cent per pound. Only keeping a few saddle horses. We also had to reduce our beef herd.

Our life on the Red Deer was complete. We loved the place dearly and lived very happily there with our son, Allan and neighbors. We never loved a place before or since as dearly as our home on the Red Deer. Visitors to our place often commented on the beautiful scenery as we lived on a hill overlooking the flats and the winding river, with coulees and hills as a background.

One Sunday morning as we were getting up early to go picking berries at the Earl Hayes place, near Atlee, we heard an explosion

Cars used by the escaped prisoner who spent days hidden in the cotton-wood trees on the north bank of the Red Deer River.

and when we went outside we saw smoke near the river on our land. We hurried there to find a car burning and another pushed part way into the river. The fire and explosion had been caused by the two gas tanks involved. Leaving my husband, John, to fight the fire, Allan and I drove to Buffalo to notify the police in Brooks. By noon we had several policemen and a tracking dog from Calgary on the scene. They continued the search all that night and early next morning they arrested a man and his boy near Atlee.

We were told later that this man had been in and out of jail many times in the past few years. This time he had stolen two cars in order to put a second gas tank on one which he was going to use to get away in. He'd spent quite a few days down in the bush by the river repainting one car and making it ready, but when he tried to destroy the other one by pushing it into the river his get-away car exploded. One of the cars had been stolen from a young couple just married. It was a wedding present from the bridegroom's father.

The river coulees and flatlands are a natural shelter for stock and wildlife. As I (John W. Smith) had been a Game Guardian at Wawaskasy Park, now part of the British Block, I am still very fond of wildlife and hate to see them destroyed needlessly. However, on the Red Deer I have seen antelope by the thousands come down onto the flats for shelter during the winter. We have often seen packs of coyotes chasing and taking down animals in the heavy snow. In summer antelope will make a circle and stand their ground against predators, but if they are on the run, coyotes can easily take one out of the herd and run it to death. It is interesting to watch antelope circle around and stand there until the coyote gets tired and leaves them.

Several years ago of the most interesting drama of nature that we have ever witnessed concerned a bobcat treed atop a power pole by a coyote below. As we arrived on the scene the coyote was frightened away allowing the bobcat to slowly work his way down to freedom.

By observing the wildlife we realize how smart they really are in their own way. One can always seem to predict the weather by the action of the wild game and livestock.

The Red Deer River could act up on occasion though, but most times it was benevolent. Cattle and deer drink from it in the heat of the day and rest beneath its towering cottonwoods. In fall thousands of geese dabble in the shallows and along the sandbars, while pheasant and grouse can feast on ripe saskatoon and bullberry fruit. The spring breakup of 1946 was unusual. An extremely heavy ice formation floated from its bed by a flash runoff came crashing to the forks at Empress. Ice built up and jammed, the current slowed and upstream ice jammed the river again north of Cavendish. In a short twelve-hour period all the lower flats were under water. Ice cakes two to three feet thick were eventually left to melt all along the base of the hills. At crest, the water reached our corrals and other buildings at the bottom of the hill and reached the foundation of Campbell's house four miles downriver from us. The approach to the Buffalo bridge was under six feet of water and ice cakes were just clearing below the traffic deck. Over the past twenty-five years I can recall only twice that flooding of this nature occurred. The other year was 1951.

In 1958 we were unwilling participants in an adventure when a gas well drilled only 300 yards from our buildings blew out of control. The lower level of the flats along which the road runs was saturated with gas which could be heard escaping through small cracks in the ground. The main surge of gas mixed with Artesian water blew a crater out of the flats some 100 yards from the wellsite. It took considerable time and many truckloads of drilling mud before they regained control of the well. All during the time the well was blowing out we were cautioned against driving cars of trucks near the area and even in having open flame in our house.

Ricky, Marnie, Roger, and Shannon Smith (Buffalo's Centennial Baby).

Mr. and Mrs. Allan Smith, parents of Shannon Smith, Buffalo's centennial baby.

In the preceding accounts I (Allan) notice an absence of stories which my folks have related to me over the years as pertaining to their earlier years in the British Block. This would more correctly be life in Saskatchewan, but it does recount much earlier times. My Dad and his oldest brother settled in the area in 1916. They established a ranch raising horses to supply the needs of a developing farming industry. Then, as today, Saskatchewan was wheat king and it was here that draft horses were always needed. From their ranch they trailed horses throughout Saskatchewan and even into Manitoba.

On a trail drive in northern Saskatchewan he met my mother. They were married in 1933 and Dad purchased his first car for their trip home. It was late fall and our Alberta weather soon took a hand in their plans. They finished their honeymoon trip by horse and sleigh.

Life here had many rewards bought at the price of many a hardship and loss. Their saddest and greatest losses were their first two children, my sister, Rose Anne as an infant and my brother John Joseph at one year.

The winter of 1936-'37 must have been devasting to their hopes and dreams. My brother was ailing as the worst winter in their recollection came on. With Mother staying in Medicine Hat as my brother slowly got weaker, Dad kept a solitary vigil at home, watching the weather and faced with a shortage of feed — wiped out almost their entire herd of cows and calves.

Spring did finally come after a winter of heartbreak and to brighten their hopes and get them moving again on March 31, 1937 I came squalling along demanding attention.

I can only vaguely recall the old ranch site, in the British Block. Ever present from June to September were the diamond-back rattle-snakes. This danger must have caused my folks many anxious moments as I can still remember their warnings about the snakes.

A trip to Medicine Hat was a rare event, although by this time we did have a half-ton Ford truck. I suppose we made this journey about twice yearly and the mail and other groceries came from Cavendish. This was a drive of some twenty miles over prairie trails which were 90 percent impassable during winter. I can recall the worry and confusion of 1941, the moving of buildings, livestock and household effects to the McCullough place on the Red Deer, north of Buffalo.

To me the Red Deer, as synonomous with childhood and growing up. Here with my trusty dog for company I explored the hawk and eagle nests, which can still be found built on the nearly precipitous coulee banks. I made my first small fortune from magpie legs at

A big catch Jim Stone and Allan Smith.

three cents a pair. The secret of course was to spot a nest of eggs and then return just before the young could fly. I would know the location of all the best berry patches and could feel quite important when my folks would ask my opinion before going berry picking.

A boy could dream of being a game scout, fishing guide or market hunter and the valley would supply the props for his play. As winter settled in, with its icy grip, the high bluffs moderated the knifing winds and browse for wild game was plentiful. Now I could trap weasel and make as much as five dollars for an extra large one. As time went on public and high school took up my time to an ever

159

greater extent, but once these were done with, the outdoor life still seemed the most rewarding.

In 1959 I married Marjorie Stone and although we do not live on the banks of the beautiful Red Deer, we have a small ranch on the former Chris Beck place south of Buffalo. We are still near enough to the river that we can spend many hours there with our four children and through them I can relive some of the happier hours of my own boyhood.

My parents rented the home place to Harry Dirk and moved to Brooks a couple of years ago. One can sense their reluctance to let go their hold on this part of our beautiful country.

In the following one can visualize what this country has meant to my father:

Over the trails I've drifted far
Over the snowbanks that there are,
No more of it for me, as you will see
For I'm leaving this wonderful place.
No more will I run the race, no more will I feed the face
Of an old range cow.
Dollars and cents go up in smoke
After all the years we're broke
But what do we care, we knew we were there
Feeding the face of an old range cow.

By John W. Smith

GO EASY

When I started up a long time ago
I thought I could make it if I went real slow.
But the harder I tried, the worse it was,
I never could figure out the cause.
I should do more my neighbor said —
But I'm still alive and he is dead.
If you go down south the strong winds blow,
If you go up north you run into snow.
So I think we are better off here between
Sometimes here the grass grows green.
But the years roll by and we older grow
The more we learn the less we know.
The hair grows thin on the upper deck
And you get deep wrinkles around your neck.
When your eyes grow dim and your nose it drips
It's just about time to abandon ship.
My advice to the young ones, save your hay
'Cause you sure gonna need it on a rainy day.

By John W. Smith

160

COW HEAVEN

When I was a youngster, as far as you could see,
The great open prairie was calling to me.
We faced all the hardships, yet thought it was fun
With a million of acres our cattle to run.
But then came the settlers, they blackened the sod,
Awaiting their fortune to come down from God.
But the drought of the ages enveloped the land,
Where cattles' Great Kingdom had once made their stand.
No more the beef herds we drive into town
Liners now haul 'em, either upside or down.
All you old cowpokes, I know how you feel,
When you have to make room for the automobile.
But soon it's all over, and I hope we may find
Some place in the Heavens, our rope to unwind.

By John W. Smith

JOHNNY SMITH ON HIS SEVENTIETH BIRTHDAY

by Violet (Bicknell) Stone

Born to a family in ninety-seven
In the state of Minnesota known as Heaven.
His mother felt truly blessed
With Johnny, Johnny Smith
Babe of the great-wild West.
Moved to Barros in ninety-four
A foothills country to explore
Ready to stand the test
That's Johnny, Johnny Smith
Boy of the great-wild West.
Grew up to become a roving man
While on a horsetrading jaunt he found his Anne.
Full of ambition and zest
Was Johnny, Johnny Smith
Romeo of the great-wild West.
The wedding over, he brought her back
To the wet paint awaiting at the old sod shack.
Could the long-johns be one of Jeff's own jest?
On Johnny, Johnny Smith
Groom of the great-wild West.
On the south Saskatchewan they made their home
And John decided no more to roam.
How nice to feather a nest
With Johnny, Johnny Smith
Man of the great-wild West.

161

After trouble a'plenty they raised a boy
As Allan became their pride and joy.
In answer to his request
Now Johnny, Johnny Smith
Was a father in the great-wild West.

Moved in the forties from the British Block
They proceeded the McCullough ranch to stock.
Settled on a Red Deer crest
Rancher of the great-wild West.

Now we find him in this great Centennial Year
Content and quiet with the family near.
With three grandchildren he is blessed
Our Johnny, Johnny Smith
Grandpop of the great-wild West.

On his seventieth birthday we wish him well
And we know he has many tales to tell.
To hear them is our request
From Johnny, Johnny Smith
Pioneer of the great-wild West

DICK STEEL was born in England in 1870 and came to Canada the same year with his parents, Philip and Martha Steele. He had three brothers who served in World War I, all were killed in action, two other brothers died of cancer and one of typhoid. One sister was still living in Ontario in 1967.

Dick came to Alberta with a carload of bulls, his wife Constance Morrison, came later. They were married in 1906. They had four children, all deceased. Dick and his wife homesteaded about eighteen miles north of Buffalo, on the S.E.¼ Section 10-24-6. He used horses and a plow to break the land. They raised horses and chickens and tried to raise crops. Dick recalled numerous incidents of horse stealing and he carried side arms when he worked at the Cochrane ranch.

Their first home was a two-room shack. He gave up farming in 1939 and worked for the C.P.R. for five weeks when he was laid off for being too old. He then worked as a chimney builder and helped in the store. He recalls of there being two elevators in Buffalo, but did not know the date as to when they were built. He started to work as a cook at the Vee Bar Vee in 1941 and left there in 1962. He lived for a few years in Brooks at the Newbrook Lodge, but spent the last two years of his life in a hospital in Medicine Hat, where he passed away August 28, 1970 at the age of 100 years and six months.

NOAH E. STEEVES STORY

I came to Buffalo in 1919. I was born in Westmoreland County, New Brunswick. I lived in Saskatchewan before coming to Buffalo. I had also served with 8th Battery C.F.A. First Division C.E.F., was wounded and sent home in 1917. I broke land with a sulky plough and four horses on the homestead I had on Section 28-21-5-4 which I got with a Homesteaders Soldier Grant. I married Grace E. Scanes.

We had cattle, horses and raised a crop. Our brand was E ⌒ .

Our neighbor to the south was a German fellow, Salzwedel. He was a sort of an exceptional character and spoke very poor English. When I was first married he came to our house and told Mrs. Steeves that he had lost his "haugs". He was unshaven and looked sort of fierce. She sent him to me over at the barn. He told me he had lost his "picks". I offered to lend him a pick. However, he managed to get it into my head that his pigs had got away and he was looking for them. He was rather excitable. Once he was out in a democrat shooting rabbits. He fired at a rabbit and shot one of his horses. 'Twas a remarkable thing, as he just had a 22 rifle, that it killed the horse. Later he told his wife that the horse dropped dead. It was quite upsetting to her as she had raised the horse on a bottle. However, to give him his due, he was a public-spirited citizen. Was mostly through his efforts that we got the hall at Buffalo built.

Scotty Bain, another man and myself were out goose hunting with Salzwedel. We drove down to the stubble field on the Gordon Flat before daylight in Salzwedel's car. We dug our pits, put out our decoys, then Salty got in his car to park it someplace farther away. He got confused in the dark. I guess he must have had his lights off. Anyway he drove in a circle and came back to our pit and decoys. He thought he saw a flock of geese and blazed away with two shots before he realized he was firing at our decoys. No harm was done except a few shot holes in the decoys.

Cecil Mode had the first post office and store. He just kept it a short time then tore it down and moved away. I kept the post office after that until my brother-in-law, Jimmy Scanes got a store going, then I turned the post office over to him. Our immediate neighbors were Ben Dart, Rufus Armstrong, Mr. Paulding, Wm. Dearing, Andrew MacKay, Olaf Skjenna, Mr. Mayhew and others. Andrew Gordon was the nearest rancher.

Our three children, Pat, Sam and Rachael were all born in the Empress hospital. We left Buffalo in 1933 and now live in Three Hills. Our three children are all missionaries, the two boys are missionary doctors. Mrs. Steeves and I celebrated our 50th wedding anniversary in 1970.

ARTHUR LOVELL STONE

A. L. Stone was born in Hawksville, Ontario, on May 29, 1889. As a young man of eighteen years he came to Clearwater, Manitoba where he worked for his cousin, Tom Stone, operating a steam engine for threshing. Arthur managed the separator while his cousin operated the engine for a crew of 28 men. The grain threshed in one day required eight teams of horses to haul it to the elevator.

While the young men were busy with the grain the young girls of the surrounding district would be going from farm to farm assisting the women in the preparation of food for the threshing crew. In the evening the young ladies would be on hand to brighten up the young men's lives and help them forget their aches and pains, resulting from a long day of threshing grain.

One member of this female group was Olive Gillispie, who has continued to help Arthur forget his aches and pains and has brightened his life since their marriage in 1913.

Arthur came to Alberta in 1912, but returned to Clearwater after he had established his homestead. He and Olive were married and following the wedding the young couple settled in their

Mr. and Mrs. A. L. Stone's home.

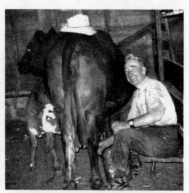
Lovell Stone and helpers.

home in Little Sweden, now known as the British Block. It was here in July 1914, a twister destroyed their barn. A. L. was just putting his team away when the twister struck. It knocked Arthur off his feet, lifting him so that he landed on the horses' backs. The winds were so strong that the young animals had difficulty in breathing, to save the animals lives Arthur and Olive had to take them into their house which was only a one-room shack at that time.

In August of the same year, a fire broke out and travelled about eighteen miles, from the Cochrane ranch where it started, north to the Red Deer River. Olive helped to fight that fire, despite the fact she was in her seventh month of pregnancy, two weeks later their only child, Edgar, was born. Because the fire had destroyed all the pasture land their cattle had to be moved to Empress while Arthur and Olive returned to Manitoba. Arthur again worked for his cousin until the fall of 1915 when the Stones returned to Alberta. They came to the Buffalo district in 1923 where they have lived ever since.

Their son, Edgar (Ted) attended school at the Lila school and in later years married Violet Bicknell, whose family lived a few miles east of Buffalo, between Bindloss and Empress.

Ted and Violet have four children, Marjorie (Mrs. Allan Smith) who has four children, she and her husband farm just southeast of Buffalo, Jim who is married and lives in Bowden, he has two children, Linda, who married Charles Mohr in the summer of 1971, and her twin sister Leona (Mrs. Tom Calhoun) she has one son, and they live at Consort, Alberta.

Arthur Stone has one niece, Mrs. John Jones living at Wetaskiwin, and a nephew, Carl Stone living at Claresholm.

Violet Stone, Rena, Mrs. O'Morrow, Mrs. Thomas, Mrs. Johnson, Ella Barneko, Mrs. Cook, Mrs. Skjenna, Mrs. Lovell Stone, Ruth Skjenna, Anna Dalbak sitting by the bush.

Olive (Gillispie) Stone was born in Wingham, Ontario, in 1890. At the age of twelve she and her family moved to Mathers, Manitoba. She obtained her early schooling at Clearwater. She rode horseback six miles to school, she still recalls with a twinkle in her eye, how friends of the family had remarked that "she rode like the wind". Olive's love for horses increased over the years and she was always known to have one of the smartest stepping horses and shiniest buggy in the district. After finishing school, Olive became a teacher.

She recalls some of the good times they used to have, especially when the young men would be doing the threshing, as Arthur has already mentioned. Olive says that one night when everyone was having a good time around the open fire, one fellow decided he would rather sleep than sit around and sing, and no amount of coaxing could make him change his mind. Olive and some of the

Christmas on the Homestead — left to right: Harvey Stone, Sam Hilstead, Chas. Winkler, Lovell Stone, Mrs. H. Stone, Mrs. A. L. Stone, Chic, Carl· and Ted.

other girls waited until they were sure he would be asleep and unbeknown to the others, took burning sticks from the fire and ran around the bunkhouse hollering "fire."

Awakening from a sound sleep and seeing the fire flickering on the walls, the bachelor lost no time ·in getting outside, but to the merriment of the girls, who by this time had innocently taken their places back with the others around the fire, he had forgotten to put on his pants. As the others didn't know what the girls had been up to they thought the poor fellow was having a nightmare.

Both Arthur and Olive had a good sense of humor and over the years have proven to be very good neighbors. They have both been active in community work and activities. The home has always been home to friend and stranger alike and the following poems written as a tribute to each of them on their 80th birthday(s), will serve to show what their neighbors thought of them.

A tribute to A. L. Stone on the occasion of his 80th birthday
Composed by Helen D. Howe:
It's with joy we have gathered this evening
In a home of warmth and good cheer.
We all deem it a great privilege
To honor this pioneer.
To know a man like Lovell
Is a priceless gift and rare.
A true husband, kind father and neighbor
When needed is always there.

166

Honest in all his dealings
As on this earth he has trod.
With a heart always full of compassion
For he lives by the Word of God.

Since he left his native Ontario
When he was just a lad
With courage he has gone forward
Through the good years and the bad.

It was while he was in Manitoba
Working hard at threshing wheat
He met a young girl named Olive
And placed his heart at her feet.

In 1912 he came to Alberta
And there on the prairie wide
Located and established a homestead
Which filled his young heart with pride.

In the hamlet of Little Sweden
Was where he had found this land
Then returning to Manitoba
He claimed young Olive's hand.

Together in their Alberta home
They had their hearts' desire.
'Til misfortune came upon them
First a twister, and then a fire.

Returning again to Manitoba
For a year they were forced to stay
While their stock was wintered in Empress
As the fire had destroyed their hay.

Following hard on the heels of misfortune
The young couple soon experienced great joy.
To ease the reverses they'd suffered
God gave them a gift; 'twas a boy.

Returning the next year to Alberta
Determined to try it again
They were filled with the pioneer spirit
To all, this was very plain.

The years rolled by so swiftly
As years have been known to do.
Lovell, Olive and young Ted were happy
As each of their dreams came true.

Then when the war broke out in Europe
Its disaster we all have known
But this family in Little Sweden
Were forced to leave their home.
They were not alone in this Exodus
By having no place to go.
While others settled elsewhere
The Stones came to Buffalo.
Soon young Ted married fair Violet
This added to Lovell's joy.
They gave him four grandchildren
Three little girls and a boy.
It's with pleasure I've related this story
Which now I must bring to an end.
As Lovell celebrates his eightieth birthday
We're privileged to call him, our friend.

A tribute written to Mrs. A. L. (Olive) Stone on her eightieth birthday
By H. D. Howe

I know you all remember,
It has not been quite a year.
On such a smiliar occasion
That we all gathered here.
To honor Lovell on his birthday
We were welcomed to this house
Now just a few months later
We've come to honor Olive, his spouse.
Olive was born in Ontario
The youngest of a family of three.
Her parents could never imagine
The changes this child was to see.
When Olive was only twelve
To Manitoba the family went.
In a little town called Mathers
The days of her girlhood spent.
Being a lass of rare beauty
Several young men came to call.
We wouldn't say Olive was flirtatious
But she certainly confused them all.
Among these young men was Lovell
Who had made a trip farther west.
It was during his absence, that Olive
Decided he was the one she liked best.

When Lovell returned to Manitoba
He spoke of his land with pride.
He asked fair Olive if she'd be willing
To return with him there as his bride.
Soon in the hamlet of Little Sweden
Each had their heart's desire.
'Til misfortune came upon them
First a twister, and then a fire.
Returning again to Manitoba
For a year they were forced to stay
While their stock was wintered in Empress
As the fire had destroyed their hay.
Following hard on the heels of misfortune
The young couple soon experienced great joy.
To ease the reverses they'd suffered
God gave them a gift; 'twas a boy.
Returning the next year to Alberta
Determined to try it again
They were filled with the pioneer spirit
To all, this was very plain.
The years rolled by so swiftly
And Ted to a man quickly grew.
Olive cared for her little family
As a mother she had lots to do.
So tonight we pay tribute to Olive
A wonderful wife, mother and friend.
Now just because she has reached eighty
To her that isn't the end.

Written in honor of Mr. and Mrs. A. L. Stone on their 50th Wedding Anniversary

by Violet (Bicknell) Stone

Just a barefoot boy from an eastern farm,
Full of fun and jokes and a certain charm.
Left motherless at an early age indeed
He turned to sister Dell for every need.
While looking for the cows one night
A black squirrel left him in a pretty plight
For alas! he fell from a tree and broke his arm.
Oh! those happy days on that eastern farm.
An adventurous spark in him awoke one day
So he started out west to Clearwater way.
He made his home with cousins, Tom and Doll
Where he worked pretty hard from spring until fall.

169

But he never minded the work one bit
For in that family he seemed to fit.
There was plenty of laughter and fun each day
Oh! those happy days out Clearwater way.
Then another spark, in his heart so young
Awoke, but alas he has lost his tongue.
For to speak all of love to Olive thought he
Lovell loved all of her, but would Olive love me?
This sounds like talk doubled, but how else would one woo
A bonnie wee lassie with eyes of bright blue.
He tried tossing peanuts at ball games and such
To attract the attention he wanted so much.
But Olive a scholar at heart so it seemed
Paid little attention when Lovell's face beamed.
When he tried serenading to strengthen his plea
She just looked at hime coldly and said, "You're off key."
Her ball playing talent was real hard to beat
When she pitched her hardest, knocked boys off their feet.
So little in common these two seemed to share
And Lovell felt almost about to despair.
When he realized that horses was their common love
It seemed that this monster was sent from above.
To bring them together, so with narry a word
Lovell borrowed from Tommy his best mare, named Bird.
He groomed and caressed her 'til she shone like a dime
To meet lovely Olive he barely had time.
"Getty-up Birdy," he shouted, but to his dismay
Old Birdy just stood there and started to neigh.
Poor Lovell, it seemed this plight never would end
So with a sound beating his whip he did bend.
But still old Birdy just stood there and shook her old head
So with his best manner quite gently he said,
"Come Birdy, nice Birdy, won't you please take a step?"
He stroked her quite gently and begged for some pep.
So away went old Birdy in a big cloud of dust
Lovell jumped the seat shouting, "Gillispie's or bust."
Just the sight of surrey all painted and bright
Pulled by that old mare, caused Ollie to give up the fight.
'Twas Lovell she wanted, there was little doubt
So plans were soon made and invitations sent out.
It was a fine wedding as old friends recall
And they were so happy that long ago fall.
Their homesteading days began in the spring
For to Buffalo then Lovell his bride he did bring.

170

The times were quite hard in those days of old
But happiness they say is neither bought nor sold.
Next year a small boy had filled their wee nest
And now the two lovers felt doubly blest.
So years rolled along and four grandchildren came
To make their lives lively instead of so tame
Then the fourth generation had added its four
So a half century together, may they have many more.
Years that is!

October 29, 1971 Mr. and Mrs. A. L. Stone celebrated their 59th wedding anniversary.

THE EDGAR (TED) STONE FAMILY by Marjorie (Stone) Smith

They say some children are born with a silver spoon in their mouth, but it seems to me I must have been born with a hammer in my hand instead. Although we were farmers, my first recollections seem to be of some building or remodeling operations going on in our family.

My first recollection was of a camp trailer my parents built for our annual summer vacation. First trip was to Banff followed by a parade in Buffalo, some twenty-five years ago. While building operations were in full swing on the trailer, Jim and I both turned up missing. Mother and Dad figured the worst had happened, and that we had fallen into one of the many deep sloughs. Towards evening Dad finally found us both asleep locked in the trailer. Several years after the trailer was built, Dad went to remove one of the light fixtures to use in the house, when he couldn't budge the first one he tried another, only to find a $20 bill hidden behind it, placed there for an emergency. It was a good thing none arose as he had forgotten it was there.

Several years later Dad was building again, this time he along with the Andersons boys, Bill and Ted, Fred Dewahl and others, was rebuilding the Buffalo Hall. They put in many hard days and evenings to have the hall ready for our annual Christmas Concert. One of my few recollections of the old hall, which is now part of

Mr. and Mrs. Ted Stone's home before hedges, etc.

Mr. and Mrs. Edgar Stone (Violet Bicknell) wedding in 1939 with Bill and Martha Bicknell.

171

the new one, was the discovery all about Santa Claus, when I happened to look in the coal shed room to find Oliver Skjenna removing his white beard and red suit. The old livery stable was used in building the present structure.

The years that followed seemed to be filled with many rebuilding operations in our own home with built-in cupboards, door changings, plumbing from crude method to modern, the same holds true in the electrical wiring from 12 volt to the 32 volt system, and then in 1958-'59 good old 'ready kill-owatt" came in. It was then that Dad became the rural electrician for the district.

One of the rebuilding operations in our home was brought on quite sudden by our boisterous bath-time upstairs when splashing water caused the plaster of the kitchen ceiling to let loose early one morning. We came down to find everything full of wet plaster. This condition was also helped by our first crude plumbing, for when some ambitious person, usually a visitor, would pump water in our kitchen, the water would also fill the barrel upstairs and soon we would find water trickling down on our heads.

In 1957-'61 Dad was on the "big build" again, when the former schoolhouse was bought and converted into a church. He was assisted by the Rev. Jack Beaton, who made the windows, Olaf Skjenna, Ken Tiegs, Leroy Callaghan and many others. The money was raised by the folks of the community putting on bazaars and a three-act play. Rev. Beaton donated the pulpit furnishings.

When my brother Jim was ready to get married in 1961 he needed a home, so Dad helped him build a lovely 10 by 40 foot house trailer. There Jim and his new bride, Lynn, spent the first part of their married life.

It seemed my married life was to be as full of sawdust as my youth. Just before Allan Smith and I were married in 1959, he had just completed a shop and barn, then on November 27, 1961 we lost our home by fire so we were now faced with building again. Again Dad was handy to give us a helping hand. In the hectic process of building our new home, our two children, Ricky aged two and Marnie aged one lived quite a rough and tumble life. One hot day, Ricky decided it was time for a bath, the only thing he could find to bathe in was a bucket of tar, which Allan and I were using on the roof. By the time I got him cleaned up he thought it was time to leave home. Another day when we were putting in the windows, a puff of wind caught the window unit and upset it with Ricky underneath, this saved the glass from being broken but Ricky's "ire" was ruffled and all he could do when he got up was shake his head and say, "Boy oh Boy," as though he was wondering just how much more he could stand.

172

Leona and Lynda Stone (twins).

In 1967 when the farmers of the district all joined together in a "farming bee" to do the seeding for my Dad, who had just returned home following a second operation. Allan and I had been at my parents' home all day and when we returned home we found that fire had struck again. All our corrals, barn, shed and feed all destroyed. There was nothing left but the glowing embers. And now our three children were started on their way again in the building business, as they were right there helping us build it all up again. Six months later our fourth child was born. To date she has escaped any building operations. But she has the unique distinction of being Buffalo's Centennial Baby.

When my sister, Leona married Tom Calhoun in September, 1969 and her twin Lynda married Charles Mohr in April, 1971, mother fashioned both of their wedding gowns and most of their trousseaus, as well as their bridesmaids' gowns. Mother passed her talents on to us girls and it seems that our entire family has to be creating something whenever we find a piece of wood or cloth.

Now as I come to the end of some 25 years of recollections of sawdust in my eyes and slivers in my fingers, Dad and Mom have just finished a beautiful Alaskan-style camper and have just returned from a trip to Prince Albert, Saskatchewan and other points.

LOUIS WILHELMSON

LOUIS WILHELMSON was born in Aalesund, Norway in 1889. He immigrated to North Dakota and then to Canada in 1913. He homestead the S.E.¼ 2-20-5, in that what was formerly known as "Little Sweden" until 1941, when he relocated just east of the Buffalo store. He did carpenter work in the district from 1941 until 1964 when he retired to the Newbrook Lodge at Brooks, Alberta.

Swen Hillsted was Louis' homesteading partner. His first home was a sod hut. He raised horses and grain. His horse brand was **LW** on right thigh. He recalls the RCMP were posted at Empress and also at the Vee Bar Vee. There was no church when he first came to the district.

He reported that they nearly starved during the thirties. In 1932 crops were fair and wheat sold at twenty cents a bushel. He helped build the bridge in 1931. Mr. Wilhelmson passed away in the Brooks General Hospital in October, 1968.

Louis Wilhelmson, a great hunter.

WOO SAM

For over forty-three years, Woo Sam owned and operated a general store in the Buffalo district, coming here in 1923, where he started in a little shack that was later used for storage. Sam remembers that when he first came to Buffalo there was another general store, blacksmith shop, livery stable as well as the post office, today there is only the store and post office. Sam's store is now owned and operated by Walter and Dorothy Heiland.

Sam came to Canada from his native China, in 1910 arriving in Victoria, B.C. where he worked in a Chinese general store, working eighteen hours a day for $18. per month. He sold potatoes for 35 cents a bushel and sugar for $2.00 a hundred-weight.

In 1916 he went to Golden where he cooked in a restaurant for three years. From there he went to Moose Jaw and Swift Current and in 1920 he moved to Jenner where he operated a general store and restaurant. He recalls that entire town of Jenner was destroyed by fire shortly after he arrived.

In 1921 Sam made a trip back to China where he stayed for

a year. On his return to Canada he was accompanied by his son, Wah Chou. They went to Bindloss where Sam again worked in a restaurant while his son attended school there.

It was August 1923 Sam arrived in Buffalo. He recalls that beef sold at eight cents a pound, hind quarters at that. Wheat was $2.50 per bushel. The elevator at that time was the Pacific Grain, the Alberta Pool elevator was built in 1928.

Sam says the years from 1923 to 1928 were very good years, but in the thirties he had approximately 41 families on relief. When asked about bad debts, he said, "All people are good people, all people pay except those who died".

He recalls when the Buffalo bridge was built in 1931, he ran a cafe and had sleeping rooms for rent. Asked if he ever had any trouble with rowdy construction workers or boisterous cowboys, his only answer was that all people are good people.

During this time Wah Chou had returned to China and Sam shared his home with Howard McCullough and family. Scotty Bain ran the Delco plant for Sam. This was before hydro. Bill Wemp and Bill Thompson and family also shared Sam's home.

In 1951 Sam was joined by another son Kai, and later the same year by two grandsons, Wing and Sang. All three attended the Buffalo school and later went to university.

Sam's wife came to Canada in 1954. She was accompanied by a companion, Mrs. Chin, who stayed on with Sam after his wife passed away in 1964.

In the late sixties Wah Chou, who in the meantime had changed his name to Roy, returned to Buffalo with his wife and their youngest son. Roy operated the store for Sam who due to poor health moved to Calgary to live with his sons. Roy and his family also live there now.

WOO SAM
by Violet Stone

From the opposite side of the world came he,
To make his home here with you and me.
He was young and ambitious and full of grit,
Had a clever philosophy spiced with wit.
His advice is worth taking we are told,
This modern Confucious from a world of old.
He left his family, friends and came,
In '23 to find wealth and fame.
He started up with the tiny shack,
Which has become a storehouse out back.

He later built his present store
With cafe and rooms on the second floor.
He was followed later by son Wah Chou
Who attended our school for a year or so.
Then came Scotty and Bill Wemp, too
The McCulloughs moved in and then Bill and Boo.
Each a few years with Sam — did spend.
Bringing lonely days to a welcome end.
Son Kai arrived to take his turn
To keep Sam company as well as to learn.
He passed all his grades with marks so high
And then it was time to say "Goodbye".
He attended Varsities far and near
To become a First Class Engineer.
If Kai's life was dull it woke with a bang,
With the arrival of nephews, Wing and Sang.
These happy faced fellows were full of life,
And they filled Woo Sam's days with both joy and strife.
To share in all this, as well as keep house,
Woo Sam was joined by his aging spouse.
And so Sam enjoyed for too short a while,
Family life in true Canadian style.
The boys fit in Buffalo like a hand-in-a-glove
As hunting and school sports became their first love.
As in our Community all took their parts,
We found they held likewise a place in our hearts.
Like Sam before them, who was father to all
With free catering service after hockey or ball
His doors never closed either Sunday or night
Buffalo without him would never seem right.
We would miss all the extras and
As to him and Mrs. Chin we would say our "Goodbyes".
But all good things must come to an end
Each of the Woos his own way did wend.
With the passing of wife and Mother so dear,
And each boy well launched with a brand new career,
Woo Sam may decide to join with his clan
Become a real city slicker on the easy-pay plan.
Now Woo Sam has given his finest and best
In depression and wartime in our woolly west,
We could laugh at the rations and poverty too
For we knew that our merchant would see us right through,
I can see by your faces you've all stories to tell
So let's wish Sam our blessings and best wishes as well.

176

Editor's Note: The following was written by Jane Havens, and appeared in the January 1956, issued of Farm and Ranch Review.

SLIM WOODS, OF HUNTING HILLS

Schooled in the ways of the West, dignified yet friendly, cautious of strangers yet one to make every visitor feel at home — that is Slim Woods as you see him today. If ever there was a ranch with a beautiful natural setting it is the YE ranch in the Hunting Hills on Alberta's Red Deer River. You reach the house by the new highway which goes north from Gregory Ferry to Wardlow, Cessford and Hanna. The road runs close to the house and Slim, with the curiosity of a lone batchelor, watches every car that passes. He quite often gets a ride to Brooks, 30 miles away, where he can spend the weekend visiting with his old-time neighbors who are still recalling the 1900's. The old neighbors include David Porteous, genial Scotch cook of the Anchor P ranch in the days of George Emerson and Rod MacLeay; John Eide who settled north of the Red Deer in 1897; Jack Thomas, cook for the Circle ranch for 16 years. Slim, whose name is Herbert, was better known among th eearly cowboys as Moccasin Foot. In his 70's, he is a tall, fine-looking chap with a heavy handclasp and a smile you remember. He was an expert roper and ranked among the best in his day.

Slim worked for different outfits such as the Circle, the Anchor P, the Bar U and the Denton which later was taken over by Mike Stapleton, with the three hooks, sometimes called the Walking Cane brand. In the early days when cattle strayed as far as 100 miles the cowboys often went for months without wages as the boss never knew where they were when on the roundup. Being from the Southern States, Slims calls a cowboy a waddy and a string of horses a remuda. He explains that if you saw some of the roundup boys at a shipping point sleeping out on the prairie some distance from the bed tent it was just as well not to ask too many questions. If there was an operator at the shipping point the boys would order jugs of liquor and if a passenger train went through in the night the jugs would be sitting besides the track in the morning.

One English lad, Charlie Harper, who was riding with the outfit one year said he had been lost all summer because the sun generally rose in the east but set wherever it jolly well pleased. When setting up camp at a shipping point the boys often rode up and down the tracks hunting iron pegs to set up their tents.

In the early days a man often took the law into his own hands. Said Slim, "One day I was driving a bunch of steers to ship for my boss. I was fairly close to the shipping point when Pat Burns and some riders showed up and took them away from me. Before long I

177

saw another bunch of riders show up on the skyline and take the cattle away from Pat. I never did find out the rights of the matter but there was some controversy over a money deal."

Slim has watched the land around him change from ranching to farming. Some homesteaders came with few effects but many plans, but after ten years of hardship their courage failed and they faded from the picture. He tells of being startled one day by music coming from the open door of a tiny shack. The couple had brought along their piano, an almost unheard of article in those days, and while her husband was away the young wife relieved the lonely hours by playing her favorite airs. But they too gave up and moved away and today nothing is left, but the root-cellar and a large flat rock which might have been the doorstep.

Slim's nearest neighbor is Alf Bradshaw, who operates the Gregory Ferry. To the north are Sam and Arthur Wiig. Mr. and Mrs. J. H. Pearson, who were among the first settlers, still live in the district. The others have gone. The Zeers, the Josephs, the Murphys, the Eides, the Saddys. Alya Saddy, who married Prime Minister Mohammed Ali of Pakistan, spent her early girlhood north of the Red Deer.

Steveville, which in the twenties was a busy town, is now deserted. As you drive through you see an old stove and Jake Schaerrer's garage — mute reminders that people once lived and worked there. Many will recall the late Steve Hall for whom the town was named and who carried on business there for many years.

Even in the early days he predicted that one day oil would be found in the district. His predictions came true. News that an oil company contemplated moving machinery across his property was thought to have brought on a heart attack which hastened the old-timer's death. At one time Mr. and Mrs. Hall owned a boarding house, a livery barn, dance hall, store and post office. In the front of the store was a hitching rack.

One of Slim Woods most prized possessions is the book, "Trails I Rode", written by an old-time Montana Rancher, Con Price, and dedicated, "To the memory of Charlie Russell, who loved the Old West and mourned its passing." All illustrations in the book are by Charlie Russell. In it is an autograph reading: "To H. Woods, my friend of forty years ago. Hoping you have no rocks or bad crossings on your trail of life. Con Price, March 10, '50".

At one time Con Price and Charlie Russell were partners on the Lazy KY ranch in Montana. In 1950 Slim Woods visited Price in his California home.

Lewis Thomas sod house, Pete Hanson, Morris Thomas.

1928 threshing crew.

1928 Harvest.

Building the Buffalo Dam.

At the ferry on the Red Deer River in the twenties.

Gus Hanson and friends in front of sod-roof barn, 1914.

Party Time — left to right — standing: Allan Gatenby, Allie Hurl, Andy McKay, May McKay, Mrs. Gatenby, Andy Ulrick, Frank Rubbelke. Sitting: Stan Hurl, Harold Gatenby and daughters, unknown, Wallace King and Mr. Gatenby.

Snow Plough, 1965.

Wintery scene at Ben Anderson homestead.

Atlee Ferry.

1920 wheat field.

Homestead Days, 1912.

Kirchner hay stacker.

Ed Johnson, a carpenter and wood-carver surrounded by his work.

Gus Hanson and Lewis Thomas, 1912.

181

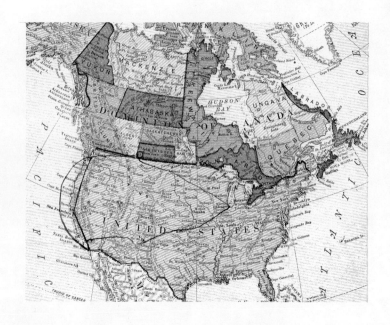

Map showing the provinces prior to 1905 when Medicine Hat was in an area known as Assiniboia.

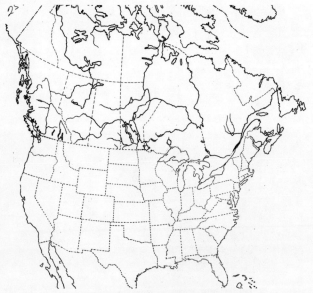

Up to date map of North America

October 5th 1970.

To Mrs. Chester C. (Helen) Howe,
    Buffalo, Alberta:
    This note will constitute, in writing, my
permission given to Mrs. Chester C. (Helen) Howe
of Buffalo, Alberta, to reproduce any or all of
the tales and poems published in the Brooks
Bulletin at Brooks, Alberta, during the
year (1970) nineteen seventy under the title
"True Tales of Days that are Gone" and covered
by copyright no. 136892, registered in the
Copyright Office, Ottawa, Canada.

                                John R. Gordon.

TRUE TALES OF DAYS THAT ARE GONE
(WITH RHYMES OF THE RANGE AND OTHER POEMS)
by John R. Gordon

Tell us a tale of the days that are gone:
Days when the West was yet young,
Days when it seems the sun always shone,
Days that were never too long.
Tell of the camps, of the herds, of the trails:
Trails that were rutted and worn,
Trails that you rode to the head of the rails,
Trails that were dim or unknown.
Tell of the men sunburned, rugged and lean,
Men who loved freedom and dare;
Some of them ornery, knavish or mean,
Most of them candid and square.
Tell of the women, stout-hearted and true,
Braving the worst of the wilds,
Sharing misfortune, inspiring the crew,

183

Raising a family besides.
Tell us a tale of the days that are gone;
Days packed with pleasure and strife,
Write it for those who are following on —
Don't let it die: give it life.

— J. R. Gordon

Gordon Ranch, the first to be established on the Red Deer River, now known as Majestic Ranch.

This is a collection of some of the stories of days gone by that I have told to my family and friends at various times. Included are a number of poems. I had been urged at different times to have these printed and bound that they might not be lost. May they give pleasure to those who read them.   — J. R. G.

CHAPTER ONE

One evening in the late summer of 1895 Father and Mother sat at the table in our farmhouse eight miles north of Moosomin, Assiniboia, with a map of some sort spread out between them. I was only six years of age but I remember my Mother telling Father she heard that there was plenty of ranch land around Medicine Hat. However, Uncle J. T. who had been on most of the ranches in western Assiniboia and Alberta dealing for beef cattle, recommended that Father go to Cowley where he should contact Mr. F. W. Godsal, a well-established rancher of that district. Mr. Godsal would show him some possible locations and advise him as to their suitability. Father did as Uncle had suggested — he went to Cowley where Mr. Godsal and he looked over a few available spots, decided on one in the Pincher Creek area and Father returned to the farm.

That fall he bought stockers from other farmers in our district — going as far north as the Qu'Appelle Valley for some. He sold the farm to Andrew Moffat and in the spring moved his family to a rented house in Moosomin; the cattle were loaded on stock cars billed for Pincher Creek, Alberta.

When they were unloaded at Dunmore Junction for water and grazing a Halfbreed named Hansen told Father about the open country (no settlers) along the Red Deer River, sixty miles north of Medicine Hat. Leaving Tom Mossop, who had come from Moosomin with him, to care for the stock, the other two men set out in a "buck board" for the north country.

They crossed the Saskatchewan River on a ferry at Medicine Hat and then travelled on the Battleford Trail until they reached the Red Deer. (Early travellers on this old trail crossed the Red Deer northwest of the present village of Bindloss, then continued northeast to Battleford). Turning west they followed a dim trail made by the wagons and carts of Halfbreeds and Indians moving up and down the river and used by North West Mounted Police on their patrols in that area.

On the afternoon of the fourth day after leaving Dunmore, they reached a spot northwest of the present hamlet of Buffalo where a few tracks left the trail and found a way down the hill toward the river. Spread out before them was a large flat extending for more than five miles along the river and at its widest part having a breadth of one and one-half miles.

A large herd of antelope was grazing in the middle of the flat and as the men drove toward the western end, blue joint grass which covered at least half of the acreage, brushed the hubs of the wheels of the "buck board". Between the main flat and the river, as it looped to the north, lay lower land comprising about 800 acres. Cottonwood brush were so arranged around patches of grass land that this part trees, willows of different varieties, black birch, bullberry and other formed one of the best bed grounds along the River (its capacity depended on how the cattle were handled).

The land seekers made their camp at the west end beside a clear running spring where the hills almost meet the river. This camp ground was used by the N.W.M. Police, both before our coming and afterwards, when on their patrols. Usually there were two Policemen in a buckboard with their bedding, grub and saddles in the back of the rig (their two horses being broken to both saddle and harness). Mr. Fred McLaughlin, later secretary of the Medicine Hat School Board for several years but who, at the time of this story, was with the Police, told me that he had planned to locate at this spring but that my Father had gotten his application in first (the land belonged to the Hudson's Bay Company who owned sections eight and twenty-six in each township). After climbing the hill above the Spring from which he had a wonderful view of the river valley twelve miles east and twelve miles west, Father told his guide, "This is good enough for me" and at daybreak the next morning they started on the return

185

trip to Dunmore. Instead of following the trail east, on which they had come, they drove southeast across unmarked country for about twenty miles until they reached the Battleford Trail near the spot on which headquarters of the ranch of John Wilson was later established.

After reaching Medicine Hat, Father sent letters to Mother in Moosomin and to a cousin Alex Gordon in Manitoba. At Dunmore he and Tom unloaded their few effects and bought another team and some saddle horses. In a few days Alex, with his family and George Findlay, joined them.

They drove their "dogies" through the Hat to the ferry. Knowing nothing about swimming cattle across a stream the size of the Saskatchewan, they decided to "ferry" them over. There were bets made downtown that those farmers would never get their "dogies" over the river but the bets were lost and the men with Mrs. Gordon and three small children, their equipment and livestock began their long trek to the land of their dreams.

The big flat looked just as good to Father as when he had first seen it and many hundreds of tons of hay were put up that summer just as it would have been "down east" — each bunch was made into a nice "cock" and "topped". Mrs. Gordon being the lone lady in the group was given the honor of choosing the building site. Though not as practical as it might have been, the site she chose was a small "bench" nestled against the hills at the western end commanding a very pleasing view of the river valley for several miles east. Lumber for two houses, a barn and a cattle shed was ordered to be shipped to Bowell, about fifteen miles west of the Hat and Mr. J. H. G. Bray with two sons Harry and Reggie contracted to haul it from that point to the ranch. They formed a small caravan: each of the three drove a four-horse team hitched to a load of lumber. A third son, eight year old Colin, drove a two-horse team hitched to a wagon upon which was loaded their camping equipment and other articles any of which might be needed along the way. The route, afterwards, was known as Bray's Trail. Their camping grounds included "East Spring," "Bray's Spring," "Bray's Lake" and the "Bone Pile Spring."

Alex's house was built and Andrew's, which with an addition still stands (1959), was started. A carpenter named Connor from the Hat was working on our house and when it was "closed-in" Father sent for Mother and the children. (Alex who was a first class carpenter built his own house).

I don't remember the exact date but I believe that we left Moosomin about the first of July, 1896. My oldest sister attended school while we were in Moosomin and though the gooseberries were still green, they were fit to eat. Another boy and I got into an old man's garden one day while he was away and were eating some when he returned and caught us. I was a green country youngster not yet seven years old and when the man said that he was going downtown to tell the Police I was "scared stiff." Mother was at the store and when she returned she found me hiding under the bed in the bedroom.

Father met us at the station in Medicine Hat and the first thing we saw after passing the Indian camps on Muskeekeeatin or Moccasin Flat, were cages beside the station platform in which were a bear, a coyote, a badger and an eagle. There may have been more animals: those are all that I remember.

Each day when the passenger train arrived from the East, Indians in different colored blankets would be squatting on the platform beside the guard rail west of the caged animals (the station house at that time was on the south side of the track) displaying different articles for sale. Their black hair was in long braids and some had dabs of paint on their faces. They displayed hat racks of different styles formed by arranging polished horns on wooden bases. Buffalo, antelope, deer and, occasionally, mountain goat horns were used. I still have a pair of horns taken from the head of either a buffalo cow or a young buffalo. These with a set from a mature male were attached to a wooden base which was covered with red cloth. Buckskin moccasins and gloves trimmed with colored porcupine quills and (or) beads, or just fancy colored stitches were also offered for sale.

We stayed at the American Hotel overnight and the next morning started for the Red Deer in a wagon with spring seat for Mother, Father and the baby. After crossing the river on the ferry two blocks west of the present City Hall, we turned east, went through an underpass at the end of the C.P.R. bridge and farther down the river flat climbed a hill toward the Police Point, passing a house on top of the hill owned by and formerly occupied by Mr. J. H. G. Bray. From here we turned north and made our noon camp at the "Box Spring" fifteen miles north, northeast. Because of rattlesnakes we children, who had never seen one, were warned to not wander from the camp. It was the first time that we saw tea made in a syrup pail over a camp fire.

During the afternoon we travelled about eighteen miles through the "Little Sand Hills" and camped that night at a spring beside the Battleford Trail about one and one-half miles south of a larger spring later known as "Shannon's Spring." Besides these sandhills another group south of the present village of Cavendish were also called the Little Sand Hills. The two groups are about thirty-five to forty miles apart.

187

Again there was a first for us youngsters as we helped (or hindered) Father pitch the tent. Again a hole was dug, the sod turned, with grass down, on one side of the hole: other grass close to the hole was removed with the shovel. A fire was kindled with wood, which we carried in the wagon, and kept burning with "buffalo chips". The horses were hobbled so that they could graze and for another "first time" we went to bed in blankets rolled out on the grassy floor.

The next morning we followed a few wagon tracks which led in a northwesterly direction past "Eagle Butte," a high pyramid-like hill on which was an abandoned eagle's nest and from which, on a clear day, could be seen the Sweet Grass Hills in Montana (looking

past the western end of the Cypress Hills) more than one hundred miles distant. These tracks which Father had made were designed to mark out a trail which would save us from going so far northeast on the Battleford Trail and would shorten the distance from the ranch to the Hat by at least ten miles. They led almost directly north from the Butte for twenty-seven miles.

We crossed the Twenty-Five Mile Coulee which appears to have been, long, long ago, a river valley. There are some wonderful springs in this coulee and in later years we built a barn and cabin beside one to furnish overnight shelter on our many trips to and from Medicine Hat. The stream which at one time flowed down this valley must have emptied into the bed of the Saskatchewan River near the "Drowning Ford" (called by some the Rapid Narrows). South of this spot a few miles there was and, I presume, still is, an eight foot seam of coal which for a number of years supplied fuel for the early settlers.

The trail for the next ten miles led through a wide range of stony hills where there was always excellent grass. At noon we stopped at the Bone Pile spring, a large spring, fifteen miles from the ranch, on the edge of a group of sand dunes partly covered with willow, chokecherry and bullberry brush. All this area that we had traversed since morning, was open country: it belonged to the wild animals. There were no cattle in it, though cattle, black Galloways from the "76" ranch at Stair, were seen twenty-five miles north of their home range. On his way to town Father had camped at this spring and had in some manner lost some silver coins. My two sisters and I searched in the grass where, we were told they might be, and found them.

We were captivated by the two huge piles of whitened buffalo bones near the spring. About fifteen miles east similar piles were heaped at a camping ground beside the Battleford Trail. These bones had been gathered by Halfbreeds and Indians for contractors who were shipping bones to Chicago where they were used, in some manner, in a sugar refining process. A new process was developed and the shipping of bones ceased. Years later they were picked up and shipped, this time to be converted into fertilizer.

Those two days were never forgotten. On almost every slough wild fowl of some kind, mostly ducks, would be seen. Antelope in small bands of from four to twenty appeared often and once in a while we would catch a glimpse of a coyote. Because we were in rattlesnake country the first day we did not see any gophers. The common gray-brown gopher is not found where there are rattlesnakes and the Twenty-Five Mile Coulee seemed to form a northwestern limit for the snakes. The snakes were plentiful along the route of the Battleford Trail and in that area east of it to the Saskatchewan River. Not until twenty years ago were any seen north of this wide coulee nor closer to the ranch than twelve miles east of the buildings where soil was sandy. Striped gophers were seen often in the Coulee; but north of it, all the way to the Red Deer, the common gophers had their holes.

The balance of the trip was uneventful except that somewhere in the last five miles Mother's "satchel" dropped from the load. Neil Swinton drove out from the ranch after our arrival and found it. When we reached the top of the hill and looked down into the wide green valley with the river winding through the brush and trees, it seemed to us that the Garden of Eden must have been like this. It was our home until the spring of 1898 when a house was rented in Medicine Hat and we were moved to town so that my oldest sister and I could go to school. Each year Father would be in the Hat for the last day of school and the next morning we were on our way to the ranch and each year, as we neared the ranch we youngsters strained anxiously for the first glimpse of that green valley.

DAY DREAMING

I wish I could unroll my bed
Upon the prairie sod tonight
And lie and watch the shimmering stars
Grow brighter in the fading light.
How oft I've watched them, one by one,
Break through that dark gray dome on high
Or, intermittent, duck and peek
As fleecy clouds went drifting by.
How oft I've watched the Polar Bear
Plod nightly round her picket pin
She never lags nor seems to tire:
I've wondered what she hopes to win.
I've felt my brow and hair caressed
By gentle breezes soothing breath
While round about me for a trice
All nature paused — as still as death.
A sleepy twitter broke the hush
As graybird wakened from a dream,
Then nestled, trembling, as she heard,
From close at hand, the nighthawks scream.
A lonely coyote on a butte
Threw back her head, half closed her eyes
And poured a pleading mating call
Toward the star-lit, vaulted skies.
A scout mosquito ventured near
And settled lightly on my hand
Then rose and sent a radar call
That brought his whole bloodthirsty band.
I pulled my tarp up o'er my head:
They buzzed about with baffled cries
While I besought my angel guard
To sprinkle sleep dew on my eyes.

CHAPTER II

When we arrived at the ranch the men were putting up the hay on the flat and a day or two later I was allowed to go with some one over a mile down the flat to watch them. It was a warm day and I climbed up on a large rock, curled up and went to sleep. When I awoke a garter snake was lying on the warm rock with me. Garter snakes are harmless but I didn't know that then and was quickly off the rock and running.

A barn had been built partly in the side of a hill. The only windows were in the end facing north. It had stalls for twelve horses and the hay was poked through a hole in the roof at the south end. That winter Eddie McKay and I were prowling around the coulees with his dog one day and startled a coyote which the dog chased into a yard where men were unloading feed for a bunch of cattle. As the coyote ran through the herd and close to a team and wagon, George Findlay threw his pitch fork into it. He believed that he had finished it with a club so took it to the barn and laid it on the hay at the far end until he should find time to skin it. Eddie and I went into the barn a few minutes later to have a look at it. As we got near the pile of hay in the dark barn we saw two eyes coming toward us. We ran out of the barn, closed the door and called George who came and made sure that it didn't move again. (When we arrived at the ranch for summer holidays three years later the old barn was being replaced by one that held twenty-two horses and had a box stall at each end with separate entrances.) Corrals and a large shed had also been built and with at least twelve hundred tons of good hay on hand the men felt ready for the first winter.

The loss that first winter was not light due mostly to the way the cattle were handled. Both Father and Alex had been accustomed to "stabling" cattle in winter and so at night they put the thinner and smaller ones in that large shed and herded them with lanterns to keep them from "piling up." The cattle were too warm in the shed and when they came out in the day time caught cold. Almost every day for a few weeks a carcass would be hauled to the "graveyard." Billy McKay, an uncle of "young Billy" (who as W. H. McKay is well known to readers of Canadian Cattlemen) told Father that if he would turn the cattle out and feed them in the brush they would "do" much better. They did as advised and there was no more loss due to the winter though quite a few of those "dogies" developed "lump jaw."

That first winter was long remembered for other reasons. Due to lack of experience the stock of flour bought in the fall was not sufficient to feed fifteen mouths 'til spring. So, in January 1897, Father started for Medicine Hat with a team of horses hitched to a sleigh. He took all the bluejoint hay that he could tramp into and tie on the double box on the sleigh. His road was to be down the Red Deer, on the snow-covered ice, to "the Forks" and then up the Saskatchewan to Medicine Hat.

During the previous summer and fall many of their trips had been made by going southeast to the Battleford Trail and then

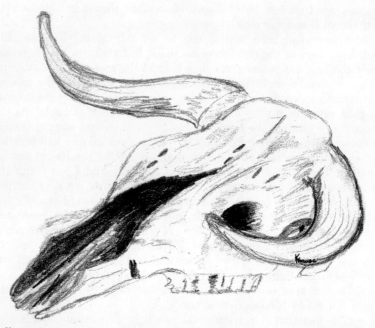

following it to town. The direct trail from the ranch to "the Hat" over which our family had been brought, was as yet only a few tracks. There was quite a bit of snow in January of that year and either of these overland routes across sixty-five miles of snow covered, shelterless prairie was extremely hazardous especially for men who had been in the territory for only a few months.

It took two weeks to make the trip to town, get the flour and some feed for his horses and return to the ranch. There he found that the folks had for several days used shorts as a substitute for flour. It never happened again: so long as the ranch existed the larder was always well filled each fall with all the provisions necessary for a long winter.

Due to the winding course of each river, it was estimated that Father had travelled a total distance of at least three hundred miles in the worst month of winter. With three exceptions, he made camp each night in the brush along the river yet so little was thought of it sixty-three years ago that I doubt if the story has ever before been told. He gave us few details. Having homesteaded eight miles north of the present town of Moosomin, Saskatchewan, ahead of the C.P. Railroad and having worked in lumber camps in the Rainy River district several winters where they were cutting and hewing ties for the Railroad, Father had already spent sixteen winters in the West and knew how to take care of himself in cold winter.

Three winters after Father had made this trip his brother Robert, who was buying beef cattle for Gordon, Ironside and Fares, had cause to travel from the Hat to the ranch in winter. He had been over the trail before but had been warned never to risk the trip at that season of the year without a companion who knew the way. However, he hired a saddle horse from Jim Sanderson, who ran the livery barn, and started out early one morning. Just before dark he reached some hay stacks which were thirty-five miles north of town. They had been built, fenced and fireguarded the previous summer by the hay crew from the "76" ranch at Stair. Here he found shelter for himself for the night and feed for the horse. Early in the morning he continued on his way. The trail was dim when compared to the well worn Battleford Trail which he had followed the day before and the few inches of snow on the ground made it difficult to be seen by a person who didn't know where to look for it.

Sometime in the forenoon he realized that, for him, the trail had disappeared. The sun was shining part of the time so he was able to keep on in a northerly direction. During the day he would dismount when his feet would get cold, and walk for a time. He made the mistake of walking until he was quite warm. His feet would sweat and of course his socks became damp but he did not realize his danger. Suddenly his feet "quit getting cold" and he thought that the temperature had risen. That night after having travelled thirty-five miles from the hay stacks, he rode into the "calf camp" twelve miles east of the home ranch with both feet frozen.

The man at the camp rubbed his feet with snow for some time to draw out the frost and restore circulation. In the morning he took his patient up to the ranch and from there he was taken as quickly as possible (a day and a night) to the Hat. There the Doctor found it necessary to remove most of the toes but uncle was fortunate in that he didn't lose both feet.

THE PHANTOM ON THE BUTTE

On the top of a butte by the bank of the river
'Neath a mound, a lone warrior sleeps during the day;
No disturbance around him unsettles his slumber
As he peacefully rests 'neath the rocks and the clay.

When the last of the day merges into the shadows,
And the stars light their lamps in the heavens of blue;
When the innocent deer venture out of the willows
And the maid in the moon coolly drifts into view;

193

When the coyotes call echoes out of the canyons,
And the ground squirrels have holed and the birds cease
    to sing;
When the grey owl glides silent on down-padded pinions,
And the nighthawk and bat swish about on the wing:
Then the night wind winds stealthily over the prairie,
To the lone charnel house on the butte's top it creeps;
Soughing softly, beside the rough cairn it must tarry
To awake, with a whisper, the tenant who sleeps.
Though his bones and his flesh many years have been
    moul'ring
Still his spirit retains to this mansion its right,
But, bestirred, smoothly sifts through the roof of the dwelling
And then, hov'ring above it, keeps vigil each night.
He can hear the faint lap and the "squish" of the river
And the least quiv'ring move of the leaves on the trees;
The one shriek of the prey of some daring marauder
As its sound drifts away on the waves of the breeze.
If the north wind, snow laden, blow fiercely and bitter,
And the night life seek shelter away from its blast
This thin spectre, unswerving and fearless as ever,
Grimly faces the storm as in days of the past.
But, on warm summer nights when the breezes are gentle,
When the buck brush and roses perfume the soft air,
Ghostly eyes, never tamed, glint from brows rare and noble
Seeking past the horizon, the lands that are fair.
"Shall I follow the crimson that leads to the sunset?
Shall I dwell in the land where the west wind is born?
For how long must I yet linger on at this billet
With impatience, uncertainty, idleness torn?"
But the morning has signalled that light is returning
And reluctant he slowly sinks into his tomb.
Must he bide in its depths, though for other lands yearning,
'Til his summons is served on that sure day of doom?

CHAPTER III

    The Federal Government had not yet made it clear to the Indians
that they must stay on their reservations. Large bands visited their
old hunting grounds. Deer, antelope, beaver, rabbits and prairie
chicken were in good supply along the Red Deer and at one time
during that first winter at the ranch about fifty Indians set up their
teepees one hundred yards from the buildings. Father had been in the
West since 1881 and Alex Gordon almost as long as they were quite
accustomed to dealing with these people.

While Alex was away from the house one day, an Indian pushed open the door and walked in. Ignoring the strong protests of Mrs. Gordon, he took a ham which was hanging from a rafter and left. Mrs. Gordon was able to tell her husband which Indian it was and Alex, a cocky little Scotch-Irishman, went over to the camp, entered the teepee, got what was left of the ham and literally kicked the fellow out of his tent while the others stood around laughing.

Shortly after the Empress-Bassano line of the Canadian Pacific Railway was built in 1912-13, a ferry was installed at the east end of a river flat north of the present hamlet of Cavendish. At the west end of this flat, in 1896, we had a branding corral of poles built against a steep hill which is almost a cut-bank. Its distance from the ranch for a saddle horse was fifteen miles.

Some of the men were branding cattle there that summer shortly after the arrival of our family. One afternoon Father started out with a team and democrat to take some grub to them and to see how they were getting along. I was allowed to go with him. There was no trail and the route along the river that would have been taken by a saddle horse had too many soft spots, caused by the flow of water from many springs, to be traversed with a team and democrat. Twice Father was forced to detour around deep coulees which ran back south from the river for a few miles. Consequently the trip took more time than he had expected.

When we were returning and were about eight miles from the buildings it became quite dark. There was no road for the horses to follow but Father believed that he was going in the right direction. He was worried that he might by-pass the spot where the dim trail went down the hill at the east end of the flat. As he drove over a high piece of land about six miles (he learned later) from home we saw a steady light far ahead of us. It was not the flickering light of a camp fire and there were no other settlers in the district so we knew that it might be a light at home. Father was now able to judge his approximate location and we got safely down the hill.

At home Mother had been watching for us; she could have seen a vehicle coming down the hill four miles east of the house. When it became dark and we had not come in sight she hung a white sheet across the east window, polished the glass of her kerosene lamp, trimmed the wick to shed the brightest light possible and then placed it in the window with the white sheet behind it. It was our beacon and the thought that Mother was trying to guide us home gave us such a thrill that neither of us ever forgot it.

The next year a cabin, barn, sheds and corral were built three miles closer to the ranch beside a spring which flowed through a

grove of "Manitoba Maples" or "Box Elders." The spot now is occupied by Don (Happy) Campbell. Seventeen springs within a span of less than two miles spread their overflow over a good part of the flat and a good crop of hay was harvested every year. There were hay sloughs south and southwest, a hay flat a mile west and one across the river. This camp with its well brushed two miles of river frontage and available hay made an ideal spot for many years in which to winter the calves.

Father spent the winter of 1898 here while Alex with his family and a few men stayed at the home ranch. (In the spring they dissolved partnership and Alex located about twenty miles west on the same side of the river, across from what is now the V-V Ranch). After dark one evening as Father was washing the dishes and preparing for the night, a tall elderly Indian pushed open the door and walked in. He made signs that he was hungry so Father put some food on the table, including a large roast of beef which he had just cooked in a two gallon iron pot, a utensil which was quite common at that time. The Indian disregarded the other food, except the tea, and made a meal of half of the roast. Father feared, as he watched him, that he would make himself sick and once rose to interfere, then thought: "You're an old Indian; I guess you know how to take care of yourself." When he had eaten all that he wanted he squatted in a corner, drew out a pipe and some "kinnikinic", had a smoke, then lay down on the blankets that had been spread for him.

In the morning he almost finished the roast, made a farewell gesture and left. No Indians were near and Father supposed that this man had been following the track of some game animal when darkness had overtaken him miles from camp. He had smelled the wood smoke coming from the cabin and decided to investigate. (The Indians took the inner bark of the dogwood, popularly known as the red willow, dried it and smoked it in that form or mixed with tobacco.

They called it kinnikinic. The smoke from it was very pleasing to smell.)

Dick LaRoche, a Sioux halfbreed, who came west from Manitoba at about the same time as "the Railroad" and who lived and worked for many years along the Red Deer, spent the winter of 1901-02 with his family of four, beside the river, north of the present railroad siding of Halsbury. One morning when he was up "on top" looking for game, he saw a wolf (not a coyote) spring up from the sunny side of a large stone and start running. Dick's shot missed and the wolf sped away toward the southeast.

At a distance one of those wolves would put you in mind of a small buckskin pony both as to size and coloring. When you got close to it gray was the predominant color.

All that day Dick followed its track. A few times he saw it far ahead and, through he was unable to get another shot at it, he kept on in the hope that he should. He knew that if he got the wolf he could collect a bounty of at least twenty-five dollars from ranchers and he would have the pelt to sell. That would be a lot of money (he had started into the winter with ten dollars in cash and one hundred pounds of flour). That night after having trailed the wolf for thirty-five miles across virgin rolling prairie on foot, he stopped at Mr. Tinney's ranch on the Saskatchewan river a few miles west of the "Rapid Narrows." The next day he walked back to his camp. There were fairly good men in those days.

Seven years later Dick was more successful in his contact with another wolf. I had found a yearling steer, dead, with a huge steak eaten out of one hind leg. He was one of the milk cows' calves; they hand wandered about two miles up the river that day. The next night a colt belonging to George Howe across the river, was killed in the same manner — by "ham stringing." A day or two after that we found two of our colts badly bitten. They carried the scars on their hind legs for the rest of their lives.

Three bunches of mares and colts were "running" in separate fields a few miles southwest of the buildings and we believed that the wolf would attack again. (These marauders would not return to a "kill" for the second feed — they always looked for fresh meat. It was practically impossible to trap or poison one.)

In our saddle horse bunch we had a pretty, quiet horse with flaxen mane and tail. Dick had tried several times to buy the horse. When Father heard and saw what this wolf was doing, he told Dick that if he would get the wolf he, Father, would give him "Flaxey." That night Dick took a good saddle horse, a pair of wire cutters and his rifle and lay in a field near the mares and colts.

Dick LaRocke, Gordon Dafoe, Johnny Gordon and Lincoln Howe on horse — 1913.

At dawn he was roused by the squealing and roaring of the mares, a blood chilling racket which only those who have heard it, can appreciate. Dick sprang on his horse and raced toward the noise. The mares were running back and forth in a frenzy, fighting to keep the wolf from the colts. As soon as it saw Dick it started to run. As he came to them, he cut the three wires on each of two barbed wire fences, a mile apart, and as soon as he was within shooting distance started dropping bullets around the wolf.

The frightened animal was doing its best running but Dick was gaining on it. He chased it about four miles then, when it turned and faced him, shot it between the eyes. (There is a lot of room between a wolf's eyes.) Besides Flaxey and the pelt, Dick received one hundred dollars from neighboring ranchers for his night's, or rather morning's, work.

Chester Barber, who lived in the Gleichen and Strathmore districts for many years after leaving the ranch, was the "day wrangler" on our wagon in 1903 when he was in his teens. His father, Jeff, who came to Canada as wagon boss with Connor Brothers when they brought in 2,500 Mexican Steers, held the same job with us for three years.

One morning when the outfit was camped near Cabin Lake, Chester rode out from the camp toward the saddle herd. As he "topped" a knoll two wolves sprang away from a yearling which they had pulled down and were eating, and Chester gave chase. He was riding a grey gelding that ran like an antelope both as to manner of running and speed. The wolves were full from their gorging and Chester quickly ran upon one, roped it and shot it with his six gun, then, after a longer chase, did the same to the other. When they were skinned he had two pelts to sell and the promise of about two months wages in bounties. Needless to say he received loud acclaim from the other riders when they returned to the camp.

Later that fall one of these riders, without being seen by the wolves, spotted a pair stalking a small herd of cattle. He returned to camp, told the others and they decided to run the wolves in relays. Two men, so that the wolves would not split up, took after them, ran them a short distance, then two others took over. There were eight men. They ran the wolves in a large circle of several miles as fast as they could and before long were able to catch and kill them. They had the hides, with head attached, tanned and mounted as rugs and gave them to Mother. For years they graced our living room in town and provided a very interesting theme for conversation.

One of those riders, George Bell, later bought two saddle horses from Father. "Babe" and "Snorter," known for their ability to run long and fast, moved farther west and with a few hounds made hunting wolves a full time job.

CHAPTER IV

Another hated marauder of those days was the eagle. This large bird would light on the hind end — usually of a cow. With its strong sharp talons clutching the hide it would ride there in spite of the wild efforts of the beast to dislodge it, and do so much damage with its beak that the animal had to be shot or, if undiscovered for some time, died. Father paid a bounty of fifteen dollars for each eagle that was killed.

These birds were bold — had little fear of a rider. One day when Dave Laframboise was on herd about eighteen miles south of the present town of Chinook, an eagle circled over the herd and dropped on a cow. It was so intent on keeping its hold and getting a meal that Dave was able to slip up on his horse and throw a small loop that settled over the neck and one flapping wing. With the eagle plunging and bouncing on the end of the rope he raced half a mile to the camp where the cook finished it with the axe.

Will Mossop was hauling poplar poles from a grove a few miles west of the ranch buildings one fall when he noticed a lone antelope walking in a circle with its head cocked to one side as though it were looking at the sky. High above it an eagle soared, around and around, moving, at the same rate as its intended prey. The antelope began to stagger — evidently dizzy. Soon it fell and like a bolt of lightning the eagle dropped on it.

The river floods of June had passed and wild gooseberries were beginning to color on the bush. In a few days ranchers would be branding their calves. Leslie Shannon and Duncan McKenzie rode up the south side of the Red Deer to look through a herd of cattle grazing on the river flat northwest of the present village of Bindloss. As they rode along talking about one thing and another, Dunc suddenly exclaimed, "There's a bear!" At the same time the bear, an old grizzly, reared on its hind legs, took a good look at these strange animals, mounted men, and then dropped to the ground and started hopping away.

Dunc pulled out the 30-30 rifle which he was packing and started after it. He shot two or three times as his horse loped along and was getting close to the beast when suddenly it stopped, wheeled, took one or two hops and lunged at the man on the horse. The terrified horse half turned and leaped sideways and the bear's powerful paw struck the skirt of the saddle behind the man. (Les said that it didn't aim for the horse — it aimed for the man.) Its sharp claws ripped through the leather and the saddle blanket, which luckily was a thick one but only scratched the horse. Then the bear turned and went loping away over the flat toward the east.

In his panic Dunc had dropped his rifle. Les watched 'til he considered it safe to dismount, then picked up the gun, handed it to Dunc and they started after the bear once more. Evidently one bullet hit its spine; it began to drag its hind legs and, after another shot, fell over on its side. The two riders, quite cautious now, circled the animal a few times, then Les threw his rope, caught the bear by the head and rolled it over. They were satisfied it was dead.

The front half of the bear's body was covered with fur but the rear half was bare as though it had "shed." When the head was skinned, five chunks of lead which had been unable to pierce the skull were found under the hide.

This happened before 1900 and it is impossible that this animal was one of the last of the prairie grizzlies which at one time roamed these parts with the buffalo. A few are now known to be in the Swan Hills west of Edmonton.

On the north side of the Red Deer, nine or ten miles west of the ranch a dry water course joins the river bed. It drains a large area north and west and, in the time of the spring thaw, carries a lot of water. When the river floods, which usually happens in June as the snow in the mountains is melting, or when the river ice goes out in the spring, the water backs up some distance in this gulley and overflows the banks.

About 1901 Dunc McKenzie was riding along the river on his way to the J. L. Sparrow ranch located beside Blood Indian Creek near the site of the buildings of the present V-V ranch. When he arrived at what was usually a dry creek bed he found it full and the water over the banks hiding the dip, on each side, when the trail crossed. It was thought afterwards that he must have ridden over the bank on one side of the trail, into the flood. When they found his body there was a mark on the side of his head as though the struggling horse had hit him.

The body was buried on a knoll at the ranch where, two years before, the body of Hector Prince had been buried. A somewhat similar fate had met Hector and it is a strange coincidence that they both were from the vicinity of Prince Albert, Saskatchewan.

For two years James Rae was located across the river north of Bindloss. This ranch was later owned, in succession, by Fergus Kennedy and his sons, Joe and Frank, Clint Jarboe, Owen Stringam and then Willis McLennan. In 1899 Bill Rae, a brother of James, and Hector Prince were trying to cross some cattle from the south

Tom McCarthy, Mrs. W. D. McLennan, May McLennan, George Campbell, W. B. Campbell at McLennan's ranch. Essex car.

side. The cattle worked their way down stream into swimming water. Hector was on the down-stream side trying to keep them from turning back. He was riding a young horse and when he turned it up stream in deep water it fell backwards. Bill saw Hector quit the horse and drop into the water. When he didn't come up and the cattle and horse swung around and headed back to the south shore Bill let his horse turn too.

Bill, who was a raw-boned six footer, couldn't swim a stroke. His horse was small and when he saw that it was being forced farther east by the strong current to where the landing, if any, would be against the steep shore which for some distance was a cutbank, he decided that he was too heavy for the little fellow and that if he stayed in the saddle they probably would not make it. He took a firm grip of the mane with his left hand, slipped out of the saddle, grasped the tail in his right and, by pulling on the tail and pushing against the pony's neck, kept it angled across the current until they reached land. When he was out of the water and could see no sign of Hector he rode the twenty-five miles to our ranch where the men shaped some grappling irons, loaded a row boat on a wagon, went back with Bill and found the body. There were no marks to show that he had been struck by the horse and it was supposed that Hector, who was an excellent swimmer, had been seized with cramps. The body was taken to the ranch and buried on the knoll where two years later Dunc McKenzie's body lay for a few months. In the winter Hector's brother came from Prince Albert with a dogteam and took the remains back with him. A few years later it was the task of someone else to take Dunc's body over the same route in the same manner.

I don't know when the ferry at the point where the Medicine Hat/Battleford Trail crossed the Red Deer was installed but about 1900 it was necessary to stretch a new cable over the river. Someone had brought it out from the Hat but nothing had been done about getting it in its place.

Our cattle, at that time, ranged from west of Blood Indian Creek to east of Lonesome Coulee (Alkali Creek on the map). We always gathered the first week in July for calf branding and turned the bulls loose at the same time. The bulls, 120 to 130 in number, half of them Shorthorn and half of them Hereford, were wintered at a camp on the river north of the present hamlet of Buffalo.

We called this the "Dry Tree Camp" because when we arrived in the country the flat on which the camp was later located, was covered with dry cottonwood trees which had been killed at some time by a prairie fire and had lost their bark. Some of the trees were lying on the ground but many were standing and their white trunks and limbs could be seen for many miles. For several years they supplied us with much of our stove wood.

Fergus Kennedy had asked us to help him to stretch the new ferry cable. (In those days people didn't run to the government for everything that they wanted done.) It was time to turn out the bulls and brand the calves. Instead of putting the bulls across the river at the ranch as usual, we moved them from where they were being herded at a spring twelve miles southeast of the ranch, to the flat northwest of Bindloss and set up camp where Gene Fitger's buildings were built many years later. I was eleven years old and I have never

202

seen nor tasted gooseberries like those we picked that summer along the river west of the camp. They were ripe and sweet and looked like large black grapes.

Besides our outfit Fergus Kennedy and his two husky sons were there, also a man named Canfield and his son. This man who stayed in this area only one or two years, was from the timber country in Michigan and had located on the Charlie Martin spring eight miles west, a site occupied the next year by Clint Jarboe, held by him for about fourteen years and then sold to the late W. D. McLennan.

When everything was in readiness the eight or ten younger men, stripped to their underwear, carried a rope attached to one end of the cable across the river and fastened it to the capstan. While they were in the water working with the cable, one of the men, Dave Henry who was a "rep" with us from Black's ranch (later John Wilson's) took cramps. He didn't cry out but we on the bank saw him struggling and Fergus Kennedy who knew what was happening, called to the others, "Go to him!" Saul Boyer, who at that time was about as active as a man can be, got to his side just as he keeled over. They carried him to shore and, needless to say, he didn't go back into the water.

The job was completed and the ferry, which had been pulled out on the north bank, was put in operation. We threw our cattle across the river and herded them northwest for seven miles. From here we drove almost directly west and the next day made our camp at a spring in Lonesome Coulee, eight miles north of the river which in this area runs northeast for nine miles from Alf Campbell's buildings, makes a sharp turn and flows east southeast for another nine miles.

My cousin Norman Gordon, who was three years older than I and who came out from Winnipeg during school holidays each year for four or five years, two men and I moved the cattle and saddle horses. Father and the other men, except the cook who drove the wagon, "rode circle" north and south of us. When we left the camp ground in the coulee and moved west the next day we had three times the number of cattle we had started with.

One of the men who was helping to trail the herd was "green." He was ambitious though and chafed at not being allowed to ride circle. Father told him that he had not had enough experience and that he would get lost but he was confident that he was being under-rated. The day that we moved west from the Coulee, Father told this man that he could ride that day with him. They rode northwest from the camp for five or six miles, then Father gradually swung in an arc toward the east. About noon they were coming into the Coulee over almost the same route on which we had moved the day before. Father asked him if he had ever seen this part of the country. "No,"

203

he had never seen it. They rode on down to the campsite but not until Father had let him have a drink at the spring and had shown him where he had unrolled his bed the night before, did he know where he was. "Now," Father asked, "do you understand why you are not ready to ride circle?" and the poor fellow manfully admitted that he still had a lot to learn.

THE ROCKIES

You rocks of ages with your snowy brows
That pierce the clouds, aspiring to the stars,
How pure, untrammeled, silent are the snows
That smooth those brows and shroud your stoney scars;

That thwart the most intriguing smiles of Sol
To penetrate, disrupt your changeless veil,
And have withstood through time, the fiercest squall —
Are there some secret springs which you avail?

Each morning, long before his rising rays
Have made the roofs of city dwellings bright,
The smiling sun to you his tribute pays
And tints with pink those peaks of purest white.

How pure and deep your aged whiteness is!
For in its depth and pureness disappear
Those short lived blushes rising with the kiss
Of Sol's red rays, bestowed year after year.

How many times your flashing drapes are changed:
At evening purple, midday grey or green.
When snowy clouds about your breasts have ranged,
In transitory ermine robes you're seen.

Down steep ravines, impetuous icy streams
Plunge headlong to your valleys far below
Where humans implement their dearest dreams
And Eden's varied vegetation grow.

The humble foothills kneel about your feet
And to your greatness lift adoring eyes.
Did e'er such faithfulness and grandeur meet
Beneath creation's universal skies?

What monuments of the Creator's art!
What inspiration for His creature, man —
Serene and steadfast, strong and pure in heart;
Continued upward look since time began.

CHAPTER V

News that Andrew and Alex Gordon had settled in wild, open country in western Assiniboia spread among friends and relatives in Ontario and in 1897 four of these arrived at the ranch for a visit. There was a cousin of Father's, Lindsay Elliott, who later settled northeast of Calgary, a more distant cousin, Frank Campbell, who returned to his carriage business in Ontario, and two brothers of Alex, Charlie and George Gordon, both of whom in after years, settled in British Columbia.

A few days after their arrival Father took them south and west of the buildings for several miles then circled toward the east to let them see the country and perhaps have a shot at an antelope. I was allowed to go with them. I have forgotten what they shot but remember two things; out in the rough hills southwest we saw a deer with a spotted fawn and when, on the way back, we were five miles from home we saw a dark object more than a mile farther east. Father told the men that it was a large rock but the wishful hunters

A herd of fast disappearing species of the prairies, 1969.

Rattlesnake.

Cowboy and his horse "Ribbon".

were sure that they were looking at a bear. Two of them went on foot around a large slough to stalk it. Father let them go and then drove around the other end of the slough, which covers about 300 acres, to meet them.

The "bear" is still there. It is one of those large rocks which appear here and there on the prairie — possibly deposited by glaciers. They are partly buried in the earth and have been used for centuries, probably, as scratching posts by buffalo and, later, by cattle.

Through the years beasts tramping around them have cut up the soil with their hooves and winds have blown away the loosened dirt until, in our time, as much as four and five feet of the sides of the rocks, once buried, have been bared and the rock left sitting in a large wallow.

That winter Father and another cousin, Sam Elliott, drove overland from the Hat when the prairie was covered by quite a depth of snow. When they left their last camp Father realized that he was becoming snow blind. Sam knew nothing of the country and so could not drive without direction. He would hold a coat sleeve so that Father could look through it and spot some landmark. When it was reached the act was repeated. Part of the time Sam must have walked on the road ahead of the team because I remember that when they came down the hill at the ranch he was walking ahead and Father was driving. Sam's eyes had played out too and they spent several days in a dark room with tea leaf poultices applied to their eyes.

Snow blindness is very painful and miserable. Your eyes seem to be full of sand, burn and water keeps forming a film over them. Things within your vision become distorted. To be driving a black team or riding a black horse helps to prevent it. When I was riding the prairie in winter I carried a strip of black velvet which I could tie across my face just below my eyes. One winter I used a green mosquito netting. Colored glasses with the sort of frames that we have today would have saved us from its torture, but if your face was exposed all day to from twenty to forty below zero temperatures, usually accompanied by wind, it would almost certainly freeze wherever the ordinary metal frames touched it.

Ranching in those days demanded a great deal from men, especially in winter. At the ranch in the first years were men like Tom Mossop, George Findlay, Billie McKay, Billie Bracey, Neil Swinton. Jesse Bishop was in charge of the drive when the S C cattle, which Gordon, Ironside and Fares bought from Stewart and Christie of Pincher Creek, were moved to the Red Deer River range. I believe Lew Rizzly and Dave Williamson were with him. Billie Henry and Percy Stimson also each spent a short time on the ranch. With the exception of Tom and George, all had been in the West for some time. There were others who had come from the "East" or from the "Old Country." All had stamina.

As the number of stock increased, more water holes had to be opened each day every winter on a river frontage of twenty-five miles. There were several good springs that flowed all winter but on the north side they were not so plentiful and had to be supplemented with holes in the river ice at strategic spots. You didn't just open a hole anywhere; it was usually where the water was not deep but swift. Such a watering spot would stay partially open, at least, all day even in very cold weather.

Those watering places east, were looked after by men at the two camps — one six miles east and the other twelve miles. Those near the ranch and west for six miles were cared for by men who rode out from the home place each day. Seven and eight miles west were two excellent springs, later part of the ranches of Magnus Bjork and Fred Nelson.

The more adverse the weather the more necessity there was to get out among the stock. Many days a man was out from morning until night fighting the elements, without any food for himself or his horse. The man had to know how to keep both hands and feet from freezing without getting too warm. Despite the hardships I never heard of any man during those first ten years, objecting to going out because it was "too cold" or "too stormy."

George Findlay was a young man who had come from the East to Manitoba and then farther west with Alex Gordon. He was a good worker, always willing and reliable. He liked to ride and for the winter of 1897 "kept up" a tall, partly broken, bay gelding. Each morning, when George got on it, it would try to unload him. George was not a bronc rider but he would get a good grip on the "goose neck" and stay on top. The horse was not getting much quieter and soon, each morning, George was taking longer to climb on. One morning, as he was "fooling around" before mounting, Father went over to speak to him. It was a cold winter morning but the sweat was running down George's face. He had "lost his nerve" and was afraid of the horse but had not complained. Father told him to put the horse back in the barn and take another. It would not have been fair or reasonable to ask a man in George's condition to ride a half broken horse, especially at that time of year. Besides it was doing the horse no good — it knew that the man was afraid of it. Down through the years Father had the reputation of always being concerned for the welfare of those who worked for him.

Not many days after the above episode I heard Alex say to Father, "I think we should sack Findlay." I didn't know what they meant but was sure it was something that would hurt George and he was a good friend of mine so I, eight years old, found him and told him what I had heard. They did fire him but he would not leave (it was sixty-five miles to town) and was re-hired. When the partnership between Andrew and Alex was dissolved George went with Alex but returned twice in later years to work for us, mostly as a teamster.

On the river flat northwest and three to five miles from the ranch buildings there are several patches of alkali. When wet these spots are quite slippery. One day in the summer of 1897 Father was alone on the flat moving some cattle. He was chasing an animal when his horse slipped on some alkali and fell. Father's right foot was trapped and twisted so that the toes pointed backward. He took hold of it and managed to get it back into normal position but of course could put no weight on it. Standing on one foot he wrote on the saddle, "leg broken three miles west." He tied the reins to the pommel of the saddle so that the horse could not feed and turned it loose. It started for home but by the time it had gone a mile the horse had worked the reins loose and began to graze. It would feed for a while and then with reins dragging move a little farther.

At this slow pace it finally reached some higher land about a mile from the buildings. Some one saw it and three of the men hitched a team to the democrat and went to investigate "a loose saddle horse." They didn't notice the writing on the saddle but knew the horse and with one man mounted drove west until they found Father.

Ready for work, 1912.

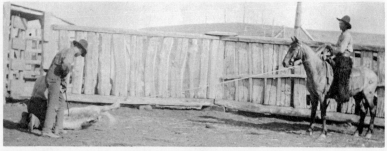

Branding — Gordon Ranch.

208

When he had turned the horse loose he had watched it as it moved toward the buildings and when he saw it start to graze he knew that it had either loosened the reins or rubbed off the bridle. With plenty to eat it might decide that it was close enough to home so he began to crawl. When the men found him he had crawled more than a mile on his hands and knees dragging that foot.

He didn't go to a doctor — it was sixty-five miles to the nearest one. Mother took care of it and he was soon around on home-made crutches, but that ankle bothered him the rest of his life.

The next summer they began building a large branding corral on the north side of the river where we now ran the cows and calves. A wonderful stand of tall cottonwood trees supplied abundance of material and three or four men who had been raised in Ontario and knew how to handle an axe were busy felling and trimming them. Father had just finished one and was moving to another when someone yelled — one of those tall trees was falling toward him. The man who felled it should have known which way it would fall but gave the warning too late. Father saw the tree coming and ran but one of the branches crashed on his head and, as he said "drove him into the ground." The men took him across the river in a row boat where a team and wagon had been left that morning, and then home.

Mother was in a coulee about half a mile from the house that afternoon picking berries. Something told her that she should go home and, always obedient to such promptings, she arrived there just as Father was being carried into the house. She nursed him for a few days, then he was "on the go" again — a very hardy man.

MARCH

Faithful old Sol, climbing higher each day,
Persuades her to try her own hand —
"Stir up old nature and call back the birds,
And flush all the frost from the land."
Decked in her own gorgeous garment of green
With pussies and crocuses trimmed
Wonders of Winter she'll fade with her charms
And reign for a spell in their stead.

SPRING

When the frost king yields his tenure
To the rule of eager spring
With her open skies of azure
Filled with wildlife on the wing.

209

Mother earth prepares her garden,
Renovates the greening leas,
Rids the waters of their burden
Sends the sap up through the trees.

A bunch of cattle were being fed in the brush below the buildings, during the winter of 1916-17, as usual. For hauling a small load of sheaves, a sleigh with a platform 8 x 16, having a gate four feet high at each end, was often used. Father had taken a load into the brush, had spread it about a mile and one half from the buildings and was returning. It was a stormy day and a strong, cold wind was blowing. He was standing a few feet behind the front gate with his coat collar up and his face turned away from the wind. The team was following the track through the brush when a large willow caught on one corner of the front gate on the sleigh. As it slipped off, it whipped Father across the face, knocking him down and injuring one eye. I saw the team stop at the gate below the barn but could not see Father. When I got to them he was just getting to his feet. He had lain unconscious while the faithful team had walked at least a mile.

The Empress-Bassano branch line of the C.P.R. was operating then within two miles of the buildings and we were able to get him on a freight train of which Pete Robertson was the conductor. He was taken to Medicine Hat for treatment but never regained sight in that eye.

In telling of Father's accident while they were building the corral on the north side of the river, I mentioned that they were building over there because the cows and calves were now ranging on that side. They had been running in the country southwest and we had built a camp for the 'linerider' about twelve miles southwest of the home place.

The linerider was expected to know where the different bunches were grazing and watering and to see that they didn't stray from the range. Charlie Robertson held this job in 1898. He heard that a few of our cows with calves had been seen sixty miles west and made a trip to investigate. While up there a certain rancher suggested that if Charlie would let a few of our cows drift in that direction once in a while he, the rancher, would take care of Charlie. But Charlie was not for sale. When he returned to the ranch with the cows and calves he reported the offer to Father. Sometime later Father was in that area, met the rancher and hold him what Charlie had said. The fellow was still chagrined because of the rejection of his offer. Stretching out one arm and hitting the wrist with his other hand he said,

"Andy, if I had had a knife that long I'd have driven it into Charlie Robertson's heart."

In September just before we returned to the Hat for school, I heard Charlie ask Father for a raise in wages. He was getting twenty dollars per month and asked for twenty-five. Father said, "I know you are worth it Charlie but if I pay you twenty-five I'll have to raise all the wages." Charlie felt sure that he could get that wage somewhere else (perhaps it had been offered to him for he was a better than average man) and he left.

The cook, who drove the 'mess wagon', rarely knew where the springs and waterholes were located, so whenever they moved camp, someone, called the pilot, who did know, rode ahead and the cook followed. Behind him was the day wrangler with the saddle herd. As the number of cattle increased and more men were needed to handle them, a second wagon called the 'bed wagon' was added and was driven by the 'night hawk', the man who herded the horses at night. Each wagon was pulled by four horses over the virgin prairie, sometimes following a 'buffalo rut', (which almost always led to water) often with no track at all to follow.

It may have been in the same year as the Charlie Robertson episode, that Father was piloting the wagon in the area between the Rainy Hills and the Crow Buttes. As he was riding along his horse 'pricked its ears', lowered its head and snorted. A few yards ahead of them a horse's head seemed to be lying on top of the prairie. Father, seeing that there was life in the eyes and that they belonged to a horse in a 'soaphole', loped his horse to the nearest bit of high ground and rode in a small circle. This was a well-known signal recognized by riders as a sign that the person signalling wanted the presence of whoever should see the maneuver. The cook and the wrangler were soon there. They pulled the horse out of the mire and, when they had helped it to its feet, it staggered away a short distance and began to graze.

George Maxted was a short, red-headed Irishman born in Ontario, who had for six years looked after the stable, wrangled the work horses and saddle horses at the ranch each morning, saw that there was always a supply of stove wood for the cook and handled the hounds and the stallion, at that time a tall chestnut standard bred that could trot as fast as some horses could lope. It was not mean, but it didn't like to see a man on a horse. One day George rode out to its bunch. When it saw him coming it started toward him with its head swung around to one side (a danger signal) and moved faster than George expected. Before he had time to dismount the stallion had reached him, its neck now straight and mouth open to grab him. George happened to be carrying an unloaded shotgun. He

211

shoved the barrel into the stallion's mouth and yelled as the horse he was riding sprang away in fear. (Did you ever hear a frightened Irishman yell?) After that he always made sure to dismount in time.

When I was eleven years old he had me on the other end of a cross-cut saw a few times, teaching me how to cut wood. Handling one of those saws looks easy but when you have someone on the other end who doesn't know when and how to pull and when to 'let it ride', the job can be exasperating. The saw would go back and forth several times over a log, then George would stop, push back his hat, swear 'like a trooper' for what seemed a few minutes, pull his hat down again and tell me nicely how I should hold my hands. We would try it once more but soon George would be 'letting off steam' again. This would go on for an hour or more, then George would think of some other chore that needed doing. His labor was not in vain for, even if I do say it myself, I did learn to handle one of those saws, at least as well as the average person.

We had, at three different times, a pet antelope. Someone would find a little fellow stretched out in the grass believing that it was hidden, catch it and bring it home. Each one, in turn, was named 'Jerry' and each one had the run of the ranch, even into the cook's sanctuary — his kitchen. Teased and played with by the men, they could be, at times, dangerous. Their horns were sharp and they knew how to use them. When the first one had been there two years the hounds took after it one day and mauled it so that, even though the cook, Jack (Fatty) Richardson, nursed it for several days, it died.

Kid and Bob Howe at the Gordon Ranch, 1924, breaking a horse to team work.

The horse stable was a long 'bank barn'. A heavy stone wall formed the side next to the bank. It was roofed with willows and sod. There were stalls for twenty-two head and a large box stall, with separate outside entrance, at each end. A feed passage six feet wide ran the length of the barn in front of the mangers and the passage behind the horses was ten feet wide.

In summer there was usually a good sized pile of manure outside, a few feet from the stable door (the barn was cleaned every morning, winter and summer). Someone would be leading a pair of horses out of the barn when suddenly there would be a 'ping' as the antelope landed, from the roof, on the manure pile and away would go the horses. The air would be blue as the man took after Jerry with whatever was at hand. Sentence of death was passed on him many times but never executed.

Each of these pets, while we had them, would stray away for as long as a week at a time. The first day or two everyone was glad that he had left but when he returned he received a royal welcome. The second Jerry had a wide red rag fastened around his neck as a protection against hunters — anyone, we thought, seeing the rag would conclude that the antelope must be someone's pet. However, one day two strangers drove into the ranch and confessed that they had shot such an antelope on top of the hill where the road led down to the ranch. They were the most unwelcomed people ever to visit the ranch and were told in emphatic language that if they could not see a red tag at that distance (Jerry had stood about one hundred yards from the trail) they had no business using a gun. He was buried with full honors.

The third Jerry was with us until he was three years old and quite strong. Father and an old man named Guardipie, were setting up sheaves one day and Jerry thought some of the stooks were not made properly so wrecked them. When he grew tired of playing with the sheaves he turned to Mr. Guardipie and proved too much for him. He got the old man down and Father had to go to his rescue. While Father held Jerry by the horns, Mr. Guardipie tied the rope from the bundle of binder twine around his neck. They pushed and dragged him to the fence and tied him to a post. About half an hour later they saw Jerry going east on the flat dragging the rope.

Ranchers travelling from the Red Deer River country to the Hat over the Battleford trail almost always stopped either at noon or at night at the ranch of John Wilson, 18 miles south of the River. Two or three were at that ranch a few days after Jerry's escape. One of them, Chris Gallup, who was on his way to town, told the others that he had seen a buck antelope with a rope around its neck about five miles north of Wilson's ranch (that would be eighteen miles from our place). That was the last that we heard of Jerry. He was unafraid of a saddle horse or team and probably proved too great a temptation for someone with a gun.

When, in the fall of 1899, the South African war broke out between Great Britain and the Boer Republic of South Africa "an electric current" flashed across the continent from Halifax to Victoria,

213

thrilling all English speaking hearts at any rate, and a cry went up that the war was Canada's as well as England's. "The enthusiasm of the Canadians took England by surprise," said the Prince of Wales, later King Edward the VII. "It took the world at large much more by surprise," added Lord Salisbury. From Halifax to Victoria, Canadians promptly answered the call for volunteers.

THE OUTCAST

(Not Bill)

Dark and handsome and tall,
Blood of earls in his veins,
Born and reared in a titled hall,
Bred to govern domains.

Stormy weather or fair,
Dawn 'til dark on the range,
Seasoned cowhand, embrowned and spare —
Forty dollars his wage.

By his family disowned,
(Social sins caused his fall);
All old ties seemed forever tombed —
Then came Motherland's call.

'Neath the sod on the Veldt,
Far from Albion's strands,
Soundly sleeps one whom Fate had dealt
One of many 'stacked' hands.

Word, that a mounted regiment to be known as Lord Strathcona's Horse was to be formed, reached the ranch and three men, Bill Hammond, Billie Goodfellow and Tom Greaves enlisted. Tom Rutherford and Dunc Sanderson also joined but I am not sure that they were working there at the time of enlistment. Tom Greaves and Billie Goodfellow were reported killed in action. Tom Rutherford and Bill Hammond joined the Transvaal Police force at the end of the war and we heard that both found mates over there. Dunc Sanderson returned to the West and later was well known around Banff.

The cook, who held that job with us, not of necessity but as a new experience, was an Englishman named Sydney Hyde. When he heard that his regiment in the Old Country had been called up he left at once and joined it in South Africa. After the war he returned to his native land and when last heard from was working at his old job — chef in a hotel in London.

214

The regiment of Lord Strathcona's Horse was manned by men from the prairies — men who could ride and shoot. Many were colorful characters. It was said that in Africa some of the British regular officers complained that members of this regiment failed to salute when met by these officers. Lt. Col. Sam Steele was reported as having replied that he had not brought these men to Africa to salute officers but to fight. Bill Hammond was scouting one day when a Boer got the drop on him and started riding to his camp (the Boer's) with Bill as his prisoner. He made the mistake of leaving Bill's rifle hanging on the side of the saddle. After they had ridden some distance the Boer happened to turn his head, Bill tipped up the rifle and shot him. He found some loose change on the fellow, took it, his rifle and shells, and rode into Ladysmith. Here he spent a few days celebrating. One officer got him to the edge of town, then Bill decided that he was going back. As reported later, the officer (of the Imperial Forces) said, "Come with me or I'll shoot you," to which Bill calmly replied, "Shoot! I've got a gun and I can shoot too." He went back.

Bill came back to Canada for a visit before joining the police. He came to our house in town to see Father and gave him a bullet which he said was one of those he had taken from the Boer scout. When he returned to the Transvaal he served a term in the police force and then married a widow who owned what in this country would be known as a ranch.

Bill had come to our place from south of the line. He was one of those men who never passed through a doorway before 'sizing up' those who happened to be in the room — apparently watching for someone who might be looking for him.

CHAPTER VI

Father was a member of the Methodist Church. For many years he was one of the trustees of that church in Medicine Hat. When Mount Royal College was founded in Calgary under the leadership of the late Dr. G. W. Kerby, Father was a member of the original Board of Trustees.

The ranching country north of Medicine Hat from the forks of the Red Deer and Saskatchewan River to Brooks on the west was without any kind of church service. Father discussed this with Rev. J. W. Saunby who had succeeded Rev. R. A. Scarlett as Methodist minister in the Hat and the Church decided to send out a man each year as a "summer supply". I will not record the name of the first one, as he was a disappointment. He did not move from the ranch during the entire summer and spent most of his time lying around

215

reading light literature. Needless to say the men had no use for him and when, in the fall, one reported having met the "preacher" on his way "out" he was asked, "was he reading a dime novel?"

Father told a representative of the Board of Home Missions that if they could not send some one better, to not send any. Men of very high caliber followed — one each summer for six or seven years. Among them was W. J. Spence, a professor in Wesley College, Winnipeg, and later for many years, Registrar of the University of Manitoba. Others were (not necessarily in chronological order) Warren Rothwell, George W. Sparling, Joseph F. Woodsworth, Robert H. Davis from Wesley College and William Vance from Victoria College in Toronto. Mr. Sparling went to West China as a missionary and for many years was head of the Methodist College in Chengtu. Mr. Woodsworth, whose father served a long term as Superintendent of Home Missions for the Church, became principal of the Indian Industrial School at Red Deer, Alberta, a position which he held until retirement.

These men made their headquarters at the ranch. We supplied a horse and saddle and they visited the ranches on each side of the Red Deer from the Forks to the P.K. Ranch, north of Brooks. It took two weeks to make the circuit. I believe that each one of them, at least once, also visted the ranches on the west side of the Saskatchewan between the Forks and the Hat.

THE SKY PILOT

"I wish you'd move a little faster, Buck
You make me so annoyed! Have you no pride?"
Old Buck cast one ear back then, satisfied
He need not fear the sting of spur or quirt,
Jogged on at his smooth, self-appointed gait.
Behind him, coming in a cloud of dust,
The Pilot saw another man and mount.
  "Jim Swan" rode up, his rangy bay all wet
With sweat and fretted by a heavy bit and spurs.
"How do."
  "Good day, you must have ridden far."
"Just from the Creek," and backward tossed his head.
"Is that a bronco?"
  "Kinda. Been so mean
I thought I'd drag it outa him to-day."
The Pilot glanced in admiration at
The graceful, youthful figure at his side
And wondered such a man could be so cruel.

216

"You going over to the ranch?"
                    "I am."
"You working there?"
                    "No, preaching is my job."
"I see! Don't look like we would get much rain."
The flimsy veil, which for a moment dropped
Between the men, was quickly raised again.
"You know the ford?"
                    "I don't, I've wondered how
I'd get across."
                    "Just follow me, and keep
Above the riffle. Might get wet below."

Each year, from east or west, the Church had sent a student
missionary to this "field" to serve the ranchers of the open range.
To those who came it seemed their "parish was the world." With
horse and saddlebags they rode two weeks to close the circuit.
Welcome beamed from every unlocked door; it mattered not what
kind, what creed — there's but one Book, one Lord.

The love of God dwelt in each pilot's heart. They passed none
by, and sunshine lingered in their wake. "When will you come this
way again?" In feeding others, they themselves were fed. With
gratitude to God for open doors and open hearts; for opportunities
to show the likeness of the One they served, they travelled o'er the
prairie trails and paths. To them goodwill and aid were freely given.

"Your pony's getting tender underfoot —
I'd better tack some shoes on him right now."
So Buck was laid upon the ground and tied.
'Twas 'Happy Jack' who shod the Pilot's horse
And proved that underneath a hardened shell
The most of men are courteous and kind.
"This mount of yours has made a lot of miles —
He must be tired, and there's nothing more
Fatiguing than to ride a horse whose legs
Are weary. Take this Pinto horse of mine
And let Buck rest. Then pick him up next week
When you have made the loop." The one who spoke
Was Alex, he who had a golden heart."
He did not call it love for fellowman —
In fact, with him, such actions had no name —
To help another his innate desire:
This time his thought was for both man and beast.

217

The gentle lady, years and seas from 'home.'
Was greatly pleased to have each share with her
Her 'pause for tea.' "Unless you pour," she said,
"The water on the tea, the 'cup' is spoiled."

Where'er the Pilot called, a portion of The Word was read. Then knees were bent, all heads were bowed, and, led by him, they raised their hearts to One from whom no thought, no word, no deed is hid; who watches over all. They thanked Him for his love and care; his mercy craved for any evil found in them. "Forgive us Lord, you know our frame. Teach us to know Your will, and grant that we may follow where we're led. Keep all from harm and ill until we meet again." A simple word with God.

The open range is but a memory now, and each year when the roll is called, one more of those who rode and loved it, fails to show or answer to his name. The shadow of a portion of a trail may here or there be found.

The "men of God" who in the few short months allotted each, sought out the Master's sheep to nurture them, renew their faith and draw them to that straight and narrow road that we so often lose, are fading memories too. In later years they, each to manhood grown, rode other trails, some worn well by those who'd gone before — a few were barely blazed. One pioneered upon a foreign field and left his body there — pierced like his Lord's.

Those pilots served their generation well and, having run his race, each fell on sleep. The last to leave for Home was Little Joe — a mighty spirit cramped by walls of clay. Endeared to all he met by selflessness, concern for others, and a simple faith, he did not say, "A leader I would be!" That he might follow in his Master's steps and be as one that serves — this was his prayer. One day "the papers" said that Joe had died. But that was not the case. True, they had laid his body 'neath the sod: that body which for many years had housed, and been controlled by, One who was his constant Counsellor, his Comforter and Friend. But he, his stint of earthly labor done, has been transferred — gone up the ladder to the Master's door. He truly "made his life sublime" and "left behind him footprints on the sands of time."

CHAPTER VII

We always had a few hundred head of our own cattle on the ranch but the large herd which was there for nine years and numbered, at one time, approximately 12,000, belonged to Gordon, Ironside & Fares Co. Ltd. The 'Firm' had no interest in the ranch or the horses. These belonged entirely to us. We were paid a certain

Gus Hanson — 1914.

sum per head per year for running their cattle which were all branded S C (ess cee) on the left ribs. This brand and the ear mark, 'crop the right and undercrop the left,' were obtained from the Stewart Ranch Co., of Pincher Creek, Alberta, when the Firm bought their cattle in 1896 and moved them to the Red Deer ranch.

Toward the last of June each year we shipped a train load (at least twenty cars) of five and six year old steers (18 to a car) to England.

"What better proof," asked the Medicine Hat News, "can we ask as to the adaptability of this country as a cattle range, or what better advertisement of its values for beef producing be given than was furnished this week when Gordon and Ironsides shipped to the British markets two trainloads of beef cattle taken off their Red Deer range — 562 head of as fine beef as ever left the range, and this in the month of June."

(From the Calgary Weekly Herald for July 5, 1900).

These steers received no supplementary feed either in summer or winter except as calves. There was an abundance of cured prairie grasses, excellent shelter in the coulees and along the river, and no fences to prevent the cattle from drifting with a storm until they found shelter. Another lot was shipped the last part of September. This shipment went to Winnipeg where it was re-sorted and part reshipped. It consisted of five and six year old steers that had been missed in June, or were not in condition for export at that time (to be fit for export a steer had to have "his britches tied"), a few top four-year-olds to fill out a car, and some dry cows and bulls which had been on the ranch long enough.

Cattle were wild in those days and, once located on a range, needed no one to tell them when a storm was coming; they themselves were the best of weather prophets. If you saw the cattle working toward shelter you could be sure that a storm was brewing and when you saw them leaving the shelter and climbing the hills to graze, even if it was cold, you knew that better weather was on the way.

It always took at least three days to move the beef herd to the stockyards at Stair (in later years at Suffield) starting from a camp a few miles south of the ranch. There would be 350 to 400 steers in the herd. Shorthorn, Hereford and Shorthorn-Hereford cross — almost everyone horned. When they were being gathered on the range there would be some great fights as the different small bunches came together, meeting perhaps for the first time in a year.

As we were leaving the ranch one year we had among the five- and six-year-olds, a gray roan steer with white markings and a pair of horns set just right for fighting. He was a Hereford-Shorthorn cross and one of the prettiest beef animals that I have seen. He had won all his encounters. The herd was moving along quietly about seven miles south of the buildings when one steer with whom he had had a tough fight, apparently thought he saw a good chance to get the jump on him and they tangled again. As they were butting and straining, each trying to get that winning 'hold', two others started hooking the 'champ' in the hind legs. He broke from them and raced as fast as he could toward a small knoll with the entire herd running and bellowing after him.

When he reached the top of the knoll, like a flash he swapped ends, threw his head in the air and with his four feet close together, his tail hanging straight down, was ready to meet 'all comers'. That herd split like a stream of water hitting a large rock — not one had enough nerve to tackle him. It was one of the most courageous and thrilling acts that I have ever witnessed, and he had to go for beef!

The trek to the railroad through wide open country, making a new camp each night, night herding both cattle and saddle horses, was just part of the day's work for men who were in the saddle, day after day, from May until October. The nights were usually cold in September. Often when you awoke in the morning, if you slept outside of the tent, your hair would be frozen to the tarp. When you were dressed you took your towel, went down to the slough or spring, broke the ice near the edge and washed the sleep

220

out of your eyes. Then, after rolling your bed, you were ready for hotcakes, slices of bacon (not these thin shavings that you get today), biscuits and coffee. If you wished any, there was always a pot of cooked prunes, cooked dried apples, cooked dried peaches or perhaps a mixture of dried apples and apricots.

The train of empty stock cars was 'made-up' in the Hat and, on the shipping day, moved up to Stair or Suffield with the Brand Inspector, J. H. G. Bray, an ex-N.W.M.P. Sergeant-major, on board. We always tried to have the cattle in the stockyards before the train arrived. If there was a misunderstanding regarding the time of arrival, the crew and any spectators were asked to stay in the caboose out of sight until the cattle were in the pens. As I said, they were wild and a small thing could make it almost impossible to corral them. When the cattle were loaded the train moved back to town where another crew with their engine and caboose took over. In those days stock trains moved at the same rate of speed as a passenger train — beaten in the long haul by the 'silk trains' only. They stopped at divisional points for change of crew and engine, and at some of the others for 'orders'. When they arrived in Winnipeg the cattle were unloaded, fed, watered, reloaded and shipped to Montreal where they were placed on a cattle boat bound for Liverpool, England.

The shipper was required to send at least one man with each shipment, both on the train and on the boat. The man was given free passage by the railroad to destination and his return ticket was purchased at a rate below regular fare. The crews on these stock trains were always hospitable and friendly; so long as the stockman was reasonable, he was made quite at home in the caboose.

WHERE ARE YOUR THOUGHTS?

How often in the day's decline
My thoughts play truant from my books
And to the plains for which I pine,
To which my spirit ever looks.

They hie away and view their vast,
Unbounded home — a land of hills,
Of vales and plains. In days now past,
The cooling water formed in rills.

And trickled downward from the springs
Hid 'mid the hollows of the hills.
No wonder that my spirit clings,
And, with the memory, ever thrills.

221

Of those domains, where, once at will,
Unnumbered herds of bison strayed
With creatures of their kind, until
The white man came and claimed, and made

That free and glorious realm his home.
Where once the Red man grazed secure
There now the white man's bison roam;
The scenes may change but not the lure.

MY MOTHER

Of all my memories there's none more dear
Than of Mother. Inborn queenly grace,
A stately step, a kind and peaceful face,
Revealed a constant inner light — so clear.
Those open, smiling eyes, devoid of fear,
Approved of neither work nor deed — if base.
Her understanding heart could find a place
In which to counsel culprits, cheer and steer
Them to a straight new path. How oft I tried
Her love and tol'rance; still she never changed.
So soon as I could speak she taught me how
To pray, to reverence God, His Word to know.
Though life did soil my soul with many stains
The blessing of her love and life remains.
I know I've failed your hope and caused you pain,
And yet I'm sure that when I leave this shell
And stray, a stranger, through the "golden gate,"
The heart which here forgave so many wrongs,
Will once again speak through those lips, those eyes:
Again, beside your knee, I'll find my peace.

For two summers my cousin Norman, three years older than
I, and I night herded the saddle horses. I would go on guard until
12:30, then call Norman and he would take over. When he saw
the cook moving around in the morning, he would drive the herd
in, place them in the rope corral and have breakfast. It didn't give
two youngsters much time to sleep so, if we had a chance at noon,
we would crawl under the wagon and sleep 'til called.

We were not allowed on the cattle herd at night at first
because only experienced men were used there. After we had night
herded the horses for two summers each was given a shift on
cattle guard with a reliable older person. The flick of a match, the
rustle of a slicker, a sudden noise such as a sneeze or, a sudden

move could start a mild stampede. Singing or talking in a normal manner as you rode around them seemed to quiet them; they would lie down and chew their cuds but be always on the alert for a sudden change of any kind. Those on guard had to know when to let the cattle spread a little to feed and when to bunch them again to bed down.

The first time that I, twelve years of age, was on night guard with the horses, Father and another man were guarding the cattle. After I had been out there about an hour I just couldn't keep awake. I rode around and around the horses, tried to sing, but my eyes would not stay open. The horses were quiet at that time of night and I thought that if I got off and laid down for a few minutes it would help. Soon someone was shaking me. It was a moonlight night and Father, who had a good idea of what would happen, had left the other man with the cattle, had watched the horses and let me have a few minutes of sleep. I was able to stay awake the rest of my 'turn' and never again went to sleep on guard.

Night herding was not a bad job so long as the weather was fairly good: we took it as a matter of course. The outfit was camped one night eight miles southwest of the ranch when one of those blustering thunderstorms came up. The thunder roared, lightning flashed, almost continuously; the cold rain, driven by a very strong wind, was like a flail and of course the darkness was black except when the lightning laid everything bare. One of those on guard with the cattle came to the camp and called for all hands to get out and they were out till morning, mainly because when the storm did stop they weren't sure, in the darkness, where they and the cattle had drifted to. (Each rider had a saddled horse tied to the wagons for use when the guards were changed.) Only the cook and I were left. The tent blew down and the beds were soaked; the grub was safe in the grub box.

The grub box was four feet high and just wide enough to fit into the back of the wagon box (usually on a 'wide gauge' wagon). It was held there by the rods which ordinarily held the end gates in place. It was divided into nine compartments each fitted with a drawer for holding food or utensils. The three lower drawers were deeper than the top ones so that when the door, which was hinged to the bottom of the box, was closed it sloped from top to bottom. A hasp and harness snap secured it at the top. When the door was opened down, it formed a work bench for the cook and rested on a skeleton platform protruding from the end of the wagon box and supported by two guy wires or rods from the top end rod. When the grub box was closed for moving, the stove was made secure on this platform.

One of the riders that stormy night was a young Englishman of excellent character, a member of a large choir in the "Old Country." He had come west for experience on a ranch. He had with him a large stock of sheet music and songs and sang a very good baritone. When he returned to camp in the morning thoroughly soaked and cold, he declared that he was through. "The blooming country is a perfect fraud; I will not ruin my health for any man." However, when he had dried his clothes, had had a good breakfast and got warmed, he felt better, changed his mind and stayed with us all summer.

The 'night hawk' did not fare so well. He did not appear until almost noon and we had only the horses that had been used all night. He had stayed with his herd and somehow kept them together as they drifted with the storm which had come from the west of southwest. In the morning he was on the hills above the river valley ten miles east of the ranch. No fences in those days except small pastures near the buildings. He had breakfast at the ranch (his clothes had dried on him by that time) and someone helped him to get back to camp.

In the first part of the century settlers taking up land south of the Hat and in the Lethbridge-Macleod area made some of the 'originals' with small herds feel that they were being crowded. A few of them moved into our part of the country and some travelled farther north toward the Neutral Hills. One of these men, Phil Miller, drove into the ranch one day with hay rack, mower, rake and a few horses. He wanted to cross the river and asked us to show him the ford. Only the foreman, the cook and I were at home and the foreman, Tom Mossop, asked me if I knew the ford.

It was a crooked ford; you angled downstream from the south bank to a large island. Here you turned sharply to your left to a smaller island and from there it was only a short distance to the north shore. I had crossed the river often at a different spot in a rowboat with the saddle horses swimming, behind at first, and then often ahead as they outdistanced the boat. Because of experiences in their early lives, neither Father nor Mother would let me go into the water and I did not know how to swim.

Earlier that summer I had ridden past the ford with a rider who thought 'kids' were a nuisance. I had watched them take cattle across and had a hazy idea as to the approximate route. A log lay on the small island and as we rode along the south bank I said to this man, "The ford is between here and that log, isn't it?" He answered "yup" and I thought that I knew where the ford was.

The day that Phil wanted to cross I had two saddle horses in the barn. One was a showy little white horse called "Ribbon";

the other was a cool-headed steel gray that proved himself many times in later years to be a very valuable horse. I started to saddle Ribbon but Tom told me that I had better take "Maj'.

When we arrived at the ford I rode into the water and steered straight for the small island. At first the water was only up to the horse's knees but as he went on it rose higher and higher. Phil saw that I was getting into deep water and, being suspicious, he stopped.

Suddenly my horse took a 'flat dive' and the water was up under my arms. I had plenty of nerve in those days and didn't pull on the reins — just clinched the horse a little tighter. He rose and rolled from side to side as he swam out. He was an excellent water horse, a high swimmer — if you took him into swimming water in a normal manner the seat of the saddle would never get wet. When I reached the small island, Phil, who had by now sized up the river, told me to cross to the large island but to "keep above the riffle." I did as he told me and after reaching him turned around and rode before him, above the riffle to the large island then to the small one and from there to the north shore. When he was out of the water I rode back to the south side. If I had taken my showy little Ribbon who was a bit "rattleheaded" it is almost certain that these words would not have been written.

Almost twenty years afterward a veteran of the First World War was hauling wheat across this ford and one day decided to take a short cut. He dropped into this hole with a load of wheat and four horses, lost all, and barely saved his own life. He had only one arm but said afterwards that when he was struggling for his life in the water he was swimming with both.

The year before, the outfit was crossing a large bunch of cattle from south to north. I was not allowed in the water and was along the south bank below the ford with Jim Ward, Pat and Johnnie's father. The wagon boss, Allen Robinson, was riding a pretty, half-broken smoky colored horse which he was grooming for a 'private' for himself and was making a pet of it. He was on the downstream side of the herd and had almost reached the large island with the 'point' of the herd when he saw that some of those behind were getting into swimming water below the ford. The horse was unaccustomed to carrying a load in water and when Allen turned him in the deep water he was upset by the swift current. Allen, wearing a coat and chaps (it was late summer) was thrown into the swift flowing stream and quickly carried away. He was fighting his way gradually toward the south bank but the heavy clothing proved a serious handicap. When he was within thirty feet Jim threw him a rope. After crawling out of the water he lay on his side till he got his breath then, propping himself on one elbow, called, "Here Smokey!" The horse was swimming around and around near the spot where he had lost his rider. As soon as he heard Allen's voice he whinnied and swam directly to him. Jim had to grab the reins and hold him back in order to keep him, in his excitement, from trampling Allen.

CHAPTER VIII

There was quite an influx of ranchers, cowboys, cattle and horses into Canada from south of the border in 1902 and 1903. Among them was a tall thirty-year-old cowboy. Texas-raised, he had spent most of his younger days in that State, New Mexico and California. Hard and 'wise', rough on the outside but true, he sometimes was more kind than the average man.

Jim Spratt was born in England. When he was two years old the family moved to the United States and joined a group of people bound for California by covered wagon. Some of them did not get there. They were attacked by Indians and Jim's parents were among those killed leaving him and a sister to be raised by survivors. As soon as he was big enough to climb on a horse he was riding and from that day until his death, like many others of his 'breed', his life was spent in the saddle. Growing up in the southwest, he learned to ride, to rope, and to handle cattle. He also learned how to pull out a gun and use it. Jim became a good shot with both rifle and six gun which, when he wore it, was in his left arm pit. He could tell many tales of work in California, of riding the Gulf Coast, of trailing beef herds through the Panhandle and up to Abilene or Dodge City. He worked in Wyoming and moved from there to the Dakotas and Montana.

One fall when an outfit in Montana for which he was riding, made the fall shipment of beef he went with it to Chicago. Here he spent a week or so on 'the loop' getting rid of his summer's wages. There were many youngsters in the large cities in those days who seemed to exist as did the alley cats. These little waifs would hang around the saloons and beg coins from patrons as they came or went through the swinging doors. Almost every day while he was in Chicago on that trip, Jim would get a handful of coins from the 'Bar-Keep', toss them into the streets and watch the little beggars scramble for them. One day while he still had a few dollars, he took half a dozen of them into a shoe store and bought each one a pair of shoes. The next day none of them had shoes; they had traded or sold them. He could be just as ornery as it is possible for a man to be and yet he had a good sense of humor and a kind heart. I knew him for forty-five years. I remember that in his later years he gave a pony and saddle to a little girl who was always friendly and pleasant with him.

When Jim first came to Canada in 1902 he worked for the 'Turkey Track' south of the Cypress Hills. When he was on one of his prolonged sprees in the Hat the editor of 'The Times' one day published an appeal to the 'decent citizens' to get together and run this 'social nuisance' out of town. Father happened to be in that day and saw this 'bit' in the paper. He went downtown, met Jim on the street and offered him a job. Jim worked for us for the three years following, knew his business and was always reliable.

On the walls of the house in which he lived for the last few year of his life as range rider for the Special Areas Board, were some clippings that you might expect someone, more interested in the better things of life to collect. Jim had his wild times and his quiet, thoughtful moments too.

Our outfit was camped a few miles north of Medicine Hat one summer and the cook had decided that he needed to spent the wages that were coming to him. He had been taken to town and a new one brought out. This new chef was a well built man and did a lot of talking about the 'chalk-lines' he had monkeyed around. According to him he was quite handy with his 'dukes'. He got in wrong with the men from the start by giving them tea each morning for breakfast instead of coffee! At that time Jim Spratt was the 'night hawk'. On the third morning of the new cook's regime, Jim put the horses in the rope corral as usual and turned to the cook tent for breakfast. A friend from eastern Canada was visiting Jesse Bishop that summer and they happened to be in the camp this particular morning. The young stranger was sitting on the ground just inside the door of the tent. Jim entered the tent and walked over to the stove, lifted the lid of the teapot and growled "tea again". Then he pulled out his gun and put a hole through the teapot remarking, "if we can't have coffee we'll have tea in the coffee pot." When the shot was fired the young easterner threw himself backward through the doorway. Perhaps he thought that he was getting a first hand view of the old west and had better get out of the way of any lead. However, there was not even a comment from the cook and the next morning they had coffee in the coffee pot.

In 1902 Gordon, Ironside and Fares Co. Ltd., shipped 2,500 head of longhorn two-year-old steers into Alberta from their ranch in New Mexico. To receive them we set up camp south of Bowell and west of Stair, to which latter point the cattle were billed. Grass was very scarce in 'the South' and when they arrived here many were quite weak — a few were dead in the cars. As each train was un-

227

loaded the cattle were moved to grass between Bowell and the Saskatchewan River. Most of western Assiniboia and Alberta was still 'open range'. Though these cattle were thin and weak they were ornery brutes, full of fight. There were a few mud holes where we were grazing them. Once in a while one would get into the mud and have to be pulled out. The fellows learned that after they pulled out a critter they had to swing it around so that it faced the mudhole because when they 'tailed it up', just as soon as it had its feet under it, it would turn, make a dive for the man and, if ends had not been switched, land back in the mud hole.

When the last shipment was unloaded, rested and filled up on the good grass, we started north with them. They did well on the range along the Red Deer but the second winter, which was a hard one in our area, was too much for the short haired, thin skinned longhorns. When that winter arrived there were about twelve thousand head of cattle on the ranch but not enough feed for the long siege that followed. Incoming ranchers had settled on some of the meadows which for years had supplied us with some of our hay, and the growth in the sloughs that summer had not been as good as usual.

The large native cattle made it through the winter though we lost many thin cows, yearlings and calves. Of the longhorn herd of twenty-five hundred animals only eight hundred were alive when spring at last arrived. The mental strain — watching cattle gradually die, day after day, while being unable to do anything for them, was too much for Father. He told 'the Firm' that he would not risk going through another winter like that one and asked them to move their herd.

That summer they were turned over to the Bar U Ranch, partly owned by Gordon, Ironside and Fares Co. Ltd., and operated by George Lane who, with Billy Henry, took delivery of the cattle at Brooks. When our men had been relieved of the herd someone had a cargo of liquid refreshment shipped to them at Brooks. They soon made the little town a small replica of one of those of the old frontier. Chickens were shot on the streets and the people stayed inside as the fellows rode back and forth on the one or two streets. One of the citizens who could handle a telegraph key managed to get into the station and wired to Calgary for militia. The agent was sensible enough to know what this man was doing. When he told the boys they pulled out of town and camped that night about four miles northeast by a large slough now part of the Johnson property. They still had some refreshment so were in no hurry to go to bed. Jim Spratt, who was the 'night hawk' came into the camp sometime before midnight and offered to bet anyone a month's wages that Dan, the horse he was riding, could smell whiskey half a mile away.

1914, Thomas Owens.

Howe Brothers throwing a bronc to saddle.

Lincoln Howe.

Grant Howe.

229

Two of them took him up. He tied his reins to the horn of the saddle and one man rode on each side of him. Dan led them out to the horse herd, travelled almost completely around, went off at an angle and stopped about sixty yards from the herd. Jim got off and pulled a jug out of a badger hole. He had cached the jug in the hole. Each time around he rode out there, stopped for a few minutes and had a sip. Dan had a rest and a chance to munch a few mouthfuls of grass. He was a tall, well-bred bay with lots of room between his ears. He soon learned to go there and stop without any help from Jim. In their condition, Jim's companions willingly admitted that Dan had a nose for whiskey. Though Jim had two months wages coming from them, I believe that he never collected.

Over seventy years I have ridden the range
From the Mexico Gulf to this Canada land,
Herding swing bags and broomtails — sometimes day and night:
From the Red Deer to Texas I've seen every brand.
Those wise orn'ry longhorns I've humored and cussed,
As we hazed them along up that old Chisholm trail
Through the thick clouds of dust and the sweltering heat
'Til we penned them at last at the head of the rail.
With the rattle of horns and the clicking of hooves
Mixed the bawling of herds and the cowpuncher's song.
We were happy and young and we never complained,
Though the wages were small and the hours were long.
Through Dakota, Montana I trailed other herds
And then over the "Line" to the Alberta lands —
To the happiest home of the buffalo hordes
And a heaven on earth for the antelope bands.
Every night in the spring as I lay 'neath the sky,
I could hear the wild geese, from twilight to dawn,
On their way to their nesting spots up in the north
With the hell-divers, ducks and the 'graceful white swan.'

Johnnie Eide was with the outfit for a time that summer and there was a young fellow who believed that he was tough: the boys called him "Buffalo Bill." He had a bad habit of staying in bed as long as he possibly could and was always late for breakfast. One morning when Jim had coralled the horses Johnnie took this fellow's rope from his saddle, slipped a loop around the foot of his bed, handed the rope to Jim who took his "dallies" and loped away from camp with this fellow's head and arms bobbing and waving as he bounced over the prairie. He was dragged a quarter of a mile from camp and left to pack his bed back. Next morning he was up with the others.

The Steersford ferry was anchored to the North bank of the Red Deer and Joe Kennedy was sitting on the apron fishing. (Steersford was a name given, after the turn of the century to the ferry located where travellers on the Battleford-Medicine Hat trail crossed the Red Deer river). It was a warm Sunday afternoon. Someone called from the bank and Joe turned to see Jim Spratt sitting on a horse. Twice Jim called "Come here —" and twice, Joe, who knew him well, gave him a smart, delaying answer. Then two bullets hit the apron, one on each side of Joe. Telling about it afterwards Joe said "I didn't wait any longer I got up and went to him. He was sitting there chuckling, beckoning with one finger and saying "Come here boy." They chatted a few minutes then Jim took his coat from the back of the saddle where he had tied it, laid it on the ground and carefully unrolled it. Then he started to swear. When he had used a considerable amount of his colorful vocabulary he pulled out his jackknife and cut the coat in ribbons. "A coat that won't hold a bottle of whiskey", he declared, "isn't worth having."

He had a bottle (or rather part of a bottle — the other part was in him) rolled in the coat but had failed to tie the strings on one side of the saddle tight enough and somewhere the bottle had slipped out.

Jim was an excellent shot with either six gun or rifle. He was riding through the brush one day with Father when a startled prairie chicken flew and lit on the branch of a tree. Jim pulled out his gun and shot off its head.

Another time a line of men were standing at the bar ("the longest bar in town") in one of the hotels in Medicine Hat. At the other end of the line was someone whom Jim did not like, but evidently it was someone who didn't believe in trying to see if he was quicker on the draw than the other fellow. Jim, who by that time had enough in him to make him reckless, from his end of the bar, shattered that fellow's glass with no exciting consequences.

In the "hungry thirties" I operated a country store and post office with all the agencies that often are part of such a set-up. One evening about nine o'clock while the lone clerk was serving some later customers and I was working in the office at the rear, Jim walked in. As he walked toward my end of the store I knew that he was drunk and that he was wearing his gun under his arm: he was dressed up, was holding his head high, looking straight ahead and his shirt was open in front.

He came into the office and told me that someone in the community was spreading a very low down story about him which was not true. He wanted me to tell him who it was. I said that I had not heard anything and that I did not believe anyone would tell such a story about him. He was not in the least impressed. Putting his hand on my shoulder he said, "Johnnie, I've known you since you were knee high to a grasshopper and I know you won't lie to me." "Now," he pleaded, "tell me who it is and when I find him I'll cut him in two." He was drunk enough and mad enough to have done just that, if someone had been named.

It took more than an hour to get something else into his head. Then he decided that he needed a new tire for his light delivery truck. We picked out two tires and two tubes — they were wrapped in those days and had my name on the wrapper. He handed me a roll of bills, told me to take my money out of that and keep the rest for him. I threw the tires and tubes in the back of the truck, gave him some "gas" and away he went, into the night.

A week later he stopped in front of the store again, normal. When I had put gasoline in the tank of the truck he said, "I guess I owe you for two tires; I found these in the back of the truck with your name on them." "Oh," I replied, "you paid for them. Do you need them?" "No, I don't." As I put them back in the store I remarked "I have something of yours here." When I brought his roll from the safe undisturbed, he had to take my word that it was his. He couldn't remember giving it to me — thought he had spent it.

When he was seventy-six years of age, Jim was range rider for the Special Areas Board in charge of a large community lease. He came to town one day for groceries and a friend offered him a drink. One led to another, suddenly Jim turned pale and grabbed his breast. They put him in a car and started for the doctor's office but before they got there he was gone. Those old fellows were tough. Jim was riding and holding down a responsible job at seventy-six and if he had been able to control his appetite might have lived for several more years.

"They can talk of the hills down in Oklahoma,
Of the grass in Wyoming where I used to ride,
But I'd settle for some of that prairie wool range
Spreading north from the Boundary on Canada's side.

"If the Lord had a land as good as this was
I'd go there tomorrow and never more roam,
But I reckon the only one left is above
And some say I ain't fit for that heavenly home.

"God must know I have broken 'most every command:
I have chosen my way and have run my own race.
Now my body is broken, I'm useless and old
And I ain't coming crying to Him for His grace."

232

He believed that some day he should stand to be judged,
And was ready to take what that judgment might bring.
He was ever reliable, generous and true —
Shouldn't that bear some weight with the Heavenly King?
He was "pulling down" wages at seventy-six
When he took "one" too many and started to fall.
'Twas too far to the doctor; he'd made his last ride
But he still wore his boots when he answered Death's call.
On the side of a hill with his face t'ward the "South,"
In a six foot three casket he's taking his rest:
Just one more of those men, soon of legend and myth,
Who were part of the vanguard that opened the West.

CHAPTER IX

Connor Brothers, with Jeff Barber as wagon boss, brought twenty-five hundred three- and four-year-old longhorn steers into Canada in the summer of 1903. They were trailed across the line (I don't remember from which point) to "the Hat" and from there to the range that they had located in the Neutral Hills country, crossing the Red Deer River three miles west of our buildings. Father and some of the men gave them a hand to cross the river. They began "stringing out" the herd about two miles south of the top of the hill leading down into the valley. (This hill is a long, narrow ridge or 'hog's back'). Two riders cut off a 'pilot herd' and the rest of the bunch followed in a long, narrow file with riders at intervals on each side. Two or three men brought along the 'drag'.

As they started down the hill something frightened the cattle, (possibly a rabbit jumping out from under a sage bush or a prairie chicken 'taking off') and they began to run. That long line of steers with cowboys on each side came down the hog's back on the dead run. At the bottom of the ridge the lead rider on one side slowed down as the man opposite him swung 'the point' sharply around the head of a deep 'washout'. They were swung back about half way and were soon out on the flat where they were 'circled' until they stopped running.

From the top of the hill to the place where the cattle were circled is about two miles. It was no spot for any but experienced men and as I was not yet fourteen I had been left at the camp near the river to keep an eye on a small bunch of our cows with calves that were to be used to spearhead the crossing. I thoroughly enjoyed watching that long string of steers with the riders, most on Mexican ponies, on each side, racing down that long hog's back, swinging around the danger spots and being 'wound up' out on the flat.

M∞ M.Bjork   Z L. Krause
07 Happy Campbell   ꟻ J. Longmuir
UR Cicon Ranch   ꟽ G. Mercer
-O- A.B. Dawson   OS C. Rinker
   C.B. Howe   G. Silverthorne
G2 Geo. Howe Sr.   JS J.B. Squirrell
   George Howe

GV G.Anderson   OS C.Danielson   N-T J. Howe
AB T. Anderson   7 Mr.+Mrs. A.Davidson ƏT L. Howe
KO T. Barneko   -O- A.B. Dawson   ZT R.+R. Howe
MM M. Bjork Sr.   UF V. Dearing   TX J. Ignatius
MM M. Bjork Jr.   D J. Dziatkewich   L17 L. Krause
5M L. Callaghan   III C.B. Howe   Z S. Krause
6-9 Happy Campbell E Chester Howe   EK E. Kulyk
CX Cicon Ranch   T-V George Howe   FO J. Kulyk
C Crooked Tree Ranch   FK Mike Kulyk

XT J. Longmuir   HR L.+H. Rinker   7 A. R. Smith
MM Mr+Mrs. K. Love   LL A. Rubbelke   OL Mrs. Annie Smith
LIX Majestic Ranches C B. Rubbelke   -SJ B. Squirrell
GM G. Mercer   FR- Mrs. E. Rubbelke U A.L. Stone
I Minor Cattle Co. EJ Mrs. E. Silverthorne -LS E. Stone
                        Mrs. E. Barros   LSL J. Stone
XM Bob. Monkman   SU G. Silverthorne   XJ J.W. Thompson
JE J. Monkman   OM O. Skjenna   TT W.M. Thompson
W-M Mrs. R. Monkman   V Vee Bar Vee Ranch
P F. Peterson
OS C. Rinker

234

There were many rocks and clumps of sage brush on that ridge and the ponies showed that they were just about as sure footed as goats.

Soon after the cattle had settled down they were strung out again and headed for the river. Some of the calves in the herd which I had been watching, had been caught, hog-tied, taken across the river in a boat and left on that shore. Their mothers, who had been thrown into the big herd, could hear their offspring bawling and without any urging 'hit the water' and led the herd of steers straight across. Both cattle and saddle horses had to swim for a short distance in mid-stream but the twenty-five hundred head were crossed without incident and next day started north for their new range.

That recalls an attempted crossing. On the north side of the river, a mile west of the buildings, we had built branding corrals. Each year at the last branding, the side of the corral near the river was opened and the cows and calves driven into the water to swim to the south side. There scarcely ever was any trouble — we always waited until the sun was getting low in the west so that it would not shine in the cow's eyes when they were swimming. My grandfather from Ontario was visiting us that summer and on this particular day he stayed at the ranch instead of crossing to watch the branding. Towards evening the cows and calves were driven into the water as usual but refused to cross and were soon out on the bank in spite of all that the men could do. Again and again they were corralled and crowded into the river but they would go only a few yards from shore and then break back. Finally the men quit trying. They couldn't understand it: the sun was far in the west and a nice breeze was blowing from the south side.

Father crossed in the boat that night and went down to the ranch feeling quite tired and dejected. As soon as he stepped into the house Grandfather greeted him with, "You couldn't get your cattle across the river." "How did you know?" Father asked. "I was hiding in the willows on this side watching you." Father told me some years later that that was the first time in his life that he had spoken crossly to his father. I don't remember all he said but he told Grandfather that his being in the willows was the reason they could not cross the cattle. The wind was blowing from the south side directly off him and the cows, which were almost wild animals in those days, could smell him. They decided that there was danger over there and that they were near enough on their side of the water.

In 1903 A. P. Day brought sixty head of saddle horses across "the Line" and offered them for sale in Medicine Hat. Father bought the bunch in which was a pair of bay geldings, apparently top saddle horses. Ad knew the horses and when he offered Father a work team for them, a deal was made. Those two geldings were well known throughout the west during the next ten years as "Scarhead" and "Rooster", two of the best in Ad's string of bucking horses. Though hard to ride they were gentle to handle and Mrs. Day often drove them around town hitched to a buggy. They made a very nice, above average, driving team.

Usually the not so good is mixed with the good whether the subject is horses, men or apples. Most of those men who came north into Canada during the first part of the Century were good citizens. There was bound to be a few of the other kind. Three of these had a 'hangout' on Sounding Creek. Two of them were Johnson and Nicol: I have forgotten the name of the third man.

Many horses were being raised in Western Canada at that time and these men made some easy money running bunches across the Line. One of the largest drives with which they were credited was made from the Brooks district. As often is the case, the police were reportedly satisfied as to who were handling the horses but for some time were unable to get definite proof.

Johnson was in the bar room of the Assiniboia Hotel in the Hat one day in the summer of 1905 when Sergeant Quinn of the Mounties got the drop on him. Johnson stepped back and forth with his hands in the air, crying out, "Haven't I any friends here? Haven't I any friends here?" Evidently he hadn't any who cared to identify themselves as such with Sergeant Quinn, a stern old-timer of the Force on the other end of that gun. Johnson went to the cells. The police couldn't dig up enough evidence to warrant holding him so the next day they had to turn him loose with an order to get out of town.

The plank platform at the C.P.R. station was poorly lighted and a garden with some trees bordered the north side of it. Late that night as Sergeant Quinn was on his way home from 'up town' two men jumped on him in a dark spot, took his gun and gagged him. They stretched him out on the platform, spread his legs almost as far apart as possible, and stuck the shank of each spur (straight shanked police spurs) in a crack between planks. Tied and apparently helpless, they left him.

The next day just before noon, Johnson rode into our ranch sixty-five miles north of town. He would not put his horse in the barn but hobbled and tethered it to the fence below the corral where the way to the brush was clear. The saddle was left on and the bridle handy. When he came to the house with the other men for dinner, he stopped in the doorway, glanced around and said, "I'm Ed Johnson". He told us that he was going down the river to McGowan's about sixteen miles east. Father gave him a pair of

236

halters belonging to McGowan and asked him to deliver them. McGowan never received the halters and we found out that Johnson crossed the river two miles east of our buildings on a good ford and went north. Several days later we heard of the treatment received by Sergeant Quinn who was certain that one of those who had attacked him was Johnson but had no idea as to where he had gone. Eventually the gang was broken up but I have forgotten the details.

THE VOICE

Hark! do you hear that gentle whispering,
    That faint, mysterious call,
Despite refusals still persisting
    As though 'twould conquer all?
Softly it steals upon the night wind
    And taps my eager ear.
Fiercely it comes upon the west wind
    And bids my spirit hear.
Hidden within the budding willow,
    Concealed amid the grass,
Calling from every distant hollow —
    It will not let me pass.
Mingled with every changing bird call
    That's wafted from the tree;
Echoed from every rising earth wall —
    It will not let me be.
Mingled with each companion's sorrow
    It seeks my pitying mind,
Bidding me rise at once and follow
    And leave dull books behind.

Any man who was a bit 'green' was a fair target for practical 'jokes'. When it came to thinking up such and 'stuffing' the intended victim with a line of 'malarky' in preparation, those cowpunchers could hold their own with the best.

A young man with quite a green tinge had been picked up in the Hat to act as day wrangler when the outfit was in the Little Sand Hills about twenty miles north of town. This was and still is rattlesnake territory. The fellows found out that this newcomer was afraid of snakes.

That evening, before bedtime, a wonderful assortment of snake stories were told and one of the men managed to place a dead garter snake in this fellow's bed. So by bedtime the stage was set and the victim well primed. The tent was large and had a tall combined pole and stove pipe in the centre. Each one was holding his breath as the young fellow crawled into his blankets. When his bare feet touched the cold snake he let out one terrifying scream, left the bed like a bullet and climbed the tent pole.

Someone opened his bed, took out the snake and showed him that it was dead but they had to make a light and turn over all the blankets to assure him that nothing else had been hidden between them, before he would venture into them again. I don't know whether he slept or not.

A tall, tanned cowpoke with several 'under his belt', walked into a store in Brooks one day. Standing beside the counter was a sedate lady who had arrived from Ontario a few days before. As this long, rough looking critter made his way toward her, he drawled, "Look out! or I'll step on you." She immediately forgot her sedateness: for the moment she was an active young girl again as, placing her hands on the counter she vaulted over it like a seasoned athlete — long skirts and all.

A young man whose first name was Ainsley, was with us for three years. He was eighteen years old when he came to the ranch from a city in Ontario. As the name Ainsley was scarcely ever used by anyone except Father he soon received the well worn cognomen of 'Kid'.

Ainsley was made of good material and had a sufficient supply of intestinal fortitude. At first he moved from one job to another: cutting wood, pitching hay, wrangling the horses, cooking, driving the mess wagon. The horses he rode were well broken except one or two that could be persuaded to 'crow hop' when 'thumbed'. It takes a lot of practice and experience to make a top rider but, like most inexperienced, Kid thought that he could ride just about anything that anyone else could.

The wagon boss, Allen Robinson, had a tall bay in his string which he called Dandy. Dandy would 'turn it on' once in awhile and was not easy to ride. Kid got it into his head that he could ride this horse and one day wanted a chance to prove it. After some argument Allen said, "O.K. Kid you can get on Dandy". They caught the horse, put Kid's saddle on it and when he mounted, turned them loose.

After about three jumps both of the reins were gone and Kid was choking the 'goose neck' with both hands. His spurs were pressed tightly against the horse's ribs and Dandy was doing his best. Kid's hat was gone, his head was flopping back and forth, his shirt was torn in front, his chest was being pounded and he was yelling "Stop him! stop him!" Saul Boyer figured that he had had enough so rode alongside the horse and pulled up its head. When Kid got off he humbly admitted, "I can't ride him."

Sixty years ago there was not much excitement in Medicine Hat on Sundays. In the afternoon, after Sunday School, if it was a nice day most young people went for a walk across the railroad bridge (there was no traffic bridge) and up the track to the 'gravel pit'. Those who had a horse and buggy or could hire one, went for a buggy ride. There were few places downtown for the young men to gather. One of these was the station platform. Kid happened to be in town one Sunday and wandered down to the station. While he and some others were standing around the big stove in the waiting room, three or four young fellows from around town came along. Kid heard one of them speak disparagingly of one of my sisters. He had been raised in a large city and was handy in more ways than one. Stepping over to the young fellow he said, "The Gordon girls are friends of mine. If you don't like them keep your 'so-and-so' tongue off them". That was that.

Another time Sam Cunningham, one of the few Irish-Indian half-breeds, quite a solid man, heard another on the street say something uncomplimentary about Father. Sam, who had a few "shots" in him, took off his coat and threatened to clean up on anyone who said anything against Andy Gordon. Others got in between them and they decided that it would be a good idea to go back to the bar and 'have another.'

About 1903-1905 several other ranchers settled along the north side of the Red Deer within fifteen miles of the ranch, both east and west. Among these were Steve Cicon, Fred Nelson (both bachelors), Magnus Bjork with his family, George Howe with six of his boys and Mrs. Howe, Wozeski Brothers (three — Adolph, Otto and Fred), Howard McCullough and R. S. Gravett.

Our teams went to Medicine Hat more often than any of the others and, when we made a trip, usually carried letters from the neighbors to be posted. There was a box in one corner of the bunkhouse where these letters were placed, to be on hand when a team went to town. On the return we brought mail, orders of groceries, tobacco, often gloves and overalls; nails, fence staples, repairs were also included.

One fall the foreman, Tom Mossop, was coming out from the Hat with six horses and two wagons. He ran into a snowstorm and had to leave one wagon at the 'Coulee' twenty-five miles south of the ranch where we had a cabin and a shed for the horses. When he arrived home one of the neighbors, Steve Cicon, was waiting for tobacco which he had asked Tom to get for him. Unfortunately the tobacco was in the wagon which had been left behind. Steve, who lived twelve miles west on the north side of the river, had come down with one horse hitched to a 'stoneboat'. Tobacco was a very necessary item and when he heard that it had been left at the Coulee he decided to go after it. It took all the next day for him to get there and it was just his bad luck that another storm blew up that night. It lasted for three days. Steve burned all the wood he could find around the buildings. Finally he chopped up the stoneboat and used it for fuel. When the storm was over he climbed on the horse and rode the twenty-five miles to the ranch 'bareback' but he had his tobacco.

Picture of early transportation methods used for a grocery trip to Medicine Hat. Pollution was at a minimum with these four horse power outfits.

Many trips were made over the trail between Medicine Hat and the ranch before the Empress-Bassano line of the C.P.R. was built. Usually we had four horses hitched to a double-boxed wagon but often used six with two wagons. We enjoyed being on the trail so long as the weather was good. If caught in a rainstorm the going would be heavy and when it was cold there was very little pleasure.

You sat up on that load juggling four or six lines and trying to keep warm. Of course we were dressed for the cold and knew how to take care of ourselves: any man who didn't, had no business out in that kind of weather. When you face a sharp wind all day with temperatures of fifteen to twenty-five below zero, you have to get off and walk once in awhile to keep the blood moving. The horses would be gray with frost, icicles would be hanging from their noses and as your outfit crept along, the wagon wheels would screech, screech as they rolled slowly through the shallow snow. When you reached camp at night you took care of your horse first. Then you started a fire, got some water from the water hole and carried in your grub. Some of it had to be thawed. I have often cut slices of bread with an axe and thawed them in hot grease in the frying pan; tasted mighty good too. You unrolled your bed and before crawling between the blankets you placed your socks and mittens near the fire to be dried in preparation for the next day. In the morning both horses and harness were cold, the tugs and lines stiff. The bits had been dropped, moist from the horses' mouths, into the snow, if there was any. It froze on the bits and when they, covered with the frozen snow, were placed in the horses mouths the next morning, the frosty steel did not burn their lips. If there was no snow you dipped them in water in the morning or else did a lot of blowing on them, to draw out the frost, before asking the horses to take them.

THE END OF THE TRAIL

Guess I've come to the end of the trail,
To the place where old wrecks are piled,
To the place where the schemes of the men
Are received and approved but — filed.
O'er the heap there arises a moan
From the souls of the might-have-beens.
And their murmurings reek of the whiner's tone,
In the stead of the victor's paeans.
And must I meekly lay on the heap
What is left of the soul of man?
Must I yield and admit that I cannot reap —
That I'm merely an "also ran?"
No! There's somewhere a path, a detour
That the ones who have won have trod;
It will never be easy or smooth I'm sure:
'Twill be rocky and strait — not broad.
Past occasional springs of delight
It will lead; through the fields of work;
Up the steeps of rebuff with depressions bight
In which quitting apologies lurk.
It will carry me over the hill
If I turn not aside to rest.
With my eyes on the goal I must toil until,
With my dreams, I attain the crest.

DON'T QUIT

Though they say you're no good, you're a quitter:
That your head is too big for your hat.
Though your name to your own folk is bitter,
You need pay no attention to that.

You must buckle your belt a bit tighter,
Firmly pull down your hat o'er your ears;
Because really, you know, you're a fighter:
You were meant not for cat calls — but cheers.
Yes, you're bruised and you're sore and disheartened,
And you sure hit the earth with a thud.
What if you and your business are "busted?"
Pick yourself up and brush off the mud.
Now, this life is a race each must enter,
And for each one the rules are the same.
Though you seem to have lost, do not falter:
Keep on running and show them you're game.
Then, it may be that you are a winner,
That you seem to be leading the pack;
If that's so you're not out of danger:
Keep your eyes front and never look back.
You know, many a race that is finished
Has been lost when it should have been won.
Yes, and many a man who is shadowed,
Should have stood in the light of the sun.
So, 'tis true, if you would be a rider,
You can't ride if you've never been "throwed."
Better climb up again, hit the leather
And now, ride to the end of your road.

CHAPTER IX CONTINUED

Before we had built that stopping place twenty-five miles south of the ranch, Father was caught in some bad weather on one trip. He camped in a group of small sand hills where there was some brush. The horses were blanketed with the harness over the blankets to keep them snug and in place, and tied to the wagon in a sheltered spot in the brush with feed before them. Father rolled out his bed nearby. In the morning everything was stiff. He got the four horses hitched but, when he was ready to go, the lead team, a pair of thin skinned, short haired Standard Breds, would not tighten the traces. They were so cold that they just moved back and forth with their heads up, ears back, backs humped, and shivering. Finally the heels of one came in contact with the singletree and with a snort, they went out of there like a team leaving the barrels in a chuckwagon race.

In the late fall of 1908 or 1909 Tom Mossop, with six horses and two wagons, and another man with four horses hitched to a third wagon, were on the trail to the Hat. It was one of those falls without snow but cold enough to keep a carcass of pork in the wagon frozen for two days. The days are short in November so it was almost dark as the outfits started down the north side of "Rae's Coulee", five or six miles north of town. Tom, who was ahead, had gotten only a short distance down the hill when he heard a terrible racket behind him. Looking back he saw the other outfit coming down the hill as fast as it could travel. The brakes must have been set because sparks were flying from the wheels as they skidded over the gravelled road. Above it all he could hear the terrified driver yelling like a mad man. Tom swung his horses to the right, off the road in order to let the others pass, but they must have been completely out of control. When they saw Tom's team turn off to their right they left the road to follow and swerved so sharply that the carcass which was in the wagon of the second outfit was thrown into Tom's rear wagon as they passed. The man jumped or was thrown out and the four horses tore past Tom's six. These caught the same spirit and the two outfits raced to the top of a small hill. Tom didn't dare turn to the left because of the steep grade. If he had had a little more room he could have brought his under control but from the top of the hill, to which the horses raced blindly, was a steep drop of one hundred and fifty feet — almost a 'cut-bank', — to a dry creek bed below. He knew what was ahead, jumped and the ten horses and three wagons plunged headlong.

When the men got to the heap at the bottom of the cut, one horse, a nervy black gelding was choking. He was lying in such a position that the collar was shutting off his wind and the tugs were so tight that Tom couldn't unhook them. When he cut both tugs with his knife (the lines were broken) the horse sprang up and away. The next morning a rider from the ranch who happened to be riding in that direction, found the horse with bridle and harness still on it, grazing four miles south of the buildings. It had travelled fifty-five miles during the night in the right direction: there were no fences across the road, at that time, to stop him.

The men managed to get the rest of the horses and one wagon into town that night; they returned in the morning to clean up the mess. None of the horses was maimed though there were several scars. The driver of the "four-up" quit, so Tom rigged up three wagons, loaded them, strung out eight horses in front and went home alone.

If you should look at that hill today (1959) you would marvel how ten horses with three wagons could come down it in that fashion without some of the horses being killed or at least crippled. The driving wheels cut deep scars in the face of the cliff that remained for several years.

CHAPTER X

Usually freighting in summer was a pleasure. It took two days to go to town empty and three to return loaded. After we had built the cabin and shed in the Coulee we kept a supply of oat sheaves piled on top of the shed. It had four large stalls for eight horses. The cabin was the size of a one thousand bushel granary. Sitting on blocks it was not too comfortable in cold weather but its shelter was always looked forward to eagerly by those on the trail in winter. North of town twelve miles, Mrs. Walker had accommodation for and, for many years accommodated, most of those travelling north from town with teams.

Before these stopping places existed our first camp after leaving town was made at the Box Spring, fifteen miles north, northeast. This was rattlesnake country and we never enjoyed our stay very much especially if it was a night camp. On one trip when I went to the spot where we got the water for tea, I saw a graybird fluttering in the air and crying. Near it was a rattler, coiled with head up and its tongue flicking in and out. The bird, which seemed to be held under some spell, as it fluttered and cried in an agonized

244

manner, drew closer and closer to the snake. It would soon have been in the charmer's mouth if I had not destroyed the charmer.

The first thing we did at a campsite was to unhitch the horses, water them and tie them, two to each side, to the wagon and give each a feed of oats either on the ground or in "nose-bags". These were canvas bags with air holes in the front. The horse put its nose and mouth into the bag which was held in place by a strap or strong string passed over the top of the horse's head. When the horses had been taken care of you took your grub box, frying pan and ten pound syrup or lard pail (for tea) and some kindling out of the wagon. There were always plenty of 'buffalo chips' around the watering places to keep the fire going. Before you started the fire you brought the pail of water so that you would not need to move very far from the fire in case a spark should be blown into the nearby grass. (When you had no more need of the fire you threw the remains of your tea and some water on the embers and then covered them with dirt.) If it was windy you arranged a horse blanket as a shield between the wind and the fire but if the wind was strong you did without fire.

The usual fare was bacon or canned corn beef (usually from Argentina), canned corn, bread and tea. If you were coming from town you probably had a can of fruit. Canned tomatoes were a standby and were greatly enjoyed in hot weather.

As a rule a tent was pitched at a night camp though often you rolled out your bed on the sod and watched the stars for awhile before pulling the "tarp" over your head. The bed was made up of a few pairs of blankets and a large tarpaulin, folded, with the blankets between folds. These 'tarps' had snaps and rings sewn on them so that the bed could be made into a snug sleeping bag, fairly safe against snakes. If camped for the night you hobbled the horses after they had finished their oats, so that they could graze. Sometimes you would walk as much as two miles in the morning before you found them. If the mosquitoes were out in force you built a "smudge" of "buffalo chips" and sagebrush. The horses would not move very far from the smoke until the chill of early morning caused the mosquitoes to look for shelter.

Coming home from the Hat we had two night camps and three stops for noon; that is, when we had loaded wagons. Many trips were made with a good team on the democrat (rarely on the buggy). Some of these trips took one day and one half but we had a few purebred Standard Bred teams that seemed to enjoy travelling the sixty-five miles through rolling and hilly terrain in seven or eight hours. They needed no urging: all that was necessary was to slacken the lines a little and they would break into a trot.

Father drove a pair of registered bay mares for a number of years. His brother Elliott was with him on one trip and as they were both horse lovers they spent a great deal of time discussing their merits. Father told Uncle that he could not take the lines from his hands without the mares knowing it. Uncle was sure that he could. Father said, "As soon as I let loose of the lines, that "off" mare's left ear will come back." So, as Lorna and Minnie (their registered names were Lorna Doone and Minnie Johnson) were trotting along, Uncle took the lines as carefully as he could and as soon as Father took his hands away Lorna's left ear came back. One of the very few times that I ever saw my Father in tears was when Lorna died.

Two other teams were Bouncer and Maginty, bay geldings, eligible for registration, and Joe and Sealim. Joe Gail was a gray registered stallion, also Standard Bred. He was a pacer and before he was born, Mr. Ryan of Ryan and Fares, Winnipeg, (from whom we had purchased the bunch of Standard Breds) told Father that if that mare, Madeline, had a horse colt he would give Father five hundred dollars for it. That would have been a lot of money at that time. Unfortunately when Joe was two years old he got into a manger on his back and knocked down one hip. He and Sealim, a bay gelding, mated very well and like the mares would travel mile after mile holding their heads steady, while Bouncer and Maginty kept theirs going up and down in rhythm with their gait.

Young men, some of them from families connected with Allan Steamship Lines in which Gordon, Ironside and Fares Co. had an interest, came to the ranch from the Old Country. Two that I remember were remittance men who did as they pleased and paid for their board. They were very pleasant fellows and always ready to help when they could. Inability to leave liquor alone was their great handicap.

Others who came to learn the business, were first-class men and soon had something of their own or turned to other employment. One of these was Ted Harrison, a man of first-class character and able in many ways. After two years he returned to Montreal and I believe entered the offices of the Steamship Company.

A young man came out from New York one summer for a holiday. Father took him to the ranch in the democrat. When they stopped for noon Father relieved the horses of their harness while they ate their oats (it was a very warm, sunny day). After the men had had their meal and the horses had rested, Father told this man that he could harness the one horse while he got the other ready. When Father had finished he went around the democrat to see how the man from New York was getting along. He had the collar on upside down and was struggling with the harness, wondering what to do next. "Why," exclaimed Father, "I thought you told me that you were accustomed to driving horses." "Yes," was the response, "but the coachman always brought them to the door."

I spent much of one summer on the road with six horses and two wagons equipped with special boxes, hauling page wire from the Hat to fence a township of grassland. It took two days to go to town, one to put on the loads and three to return. I travelled alone and put on the loads alone. I was quite independent in those days — not very big but tough and wiry. On one trip the year before, my load consisted of seven eight inch (inside diameter) cast iron pipes eighteen and twenty feet long. A heavy thunderstorm crossed my trail one afternoon and that was the only time in my life that I was afraid of lightning. There was a very strong wind with the storm and my four horses were not "old plugs." With the wind and the driving rain, the thunder crashing and lightning flashing, I didn't dare get off the load because it was all that I could do to control my team while up there. I had to stay on top of those iron pipes and hang on to the four lines which the wind forced into great bows, first one way and then the other, even though they were tight and the horses off the road with their backs to the storm. The bolt of lightning didn't happen to find the pipes but the rain soaked me to the skin. It was one of those sudden summer storms. It quickly passed, the sun came out and I was soon dry again.

There were many accidents through the years; though some were serious most were not considered so. Alf Winterburn's leg was broken one evening when a few of the fellows were wrestling. There was neither airplane nor rural telephone; nor were there any automobiles to take him quickly to a doctor. He had to be laid on a bed in the back of the democrat and jolted behind a team of horses on a sixty-five mile jaunt to the Hat.

Tom Mossop, who was very handy with an axe, as with most tools, was sharpening some sticks to be used as tent pegs at a new camp site to which the haying outfit had moved. He held each stick with his left hand while he sharpened it. As he brought the axe down fairly close to his finger the thought passed through his mind, "Suppose I should hit that finger." The next time that the axe came down, Tom looked at the finger and struck where he looked. The finger was almost completely severed from the hand. One of the men helped to wrap it up and he drove, alone, twelve miles to the ranch. A good team was always in the stable and soon (it was late in the afternoon) Father and Tom were on their way to the Hat.

SPRING

Willow buds will swell to bursting,
Setting all the pussies free:
In their silky, pearl grey dressing
Gowns, they beautify their tree.
In the dew a fearless flower
Pushes boldly through the sod;
Greets the early April shower
Raining from its crowded cloud.
Brave anemone comes calling
In her 'lavender and lace';
Whether sun is hid or shining,
Shows a placid, smiling face.
All of this is set to music
By the singing of the birds;
Stirring up within the rustic
Feelings much too deep for words.

THE RETIRED RANCHER (J.S.S.)

(From "Rhymes of the Range" by J. R. Gordon)

He didn't sell the ranch because he wished to:
    It wasn't that he longed for urban life.
It wasn't that his mate was growing feeble:
    He'd toiled alone — unaided in the strife.
There was no money problem now to vex him
    For Fortune through the years had kindly smiled;
But brutal Time, by never ceasing nagging,
    Had rendered him unfit to fight the wild.

No more he'll watch the cattle in the springtime
    Climb up the hills and scatter far and wide
In eager search for springing blades of green grass.
    Or resting on some hillock's sunny side.
No more shall he experience the elation
    That comes the time the first new calf is found:
Nor carefully keep watch on every mud-hole
    For fear some weak old cow would bog and drown
He'll miss the fun and festival of branding:
    The noise, the dust, the labor and the sweat.
He'll not be kept awake this fall at weaning
    Nor shall the threat of winter make him fret.
For cosily beside some old friend's fireplace
    He'll rest and bask before the dreamy glow.
Imag'ning pictures in the flames and watching
    The scenes of other days pass to and fro.
He scorned security and sheltered comfort
    To be another hardy pioneer
Who dared to face the worst the wild could muster —
    A breed of man that soon must disappear.
His given task has duly been accomplished
    And by the western gate he calmly stands.
Awaiting, now, a signal from the Pilot
    To move his camp to the Elysian lands.

THE OLD TRAIL

The old trail is long and awinding;
The hills are many — some steep.
You start from camp at the dawning —
The night alone is for sleep.
You watch the glad glow of the morning
O'er heaven and earth quickly creep;
The birds fill the air with their warbling
While thrills, none can tell, o'er you creep.
Your steed's in rhythm, wagon wheels creaking,
Your heart's attuned — nature is singing.

THE ROBINS

strayed by a brook one bright day in spring,
When the robins were building their nests,
And listened as each, then the choir, would sing
Of the joy that was fililng their breasts.

249

I saw mid the throng, one busy red breast
Whom I thought to be toiling alone.
Yet he gathered the twigs and sang with the rest,
As though it were done for "someone."
I drew near and asked the bright little man
If he hadn't yet chosen a mate.
"I'm working, dear sir, as hard as I can,
For I've asked my own birdie to wait
"Until I've for her a nice little home
Fixed cozy and neat just for two,
And then, I've no doubt, that my darling will come,
For there never was a birdie more true."

Our house in town was one block from the ferry and about two
o'clock the next morning, my mother who seemed on more than
one occasion to be psychic, woke up, went to a north window
and looked out just in time to see the team coming into the yard.
The finger was amputated between the hand and the first joint
without benefit of anesthetic, and after resting one day they returned
to the ranch. Tom used to say that whenever his hands got cold,
the part of the finger which had been taken off got cold too.

Another year when the hay gang was putting up the hay at
the calf camp, twelve miles east of home, Tom started for the ranch
with one broken horse and a bronc hitched to a single boxed
wagon. When he was "on top" four miles from the camp the bit
on the bronc broke and the horses began to run. There was plenty
of room so for awhile he ran them in a circle. This did not seem
to accomplish much so he managed to get them back on the road.
The "broke" horse held the road and they raced towards home. They
had a steep hill to go down descending to the flat, four miles from
the buildings. They were half way down the hill, still running,
when the bronc and wagon hit a very large rock and everything
was piled up. As the wagon started to turn over Tom jumped. The
bronc was down so he got on its head and held it there 'til he
fitted a bit out of the halter shank. The draw bolt was broken and
the only piece of iron that would fit was the brake rod. He got
one end of it through the doubletree, bent the rest back over the
box and drove the rest of the way with a rope bit.

The bronc had a run but did not get away so no harm was
done to it.

One year when we were cutting out cows and calves at branding
time, Adam Rutherford was one of those holding the big herd. A
cow ran back toward the herd from the "cut" and Adam raced
up to head her off. As she plunged into the herd the front feet of

250

the horse, which was travelling at full speed, hit her hind legs. He turned a somersault and his sudden stop sent Adam out of the saddle as though out of a catapult. His head hit the ground and bounced; he drew his knees up towards his chin and lay still. The soil was light: had it been heavy clay, gravel or stony ground the fall might have proved fatal. They took him across the river in a boat and down to the buildings where he was put in bed. No marks could be seen and by this time he appeared rational. Father asked him if he knew where he was. He replied, "I'm on the —— ranch," naming one in the Cypress Hills south of Medicine Hat. That was enough to make them fit a bed in the back of the democrat and with a man beside Adam to watch him, Father left immediately for the Hat (sixty-five miles). The next day before leaving town, Father went to see him in the hospital. They discussed the accident and Adam seemed quite normal. Father asked him if he knew where he was. He was lying between white sheets on a hospital bed but his answer was, "I'm on Andy Gordon's ranch on the Red Deer." I don't remember when he got out of the hospital but he was at the ranch, riding again, when the fall shipment of beef was made.

We had just made camp at the Bone-Pile spring, fifteen miles south of the buildings, on our way to the railroad and all except the two on herd had had their supper. Adam and another man were about to go out to relieve those two until it would be time for the first night shift. He had saddled a brown gelding which we called Cinchbuckle — that was the brand on his right shoulder. The horse was comparatively gentle and a very useful horse when he got going, but it was very dangerous to get on him after he was first saddled if the cinch was tight. He would brace himself and if you urged him instead of getting off and loosening the cinch a little, would flip over on his back. This attitude was galling to whoever his rider might be and he was called many uncomplimentary names when the fellow got off to let out the cinch.

This particular evening Adam was feeling "out of sorts" when he got on the horse. As he applied some pressure with his legs as a sign to get going the horse braced itself, turned its head and looked at him. Adam cussed and hit it in the shoulder with his spur. The horse ducked its head and flipped so quickly that Adam hadn't a chance to move. He happened to be sitting a bit to one side and when the horse threw itself the horn of the saddle just scraped Adam's ribs. Cinchbuckle was uncocked now. He leaped to his feet with the man on his back and set out on the "dead run" for the herd.

Saul Boyer who, when he was young, could have more patience

with a horse than most men, used to ride Cinchbuckle without any trouble. He would get on him with the cinch a bit slack and when he had ridden a short distance, get off and tighten it. He was possibly the quietest horse in Saul's string and was even used by him as a rope horse in pulling calves up to the branding fire.

Father and a young man named Russell Dodd, were working on the farm land one day. Each had four horses hitched to a disc harrow. Russell was driving three broken horses and a green one. When they were coming in for noon Russell, who was ahead, stopped his team, wound the lines around a lever and went in front to throw a branch of brush from the road. The "green" horse, sweating and itchy, began rubbing her head against the next horse. The halter shank with which she was fastened to the other's hame, caught on a blind of her bridle and pulled it out of place. When she saw the disc behind her she whistled and jumped. The others went with her and ran straight toward Russell. Instead of stepping aside out of the way, he grabbed the bridles of the two inside horses in an attempt to stop them. They picked him up and carried him along until he managed to straddle the end of the pole. They swerved off the road into a cultivated field. He clung to his roost for some distance but finally was jarred loose and fell under the horses feet. They and the disc harrow passed over him. The harrow was set so that the discs were running straight and the machine happened to be one of those with two low slung drag bars in front. These bars and the fact that the ground was soft probably saved his life. When the outfit had passed over him he got up and walked around. By that time Father had caught up to him. He was badly cut in several places by the discs; one ear and one eyebrow were disfigured but the deepest cut was on one side of his head. He was fortunate indeed to be alive and able to make the journey to the Medicine Hat Hospital.

I was at the stable when I saw Russell walking around in the field and his team running toward the barnyard gate. I ran down to open it but before I had it opened the horses were away again. They ran between two posts, upset the mare, broke her leg and ripped the harness off her. A bullet quickly put her out of pain.

About the beginning of the century Norman and I were left to keep tab on the main herd while the men took the "cut" of about three hundred cows with their calves to the corrals to brand the calves. Each year we branded between 1200 and 1500 calves. The first few years my job was to sit on the top rail and keep tally. The river made a horse-shoe loop here with the heels of the shoe to the north and two miles apart. Inside the horseshoe were many cottonwood trees, brush of different kinds and small meadows. While cutting out we always held the bunch on the "bench" northwest of the horseshoe because it was level and gave us plenty of room to work the herd. Left to ourselves (15 and 12 years old) Norman and I thought that we would let the herd move east to grass that had been grazed very little. There were about twenty-five hundred head in the bunch, half cows with calves. We started them in the right direction but we had a lot of cattle to handle and while we were back getting the stragglers moving, the leaders who should have kept working east, decided to go south following the trail made by the bunch in the corral. I went up to turn them.

Scattered through the brush and open spaces were a few holes hidden by small brush and grass. These holes had been made years before when prairie fires, consuming dead trees, had followed the roots into the ground. They were more dangerous than badger holes because they were larger and camouflaged. When Norman saw that the "point" was not turning and that more cattle were going where they should not go, he decided that I needed some help. When he rode around a belt of trees and brush he saw my horse standing and me curled up in a ball on the ground.

We supposed, later, that I had been running my horse and had ridden into one of those hidden holes. Norman finally got me on the horse but had trouble persuading me to go with him to the camp. He got me there and left me with the cook, Jim Ward, while he rode to the corrals for Father. They took me across the river in the boat and down to the ranch. There was no blood on me but my neck was badly swollen and my head was sore. Later I could remember having left Norman while I went to turn the point but from there all was a blank until I was crossing the river. In a few days I was back at the camp.

Either the year before or the year after the above episode I was helping to pitch a tent near the house to be used for extra sleeping room. As I was driving a peg the axe caught on an overhead clothesline and the heel dropped on my head. It cut through my felt hat and made a gash more than an inch long in the top of my head. They packed flour in and around the gash to stop the flow of blood and wrapped my head in a long bandage. It soon healed but there is still a scar an inch long.

Fifteen years later a farmer near Jenner asked if I had a good work horse that I would trade for some oats: he did not have cash to pay out at that time. We had a large "sway-backed gelding", broken, but because of his deformity difficult to sell. I agreed to deliver this horse on a certain day. It was in the month of December but there

Walter Heiland at Calgary Stampede, 1947, on horse called "Don't do it".

Jack Coates chuck wagon outfit under the name Burkenshaw. Walter Heiland with the horse.

Howe Boys around 1914.

was no snow on the ground. I knew that this horse should be in a bunch which was grazing on some "open" land about twelve miles southeast of the buildings. (We turned some of our horses out of the pasture in winter to graze over public lands.) When I rode out to get it I found the bunch easily but they were mixed with a number of horses of other brands. As usual I was riding a good horse so cut our bunch away from the others and chased them through some hills in an effort to lose the others. Running them as fast as I could and dodging around the small hills I looked back to see if the others were close. That was the last thing that I remembered for a while. My horse must have hit a hole or a stone hidden in the grass just as I looked back. He evidently turned a somersault because there was dirt on the horn and cantle of the saddle. I don't know how long I lay there; I had one rein in my hand when I got up and remember that as I climbed into the saddle I said to my horse, "You almost did for me that time." In all the many falls that I had, I never had a horse get away from me — always had one line when I got up or woke up.

I forgot all about the bunch that I had been chasing — no horses were in sight — and rode two miles to a gate in our fence which was seven or eight miles from home. I went through the gate and had followed the fence a mile or more when I happened to put my hand to my face. When I looked at my mitten there was blood on it. "I must have got hurt," I said to myself.

Soon I remembered about the gray horse and that I was supposed to deliver it the next day, so turned and rode back. I found the bunch and started to drive them but my head was so sore and my stomach so sick, that I left them and rode to Olaf Skjenna's house nearby.

He was just coming out of the barn with a harnessed team preparing to go to town. I greeted him with, "Aren't you going to eat?" He took a look at me, sized me up, and said, "Yes", though he had already eaten. He put the team and my horse in the barn and took me to the house. While I lay on the bed (he was batching at that time) he prepared a good meal for me. I tried to eat but nothing would "stay down" and I told him that I was very sorry to have put him to so much trouble.

Olaf tried to persuade me to stay with him but I had to deliver that horse so struck out again. I found the bunch, got them down to the ranch that night and delivered the gelding in Jenner the next day but afterwards it seemed as though I must have dreamed the entire episode.

OLD COWBOYS

Old cowboys do not die — they change their range.
For them the winters grow too long and cold:
The summer sun too hot. Their dimming eyes
Too oft have strained to read defective brands.
Stiff are their joints: they scarce can fork their mounts.
For years they've ridden circle here below,
Stood guard at night and trailed the moving herd.
So many snows and rains have soaked their hides,
And summer suns and winds have seared their skins
That wrinkled, weathered, worn, crippled and lean
They seem but fit for Tutankhamen's tomb.
Old cowboys do not die — they drift away.
They wait until the roundup in the fall,
Until the beef is shipped, the calves are weaned.
Then, when the river's edge is fringed with ice,
When whining, bleak northwesters swell with snow,
They stow their sack and saddle up their "top,"
Then, mounting, turn his tail toward the blast
And fade into the wily, swirling storm.
The darkness falls; no pathway can be seen,
But, fearless and alone, each drifts away
Toward that unknown range beyond his dreams.

A TRAGEDY

Came a murmur drifting eastward
    From the prairies and the plains;
Came a throbbing o'er the greensward
    Like unnumbered, rumbling trains.

'Twas the remnant of the bison
    Fleeing from the blood-soaked south;
Slaughtered wantonly, a million
    Lay amouldering on the earth.

To their northern refuge, Winter
    Came with all his lethal might.
Spring sprang up to save a meager
    Handful from their deadly plight.

Monarchs of a grassy ocean,
    For the Redmen all in all:
Victims of rapacious Whitemen,
    Partial progress caused their fall.

When Saul Boyer was in his twenties I believe that he could ride any horse, so wherever he worked he was given the "rough string" to ride. He rode in only one "stampede" and that was not a Calgary Stampede. Saul drew what was supposed to be the hardest horse to ride that the management had. He rode him with no trouble and when he figured that he had been up there long enough, jumped off. The judges declared that he had been thrown. Saul never rode in another bucking exhibition or contest except the smaller ones at community affairs.

(By most people he was known as "Sol", short for Solomon. He told me at one time that his name was not Solomon; that it was "Saul".)

The flat two miles west of the buildings had on it a good growth of brush and some trees. In winter it was a first class feed and bed ground with good grass adjacent to the brush on the south and west sides. The June floods almost always covered the brushed part and some of the grass land with water and left in the brush a deposit of very sticky mud. In the lower places this sticky mud would be quite deep — it took a lot of dry, hot weather to dry it.

Saul was among those who were hazing some cattle out of the brush one summer after the flood had disappeared. He scarcely ever rode what would be called a quiet horse. It was said that he could take a bronc and do more with it than many men could do with a "broke" horse.

This day he was riding an excitable, half broken bay gelding. When he rode on to what appeared to be dry ground the horse broke through the thin dry crust into heavy, sticky clay. In struggling to get out he reared, his hind feet slid farther under him and as he appeared to be on the way over, Saul put both hands on the fork of the saddle and, throwing himself backward, turned a complete somersault, landing clear of the horse. We used to say that if Saul could get one arm and one leg free he would get out of any "mixup".

Years later he was riding east along the south side of the railroad between Majestic and Buffalo in winter. The rails run through several long "cuts" in this stretch and it is all down grade. I believe that this "down-grade" extends from Majestic to Empress, a distance of forty miles. Trains could slip along with very little noise.

As a long freight slipped out of one of these cuts just behind Saul, the engineer pulled the whistle cord and the horse bolted.

257

Saul didn't have a bridle on it, just a hackamore which was well up on its head instead of low on its nose, and he could not control the horse. There are several small coulees within a span of two miles and the snow was deep. When he saw that the horse was going to take him into these coulees at blind speed, Saul jumped with the hackamore shank in his hands and upset the horse. It is not an easy thing to do and I have seen very few men who could do it.

There was a very heavy storm in the spring of (I believe) 1938. Saul, who was no longer young, had wintered a bunch of cattle for us on our lower place, northeast of Buffalo. There was a very poor growth of grass in the fields along the river and, as the weather seemed settled Saul cut fifty head of two-year-old steers into the larger field north of town in preparation for a move south to the community lease where there was much better grazing.

Then this storm struck without a warning. I have seen others just as bad but none worse. A very strong wind blew from the north bringing with it a heavy fall of wet snow, which as it grew colder, was blown into large drifts. So strong was the wind and so thick the falling snow that it would literally, steal your breath.

These steers were south of the coulees when the storm started and, not liking to face it, drifted against the five mile long south fence, where the wet snow, freezing, turned them into blind white statues.

An ordinary man would not have done what Saul did. The cattle were not his. He was just working for wages but, he was a man. Dressing as warmly as he could, he tied a scarf over his mouth and nose, something that I suppose he never did at any other time in his life. Without the scarf it would have been very difficult to keep from being smothered. He rode three miles along the river through the storm and then one mile south with his back to it before he reached the first steers. They were in small bunches of from three to six head, scattered along the five miles of fence. They were standing in snow with their eyelids held closed by the frozen sleet and could not see anything.

Saul would ride up to a bunch, get off his horse and rub the frozen stuff from their eyelids. As soon as they saw him they would wheel and run toward the coulees and shelter. When he had covered the five miles he turned homeward and had to ride northeast for nine miles practically against the storm beating in from the north. Four or five of the steers were down and dead or dying when he reached them — probably smothered. They were neither weak nor thin. It is impossible to tell how many would have perished if Saul had not gone out there.

MOTHER MALLARD

Where the cherry tree's limbs overhang,
Mother mallard has hidden her nest.
In her dress, mottled, pale buff and brown,
She hopes that no foe will molest.
As she nestles amid last year's grass,
She cuddles her eggs 'neath her breast;
And she dreams of the day, with her brood,
'Mid the reeds of the slough, she can rest.

CHAPTER XI

During those early years Father always managed to be in Medicine Hat on the last day of school and, as a rule, we all left for the ranch the following morning. One summer, possibly that of 1899, a few head of Manitoba stockers and some bulls had been shipped to Stair where they were unloaded and started for the ranch by two riders. Father was driving four horses hitched to a double box wagon carrying some supplies with the camping equipment, tent and beds, etc., on top. He was leading a half broken horse behind the wagon. A long rope reached from the halter to the wagon seat where Father sat on several coils. He told me to not touch it but I could not understand how he could hold that horse by just sitting on the rope. When the team started to trot down a slope and a coil of the rope "paid-out", because the mare did not start trotting at the same time as the team. I took hold of it and was jerked over the back of the seat. The rope passed over the back of my wrist in such a manner that my hand was forced backward and the wrist bones pushed out in front. While he was scolding me, Father put the bones back in place. If he had not been angry and I had not been in the wrong it is very likely that I would have cried; as it was I didn't let out a whimper.

He had to drive to the camp ground at Box Springs, throw off the camping equipment, hobble the extra horse and take me back to town — fifteen miles. When we met the men with the cattle Father told them what he was doing and they told him that a rattlesnake had bitten one of the bulls. Half a mile further we saw it, lying on its side, already greatly swollen, with its four legs sticking out straight like four table legs. The snake had bitten it above a front ankle.

Father took me across the ferry (on the north side of the river it was necessary to drive through water too shallow for the ferry) to the house, then turned around at once and started back to the camp. He returned in about a week for the family.

My sister went 'downtown' for the doctor and when he arrived I was in our back yard showing my arm to some neighbor boys. My arm from finger tips to elbow was placed in a strong plaster of paris cast. I carried it in a sling all summer but that didn't stop me from riding.

When I went to Winnipeg with the fall shipment of beef in 1908, a saddle horse was left in town for me. During my absence a neighbor boy gave it feed and water — my sisters were still at the ranch. It was the last week in September and when I left town on the morning after my return, clouds covered the sky and the wind was blowing from the northwest. Rain, which soon turned to sleet, began to fall. The wind became stronger and by the time I had ridden against it for four miles my legs above the knees were wet. It was getting colder and the sleet had changed to snow. I was wearing two pair of overalls and a short sheepskin-lined coat. (During one winter I wore chaps for the only time in my life. When I would get off to walk my body would be too warm by the time my feet were warmed. Besides the chaps were too heavy if I had to get off to chase a cow out of brush too thick for the horse to get through with the saddle. I sold them.) I had sixty-five miles to ride and knew that if I kept going I would freeze stiff before night. I returned to town.

All day the wind blew fiercely, piling up snow until there was six inches "on the level" with drifts two feet or more in depth. I dried my clothes and, though I knew of no reason why I should hurry back to the ranch, when I went to bed that night, I set the alarm on the clock to ring at five in the morning. When it wakened me I looked out of the window and by the corner street light could see long icicles hanging from the eaves. I realized that there had been quite a few degrees of frost during the night and that there would be a thick crust on top of the wet snow. I said to myself, "No use starting out in this — it would cut the legs off my horse." Then I crawled back into bed.

THE DREAMER

Stampeding days are here again,
   My rig and boots are ready;
Been getting lots of practice in
   And soon I'll hit for Calg'ry.

I wonder if I'll see her there
   And will she still remember?
Has she been waiting for me too
   Or, has she found another?

There's nothing that I wouldn't give
    If I could only find her,
And see her smile at me again
    And hear her rippling laughter.
'Twas just the other night I dreamed
    That I had drawn Barr'lhead.
They had him saddled in the chute
    And I was getting seated.
They jerked the gate and out we came
    A twisting and a'kicking:
I scratched his hide from ear to tail —
    I knew that she was looking.
I made the ride and hit the ground
    And there stood she beside me
With her bewitching face aglow —
    A dream of charm and beauty.
I hope my dream will turn out real,
    I hope that I can find her
For she's the sweetest little girl —
    Oh, how I'd love to hold her.

JULY COMPLAINT

There's something in my bones today;
    It surely does seem queer
That it should bother me this way
    July time every year.
I get so cranky with my wife,
    The kids just drive me wild.
My life is naught but strain and strife;
    The least thing gets me riled.
My wife says, "John, you need a change,
    The grass here's getting dry.
You'd better hunt another range
    Before you wilt and die.
"I'll wash your shirt and pack your grip
    With socks, a tie, and food,
For you are going to take a trip —
    I've stood all that I could!"
I listened to my loving wife
    (I need a change of feed).
I'm goin' to where I'll find new life —
    The Cal-gar-y Stampede.

261

Walter Heiland at the Brooks Rodeo, 1945.

John Hausness and his threshing machine.

Mr. Olaf Skjenna Sr., old Hart Parr tractor, Oliver Skjenna standing on top of tractor also Olaf, Norman Hurl at the wheel and Willie Hurl standing beside the tractor.

Joe Kulyk with 145 horsepower Versatile tractor in 1971.

Chester Howe's irrigation ditch, 1971. Alfalfa field in background.

C. B. Howe's work team.

I went to sleep at once. My mother, who had been dead for four years, spoke to me. Her voice was as natural as though she were standing beside the bed. (Perhaps she was.) "You ought to go," she said quietly. "But," I replied, "that snow is crusted and it will cut the legs off the horse." "You ought to go," she repeated. Twice I offered excuses but when she spoke the same words the third time quietly, but firmly, as was her wont, I jumped out of bed and pulled on my clothes. Believe it or not I had been there five minutes.

The horse was saddled and fed; I ate some breakfast, put a can of sardines in my pocket and left town at six o'clock. For seven miles, after I was five miles from town, I had to travel in a fenced road allowance. I walked those seven miles breaking the crust ahead of my horse. It was twelve o'clock when I reached the end of the road allowance twelve miles north of town. Now I was free and could pick my way. I didn't look for the road — rode the ridges and the higher ground where the snow had not had a chance to rest so much. Even at that it was nine o'clock and dark when I reached the "half-way shack" that night. I had ridden at least forty miles but weaving back and forth as I had been doing in order to keep out of the deep snow as much as possible, it was impossible to tell exactly how many miles I had covered. The northwest wind had driven the snow into and filled the shed which was on the sheltered side of the hill. So, there was no shelter for the horse. We kept an iron picket pin, an axe, frying pan and tea pail at the shack. Leaving the saddle on the horse I picketed him where he would be sheltered from some of the wind. The sky was covered by clouds so that no stars were in sight. It would be impossible to follow the trail in the dark and the hills look very much alike after night under a blanket of snow. It would have been unwise to try travelling farther.

I chopped some chips from the rafters of the shed, made a small fire in the little box stove, ate my sardines and lay down beside the stove. When I became cold I would waken and put a few more chips on the fire. Several times in the night I heard the horse (we called him Catfish — I don't know why) running back and forth trying to keep warm. He happened to be the most thoroughly "picket broke" horse that I have seen. If he hadn't been, I would have been left on foot, for in the morning the pin was almost out of the ground and I believe that one more jerk would have pulled it free.

That part of the country between the Coulee cabin and the ranch is hilly. The snow was deep, making the travelling very

263

difficult. I left the cabin at six o'clock and at four in the afternoon I was still six miles from the ranch. As I moved out of the big hills at this point I could see that from here the snow grew less and less and that the hills across the river, north, were bare. A mile west a four horse team, hitched to a democrat, was going south on the trail. It was my Father starting for the Hat with my three sisters.

It would have been impossible for him to have reached the Coulee cabin that night. I had been ten hours travelling that part of the road with a saddle horse. When I told him what the road was like and at what time I had left "the Hat", he turned around. There was and had been, no snow at the ranch. If he had had any idea of what lay before him, he would not have set out. No weather reports were broadcast on the air in those days. I believe that, though our bodies perish, we do not, and I know that this was an intervention of my Mother.

At least thirty-six hours before I met my Father and sisters on the trail, my Mother knew what my Father was planning to do but evidently could not cause him to change his mind. She spoke to me in town and started me out to prevent a tragedy.

If I had not gone, only those who are old enough to have had similar experiences in the wide open spaces, will be able to imagine the tragedy which could have and, almost certainly would have happened.

Prairie fires have always been feared and hated by stockmen. In those early days they would sweep from the main line of the C.P.R. to the forks of the Red Deer and Saskatchewan Rivers. In destroying the feed they also removed the protective covering from the soil allowing what little moisture there was in the ground to escape. In many of the sloughs the tall grass had been tramped down by stock and winter snows each year for ages and had been formed into a peat-like substance, in some places a foot deep. After a fire had swept the prairie, small fires could be seen smoldering in dry sloughs for a week. Harm was often done to livestock caught between two fires. Horses had their tails and hocks burned; cows' udders sometimes were so badly burned that they were useless. I found a cow, once, that had been in fire hot enough to blind her. She was singed all over; the long hair was burned from her tail and her udder was ruined. She was put out of misery.

Fences, in later times, often proved to be traps. A quiet pet mare belonging to a neighbor was trapped in a fence corner. The hair was singed from her legs and the inside of her hind legs badly burned. Her udder was ruined and much of the hair was burned

264

from her tail. Because she was so quiet the owner was able to care for her. The only part that could not be restored was her udder.

Before there were fences much of the stock (half wild) seemed to know enough to run toward water. When one fire was sweeping east through the country south of the ranch, bunches of horses could be seen running down the hills toward the river on a frontage of many miles. You would often find small bunches of cattle on the safe side of a large slough or lake.

When we were on our way to the railroad with beef one year before 1900 we made one night camp at Bray's spring thirty-five miles south and a little west of the ranch. We could see clouds of smoke to the north being carried east by a strong wind. After dark we watched the side fire as, for many miles, the flames would run up and over a hill like so many racing, fiery demons, then disappear in a low spot only to reappear on the next hill.

It was an awesome sight but you could not help thinking of the acres and acres of grass being turned to black dust. We were fifteen miles from our side of the fire and supposed that the north side was not far from the ranch. I remember Father remarking, "Tom and the boys will get little sleep tonight." He presumed that they were out fighting it.

At one time a fireguard, paid for by the government, was plowed from Tide Lake to a coulee a few miles west of the present village of Iddesleigh. This coulee, whose sides were practically barren of grass formed a natural guard the rest of the way to the river. Harold Keay, a neighboring rancher, did the plowing one year and made a guard forty feet wide — twice as wide as was specified. He believed that it would stop any fire. In a short time it was tested.

Keay, Alex Gordon and some other men managed to get to the guard before the lead of a fire when they saw its smoke far to the west, possibly beyond the Crow Buttes. They had time to burn a narrow strip for about a mile along the west side of the guard before the fire reached them. They stopped this lead fire and were congratulating themselves when the wind picked up a piece of burning manure and carried it across the guard into a dry slough. The fire was away again. It was midnight; in three hours the lead fire travelled seventy-five miles to the Forks of Red Deer and Saskatchewan Rivers. When I left the house at the ranch that morning at four o'clock the main fire was long past but small side fires were at the heads of the coulees above the ranch threatening to find a way down the hills to the flat. One of these small fires could be seen from the buildings. The country from Cassils to the Forks was black.

265

TEACH ME TO SMILE

Teach me to smile, dear Lord, whate'er befall.
Whate'er the task, where'er the call;
When threat'ning clouds disperse, and skies are clear,
    'Tis easy then to wear a smile; to cheer.
    When disillusion, pain or care
The aching heart's strings chafe and tear
I'm prone to yield to gloom and dark despair.
Teach me to smile in spite of inward storm,
    My selfish habit to reform:
Why should I thrust my burden on a friend?
Why thus my melancholy mood extend?
    Each has his woe; each has his cross;
    To each will come some gain, some loss.
Dear Lord, please teach me not to horde the dross.
Teach me to smile; to let the love light shine;
    Both love and light, alike, are Thine.
A smile reveals the light that shines within;
To stifle it is wilful, churlish sin.
    'Tis in the dark that evil lurks
    To snare the soul that duty shirks
And use it to promote its wicked works.
Teach me to smile, dear Lord, to love like Thee;
    Thy love in me may all men see;
Unselfish love, a love that smiles through pain,
Though often overcome, still tries again.
    A smile whose fount is love alone,
    Does make an inward beauty known
Which only those who love can ever own.
The future of immortal souls
Is settled in the ring of time.
Redeem, then, time while yet you may
For some day time shall be no more.

THE RED DEER VALLEY

Through a valley that's verdant in springtime
Winds the Red Deer with natural grace.
Past its islands, its fords and its sandbars
It meanders at leisurely pace.

There's a pair of grey geese on the island;
Every summer they rear a new brood.
In the shade of that cherry a mallard
Hides her nest 'neath a green, grassy hood.

266

If you're silent and sly as a Redman
You may watch the wild whitetail at play,
Or, perhaps catch a glimpse of the mule deer
As he proudly goes bouncing away.

And up on the bench there's a dance floor
Where the chicken their sundance perform.
Nestled close to that sage two hungarians
Crouch to keep their full nest free from harm.

Straying warily down from the uplands
Timid antelope bands oft appear,
With a cunning old doe in the vanguard,
And a daddy-buck guarding the rear.

While the others slip down to the water,
There is one keeping watch on the hill;
And they're up and away like the whirlwind,
If he whistles a note sharp and shrill.

Ranging spirits built homes in the valley
Years before any tumbleweed came.
There was water and feed in abundance,
And their stock mingled with the wild game.

If you ride up the hill in the morning,
E'er the eastern sky is aflame,
When the musical sounds of the dawning
Weave a harmony no one can name.

Then will something seep into your being,
And abide as long as you live.
It will whisper wherever you wonder,
"There's content that none other can give."

North of the present railroad siding of Halsbury the river makes a sharp bend to the north for a few miles then swings east again. Protected by that bend, ten or twelve sections of grass across from the present V-V Ranch had been by-passed by the fire. It was part of Alex Gordon's range. Some more of his grass west of that had also been spared. We were cleaned out except for narrow strips along the river. The buildings at the camp at the "Dry Trees," seven miles east of home were lost in that fire. Practically all the cattle were on the north side of the river but we needed grass for two hundred horses. Alex told us that we could use that large patch across from the V-V, so we turned the horses up there — a camp was set up for the man who would be herding them. They were kept there until our new grass was tall enough to be of use. The prairie, green with clean new grass, is beautiful.

267

One year I saw smoke about twelve miles west and judged by the wind that the lead fire would cross our Medicine Hat trail about four miles south of the buildings. There were four to six well worn ruts forming the trail and along the west side of it for nine miles we had a fireguard of twelve fourteen-inch furrows. Three of us drove south, planning to "back fire" where we expected the fire to cross. We would then work back toward the ranch ahead of the side fire.

As we drove to the top of a small hill less than four miles south we were just in time to see the lead fire hit the guard. We watched the flames as they reached out through the air across the fourteen foot guard and the wagon ruts (another six or eight feet) grabbed the grass on the other side and sped on without even a pause.

While Tom Mossop and Bill Rae were camped for noon one day at the Bone Pile spring the wind whipped a burning ember from the camp fire and dropped it in some dry grass. They were up and fighting at once but the fire got away from them and raced northeast. They stayed with it, fighting the west side until it reached a coulee near the "calf camp," a distance of 18 miles. They were two husky men but when they had beaten out the last of it they had to lean against one another to stay on their feet. Some one was at the calf camp so they did not have to walk back to the Bone Pile.

On another occasion a fire had burned from near Suffield northeast to the Big Sand Hills. It had passed quite a few miles south of our place and our side of the fire was out. It smoldered in the brush in the Hills and when the wind changed, the fire started up again and threatened the grass between us and the "burned over" land. Tom and I and a few others went down the river seven miles and started a "backfire".

We fought our side of the blaze 'til far into the night, working southeast until we reached the black ground where the fire had passed on its way east, a day or two before. We found later that we had been about fourteen miles southeast of home. The sky was covered with clouds so that no stars were in sight and the men speculated as to the direction in which the ranch lay. No two pointed in the same direction but I always thought that if I had followed anyone it would have been Ed Cunningham.

To make sure that we didn't get lost we decided to take the long road and follow the line of the "burn" along which we had come. While the others walked one would drive until he reached that stage (which didn't take long) where he could not keep his eyes open any longer. He would then get out of the "rig" and another would drive for a time. As dawn began to break we were back to where we had started the backfire. We were tired, sleepy and hungry.

268

We didn't have any grub with us and hadn't eaten since noon of the previous day. We were not out for a picnic: we went out to fight fire and that meant fight until it was out. The fire would not rest and there would be time to eat afterwards.

CHAPTER XII

We always had a garden at the ranch. An old lumberjack, John Esplen, planted and cared for one of the earliest. Potatoes, turnips and onions were the main products of this early garden. The patch was extended until it included about two acres. A dam was built in a coulee close to the garden. Spring "run-off" and rains filled it and the overflow from a spring about two hundred yards up the coulee, fed it and kept a usable supply in the dam. Having good soil in a sheltered spot with plenty of water, we were able to grow tomatoes, melons, peas and corn besides the ordinary vegetables. A rhubarb patch was started and later a strawberry patch was added.

About 1908 two men driving through the ranch in an auto, stopped to admire the garden. They took several pictures of the tomatoes, pumpkins and tall corn. They did not tell us who they were and in those days you were not in the habit of asking anyone for his name; if he wanted you to know it, he told you without being asked.

In 1910 settlers began coming into the country around Bindloss and Cavendish. Some of them trailed in from Brooks where there was a Government Land Office. Often some of these people would stop overnight at our place. There was always room at the table for whoever came along, and feed and shelter for their horses.

Father believed that these people were making a great mistake in coming into this part of the province to try to make a living growing grain and he often told them so. One evening he was making his usual remarks. "Why," exclaimed one, "you are doing more to settle this country than any one else."

"How?" asked Father.

"Over in the Land Office in Brooks they tell people that Andy Gordon has been back on the Red Deer for years and he can grow anything. Then they show pictures of your garden but they don't explain that it is an irrigated garden." One settler from the South told me that pictures of Father's garden were on display in the Union Station in Kansas City to show people what could be raised in this area that was being thrown open for homesteading.

While many made a humble beginning there were others who with the settler referred to, spent a fair amount of money paying for the erection of good buildings, buying all necessary equipment and some livestock. They were unable to get that money back.

In 1915 and 1916 the first good crops were harvested in that area and Father remarked that it was "the worst thing that could have happened to those farmers." When asked why, he replied, "They will just sit here and wait for another." That is what many of them did. Several moved out after harvesting those two crops but many stayed until the government moved two-thirds of them to other areas. Those who remained rented abandoned land from the Special Areas Board for a rental of one-fifth of the crop. We relinquished our hold on 18,000 acres of grazing land with the proviso that the land be used for a community pasture.

Mr. Buckum of the Special Areas Board had called at my house (the lease on that land was in my name) and after talking for an hour telling me of his dream of such an arrangement, asked:

"What is the lowest figure that you will consider for that township south of the railway?" Tom Owens had offered to buy it for seventy-five cents per acre. When Mr. Buckum, who had been pacing the floor while he talked, heard me say that the government could have the lease for that purpose if they would cancel the two years rental and taxes outstanding, he sat down and gasped.

"Say that again."

I repeated what I had said and added that Father and I had discussed the matter more than once and were of the same opinion as he. That was, that if these people were to remain in the country they must have cattle and a place to run them during the summer.

Mr. Buckum often made use of a parody on one of Blake's poems:

"I will not rest from toil or pain.
Nor shall the pen rest in my hand
'Til we have built Jerusalem
From Medicine Hat to Denhart Land."

The two years' taxes and rental against the township amounted to nine cents per acre. We didn't have to give it up but believed that the right thing to do was to help these others make a living, and in our offer we stipulated that the grazing rights must not be resold to anyone but be used solely for a community pasture. Those farmers who remained in the area have become independent. During the last seven years (1952-1959) they have harvested good crops and have received a good price for any grain sold. The price of cattle has been from ten to fifteen times as high as it was during part of the time in the years 1930-1938. With the assistance of the government they have been able to build up well-bred herds of

270

cattle. Their farms are well equipped, their homes comfortable. Life for the younger generation is a wonderful improvement over that endured by their parents.

WHAT COUNTS — Author unknown.

It isn't the things you talk about
No matter how fine and true,
It isn't the way you seem to live
Nor even the things you do;
It isn't the creed you call your own,
Nor the mottoes on the wall;
The only thing that really counts
Is what's in your heart — that's all.
It isn't the many friends you make,
It's only the friends you keep;
It isn't the you that people see,
It's the real you down deep;
It isn't what people say you are,
Just let them talk as they please,
It's what you know you are inside;
What counts is what God sees.

STORIES

One day Quinton Donovan was sitting in a beverage room with some of his co-workers and their conversation was soon turned to carpentry. One of the men was telling Quinton the trouble he was having with his planer. Sitting at a table, about three away, was Ralph Rathburn and some of his cowboy friends. Anyone knowing Ralph knows that there are only two subjects which Ralph thinks are worth talking about — horses and guns. Overhearing parts of the conversation between Quinton and his friends, such as "how much lead are you going on — is your saw table set at correct angle; and finally "what have you got for power?" Quinton asked. The reply was, "1/4 horse electric motor." Ralph being very high, hearing the mention of 1/4 horse, immediately said, "No Quarter Horse could do it." Getting up he said to his cowboy friends, "Let's go and get into this argument."

One day when Pete Sulley was helping Kid and Lincoln Howe, break horses, after they had been working steady for a few hours, when they stopped to rest awhile. The trio was sitting on the corral fence discussing the corral full of horses, when someone brought the message that a rich relative in England had died and left the Howe boys a small fortune, something like a half million dollars. Their only reaction to the news was, Lincoln said, "If I thought that was true I would turn these horses loose and never work again." Kid went one better when he said, "Hell, if I thought that was true, I'd hire Pete here to turn those horses loose."

Mrs. Steve (Mary) Keinick and pup, Cavendish, Alta. Raised from a pup till about 3 years old, but had to be destroyed as it killed and ate the chickens.

272

Miscellaneous

Gus Hanson 1928 threshing crew on the move.

Mrs. Jim Hannaford arriving with lunch for the ground breaking crew, 1914.

Remember when a "Sunday Drive" was a time of relaxation?

Harvest Time, 1926.

Stacking loose hay.

Waiting for the Ferry.

274

Stacking bundles.

S. Hillstead hauling grain to Buffalo in 1928.

Buffalo Bridge, one span south side of river.

Harvest time, 1943.

Seven-horse-hitch on a seed drill.

Early days threshing.

Atlee baseball fans, 1914.

The old-timers at Buffalo Parade. Mr. and Mrs. C. B. Howe, R. S. Gravette, Louis Wilhelmson.

Chow time at the chuck wagon. Some of the people I can recognize are Tom McCarthy second from left, Mrs. Jarboe kneeling in front of back wheel, Clyde beside her, Fisher kneeling second from the right. Otto Wozeske far right and Fred Wozeske in the wagon seat.

Ben Dart and Joy in the covered wagon. Parade.

Some of the boys at the Buffalo Parade — Clarence Hurl, Olaf Skjenna as the clowns, Theodore Barneko the policeman, Gene Anderson with Mule as prospector. Buster McCullough as the organ grinder with a monkey.

Two early contrasting modes of transportation.

Girls' Ball team at Buffalo — Clarence and Dell Hurl as coaches.

A SKETCHY OUTLINE OF THE DEVELOPMENT OF THE HAMLET OF BUFFALO

Around the turn of century the few settlers and ranchers in this district received their mail about twice a year, this would be when someone would make the semi-annual trip to Medicine Hat, about sixty-five miles across the open prairie, over rutted prairie trails. The trip would take two days to go, stopping overnight and sleeping out under the stars, two days in town to get the supplies and two days for the return trip. Sometimes it would take the better part of a day, for those living on the north side of Red Deer River, just to get their wagons and teams across. This was a slow process as in some instances the wagons would have to be dismantled and taken across piece by piece and re-assembled and the supplies taken across in the same manner.

Around 1910 a post office (Gold Springs) was established and was located at Howard McCullough's place, on the north side of the river. Prior to this time mail was also received at Parvella, later known as part of the Vee Bar Vee. In 1914 the Canadian Pacific Railroad tracks were laid and has since been known as the Bassano — Empress line. It was about this time that Buffalo received its name. There are many stories as how the name of "Buffalo" was arrived at, but the most logic one being, as told by Mr. John R. Gordon, who arrived in this country in 1896.

He notes that a Mr. Pauling of Buffalo, New York, who homesteaded east of Buffalo, supplied the name. A Mr. Todd, the engineer in charge of construction and recommending of names, lived with the Gordons as long as he was in the area.

The train made two trips a week, going east on Wednesday and west on Saturday.

In about 1916 the first automobile came to the district and was owned by Leland Pound's grandfather, Atlee. Cattle buyers would occasionally come in by car.

In 1920, the Buffalo, Alberta post office opened for business on February first.

The following are a list of the postmasters and their dates of appointment.

POSTMASTER	DATE APPOINTED
Cecil Mode	February 1, 1920
Noah Steeves	May 7, 1921
A. J. Scanes	January 1, 1922
John Elbridge Steeves	February 1, 1929
John R. Gordon	December 28, 1929

POSTMASTER (cont.)	DATE APPOINTED (cont.)
William Marshall Thompson	April 16, 1946
Mrs. Bernice May Jeske	July 30, 1952
William M. Thompson	September 1, 1954 (acting)
Arnold Christian Beglaw	January 6, 1955
Mrs. Rita Hazel Nelson	October 1, 1968

The Alberta Pacific Grain Company erected an elevator in 1923 and the Alberta Wheat Pool came in 1928.

During all this time the community was still without means of crossing the river except by ferry, so in 1931 the Buffalo bridge was built. Many of the men from along the Red Deer worked on the construction of this bridge. Some of the names are: Matt Sneddon, (Dave's father) and it is reported that his name is engraved on a pier on the north side; Wm. Dziatkewich; Karl Dziatkewich; Bill Peleshock; Mike Holoida; Steve Holoida; Steve Lupulack; Joe Kulyk; Lovell Stone; Ben Anderson and many others.

Shipping corrals were built in Buffalo, the date is not known, but the last shipment to pass over the scales was in 1966 and later the corrals were demolished.

In about 1946 the river flooded its banks and the large pieces of ice destroyed the bridge at Empress and for a while it looked as though this district was to lose their bridge to replace the one at Empress. But several of the ranchers and farmers went to Edmonton to protest such a move.

The early settlers engaged the services of teachers to teach their children at home and later as more and more people came in and the means of transportation, as well as the roads improved, schools were established. The Emslie on the north side of the river and the Lila on the south side. In about 1942 or '43 the two school divisions, Acadia and Medicine Hat, combined and all the children went to the one school located on the south side of the Red Deer River. The families with children attending school were responsible for their transportation. In 1962 a bus was provided and Leroy Callaghan was engaged to transport the children from the north side of the river. Later when another bus was required, Eugene Anderson became the driver of the second vehicle. Today we are back to the one bus and Leroy is still the driver.

At one time the hamlet of Buffalo had two elevators, a railroad station complete with telegraph service, a pool hall, a restaurant and rooming-house, a livery stable, two blacksmith shops, two stores and a post office, a dealer in bulk Esso products, as well as the shipping corrals already mentioned. A church, as is often the case, seemed to be the most difficult to obtain, but services were held in the different homes and in the Community Hall. (See history of Buffalo United Church.)

Just when the first Community Hall was built, the date is not known, but in the fifties, the hall was moved from just west of Woo Sam's store, to its present site and remodelling job was done. Harry Muzyka recalls that Fred DeWahl was head carpenter on this job and the menfolk of the community joined together to dismantle the livery stable of Mr. King's and used the lumber from it to rebuild the present hall.

One man who had done much, driving wise, to help develop this small hamlet, is Don Olson, Brooks, Alberta, who for six years and one month drove the truck which brought the mail from Brooks to our local post office. During that time Don drove 247,000 miles and was only prevented, by road conditions or because of the weather, from delivering the mail two or three days in all that time. And as anyone can report, this part of the country can experience some very severe storms and a great deal of the time the road between Brooks and Buffalo leaves much to be desired.

Don is a married man and has three daughters. They live seven and one half miles west of Brooks, at Cassil. Don's father, Ingvold Olson, was a homesteader in the Iddesleigh district in 1912, as was his grandfather, John Myhre (mother's father). Today Don works for the Eastern Irrigation District, operating a Hi-Hoe. This is a big machine, hydraulically operated, a combined Back-hoe and Dragline, but much bigger than either.

THE EMSLIE SCHOOL by Iris Anderson

The Emslie school was named for Jack Emslie who died in England, with the flu, after serving four years in World War I.

The land was donated by Ole Kjarland, on which the schoolhouse was built, while others in the community gave money for material and labor. During the earlier years the schoolhouse was used for a Community Hall.

The only teachers we had were Mrs. Graham, she taught for three years, then William Thompson taught for seven, during which time he married Elizabeth (Boo) Campbell. Dib McManus was our next teacher, she taught for one year and until Christmas of the next year, then a Mrs. Peterson, taught the last six months of 1941. While Miss McManus was our teacher she married Del Brassard. In the fall of 1941, Mrs. Brassard taught us again and in June of 1942 the school closed. This school was located about six or seven miles north of the Red Deer River. In the fall of 1942 I went to high school in Buffalo. The school was held in one room in the

280

Emslie School in 1941.

Ted Anderson, Wm. Thomson, Dorothy Howe, Alice Anderson, Leroy Callaghan, Sheila Anderson, Maxine Callaghan, Shirley Howe, Iris Anderson, 1938.

old Buffalo Hall, which used to sit right up against Woo Sam's store, on the west side. Mrs. Del Hurl taught us until Christmas, then a Miss Dixon taught from January to June. A Mrs. Thomas from Saskatchewan taught the next year. The school was moved from the Hall to the house where Joe Getz now lives. One wall was taken out between the living room and one of the bedrooms. Mr. Klink from Jenner taught the school term of 1944 and '45, at which time the high school was closed down and a joint arrangement was made between the Medicine Hat and Acadia school division. A hardwood tree, trimmed with creeping cedar served as our Christmas tree at our school concerts. There were no trees in the homes as they were too hard to come by and were considered a luxury.

281

About 1924 Emslie Class. Left to right in the back row, second Margaret Orpen, Eileen Bjork, Sylvia Orpen, Edna Bjork and the teacher Miss Eberley. Front row: Fred Lubin, Annie Lubin, Helen McCullough, Helen Brown, Tom Lubin, Norwood Bjork, Buster McCullough and Hughie Brown.

IN PRAISE OF EMSLIE

Emslie, like Atlee has a team
And when we get started, watch our steam.

As usual we have players nine
We have a pitcher that's very fine!

Shirley our catcher is very fair,
She catches the pitches of "Teddy Bear."

Of our stunning first baseman, Dorothy Howe,
All we can say is, her catching's a wow!

The second baseman keeps the crowd staring,
And Sheila has all of Atlee glaring.

Our third baseman, Maxine, is one of the best!
She lets Kenny go, but catches the rest.

As for our good old short stop Ike,
She doesn't let Atlee do as they like!

Our left fielder, Leroy, is not very big,
But he stops the ball while dancing a jig.

282

Mary, our centre field, we insist is very good,
She'd even be better if she possibly could.

Although Alice, our right fielder, is very small,
She always manages to stop the ball.

Now that you have met our players nine,
I think you'll agree we are all very fine!

Sheila Anderson
assisted by Grade VIII.

ARETHUSA

Look up at the hill
Why, there they are,
Arethusa is coming in a car.

Tony the catcher, is in the front seat,
Look like their team is going to get beat.

Mike the pitcher, is fat and round,
And finds it hard to reach the ground.

Mike pitches the ball, but misses the base.
Look, there's Tony making a face.

Tony throws a ball. Oh where is it going?
Sister Annie better do some growing.

Her long golden curls floating in the breeze
As she springs for the ball with the greatest of ease.

Their first baseman, Lily, is quite a size,
Which helps to prevent the passing of flies.

The second baseman, Mary, is tall and dark,
And at playing ball, she's really a shark.

When Alex plays he's always behind,
Wonder what girl is on his mind?

Phylis and Stanley are light as a feather,
And when they play ball, they're always together.

Annie, the teacher, who plays short
Is the one who Harry likes to court.

Now this brings Arethusa to a close,
And if you're asleep, wake up from that doze.

We meant it to be good, but if you think it's bad,
You'll make us feel sorry as well as sad.

But cheer up, folks, there's more to come,
Here's hoping the rest isn't nearly so bum.

by Us Two.

OUR OPPOSITION

There are nine players in Atlee's team.
Tall, thin, short and fat.
And it is really a wow
To see these players bat.
There's Davie, short and also fat
With Kennie tall and lean.
And Keith, is always saying things
That he shouldn't really mean.
When the pitcher, Don
Is on the blink,
The rooters for Atlee say,
"Wink, Donnie, Wink."
And when Delmar, the catcher
Gets up to bat,
The on-lookers say,
"You fielders ought to get back."
When George is up to bat
Colette says, "murder that ball."
But George has often fanned
And doesn't hit it at all.
Gordon, the second baseman,
Lets the ball go by,
And Eileen, the right fielder,
Heaves a big sigh.
The seventh inning comes to a close,
By the pitcher fanning Dot.
They all boo her and Atlee says,
"Gee whiz, that helps a lot."
This brings the ball game to a close
It is a sorrowful ending.
And someone from Atlee says,
"The Emslie team needs mending."

by S. Howe.

LILA SCHOOL by Mrs. Rena Monkman

Lila school opened on the southeast corner of Mayhew's (now Lovell Stone) farm, in the fall of 1920, in a little shack. Mrs. Mary Allen was the first teacher and a Mr. Bignee was our second teacher. They had a new school built in 1922, but still on the Mayhew farm, but farther north opposite Dearings. The school was so named because Lila Dearing was the first child born in the immediate district.

Emslie and Lila and Atlee school children gathering for picnic in 1939.

Lila School before converted to Buffalo United Church.

Miss Anna Wilson and her sister, Clara taught in the new school in the fall of 1922 and the winter of '23. Miss Mornie Peterson taught a half term in 1924 and Miss Maxwell part term. Mary McQuarrie taught school for two years, the teacherage had to be moved to the McKay's place in 1925 as she was afraid to stay alone. Ralph Edgington taught school for a part term and Miss Boardseth finished off. Kenneth Argue taught here in 1926, Helen and Mabel Nash in 1927. Other teachers were: Arthur Slapoe, Chuck Bridgeland, Travis Newton, a Mr. Nelson, George Sackman, Mr. Miller, Miss Heather, Jean Murphy, Mr. Allen, Annie Dahlbak, Mrs. Delmer Hurl, Miss Lorraine Hubac (now Mrs. Leonard Rinker), Myrtle Silverthorne (now Mrs. Jeff Venables), Mrs. Lily Ertmoed and Mrs. Fred DeWahl.

It was about this time (1957) the Lila school building was moved and converted into a church, namely the Buffalo United, and a new building was brought in, in two sections to be used as the teacherage in 1962, but a new school had been built in 1957 and Mrs. Lily Ertmoed was the first to teach there. She was followed by Mrs. Bob Stewart, her husband used to give the children swimming lessons. They lived in a trailer. In September 1962 a Mr. Luchuk taught and he was the first to occupy the new teacherage. Mrs. John Heiman and Mrs. Myrtle Venables taught the school year of 1963 and '64. Mrs. Herman and Mrs. Marjorie Kornelson in 1964 and '65. Mrs. Herman and Mrs. Jack Thompson in 1965 and '66. Mrs. Herman and Mrs. Myrtle Venables in 1966 and '67. Mrs. Marianne Hankerson and Miss Lorraine Olson in 1967 and '68. Miss Lorraine Olson and her sister Beverly in 1968 and '69. Mr. and Mrs. Delmere Kitt from 1969 to   ?

In 1971 there were 28 pupils attending this school. The arrangement spoke of between the Medicine Hat and Acadia school divisions were that the children on the north side of the Red Deer River would be allowed to attend the school on the south side of the river.

A school bus has been provided and some of the bus drivers on the north side were Eugene Anderson, Don Hankerson and Leroy Callaghan. The latter is still active in this field. Walter Heiland and George Mercer are the drivers for the south side. Before Arnold Beglaw left here he was one of the drivers on the south side.

The pupils are taught up to and including Grade Nine, after which they have to leave here and attend school in either Brooks, Calgary or Medicine Hat if they wish to further their education.

THE HISTORY OF THE BUFFALO UNITED CHURCH

by Mrs. Rena Monkman and Mrs. Ted Stone

In the late fifties or early sixties, the old Lila schoolhouse was moved and converted into a church. Heading up this project was the Rev. Jack Beaton, who also donated the furnishings for the pulpit in 1962. Supporting Rev. Beaton were such men as Louis Wilhelmson, Edgar (Ted) Stone, Olaf Skjenna Jr., Allan Smith, Leroy Callaghan and many others, with the entire community contributing money for materials. The women shared this work by preparing meals for the working crew.

The moving of the building was marred by a very tragic accident in which a Portuguese man, who was employed by Chester C. Howe, lost his life, when the tractor he was driving overturned and he was pinned beneath the flaming wreckage.

With the completion of the church building, the opening and dedication services were held on Sunday, April 26, 1962.

A large Bible for the pulpit was donated by the Congregation and dedicated to Mr. and Mrs. John R. Gordon, in appreciation and recognition of the many years they spent in this community and for the work they did to keep the Word of God alive.

The first wedding performed in this church was in 1964, when Marjorie Louise Stegen and Gerald Peter Kornelson exchanged their marriage vows. Other weddings to date are: Gail Rosalyn Rubbelke and James Wesley Andrus, May, 1965; Valerie Ann Ertmoed and

286

Church gathering at Buffalo.

Dennis Roy Brodie, on August 10, 1968; Leona Mae Stone and Thomas David Calhoun, September 6, 1969 and Lynda Rose Stone and Charles Edward Mohr on April 10, 1971.

There have been several baptisms, but those to be found recorded in the Bible in the church are, David Edgar Calhoun, son of Mr. and Mrs. Thomas Calhoun on April 9, 1971. On the same date Jeffrey Bobbie Rempel and his sister, Karrie Lynn Rempel, son and daughter of Mr. and Mrs. T. Rempel, grandchildren of Mr. and Mrs. Clarence Hurl. Zane Wesley Andrus, son of Mr. and Mrs. James Andrus, on June 27, 1971.

Names of the ministers that have served in the church are, Rev. Jack Beaton, Rev. Harvey Murphy, Rev. John McNeil, Rev. G. Arthur, Mr. Stewart Anderson and our present Minister, Rev. James Bushel.

Some of those who served over the years prior to the opening of the church were such names as; Claxton, Steward, Craw, Irwin, Charles Lewis, Mitchell, Jones, W. P. Smetherane, Ian Killens, L. G. Harvey, Wesley Latimer, Bell, Arthur Anderson, a Mr. Gordon from Jenner, MacMillan, White, Proctor, Doug McMurtry, John T. Horricks, McKenzie, Edmonds, Quigley, Shields, Phil Cline, Hartwell Illsey, Don Parr and J. VanWalsen.

A Sunday school was held for many years until about 1965 or 1966, when due to the controversy over the "new trend" of teaching Word of God caused the split. Those who had devoted so many years teaching the children were reluctant to "feed" the children a more scientific approach to the Word which proned to deny the

Buffalo Church congregation in front of the old hall.

287

Virgin and Supernatural birth of Christ. This past year has seen financial difficulties in our little church, but with a steadfast faith in Christ and our loyal attendance, we feel that even this will be overcome.

THE ALBERTA WHEAT POOL

The Alberta Wheat Pool began operations in Buffalo in 1928, with a 35,000 bushel elevator built by R. O. Benell. This elevator was wrecked in 1947 and the salvage was used in Oyen. On October 11th, 1943, Alberta Wheat Pool purchased from Alberta Pacific Grain Company a 29,000 bushel elevator and a coal shed, both of which were built in 1923. The coal shed was sold in December of 1962. In 1967 the Pool built a 70,000 bushel elevator at Buffalo, and converted the old 29,000 bushel elevator to a twin.

Grain handlings between 1928-29 to 1969-70 at Buffalo totalled 3,428,940 bushels. The high in handlings is recorded for the crop of 1966-67, when the Pool elevator at Buffalo totalled 220,392 bushels. The low recorded was in 1937-38 when handlings amounted to only 49 bushels. The following is a list of Alberta Wheat Pool Agents, their Travelling Superintendents, Delegates and Public Relations Representatives for the Buffalo area.

Agent's Name	From	To	Superintendent
J. J. Souter	Nov. 16/28	Feb. 13/35	R. C. Armstrong
S. J. Hurl	Feb. 13/35	Oct. 30/35	From Nov. 16/28 to Sept. /29
E. H. Lewis	Oct. 30/35	Jun. 26/37	A. R. Purvis
Closed	Jun. 26/37	Oct. 19/37	From Sept. 18/29 to Aug. /35
J. R. Gordon	Oct. 19/37	Aug. 8/38	G. E. F. Johnston
R. S. Edey	Aug. 8/38	Jun. 21/39	From Aug. 7/35 to Aug. 16/47
Closed	Jun. 21/39	Jul. 6/39	A. L. Oliver
M. V. Meyer	Aug. 1/40	Jul. 1/42	From Aug. 16/47 to Sept. 1/54
G. Leishman	Jul. 1/42	Jul. 15/42	A. Christianson
W. L. Culham	Jul. 15/42	Apr. 19/43	From Sept. 1/54 to Sept. 1/56
J. N. McDonald	Apr. 19/43	Jul. 10/43	W. E. Smith
Closed	Jul. /43	Aug. 5/43	From Sept. 1/56 to Aug. 1/60
S. J. Hurl	Aug. 5/43	Aug. 16/55	J. M. Ferguson
C. E. Siewert	Aug. 16/55	Jan. 30/57	From Aug. 1/60 to Feb. 8/62
J. P. Kirwan	Jan. 30/57	Apr. 7/58	A. A. Baker
A. McMorran	Apr. 7/58	Feb. 5/66	From Feb. 12/62 to Oct. 1/65
T. D. Dixon	Feb. 5/66	Jun. 16/66	J. E. Patterson
E. H. Whitelock	Jun. 16/66	Aug. 7/67	From Oct. 1/65 to Jul. 1/69
A. R. Nelson	Aug. 4/67		C. R. Rennie
			From Jul. 1/69

Public Relations Representatives for Buffalo.

1928 - 1948	William Pettinger
1948 - 1949	J. E. Alcock
1949 - 1950	G. W. Braithwaite
1950 - 1956	J. E. Ness
1956 - 1964	B. H. Sommerville
1964 - 1967	D. L. Freed
1967 to present.	W. R. Wyse

Delegates in Buffalo District.

1923	S. S. Boyd	Brutus
1924	John G. Ellenton	Iddesleigh
1925	Harry Bunn	Atlee
1926	Wellington Yake	Cappon
1927	Wellington Yake	
1928	Wellington Yake	
1929	Wellington Yake	
1930	Wellington Yake	
1931	Wellington Yake	
1932	Wellington Yake	
1933	J. R. Hannaford	Howie
1934	J. R. Hannaford	
1935	Wellington Yake	Cappon
1936	J. R. Hannaford	Howie
1937	J. R. Hannaford	
1938	J. R. Hannaford	
1939	J. R. Hannaford	
1940	J. R. Hannaford	
1941	J. R. Hannaford	
1942	J. R. Hannaford	
1943	J. R. Hannaford	
1944	J. R. Hannaford	Bindloss
1945	John Fowlie	
1946	John Fowlie	
1947	John Fowlie	
1948	John Fowlie	
1949	Jake Frey	Arneson
1950	Jake Frey	
1951	Jake Frey	
1952	Jake Frey	
1953	Jake Frey	
1954	Jake Frey	
1955	Jake Frey	
1956	Pete Voroney	Tilley

1957	Pete Voroney	
1958	William W. Plumer	Brooks
1959	William W. Plumer	
1960	William W. Plumer	
1960	William W. Plumer	
1961	William W. Plumer	
1962	William W. Plumer	
1963	William W. Plumer	
1964	Albert P. Schindler	Brooks
1965	Albert P. Schindler	Brooks
1966	Albert P. Schindler	
1967	Albert P. Schindler	
1968	Albert P. Schindler	
1969	Albert P. Schindler	
1970	Joseph Volek	Tilley

Four of our earliest pioneers, who are also members of the Wheat Pool were on hand when the new elevator was opened in 1967, they were: Frank Rubbelke, Lovell Stone, Magnus Bjork and C. B. Howe. The honor of cutting the ribbon was bestowed on Woo Sam, a local merchant. While he was not a wheat farmer, he had contributed much towards the development of this community. C. B. Howe being the oldest member with wheat that year, delivered the first load, followed by the youngest member Bob Monkman.

Do you remember when ads were like this? The ads were taken from the 1940 Emslie school yearbook.

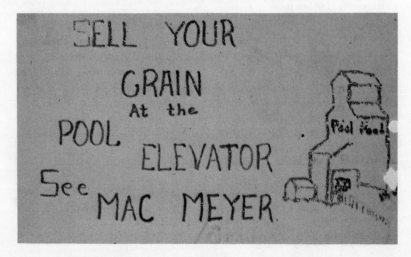

290

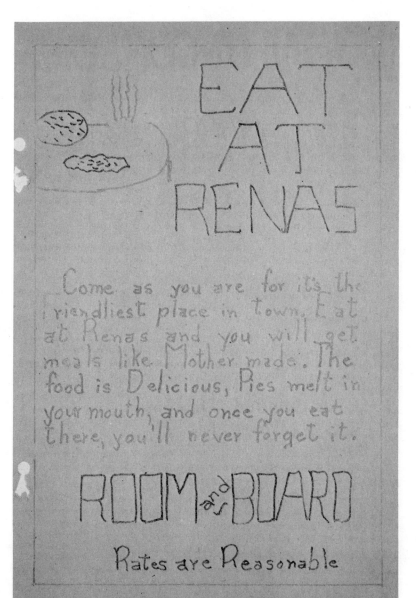

EAT
AT
RENAS

Come as you are for it's the friendliest place in town. Eat at Renas and you will get meals like Mother made. The food is Delicious, Pies melt in your mouth, and once you eat there, you'll never forget it.

ROOM and BOARD

Rates are Reasonable

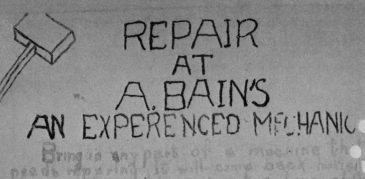

REPAIR
AT
A. BAIN'S
AN EXPERIENCED MECHANIC

Bring in any part of a machine that
needs repairing. It will come back looking
like new. Specialty, cars, tractors, plow-
shares—etc.

—Moto—
Speed and Satisfaction

TELEGRAM TELEGRAM!

EXPRESS FOR MR
GET YOUR MONEY ORDERS HERE

TICKETS!   TICKETS!

Jas O'Morrow C.P.R.

WOO SAM

The biggest little store.
Prompt service for everyone
GROCERIES
HARDWARE
DRY GOODS
GAS and OIL
ROOMS for RENT
Here's where your dollar goes farther.

KING'S POOL HALL

If the weather is wet or cold,
Go to King's for a game of pool.
If you go to put in time,
All you'll need is a single dime

SELL YOUR
GRAIN
AT THE
ALBERTA PACIFIC ELEVATOR

The highest prices are given to you
by the friendly elevator man
JIM O'BRIEN

BILL JOHNSON

Have

REPAIR YOUR SHOES

The best in the west.

Let him make your old shoes
look new prices are reasonable

294

JOAN R. GORDON

POST MASTER

MASSY HARRIS AGENT.

IMPERIAL PRODUCTS

GAS and OILS

Buy Imperial Products — Best in the west
Money back guarantee

MRS. NATTIE KULYK

Telephone Service
Groceries and Gasoline

Buy at Kulyks   We give
Prompt Service

First grade merchandise
Reasonable Prices····Buy and Save

Frank Rubbelke and Lovell Stone played a major part in obtaining the new elevator for Buffalo, Magnus Bjork has the distinction of holding the oldest permit in the district. Tribute was paid to Mrs. Pauline Anderson and Mrs. M. Cook, both widows of former pioneer members.

HONOR ROLL 1939 - 1945

For King and Country. Members of the Buffalo Community, who volunteered for Active Service with Canada's Armed Forces — Anderson, Theodore B.; Bartholow, James L.; Bartholow, Robert R.; Dearing, J. Orval (Orville); Dearing, Clifford E.; Drewnick, Steve; Skjenna, P. Oliver; Hurl, Clarence L.; Dziatkewich, Antony; Howloka, Harry; McCullough, Francis H. (Buster); Silverthorne, Garnet; Skjenna Arthur F.; Skjenna Olaf M.; Thompson, William M.; Findlay, James Daniel, killed in action.

LEASES

In this part of the province of Alberta, it is difficult to buy the land outright. It belongs to the Crown, and therefore one must lease the land from the Crown. The following will perhaps explain more fully what happens to the cattle rancher when this land is not controlled by the Crown. The Provinces of Assiniboia, N.W.T., lost their identity in 1905 when Alberta entered Confederation. The years of 1905 and 1906 saw the peak of the cattle industry in so far as the large ranches were concerned. The influx of settlers into the more productive areas and with the railway construction coming closer to this area, making the exporting of cattle easier, brought about a sudden demand for beef and offered an opportunity for the ranchers. This situation was greatly changed following the hard winter of 1906 and '07, the most disastrous period in the history of ranching. Only a small percentage of the range cattle in the country survived (approximately 25 per cent) forcing many cattleman out of the business, while a scattered few remained to rebuild their herds from the remnants of what they had the fall before. The incoming settlers were gradually creeping towards the short-grass country and in 1909 and 1910 the actual homesteading boom was on. The ranchers, in order to protect and secure their position, had been pressing Ottawa for grazing concessions and after years of effort were told about 1910 that grazing leases were available. This was, however, too late as most of the land had been homesteaded. But the rough country along the river, not suitable for farming, was overlooked and leases were granted to those making applications. Wire fences were constructed, much to the disgust of the ranchers, and the stock kept within its borders.

The period of wheat growing followed and with a bumper crop in 1915 and '16 along with war prices on wheat, spelled disaster to the rancher. It was with great difficulty that he managed to hold his leases and carry on. Nature, however, checked farming expansion after 1916. A drought period started, and it was easier for ranchers to retain their leases.

The Federal Grazing Regulations, however, compelled a rancher to overstock his lease. This combined with a drought, brought about a more serious condition. This was partially overcome by the fact that thousands of acres of homestead land were abandoned because of the drought, and this land became available to the ranchers in 1925.

The years 1927 and '28 were bumper crop years for the wheat farmer, but this was short lived, when another and longer drought cycle commenced, known as the dirty thirties.

Since 1931 the Province of Alberta has had control of her natural resources and has since administered her own grazing policy. It is now within the power of the Department of Lands and Mines to dispose of this land in the best interest of the people of the Province. Leases are granted on a 20-year basis with the understanding that the Lessee must raise stock. These leases may be sold, but the Department of Special Areas working for the Crown may stipulate the amount of acreage each Lessee may have. During dry years, wheat farmers are paid a bonus, based on acreage under cultivation. Several ranchers along the river irrigate land for the purposes of raising feed for their stock. This requires a special permit. Special Areas also grants assistance to those wishing to improve their stock watering ponds. These can be found scattered across the prairie. Rainfall, including the spring-runoff averages around 12 to 14 inches per year. Land on which the ranchers' and wheat farmers' homes are located is the only deeded land. Special Areas are the "watchdogs" to prevent overstocking of this land, allowing one animal to each 50 acres.

Many tons of grain are also grown in this part of the province. The first Alberta Wheat Pool elevator was built in 1923 with a capacity of 29,000 bushels, but 161,000 bushels were handled that first year. 1966 was the best year for the farmer elevator when 215,000 bushels were handled. 1937-'38 was the worst with only 49 bushels. A new elevator was built in 1967 with a capacity of 70,000 bushels and capable of handling 3000 to 4000 bushels per hour.

THE RED DEER RIVER

The headwaters of the Red Deer River are in the Sawbuck Range of the Rocky Mountains in Banff National Park. The river is glacier fed and begins near the foot of Mount St. Bride (elevation 10,867 feet). It is also fed from glaciers on Mount Drummond and Cyclone Mountain; Mount McConnell, and Bonnet Peak (elevation 10,615 feet). The water from the icefield on Bonnet Peak flows down through the Valley of the Hidden Lakes, in which Douglas Lake is located.

The Red Deer is about 461 miles in length from the headwaters to the Town of Empress. The drainage area at Empress is 17,300 square miles.

The widest point of the Red Deer River is about 750 feet, bankful near its confluence with the South Saskatchewan River.

A STRETCH HERE

Some other recorded widths at various centers along the river are:

Sundre — 152'; 190'; 235'; 243'
Red Deer — 279'; 293'; 371'; 471'
Drumheller — 332'; 304'; 368'; 398'
Bindloss — 562'; 667'; 739'

The Red Deer River received its name from the English translation of the Cree Indian word WASKASLOO. (Source: Geographic Board of Alberta)

The river bed is predominantly gravel from the headwaters to near Drumheller where the bed is sand to the confluence with the South Saskatchewan River.

There is a total of 21 bridges crossing the Red Deer River. Seven (7) of these bridges are on highways. The Highway Numbers are: 27, 54, 2, 21, 56, 36, and 41.

There is still ferry service operating on the river at four locations: Munson, Dorothy, Finnegan and Jenner.

This information was given by the Water Resources Division of the Government of the Province of Alberta.

Poems

THE OLD COWPOKE by J. R. Gordon

"Over seventy years I've ridden the range
From the Mexican Gulf to this Canada land.
Herding broomtails and swingbags — sometimes day and night,
From the Red Deer to Texas, I've seen every brand.

Those wise, ornery longhorns I've humored and cussed
As we hazed them along up that old Chisholm trail
Through the thick clouds of dust and the sweltering heat
'Til we penned them at last at the head of the rail.

With the clicking of hooves and the rattle of horns,
Mixed the bawling of herds and the cowpuncher's song.
We were happy and young and we never complained,
Though the wages were small and the hours were long.

Through Dakota, Montana I trailed other herds
And then over the lines to these Alberta lands,
To the happiest home of the buffalo hordes,
And a heaven on earth for the antelope bands.

Every night in the spring as I lay 'neath the sky,
I could hear the wild geese from twilight 'til dawn,
On their way to their nesting spots up in the north,
With the hell-divers, ducks and "the graceful white swan."

Let them sing of the hills down in Oklahoma
Of the grass in Wyoming where I used to ride.
I'd settle for some of that prairie wooled range
Spreading north from the boundary on Canada's side.

If God had a country as good as this was
I'd go there tomorrow and never more roam.
But I reckon the only one left is above
And some say I ain't fit for that heavenly home.

God must know I have broken most every command;
I have chosen my way and have run my own race.
Now my body is broken, I'm useless and old,
And I ain't going begging to Him for His grace!

He believed that some day he should stand to be judged,
And was ready to take what that judgement might bring.
He'd been ever reliable, gen'rous and true;
Shouldn't that bear some weight with the heavenly King?

He was pulling down wages at seventy-six
When he took one too many and started to fall.
'Twas too far to the Doctor, he'd made his last ride;
But he still wore his boots when he answered Death's call.
Those old cowpokes were rough; they were fearless and tough,
But there wasn't a hypocrite found in the lot.
It was either deliver the goods or move on,
And the fittest survived while the others passed out.
On the side of a hill with his face t'wards the south,
In a six foot three casket he's taking his rest.
Just one more of those men, soon of legend and myth,
Who were part of the vanguard that opened the West.

Editors Note: I am not certain but I feel that this poem was written about a man named Jim Spratt; as some of the incidents mentioned could fit the manner in which he died.

LAMENT OF THE OLD COWHAND

I'm just a lone cowboy, that came up from the south,
I've rode the Bow River from the hills to its mouth.

I've worked on the ranges in the palmy old days
And hope the old-timers will like my poor lays.

I've stood many night guards as wet as a pup,
While working on the Red Deer in the general roundup.

With the beef herd in the autumn 'twas not very nice
Fording at Gregory's amid swift running ice.

The mouth of the Berry to Blood Indian Creek
There was no better range land where e'er you might seek.

Then across to the Hand Hills, reaching up to the blue,
And down Bullpound Creek — there's a land that I knew.

The Circle lay south of the Red Deer's fast stream,
To the west was the Anchor P, where spring grass grew green.

Forster's ranch was at Nateby on West Berry Creek,
Its hospitable welcome old rangemen did seek.

We camped on the Nigger John, to Brooks we did go,
And blew in our cash while we put up a show.

Then back to the roundup, our money all spent,
A bunch of "broke" punchers, but we were content.

We worked the Bow River right up to the Creek
The Indians called Crowfoot, where oft we did seek,

Riders from the Bar U, the old George Lane brand,
Those were good days, says this grey-haired cowhand.

300

We rode over to Mosquito and up Fish Creek way,
And camped on the Highwood, where grew the tall hay.
Saw the mountains in splendor, their peaks tipped with light,
A background of grandeur, a charm to the sight.
The range days are over, the old cowmen gone,
Their era is past and their last roundup done.
No more in Alberta will there e'er be again,
Such beef herds, such freedom, such living, such men!

(Author Unknown)

Note: The above cowboy poem was printed in a very old copy of The Brooks Bulletin. Does anyone know the author? The Bulletin asked.

This poem appeared in the Canadian Cattleman's Magazine . . . . December 1955.

THE RANCHER by Anna M. Johnson

He sat — the picture of despair,
With face upturned to cloudless sky,
He breathed the redhot smothered air,
He saw the dust go whirling by.

He looked — his cattle from afar
Came straggling over parched plain.
He saw them near the empty draw,
He knew they sought the rain! the rain!

He cursed the luckless yesterday
That drove him to this sun-burnt spot.
Deplored the God-forsaken way
Creation seemed to die and rot.

He thought: "No breezy signs today
Of settling clouds or veering winds,
A year, a month, eternity
Shall come before the rain begins!"

Yet, yet beyond the distant waste
Of sun-dried blue and white skies,
He sights a speck that moves in haste;
He sees a stormy cloud arise!

He feels the thrill across the range,
A stir of every living thing;
He hears the voice of nature change,
And birds come batting on the wing.

He smells the dust upon the plain,
The driving dust upon the ground,
He sees the lightning flash again,
He hears the thunder's rolling sound.

"Ho, ho," he laughs to face the gale,
The wind, the dust, the howling train
Of flying grasses, breaking hail,
And then the rain — the bursting rain!

He sits — in silent wonderment,
With face upturned to cloud and sky,
He smiles: " 'Tis here that I was sent,
'Tis here that I shall live and die."

The Big Roundup on the Red Deer

Come all you cowboys if you want to hear
A story of a roundup on the big Red Deer,

Long Frank Stewart was the foreman's name,
It was on the Texas Panhandle boys, he won his fame.

Cook called breakfast at half-past four
He stood with a club at the mess tent door.

And said "Dishes in the pan, boys, I'll have you understand,
That the cook ain't a waiter in the promised land."

Long Frank looked at his watch, and his watch was slow,
He looked at the east for the wind' to blow.

He turned to the cowboys and he said,
"We are going to Bull Pound Creek or we'll all be dead.

So saddle up your broncos and cinch them tight,
For I'll guarantee them gentle before it comes night.

For you will see a lot of country if you ride with me
And all the blessed brands in the dictionary."

We gathered some cattle as we passed Lone Butte,
And there we saw a big-jaw that we stopped to shoot.

The coyotes knew and they howled with delight
For they thought of the feed they would have that night.

We gathered cattle branded ore-lock and round T
Half diamond, upset pick axe and the Bar K3,

Quarter circle over brand, that would tax the blacksmith's skill
And would take a Hebrew scholar for to read them well.

Long Frank said as he nearly cried,
"There is one more roundup, boys, I'd like to ride;

302

That is to gather up the farmers that are taking up the range,
And run them through the dip for the cattle mange.
For they'll homestead and pre-empt every acre free,
Till on the range not a cow can you see.
And they'll plow and they'll harrow to the very last stroke,
Till farmers and ranchers are both flat broke."

by Arthur Peake.

RED DEER RIVER by Robin Krause, August 1970

The endless river wanders, brown and warm,
Enjoys the well-earned leisure of its age,
The quiet saunter through the valley broad
And deep it carved through the centuries of time.
A million eyes watch briefly, blink and vanish
Age upon age, kind upon kind, until
In the last brief second one appears
Who watches shrewdly a brief time, and sees
A tool for his own use, a helper to be held,
Gently perhaps, but firmly in control,
Like a strong colt that's gently broke but well.
All this and more the old man feels and sees,
More with his bones and heart than with his mind;
And sits, the prairie seeping through his veins
As one returning soon to join the land.
The autumn sun but feebly warms him now,
Though all the yesterdays he felt its heat;
A pheasant cock screams sudden, close at hand,
An echo of thousands heard through myriad days
And nights of summers past. The pungent smell
Of ripe alfalfa brought him on the wind
Blends always with the warm smell of manure
And steamy cattle bodies on crisp days
When winds blow cold and hard snow crunches loud.
A stir of anger breaks his reverie,
A hopeless raving at advance of time,
The faceless "they" who brought about the change
That made his ways old-fashioned: anger fades
Into a sadness deep of one resigned
Although reluctantly. His mind returns
Sinking into the cloud of memories past
That wrap pain with forgetful cotton-wool . . .
How long ago, how recent were the days
When as a boy he first remembered Spring

In this small valley? Heard the river swell
And groan and break its icy prison shell:
How long ago he smelled the first wet sage,
Saw the first crocus with its golden heart,
Smelled the sharp woodsmoke from the cabin door,
Touched the first warm, wet, calf?
Was it not spring past he gathered first
The thorny pink wild rose, or cherished close
The yellow and magenta cactus flowers?
How many springs ago since first he saw
And heard the meadowlark and oriole
Pour forth their mating songs? Or watched with awe
The robins and busy swallows choose and build
Their careful nests? How often had he chased
And caught the whistling ground squirrels, flicker tailed
Or watches the silent deer steal out of woods
To feed upon the newly-sprouted grain?
He knew not now, but always through his dreams
The river ran, weaving a warm brown thread
Through all the tapestry. He now recalled
The many valley summers, green and gold,
The trees' soft rustling in the prairie drought,
Their green made vivid by the faces round
Of golden dauntless sunflowers, small and wild,
And heads of goldenrod like scrambled egg.
Ah yes, he well recalled, and lived awhile
The pride of ownership as first he gazed
At ruddy white-faced cattle, grazing full
On short rich prairie pasture, while fat calves
Played games of run-and-leap, and follow-me
In cattle ways, or nursed beside their dams.
Then too, the stab of pain felt in years lean
When cows turned gaunt and dull before his eyes
And calves lay still on hillsides with eyes sunk
And panted out their last; and in its bed
The river gurgled faintly here and there
Between the many sandbars it laid down,
And the hot wind crackled through the parching grass
And the stunted yellow burning heads of grain.
He was a youth then, resilient and stong
For whom the ripple of a strong horse flank
The tang of sage and fingers of the wind
To stir his hair were all the balm he asked
To sooth the ache within: the land belonged

304

To him and to the stream, and both were strong.
The dry leaves slowly turn to gold and red,
The evening's chill leaves water edged with rime;
The face of youth so strong now lined and brown,
The shoulders stoop more low: and now the son
Walks tall and bold, and views the hills with pride
And more the number of the autumns crisp
The aging pioneer can now recall.
The seasons come and go, and now the youths
Do call him father, but no longer wise,
The land is theirs to keep or give away —
They know not of the river in his veins
Nor how the land his marrow forms; their love
Is of machines and record-books, their hay
Is chewed by teeth of steel and spit again
Upon the fields in blocks; no more the toss
Of careless bundles on the horse-drawn rack.
The old man sighs as memory slips along
From autumn to the winter of the year,
When snow lies deep upon the river hills
And the river seems almost dead beneath its mail
Of ice and snow; Yet warming to the heart
The sight of cattle damp and warm who feed
On hay and grain close-garnered in the fall;
As steamy breathing fills the air with chips
Of diamond, and loud munching fills the ear
Fom many jaws; the crunch of hooves in snow,
The soft lowing of contented kine; the sights
Of many out-turned tails in rows while heads
Are buried deep in mangers, still amuse.
Remembered too, the silence of the morn
After the fury of a blizzard passed,
And the soft scratching in the drifted snow
Of partridges and pheasants round the door,
And after cold of storms, the warmth of friends,
And many neighbors, while the fiddler's dance
Goes on 'til dawn; as laughter rings out loud,
Good-byes are said until another day. . . .
But these friends now are gone, the neighbors changed,
The nearby ranches owned by strangers now,
Come from the cities far away; the fields
Held in the grip of huge machines, which tear
And chew the soil and spew out hay and grain,
While winter's cold is braved in heated sheds

Or costly city homes, secure and warm.
The old man spits, and stirs upon his stone:
A skein of geese wing southward, calling loud.
His heart lifts to them; they are kindred now
More close than his own kind. A yellow leaf
Drifts slowly down, and settles on his hair.
'Tis autumn now, and soon the winter snow
Will once more fill the air; but now he knows
Where e'er the old year goes, he travels too:
He is not sad, for they have long been friends,
And now as one may journey endlessly,
The goose, the year, the river brown, and he.   . . .

THE BLIZZARD by H. D. Howe

On the fifteenth of December,
In nineteen sixty-four,
The north wind starting blowing
And the snow fell more and more.

For two long days and nights
The wind, how it did blow!
The temperature kept dropping
To twenty-nine below.

The third day the snow had stopped,
The wind no longer blew.
The cattle all were hungry,
This the ranchers knew.

A rancher now, is a devoted man —
To him, his cattle rate first.
He knew they needed hay to eat
And water to quench their thirst.

On the wide and open range,
In a storm of wind and snow,
Without a tree for shelter,
The cattle have no place to go.

They can wander far in the storm —
Sometimes getting lost,
And with an anxious eye
The rancher counts the cost.

The ranchers out in Buffalo
Were fortunate indeed,
They found all their cattle
When they went out to feed.

But in the Hanna district
Their losses were very great;
By the time they could reach their cattle
They found they were too late.

The antelope and pheasant,
Which roam the prairie wide,
Could not withstand the cold
And from starvation died.

This storm will long be remembered,
As many have been before;
Varied will be the stories
Of the blizzard of sixty-four.

SIGNS OF SPRING by H. D. Howe

When it's springtime on the prairie,
And the snow all disappears,
The song of birds returning
Is music to our ears.

The crocus on the prairie
Will soon be in full bloom,
To see them in their glory,
Dispels the winter's gloom.

When we see the river open
And the ice all leaves its banks
When we know that spring's approaching,
For this we give our thanks.

When we hear the wild geese honking,
On their way towards the north,
We know the winter's waning
As the leaves come bursting forth.

When we see the gophers running
All around, like kids at play,
Then our hearts rejoice within us,
That spring is here to stay.

SUMMER SONG OF A FARMER'S WIFE by Mrs. Mae Gillatly Wyoming, Ontario

Up in the morning at the break of dawn,
My eyes half open and I give a yarn.
Out to the barn where husband toils,
Cow kicks over the pail and his temper boils.

I pour the foamy white in the separator,
Plug in the switch, the motor purrs.
Pigs to feed and pails to switch,
Then up to the house with that cream so rich.
Breakfast over and dishes done,
I make up the beds and the vacuums run.
Put a roast in the oven and also two pies,
While peeling the potatoes I look to the skies.
There's a cloud up there, sort of hazy somehow,
Oh, to combine all day, it's mid August now.
Dinner's on the table for the hungry men,
They are up from the field with an appetite for ten.
Potatoes are lifted, beets and corn too,
Ham, buns and pies and pickles a few.
I was up the dishes, reset the oven,
Grind up a meat loaf and look again to the Heavens.
That cloud is blacker and lightning streaks.
Maybe it's just heat, been hot all week.
Take a few minutes to mend those pants for Ben.
I look out the window as I hear a grunt,
The pigs in the garden I can see the runt.
I run in the house, it's starting to rain,
Hubby hollers, "Come give me a hand with the grain."
Thunder gets louder, lightning flashes about.
If the grain gets wetter, it will surely sprout.
The afternoon is most over, the helpers go home,
Won't wait for supper, "Mary's all alone."
We sit down at a table spread for more,
We eat what we can and the rest I store.
Glad to have Fridges, we'll eat it tomorrow,
Then I head for the barn again straight as an arrow.
The evening chores done, our work is not through,
There is a garden to weed and the lawn to cut too.
When all is finished and the lawn chairs placed,
The sun has set on our day of grace.
Then I envy a little as I look about,
And wish I'd had time to sit a while out.

THE PRAYER OF AN AGING WOMAN

Lord, thou knowest better than I know myself, that I am growing
    older and will someday be old.
Keep me from getting talkative and particularly from the fatal habit
    of thinking that I must say something on every subject and on
    every occasion.

Release me from craving to straightened out everybody's affairs.

Keep my mind free from the recital of endless details.

Give me wings to get to the point.

I dare not ask for grace enough to enjoy the tales of others. But help me to endure them with patience.

Seal my lips on my aches and pains.

They are increasing and the love of rehearsing them is becoming sweeter as the years go by.

Teach me the glorious lesson that occasionally I may be mistaken.

Give me the ability to see good things in unexpected places and talent in unexpected people. Give me the grace to tell them so.

Keep me reasonably sweet. I do not want to be a Saint, some of them are so hard to live with. But a sour old woman is one of the crowning works of the Devil. Make me thoughtful, but not moody, helpful, but not bossy. With my vast store of wisdom it seems a pity not to use it all. But thou knowest, Lord, I want a few friends at the end.

Example sheds a genial ray
Of light that men are apt to borrow.
So first improve yourself today,
And then improve your friends tomorrow.

A man knocked at the Heavenly Gates,
His face was scarred and old.
He stood before the man of fate
For admission to the fold.
"What have you done?" St. Peter asked,
"To gain admission here."
"I've been a Rancher sir,
For many and many a year."
The Pearly Gates swung open wide,
St. Peter touched a bell,
"Come in and choose your harp", he said
"You've had your share of Hell."

GOVERNMENT OF THE PROVINCE OF ALBERTA
DEPARTMENT OF MUNICIPAL AFFAIRS

$ 23 $\frac{40}{xx}$

RECEIPT FOR TAXES   F N⁰ 1444

Received from *Stefan Kinick*

of *Gold Spring or Empress*

the sum of *Twenty Three* $\frac{40}{}$ DOLLARS, applied as follows:

LAND DESCRIPTION	LOCAL IMPROVEMENT TAXES			District No.	EDUCATIONAL TAXES		
	$	c.	YEARS		$	c.	YEARS
Nw - 34 - 21 - 4 - 4	9	20	1912/015	182	5	00	1912/13
Sw - 34 - 21 - 4 - 4	9	20	—	—			
TOTALS -	18	40			5	00	

EDMONTON, ALBERTA, *13 Dec* 191 *5*   *Jno. Perrie*

                                                              DEPUTY MINISTER

                                              Per *B*

Buffalo School, 1964 — 65 under supervision of Mrs. R. Herman and Mrs. Gerald Kornelson.

Aerial picture Keinick Farm, 1970.

Ewan Kulyk, Leroy Callaghan, Arnold Rubbelke, Jim Stone, Gibb Gilham, Frank Rubbelke. Front row: Howard Jones, Gene Anderson, Norman Rubbelke and Jim Sewell.

Gus Hanson, 1912, making bread.

311

The original Howe house built in 1910.

C. B. Howe and neighbors moving the Carter house from north of Cicon's in 1928.

Mr. and Mrs. Olaf Skjenna Sr., and home.

Steve Kulyk's first mud house.

Bins of grain at Ben Anderson's in the fifties.

312

Typical winter scene on the prairie.

Ed Porter 1913, Cereal. Retired living in Brooks.

Wardlow Ferry (service discontinued in 1970).

Taken while the crew was moving
the hall before rebuilding.

Buffalo Hockey team on Red Deer River, 1931.

313

Red Cross Meeting — Mrs. B. Lawler, Annie Neil, Lenora Bunn, Unidentified, Christie Pound, Unidentified, Mrs. Brassard, Mrs. Eddie, Mrs. Sam Hyde and Cecil, Mrs. S. Wilson. Children in front — unidentified, Frankie, Lorry, and Helen Brassard, Lorraine and Johnny Wilson.

Threshing crew.

Bill Hendry with an Avery Gas Tractor.

Chinook Arch — 1967.

Willie, Delmer, Clarence and Norman Hurl. Woo Sam's store in background.

Russell Cicon, Elsie Hyde, Lorry Brassard, Frankie Brassard, Rita White, Dorothy Cicon, Jeannie Cicon. Second Row: Helen Brassard, Cecil Hyde, Delmar Pound, Ruby O'Brien, Louis Cicon, Raymond Howland, Cecil White, Rubin Howland, Jackie White. First Row: Ken O'Brien, Gordon O'Brien, Eileen Ohman, Marjorie Ohman.

315

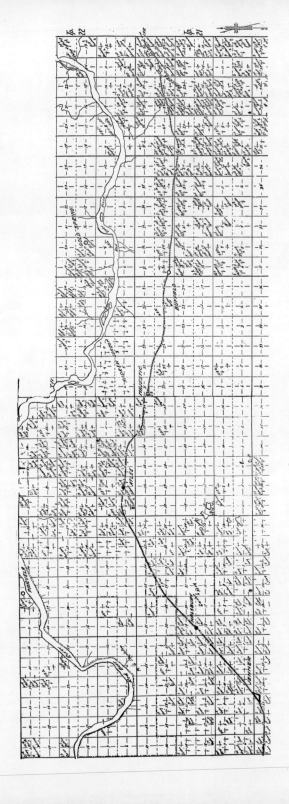

Map showing Red Deer River. Note: Jenner, Atlee, Majestic, Buffalo, Pancras (now known as Cavendish).

Articles of General Interest

THE VEE BAR VEE RANCH

This article appeared in the September 2, 1965 issue of the Brooks Bulletin: by John Schmidt, Agricultural Editor, Calgary Herald.

The Brooks area boasts the largest mustard seed crop in the world this year. C. W. Loose has grown eleven thousand acres of mustard crop on his 75,000-acre V Bar V ranch southwest of Wardlow.

His claim of the world's biggest crop is confirmed by the Montana Mustard Company of Lethbridge which has contracted the whole acreage. The biggest acreage attempted before was some 3,000 acres.

Loose, 57-year-old farmer-rancher from Vulcan area, said the crop will average 1,500 pounds per acre. Provided harvesting goes through without a hitch, he expects to harvest 250,000 bushels. It will all be exported to England and Japan for processing into table mustard.

The value of the crop will run to about $500,000, he added.

He turned five swathers loose in the crop on Friday, August 13. The swathers are each 18 feet wide.

Combining of the swaths started Monday. Eight combines will eventually be at work in the bumper crop. The average crop runs from 1,000 to 1,200 pounds per acre, although in some areas it will run up to 2,000.

Last year Loose created a sensation when he sowed 10,000 acres of flax and 3,000 acres of wheat in the V Bar V farming area. A rare type of fungus was responsible for destroying a large part of the crop.

"However," said Loose, "I discovered the fungus by accident in time to resow 3,000 acres. This flax grew but not soon enough and it froze. This year, I took cultural methods to keep the fungus from damaging the mustard crop — and we really have a dandy crop."

He said the fungus did not attack the roots of the plant but attacked the stem, causing the plant to "go down". Loose describes the V Bar V — which is all deeded land — as a "good little place."

"It is a challenge to me as a farmer," he said. "This grassland should never been broken up by the previous owners. But now that I have inherited their mistake I intend to make the best of it and bring the land back into condition."

He said it is his aim to try to pay off the land purchase price by growing cash crops, then seed it down as pasture land for cattle.

"I have only 2,200 head of cattle here now, but there is enough grass potential for more than 4,000," he said.

He indicated much criticism was heaped upon him over the flax crop fiasco last year, "but with this cheap land out here you only need to produce a grain crop every three or four years to pay your way".

Another article appeared, reprinted from the Calgary Herald, in the October 20, 1966 issue of the Brooks Bulletin.

It's not often in an age of medicare, pension plans and prepaid funerals that a man's personal initiative, enterprise and old-fashioned faith are rewarded.

But for Bill Loose, boss of the huge V Bar V ranch about 150 miles east of Calgary, at Wardlow, Thanksgiving weekend was a tribute to a dryland farmer engaged in an uphill battle against the whims of nature and the economy. The piece of land upon which he staked all his faith and most of his fortune this year justified itself — for this harvest at least. The crop is off the fields.

The 75,000 acres of Big Country grassland sprawling along both sides of the Red Deer River have lived up to the vision he gave a district court judge back in June.

In June, the stocky, out-going farmer was on the spot. He had 10,000 acres of land seeded to mustard (a great cash crop if it could be harvested)' 5,000 acres of wheat and 1,000 acres sown to oats. There were 1,000 calves roaming across the short grass area which had become almost a desert in the 1930's and once again in the 1940's.

Bill Loose had parlayed the 280 acres he started out with at Magrath in 1929 into this spread and two other large operations in Alberta. But this expansion had also brought potential ruin.

He had no money. The V Bar V was mortgaged and a large farm equipment company was threatening to seize four combines which he needed to carry off any harvest that land might produce this year.

Also hanging over his head on that day was an unpleasant memory. The V Bar V had wiped out some Americans who forgot the lessons taught by the drought of the 1930's and reopened too much land in the 1940's. A drought occurring amid a wet cycle and finished both the crop and its over-ambitious masters.

The farm machinery company was insistent on June 22. Its lawyer had applied for a judicial order which would wipe out Bill Loose every bit as surely as a drought.

Last year had been enough to make any man doubt there would be a crop harvested on the V Bar V in any year. In 1965, Bill

318

Loose had planted 11,000 acres of mustard, some wheat and oats on his land. He had also purchased a lot of machinery on credit.

But poor weather, a resultant late harvest and early snows had cut a potential 250,000 bushel crop in half. After making the mortgage payments, Loose had nothing left with which to cover the $4,000 payment due this spring on the farm machinery.

So on June 22, in the Hanna court house, the farm equipment company submitted its application for removal and sale of the equipment. Loose's lawyer, Eugene Kush, filed no material for the defence; but asked the judge to hear evidence directly from the farmer even though such an application was being held in judges' chambers, where normally only affidavits are heard.

Bill Loose was permitted to give evidence, but only after Kush argued strenuously on his client's behalf. The farmer explained his position. He had no money, but great expectations. He said he would have some money available to the equipment company from the Montana Mustard Company of Lethbridge, and if he could get his crop in, the rest would be easy.

During his testimony, it became evident there was another side to the story. When the farm equipment had submitted its application there had been no mention of the fact Loose had bought a lot of equipment other than the four combines — and for cash. Loose had also paid nearly one-third of the cost of those combines as well.

The judge later recalled the scene: "As Loose began speaking of his hopes, his aspirations, his struggles and his faith, the court seemed to light up and a cool prairie breeze seemed to fill the room."

"All present must have felt mean and small and of little faith," he added, "most of all, the company representatives . . ."

The order was refused and the company rebuked for temporarily forgetting that its power today stems partly from faith it invested many many years ago in the West when it gave farmers, equipment — "its treasures" — on credit. This faith the judge ruled, should be extended to Loose, despite the farmer's temporary shortcomings.

Loose went back to his farm, where he, his family and hired hands have watched their crops ripen under ideal weather conditions. The combines have been running day and night this fall at the V Bar V. A big farming operation such as this one can lose thousands of dollars a day if a combine breaks down.

One day just such a thing happened and Loose had to drive to Hanna, charter an aircraft and fly to Edmonton for a replacement part. When he returned a few hours later, he ran into his lawyer in Hanna, Eugene Kush, who has the biggest geographical law practice in Alberta (from Hanna to Calgary, from Red Deer to Lethbridge and Medicine Hat) then learned of his client's fate.

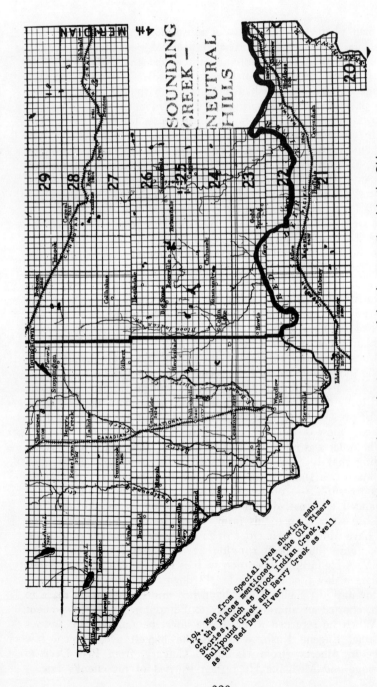

104. Map from Special Area showing many of the places mentioned in the Old Timers Stories, such as Blood Indian Creek, Bullpound Creek and Berry Creek as well as the Red Deer River.

Map from Special Area showing many of the places mentioned in the Old-Timers Stories, such as Blood Indian Creek, Bullpound Creek and Berry Creek as well as the Red Deer River.

Most of the crop is harvested, Loose told the lawyer and with luck, all of it will be combined and $500,000 gamble will have paid off. Then, turning as he hurried back to the harvesting operations, Loose added: "Oh say, if you ever see that judge, tell him thanks from all of us."

Editor's Note:

Not many details are known, but Mr. Loose left the Vee Bar Vee, following a Sheriff's Sale in 1968. The ranch was purchased by a Mr. Lou Carey in 1969 and the following year (1970) was purchased by a man from the United States, Ben Gay and is now operated by his nephew John Gay, while Blair Gay, Ben's son, is business manager. While the cow-camp is under the management of Ray Anderson, who composed the following poems.

THE MIGHTY VEE BAR VEE
by Ray Anderson

She rests along the Red Deer, for twenty miles or more,
Her grassy draws and waving trees, reach down to touch the shore,
Her rugged canyons and tangled breaks, protect the pheasant and
the deer,
From the foolish city hunter, with his guns and fancy gear.
The Red Deer is her bloodstream, and oft as twilight falls,
You can hear her throbbing heartbeat, echo off her canyon walls.
Men have come from far and near, her vast domain to see,
For in all this land there's none to match, The Mighty Vee Bar Vee.
Many men have loved her, men with ranching in their blood,
But none would stand beside her, when her name was in the mud.
But these men she views with pity, for she knows they're not to
blame,
They are only human poker chips, in a set up poker game.
So she waits with endless patience, for she knows the time will be,
When they'll wish they hadn't scorned her, The Mighty Vee Bar Vee.
For the men who ride her ranges, she gives no special heed,
For these men of easy laughter, have no driving greed.
They do not wish to claim her, to them the world is free,
They know that sweat and calloused hands, will make The Mighty
Vee.
Foreign men with whiskers came, with chisel-plow and drills,
They tore up miles of grassland and left scars upon her hills.
These men were willing workers, earned their living from the land,
But the ranchers of the district, did not wish to understand.
So they were driven from her boundaries, and will someday cease
to be,
But the grass will still be growing, on The Mighty Vee Bar Vee.

321

The mustard king with winning smile came to claim her charms,
But he also left, a beaten man, crushed by her mighty arms.
He came to take, had naught to give, her gifts to him were free,
But he underestimated, The Mighty Vee Bar Vee!
Moneyed-men from far and near, have gambled with her soul,
But each and everyone of them, have sadly paid the toll.
Men of little ethics, con men by the score,
In search of wealth and power, have come knocking at her door.
Their educated lawyers, have plotted for their fee,
But these men will be forgotten, not so, The Mighty Vee!
Men's struggle to possess her, she views with cool disdain,
For she knows their puny efforts, cannot bring the needed rain.
They cannot halt the raging blizzard, nor the drought that has to be.
Mother Nature's way of helping, The Mighty Vee Bar Vee.
Some day, a man with vision, love and gently power,
Will come to claim this beauty, and she'll blossom like a flower.
Her irrigation system will fill his bins with grain,
To feed the growing number of cattle on the plain.
The winter storms will slacken and drought will be no more,
And the waters of the Red Deer, will not freeze against the shore.
Fine mares will graze her pastures, great stallions stand at stud,
And their foals will drink in freedom, from the water of the Blood.
When these things have come to pass, and man has made atone,
This lovely Queen of ranches, will sit majestically on her throne,
And so she waits contented, for she knows the time will be,
When all will thrive and prosper on, The Mighty Vee Bar Vee.

THE SILENT VIGIL

by Ray Anderson

Crouched high above the canyons, across the Red Deer vale,
There's a hill shaped as a lizzard, long, flat head and serpent tail
At times I sit and ponder, back through our short life-time span,
And I can almost see him lash his tail, at man's atrocities to man.
Countless times he's watched the river, swell high in springtime flood,
From the run-off of the Bull Pond, the Berry and the Blood.
He's seen the grass grow tall and green, in the valley far below,
He's seen the awful summer's drought, and the winters deep in snow.
For years he's watched the red man, in his home of bison hide,
He's heard their children's laughter, saw their young braves learn
    to ride
He's watched them paint their faces, do their war dance 'round the
    flames,
But he knew to these care-free people war was just a game.

322

But as the years went by, there came different sights and sounds,
As the white man came to take away, the red man's hunting grounds.
Then came the whiskey traders, with their jugs of liquid hell,
And the lizzard watched and knew, this would toll the red man's knell.
They stole their furs, their women, in their wake, left grief and shame,
And the lizzard writhed in sorrow, for these proud people of the plain.
Then on the scene the red coats came, these men rode straight and tall,
And the filthy whiskey traders, saw the writing on the wall.
These mounted men were fearless, backed their words with fist and gun,
But for the noble red man, the damage had been done.
He saw the spurred and booted riders, come north with longhorn cows,
The farmer with his children, his oxen and his plows.
He watched them fight the elements, blizzard, drought and fire,
He saw them build their shanty homes, and string the hated wire.
Then came the years of endless drought, when dust obscured the land,
And the farmers left their homesteads, to the wind and drifting sand.
And so today big tractors roar, and jets streak overhead,
And cattle by the thousand graze, on the Red Deer watershed.
But as we look into the future, we wonder what he'll see,
Will the red man return on his pony? Will the white man cease to be?

THE COWBOY'S CREED
by Ray Anderson

When you're out alone on the open range, with a good horse between your knees,
The world may be in turmoil, but you feel you can do as you please.
Though the work be hard, and the pay be small, you'd not trade with any man,
For the price of freedom is something high, but fits in His big plan.
Some will trade their place in life, for the sake of a bank account,
But all you ask is your closest kin, your work and a good strong mount.
When your loop takes hold of a two-year-old, by the hoof or the neck or the horn,
He can plunge and fight, 'til his eyes grow white, but you'll throw him as sure as you're born.
Though your rope it sings like a banjo string, and your horse beneath you strain,
You have no fear of a maddened steer, you'll tumble him to the plain,

323

You know you can die 'neath your horse's hoofs, or by your ropes
  small strand,
But this old land has mothered, she can take you any way she can.
And as the twilight deepens, and you are homeward bound,
Though your horse is weary, should the need arise, he can run like
  a striped hound.
For you've been taught to care for him, and treat him as well as
  you can,
For a man is as helpless without his horse, as the horse without the
  man.
And as you top the last rise to home, you feel a small stab of pain,
For you know when you die, they'll take you to town, not leave you
  out here on the plain.
Though you know the day of the open range, has long since ceased
  to be,
You thank God there's still a bit of it left, on the Mighty Vee Bar
  Vee.

HISTORY OF THE CROOKED TREE RANCH by Robin Krause

Nestled against the protecting hills which form the north wall
of the Red Deer River valley seventeen miles west of Buffalo, are
the buildings belonging to the Crooked Tree ranch. The ranch itself
sprawls for ten miles like a large question mark with its base
against the river while the dot is formed by a block of land approximately eight sections in area extending four miles along and two
miles south of the river. Although it has not always been as large
as its present 25,000 acres, the ranch has occupied a long and varied
chapter in the Red River saga.

The land comprising the ranch must at one time have been part
of the hunting grounds of Indian tribes, for fire and teepee rings
can still be seen on some of the hilltops. Early in the history of the
white man in the valley, the land was grazed by cattle from the
Gordon ranch, and in the late 1890's, squatters' rights to the home
quarter were taken out by Jim Ward, a Metis from what was to become Saskatchewan. Mr. Ward erected the first building on the site,
a large two-room log cabin, roofed with sod over a pole framework.
This building still stands as the two main rooms of the house occupied by Stan and Robin Krause.

In 1905, Ward's quarter and the one adjoining to the east were
purchased by Fred Nelson, a rancher from Kibbey, Montana. In the
spring of 1906, Mr. Nelson and his brother-in-law, Magnus Bjork,
came up to the Red Deer to cut hay, then returned south to Sundial
on the Little Bow River to pick up their cattle. They drove the cattle
up during July and August; then Fred Nelson stayed on while Mr.

Bjork returned to Montana for his wife and two sons, Magnus Jr., and Clarence. When the Bjork family arrived they lived with Mr. Nelson, until a log house could be built on their own property, half a mile to the east. (This house, with additions is still occupied by the Bjork family.) Of the winter spent with his Uncle Fred Nelson, Magnus Bjork, then a boy of six, remembers picking up the insects which fell out of the sod roof, attracted by the heat of the house.

At first, the Bjork and Nelson cattle had free range, north of the river in summer, south in winter, but in 1909, as more and more homesteaders came in, Mr. Nelson took out a lease on ten sections north of the river and three sections on the south, while Mr. Bjork leased a matching piece of land to the east of Nelson's. This lease still forms the nucleus of the ranch, as it contains the river brush so valuable as winter shelter.

In the early years of this century the amenities of civilzation were only beginning to reach into the Red Deer country. The nearest post office was at Medicine Hat, and mail for all the settlers was picked up by anyone going to town. If the self-appointed carrier had a wagon he brought all the mail; if he was on horseback he brought only the important-looking letters. Often no mail was received between November and March, and Magnus Bjork remembers that his father and Fred Nelson, who subscribed to a daily paper from Great Falls, often received several sacks of newspapers alone.

Schooling presented another problem, as there were few families along the valley with school-age children. At first, a teacher was hired to live on the Bjork ranch and teach the older children; later, when Mr. Nelson's sons, Clayton and Adrian, started school, a small schoolhouse erected between the Bjork and Nelson ranch sites where both families attended. Part of an addition built onto the Nelson house around 1920 was a "teacher's room", a private bedroom for the current resident teacher.

The settlers themselves did much to make life easier and more pleasant. Mr. Nelson, utilizing natural springs rising in the hills nearby put running water into the house as early as 1914. He and Mrs. Nelson also dug up small cottonwood saplings along the river and transplanted them around the house. Today these fifty year old giants provide cooling shelter as well as beauty to the ranch house.

The original logs of the house itself were covered with siding on the outside and lath and plaster on the inside, and two major additions made to it; two bedrooms and a bathroom in 1914, and a new kitchen and teacher's room in 1920.

Mr. Nelson operated the ranch ably, and was known as well for the horses he raised as for his cattle. There were bad years as well as good and in the dry years of the 1930's, the bad years seemed to have swallowed up the good ones. In 1935, with even the weeds dried up, Mr. Nelson was forced to sell his cattle. Unfortunately, he was not able to recoup after this disaster as he had with those encountered before, for he died suddenly in 1937, and the ranch was sold. Of the Nelson family, one son, Adrian, is still living in British Columbia.

After Mr. Nelson's death, the ranch was purchased in 1938 by A. B. Dawson, a young man from Maple Creek, Saskatchewan. In 1938, the first crop in nearly ten years harvested along the river, and the ranch was on its way to recovery. Mr. Dawson, known to everyone as Bruce, stocked the ranch with Aberdeen Angus cattle, and named it Riverview ranch. During the thirty years of his ownership, Mr. Dawson added blocks of both leased and deeded land, to bring the ranch to its present size. Becoming interested in crossbreeding, Bruce introduced the exotic Brangus breed, and satisfied with the results, gradually converted his whole herd to registered Brangus. From that time, the fame of the ranch spread, as the Riverview ranch became internationally known as "The Canadian Home of Brangus".

A number of well-known ranchers along the Red Deer can claim to have belonged at one time to the fraternity of Riverview ranch hands, and several romances blossomed over the dinner table, between one of the hands and the current young lady employed as cook. Two couples living in the Buffalo district who worked at the Riverview are Mr. and Mrs. George Howe (nee Lorrie Brassard) and Mr. and Mrs. Leroy Callaghan (nee Racheal Skjenna).

In 1955, Mr. Dawson was married to Doreen Black and they have two children, Richard and Cheryl. During the Dawsons' tenure the kitchen and bathroom of the ranch house were remodelled and modernized, and two bedrooms were added. Doreen' sfather spent a summer putting in attractive patios and retaining walls of field stone, laid in the old-country manner without mortar. Also at this time extensive additions were made to an existing bunkhouse, resulting in a three-bedroom house for the foreman and his family. This house was occupied by Mr. and Mrs. Walter Heiland and their two sons, Robbie and Wade, and is now the house of Lorne and Kathy Krause.

Early in 1968, Mr. Dawson decided to move his cattle operation to Empress and his ranch was purchased by Reinhold Krause and his two sons, Stanley and Lorne. The name Riverview ranch, so long associated with the Brangus cattle, went with them to their new home, so the ranch was renamed Crooked Tree ranch, for some old cottonwoods along the riverbank which have been deformed over the years by spring ice.

Although the Krauses are new to this area, they are no strangers to the style of ranching conducted along the river, for the boys were raised on a twenty-five section ranch lying in a bend of the South Saskatchewan river west of Hilda, Alberta. They first came north in 1961 when Reinhold Krause purchased eight sections of grazing lease ten miles north of the Red Deer. (This land borders the Crooked Tree to the north.) This purchase was made from Ray Anderson, now cattle boss of the Vee Bar Vee ranch.

In 1965, Stan, having graduated in agriculture from the University of Alberta, purchased part of the "north place" from his father, and took up residence there. In 1967, Lorne also graduated from U. of A. and became interested in finding a ranch in the same general area. This search led to the Red Deer, and the decision by Stan and his father to sell the north place and join Lorne in purchasing the Dawson ranch. Both Stan and Lorne are married, Stan to Robin Baker from Cereal, and Lorne to Kathryn Thomson from Edmonton. Both families live on the original ranch site, while "Mom and Dad Krause", although officially retired and living in Medicine Hat, spend several days each week during the summer in the house trailer they have parked in the ranch yard.

FAMOUS HORSES

The world's best cowboys have ridden the Red Deer range in bygone days and still do and some of the best horses have roamed that range. "Bassano Boy" was a famous racehorse raised there and "Wild-Fire", "Hat Rack" and "That's All" to name only three of the top bucking horses from there. The following is an article written by Carl Weston Lybbert, and appeared in the Star Weekly around the early sixties.

During a late April blizzard, a sorrel mare gave birth to a colt in a brush-sheltered coulee by the Red Deer River near Buffalo, Alberta. The colt lived a normal equine life along with other colts on the ranch and when he turned three, he was broken to lead and ride. For two years he was a good "usin' horse" on the ranch — then something happened. Nobody seems to know what went wrong, but one day the little sorrel "blew up" and bucked his rider off into a clump of prairie cactus. The chagrined cowboy regained his feet picked the cactus from various regions of his body, and remounted. "Yuh can't do that again, yuh son-of-a-buck", he said between clenched teeth, and sank his spur rowels into the quivering sides. The sorrel gelding promptly "bogged" his head and repeated the performance, dumping the hapless rider into the same clump of cactus. From then on, the little sorrel horse bucked off all comers.

In an effort to bring him back into useful ranch work, the sorrel gelding was turned into a corral with another horse that had gone sour. Both received a substantial cut in rations. After a month of solitary confinement, both horses remained unridden; they chewed each other's manes off in an effort to satisfy their mineral-starved bodies which were now severly debilitated. One could now count the ribs showing through the rough coat of hair, and the hip bones protruded cruelly.

When the date for the Brooks rodeo arrived, the rancher (Archie Garrick) loaded both horses into the ranch truck, and hauled them to town. Reg Kesler, a noted rodeo stock contractor and owner of a ranch near Rosemary, Alberta, looked the two ponies over with an experienced eye.

"I'll give you 100 bucks a piece for them," he said doubtfully, "and another 50 if they're still bucking a year from now."

"You got yourself a deal, Reg" said the rancher, "I'll be back for the other 50; they'll still be bucking."

When the sorrel gelding came into the chute, the cowboy who had pulled him in the draw complained, "Hell, there ain't nothing to ride," his eyes sweeping over the shrunken frame. "What's the matter, Reg, did yuh run out of oats?"

"New horse," said Reg. "Take him out, cowboy, and make yourself a reputation. The man I bought him from said I had a bucking horse."

When the chute gate came open, the cowboy spurred the sorrel in the shoulder to "open him up". He spurred him only once. After the rider "hit the dirt," the sorrel continued to buck, kicking so high behind that the stirrups clapped together above the saddle.

"Get that flank undone," yelled Reg. (A strap fastened tightly in front of the horse's rear quarters is designed to make him buck.) "Don't let that horse buck himself out." Reg now eyed the sorrel with renewed interest. "We'll call him Hat Rack. A feller could hang his hat on him most any place." And so Hat Rack was launched into a rodeo career that is scarcely equalled by such notables as Midnight, Badger Mountain and the Mighty Snake.

Snake was a dark brown gelding raised by the Vanc Cleve outfit at Taber, Alberta.

After a few top performances at Calgary, Snake was purchased by Joe Kelsey, of Tonasket, Washington and, after 15 years, still thrills rodeo crowds. He receives top billing in any rodeo where Joe Kelsey is showing.

Badger Mountain was another Canadian bucker that U.S. head-lines with many outstanding performances at Calgary. Tim Bernard, from Moses Lake, Washington and Leo Moomaw, from Omak, Washington, purchased him and took him across the line.

After a couple of years he was sold to the Ring Bros., of Davenport, Washington. Badger Mountain was a bucker for twenty years altogether. In 1949, Ed Ring gave him back to Tim Bernard to be retired and put out to pasture. Many say that Midnight was the greatest bucking horse of all times. This coal-black gelding with unorthodox bucking style, stocky body and gentle nature, caught the fancy of the crowds. Women and children used to walk out from the sidewalk and pet this great horse as he was led in parades. From the time rancher Jim McNabb of Fort Macleod entered him in the Calgary Stampede in 1924, Midnight was destined for fame. Time after time in Calgary, Winnipeg, Toronto, New York, Cheyenne, London and other cities, he threw all comers.

Only a few men ever rode him. The greatest of these was Pete Knight of Crossfield, Alberta, who drew Midnight at the Montreal Stampede of 1926 and managed to weather the storm for a qualified ride. Earl Thode finished a ride on him around 1933. Weldon Bascom, once considered to be one of the top bull riders in the Rodeo Cowboys of America circuits, drew old Midnight at the White City Stadium in London, but was bucked off before they cleared the chute.

Now into the lengthened shadow of these great performers came a little sorrel gelding, with white stockings and blaze face. Unlike Midnight, Hat Rack has been ridden by many top riders. A cowboy who makes a qualified ride on him is almost bound to be in on the prize money.

For a ride to qualify, the cowboy must stay on for ten seconds. He must come out of the chute with both spurs over the horse's shoulder points (to open the horse up and induce bucking). Then he must spur forward and back continually for the length of the ride. Dull spurs are used so the horse is not scarred up.

To promote higher kicking with the hind legs, an "Australian flank" — a sheepskin-lined strap — is used. As the horse is turned out of the chute, the flank is tightened.

The rider is allowed one hand on his bronc shank (halter rope) but the other must be held aloft. If he touches the horse with his free hand, fails to spur the horse, or loses a stirrup, he is disqualified. A perfect ride earns 85 points for the horse, twenty for the rider. Two judges mark the ride and the average of both score cards is the mark awarded the horse and rider. If the horse he draws doesn't look good to the judges, the rider had to "outride"

329

the horse to get marked at all. If the judges so decide, the cowboy is permitted to draw a re-ride on another horse. No one has ever asked for a re-ride on Hat Rack, which makes him a desirable draw. His ability to kick high and crooked and "big behind" makes him tough to ride, but also earns top marks and cheers from the crowd. When Kenny McLean of Okanagan Falls, B.C., drew Hat Rack at the Denver Rodeo a few years ago, the judges' average mark was 83 for the bronc, 19 for the rider. A string of other near-perfect scores has won Hat Rack international fame as a top performer.

For the past three years Hat Rack has been held over for the finals at the Calgary Stampede. In 1961, Winston Bruce went into the finals in seventh place but his ride on the mighty Hat Rack put him out in front by a good margin and earned the pair of North American Bronc Riding Championship. Hat Rack missed the championship in last year's Stampede by a hair. Going into the final round Hat Rack was drawn by Leo Brown of Czar, Alberta. Their marks tied those of Duane Bruce of Calgary, riding a vicious strawberry roan named Red Pepper, but Brown drew an easier horse for the ride-off and won.

Two years straight, Guy Weeks, one of the world's top bronc riders, drew Hat Rack at the U.S. national finals in Dallas, Texas. In December, 1961, on Hat Rack, Guy spurred his way to second prize money. The same year, at the National Stock Show at Denver, Colorado, Kenny McLean won the second go-around on this fabulous little horse and chalked up top marks, competing against 150 of the world's best bucking horses and most of the top riders.

Sye Taillon, noted rodeo announcer, once said that Larry Kane of Big Sandy, Montana, could ride anything on four legs. "This boy has never been thrown," said Sye. "It's impossible to buck him off". Larry drew Hat Rack at the National finals and was thrown higher than a woodpecker's nest. Sye Taillon's only comment: "Well, nearly impossible."

No one knows what makes Hat Rack — or other top broncs who start out as saddle horses — buck. With some, it's pure cussedness — they hate anything on their backs. Like other greats, including Midnight, Hat Rack, is gentle of nature. He'll walk all over a cowboy with a pail of oats in his hand. He stands quietly while he is being saddled — but when that chute gate opens, he performs like a champion.

Reg Kesler has frequently turned down offers of $3,000 for Hat Rack, the best of his bucking string. Although the sorrel hasn't a reputation for bucking off as many riders as Midnight did, he has won more money — over $12,000 so far.

On rides that went the full ten seconds, he has never bucked out of the money. On others, many of the world's best bronc riders have taken up homesteads in some of the largest arenas in the world from the hurricane deck of Hat Rack.

From the shortgrass ranges of central Alberta, Hat Rack has bucked his way into the ranks of the aristocrats of the rodeo world. He now gets his three squares a day, winter and summer, and for this plush living he performs twice a week — ten seconds a day — during rodeo season. For the little Cinderella horse the ball still goes on.

Alfred (Alf) Campbell raised some very fine quarter horses when he ranched in the Buffalo area. His father, Billy Campbell, was an old-timer rancher in the Dorothy district around 1909, and was the owner of a famous stallion, originally owned by Ad Day, as well as many outstanding mares. Some of these mares were bred to a stallion named Sleepy Cat, owned by Jack and Allie Streeter of Stavely, Alberta.

It was this mating that brought the quarter horse industry back to life in Canada, and was the beginning of the big quarter horse business of Western Canada as it is known today.

Old Sleepy Cat died in 1959, but he was a legend long before his death and will probably hold the same position as Old Sorrel holds in the quarter horse story of the United States.

Old Sorrel is looked upon as the senior father of the breed in its era just before registration began, he was not registered, but Sleepy Cat was. Sleepy Cat was foaled in 1938, he had an ideal disposition. He was mild and tractable as a breeding or working animal and highly intelligent. He was named champion rope horse at the Calgary Stampede in 1945, he performed well and often as a cutting contest horse. He was a dun colored and weighed 1,200 pounds and stood 14.3 hands.

The quarter horse draws admirers from every walk of life — from the working cowboys along the Red Deer River, who use them as part of their business, to the millionaire who raises them as a hobby or a profitable sideline. The price of these horses can be as much as $7,000. One of the most influential quarter horsemen in Canada was George Cheatham, an oil man and who in 1960 was president of the Canadian Quarter Horse Association and in his line of brood mares were included a number of Streeter mares which trace back to the Campbell mares and the original Ad Day stallion.

To those who don't know the meaning of "Quarter Horse", to begin with he is all horse. The name had its origin more than 300

331

years ago on the North American continent when a versatile type or riding and working horse was required.

For years the prominent light horse was the thoroughbred, and most every old-time cattle rancher in the country owned at least one thoroughbred stud. By crossing these good stallions with cold-blooded mares, the result was the half-breed (half Thoroughbred and half Mustang). These horses were tough, agile and fast, and proved to fill the rancher's need for horse flesh.

As the thoroughbred was primarily bred for the racetrack, they were thought to be too fine-boned and nervous for ordinary ranch work; yet many a horseman will tell you that a thoroughbred will go further on nerve alone than most cold-blooded horses on stamina.

When someone bred a new strain into a thoroughbred line, a well-muscled horse that was extremely fast for a short distance was produced. Often horse owners would get together with their neighbors and staged short, quarter mile races. As the popularity of these races spread, so did the popularity of this short-coupled thoroughbred and thus the quarter horse breed was born, and soon became a recognized breed in both Canada and the U.S.A.

Donald McKenzie "Happy" Campbell (no relation to Alf and Billy Campbell mentioned before) who lives on the south side of the Red Deer River, just east of Buffalo, is well known as a quarter horse breeder.

Before coming to this area, Happy worked for 12 years with the Pat Burns outfit. It was while he was working for Burns that he met his wife Mary. Her Father was one of the old-time stockmen of the Airdrie district.

When Happy left the Burns ranches, he went to work with the Streeter outfit about the time they brought in the famous quarter horse stallion, Sleepy Cat. This horse instilled in Happy the desire to breed quarter horses.

Happy has registered quarter horse mares from such lines as Hancock, Saddle Tankin, Chubby, Newsboy, Narfleet and the mighty Sleepy Cat.

DICK IMES RECALLS EVENTS IN LAST BIG CATTLE ROUND-UP.

There were four roundup crews and wagons on the 1918 roundup between Suffield and Bassano and the Red Deer and Bow Rivers. They were the Bar U, Hill & Butler, Circle and Anchor P. The wagon bosses were Ernie Lane, Harry Herbets, George Crooks and Sam Howe.

We on the Bar U wagon worked with the Frank Hill wagon for a short time and Bob McIlvride (XL Bob) took over for about a week as boss of both wagons. I never heard the reason for this and no one else I asked knew either. Both wagons and crews camped together for about a week. We were always ready for the wagons to roll at sunup with cowboys walking their horses around to talk them out of bucking and to loosen them up for another pull on the latigos.

There were three of us riding a bunch of broncos from the Hatfield ranch at Pincher Creek — Howard Cowling and Clarence Blood of Bindloss, Alberta, and myself had all of the Hatfield horses split among us. Howard had Sexsmith, a brown horse with a white star on his forehead and a reputation as a bucking horse, although Howard managed to talk him out of bucking all fall. I had a big brown horse, a half-brother to Sexsmith that Howard voted the hardest bucking horse on the outfit after he stripped me of my boots one morning west of Lake Newell where we were camped.

Stone Roberts said to all and sundry grouped around me when I pulled on my boots — "The Old Kid might have ridden him if he had kept his boots on." I never knew the horse had a rep. Ernie Lane was in a vile humor as he had told the riders to get out on circle and they had all stopped on the first hill to watch the show. That was the first inkling that I was in deep trouble.

The same thing happened later out north of Cassils; only I knew what the horse — a sorrel named Bar U Fox — was like. The crew had started out east after a lecture from Ernie, who said he was not paying wages for them to watch a horse buck. But they stopped in a slough and had Clarence Blood stand up on a gentle horse so he could see what went on over the hill. Clarence told me later that about all he could see was my head popping up but he saw enough that he could report that the horse was rode. Dick Laswell picked us up, although he had trouble, for my right spur was caught in one end of my cotton hackamore rope. Ernie had told me, "I'll pick you up; if Two Bits can't catch him, nothing else can." He was on Two Bits, a bay Mexican, well known as a rope horse. It was killed the next year under Rusty Lane roping at Calgary.

Pete LeGrandeur had been riding these Hatfield horses most of the summer and they were supposed to be broke, but what they didn't know about bucking, Pete had taught them.

Mr. Lane came in one day and was there when Clarence Blood and I rode in on two broncs. The wagon was to pull out in about four days and this was a surprise visit to the ranch by Mr. Lane. There was a big crop of wheat and oats that had been irrigated and threshing was about finished. Clarence and I had been trying out those horses to get out of pitching bundles. We never knew Mr. Lane was there until we heard someone say, "I thought Pete had those broncs gentle." My horse had gone to bucking and kicking when I dismounted and it was all I could do to hang onto him.

There was a big poker game a couple of days later that lasted all night and until noon the next day. Norm Stafford, Herb Tweed and another gambler had come out from Brooks in a Model T Ford for the game. I heard that one of the men working at the ranch, farming was the big winner. He was the one who hauled the ranch wheat to Cassils using four horses on a grain tank with 150 bushels to the load.

We pulled out with the Bar U wagon about the 20th of September and finished loading out beef steers the 8th of November at Brooks. We loaded out a trainload, 12 head to a car, for Mr. Fares of Gordon, Ironside and Fares. The weather had turned bad and there was quite a lot of snow before we finished after dark.

Dick Laswell had to rope a big two-year-old farm heifer that had got in with the last bunch to keep it from being loaded. We had to get his rope off and it was snowing and cold. Dick called to me, "She is too big to wrestle down." I said, "I'll try it," and went down the rope. I got her down and had to run with Dick's rope when she got up seeing red and snorting defiance.

I caught the train to Calgary the next day and went with Archie Chadwick, a Pat Burns buyer who had helped load out the beef. Hill & Butler had to hold their beef about three weeks longer in bad weather and had only Pat Burns' word that he would take them. The war was over and Burns had to take 250 head of big cattle from Charlie Furman at Taber at $240 a head first. Charlie had no contract either, I heard, but Pat's word was good. The latter were big steers.

When we worked the Emerson Bridge country, we camped a couple of nights on Matziwin Creek, a short distance from Jap Fryberger's ranch house. Jap had an Edison phonograph and we all were over there one night. The next night there was a big crap game on and Clarence Blood lost most of his money and quit. The next morning a sorrel horse called The Fighting Sorrel bucked through the rope corral with me and scattered horses and cowboys from hell to breakfast. Then out a few miles from camp the sorrel had me about unloaded but bucked in under me and Jap was the only one who knew I was nearly grounded. About an hour later I was bucked off when Clarence and I were together. This horse couldn't stand a cinch and later on I quit riding him when the weather turned bad. We were on the CPR land all fall and all open land and a hundred brands to contend with. All of the stock were fat on the 1915-16-17 grass and all of it free grass. The PK Ranch said they had about 1,200 horses north and east of Brooks. We moved about 500 head of beef from Matziwin Creek to Cassils from 7 a.m. to about 3 p.m. I was captain as I was the only one who knew the country. We swung west of Duchess through where Jack and Alice Husband are located now. There were no fences nor anyone living there. We hit the CPR tracks and followed them about five miles to Cassils. There were four of us; it took one and sometimes two men to clear stuff (other cattle) out of our way.

STORIES by R. H. (Dick) Imes

A Texas cowboy who came north to the badlands of the Red Deer River 80 miles northwest of Medicine Hat with Lord Beresford's Old Mexico outfit in 1902 was Nate Schofield a tall courteous man will all of the mannerism of the old south. Nate stopped at our camp, the end of September in 1908, on the Blood Indian Creek, 15 miles northwest of the V Bar V ranch. He had a bunch of horses he was taking to a farming settlement near Stettler. They had been bought up by a buyer at Medicine Hat. He had help from the buyer to our place but was alone from there on, over 80 miles with no ranches in that big wild open country and no fences. During the night Nate's saddle horse pulled up the picket pin and he had to take a saddle mare of ours to take the horses to the horse pasture at the V Bar V while he went looking for his own saddle horse. They had been in our corral overnight. Nate found his horse after several days of riding hung up along the Old Mexico fence by the picket rope. Nate knew that country very well as he had rode line on 1500 Old Mexico steers during the summer of 1906. (It was near here that Sam MacKay, an old buffalo hunter, built a cabin for Lord Beresford on a lake named Cabin Lake, which got its name from the cabin which Nate lived in when he rode line on these steers.)

Nate got through with all the horses but the weather turned so bad he couldn't get back. However, about the middle of March he started out for our dug-out camp where he would only be a day's ride from the Old Mexico ranch. Nate put a stake rope on his horse at the head of Blood Indian and rolled up in his blankets. He was found later, by Jasper Demery who was driving settlers out from Brooks for Albert Maley, still rolled in his blankets. His saddle was pretty well chewed up by kitt foxes. His horse, raised by Gordon Forster on Berry Creek was found by Gordon along his pasture fence with the stake rope dragging. Our camp was where Leonard Grey's place is now. I was up there where Nate was found about a month later, at the head of the Blood Indian where the creek starts to between two little hills. The Mounted Police had gathered his 30-30 and scraps of leather scattered by the foxes so there was no sign of anything there. They buried Nate at Brooks I think. I know he was taken to Brooks. The stock of his rifle was chewed off by foxes. They would chew anything with oil on it.

Later in March, 1909 a man stopped at our place with a bunch of work mules on the way to Stettler. Steve Cicon was helping him and was to go through but he got my brother Montana to go in his place. Montana was gone over three weeks and I was alone. The silence in that wild open country was deafening. I could hear a cow bawling three miles away. Our cattle were near Cabin Lake and I could hear them plainly. Ben Howe came up and stayed three days with me and Steve Cicon stayed overnight once. I started out the next morning with Steve on his way to look for some horses and I was looking for cattle. On my way back the mare I was riding kept turning toward Cabin Lake where she knew our horses were. I slapped her on the neck pretty hard and she bucked me off and started for Cabin Lake. She had been getting oats so I put some gravel in my hat and kept calling and shaking my hat. She stopped and let me get hold of the reins. It was about five miles north of Cabin Lake and she bucked me off three times before I got there. I kept hold of the reins after the first time and caught a gentle old horse, Old Colonel, at the lake and turned the mare loose. Both of my legs were pretty well skinned up. Why I didn't lead the mare and walk I still don't know. That was after Ben Howe had went home. I was only 13 at the time and I guess Ben was afraid a storm would snow me in. The weather stayed good though. Ben was alone at their place too. His parents were in the Medicine Hat with Grant and Bob in school. Their place was about ten miles up the river from where the bridge is today. An old-time rancher, Mr. Gallup, lived on the south side of the river, his buildings were on the north side. I stayed overnight once with Mr. Gallup in May, 1913. He told me about a Metis boy of 14 years who got lost and froze to death the fall of 1906. The boy had left Gallup's place to join a brigade of Metis who were going north to the lakes and marshes east of Edmonton to trap muskrats.

They left every fall after working the summer for the ranchers. A captain was appointed and no one could join them unless approved by the captain. In this case Gardapee was the captain. The boy caught up with them 12 miles north of the river. The captain had sent him word that he couldn't go with them and waved him away. The boy was riding a good pony and evidently decided to make it on his own. Gardapee had a reward for some stray horses in sight when the boy picked them up. Jim Spratt told the boy where they were, not knowing that Gardapee knew where they were. The boy got the reward and bought some clothes with the money, two pairs

336

of overalls, a pair of four-buckle overshoes with four pairs of woollen socks, a coat and mitts and a good cap, but Mr. Gallup said he had no good underwear. A storm caught him and a rescue party headed by Jim Spratt, punchers from the Old Mexico ranch and others scouted that country for days. They figured that he had nearly reached a settlement up north but the storm had forced him back toward the river. They found his saddle by a frozen slough. He had discarded it to ride bareback to be warmer. His horse was found dead the next spring. The boy was never found. Two homesteaders from up south of Cereal in the same locality where the boy was lost, who came to a dance at Steve Cicon's ranch in the fall of 1911 were lost on the way home. They were walking the last stretch to their shack when evidently they became lost. One was found hanging on a wire of Kennedy's pasture fence the next spring. The other man was never found to my knowledge. That was a terrible country to get lost in. Experienced cowboys were careful not to get caught out there with a played-out horse.

Another cowboy who came up from Old Mexico was working for Andy Gordon. His saddle horse was found with saddle, bridle and catch rope. From the mud on the horse's legs and body they knew he had been in a soft place. They tracked him back and found the cowboy drowned in less than two feet of water. From all the signs the horse had been struggling to get out of the quicksand and had hit the rider with his head. He was knocked out and drowned.

He was a Mexican and had a complete Old Mexico outfit; silver conchos on spurs, hat, saddle and chaps. Andy Gordon was one of the men who found him and he told me all the details. He thought that his big Mexican hat had settled down over his head and on the water with the leather throat latch had shut off any air he may have been able to get. But being unconscious he would have had a slim chance of getting out alive.

When we travelled up from Bozeman, Montana in 1908 we crossed the Boundary line on the fourth of July at Spencer's ranch on Milk River and we crossed the Red Deer at Gordon's ford on July 27th. Ben. Lincoln, Kid, Grant and Bob Howe with Mr. and Mrs. Howe were at the river to help and we stayed at their cabin setting up a tent near the cabin to sleep in with the boys. They were line riding on their stock on open range north of the river. Montana and Dad had driven their cattle up in 1905 with Steve Cicon and Calamity Jane but we brought up about 25 head or more in 1908. Poor me was driving the loose horses with about 15 head of cows with calves. We had seen Lincoln and his Dad in Medicine Hat, so Mr. Howe was driving a buggy and Lincoln was on a saddle horse with a new rope buckled on. Linc milked a cow at home for

his Mother and she made us bread and milk once a day and didn't
it taste good to me. She made butter too from the one cow. Lincoln
had broke her to milk. I knew all the Howe family except Cud. I
only saw Cud a few times. I stayed overnight with the family in
1925. By this time Cud had a family of his own. In the spring of
1912 one of the Howe boys, Charlie was killed by lightning. He and
Alfred (Kid) were each driving a team of horses, hauling loads of
lumber from Medicine Hat. Charlie was in the lead with Kid close
behind him. We got word at the Stapleton ranch but too late to go
to the funeral which was in Medicine Hat. It was a terrible shock.
I met Charlie at Steve Cicon's in 1908. He had just come back from
South America. He was wearing a pair of big rowel S. America
spurs. A story about Charlie I remember was one time he had been
working in a lumber camp out of Kalispell all winter, when he came
out in the spring a man in Kalispel had a horse he said hadn't ever
been ridden. Charlie had on logging shoes so he had to borrow a pair
of boots and spurs. He rode the horse in the street and they collected
$50.00 and presented it to him. Alfred (Kid) had a similar experi-
ence at Lethbridge the spring of 1909. Someone had a horse that
couldn't be ridden. Kid rode him in the street on a $50.00 bet and
won the money. Someone who knew Kid put up the $50, as Kid was
broke. He had just come off the Waldron spring roundup and had
spent all of his money in Lethbridge. I heard Kid tell about that
myself. He said that his legs were all skinned up from that ride.

R. H. (Dick) Imes was born on November 9, 1895 at Bozeman,
Montana. There were five in the family. (But only Montana is
mentioned.)

MANY OLD-TIMERS AT ATLEE PICNIC

First such picnic was held in 1956 at Bjork's when they observed
50 years on the Red Deer River. Magnus Bjork Sr., came in 1906
and bought a ranch from Jim Ward, who was a squatter. Steve
Cicon came in 1905. Bill Kinniburgh came to Canada in 1899 and to
Atlee in 1920.

W. A. Wilson, came in 1912. He married the former Clara
Pound. They had four sons and two daughters. He joined the army
in 1914 went overseas and in 1919 he returned to farm until 1926
when they moved to Cartwright and later to Nanaimo, B.C.

W. A. Price came to Atlee as a foreman of the Cill Shaver
ranch. He took up a homestead in 1910. Price was one of the lucky
cowhands who got bucked off and was dragged by a foot in the
stirrup for several miles without being injured too seriously.

John E. Thompson, father of Bill Thompson, filed on a homestead in Atlee in 1911. He trailed to Atlee from Brooks fording the Red Deer River.

William Forrest Lawler and his wife Emily Mae came from South Dakota to Medicine Hat then to Atlee where they homesteaded in 1914, travelling with horse and wagon. Mae was a teacher and after her husband passed away in 1937 she returned to Chamberlain, South Dakota, where she went to summer school and began teaching again. E. F. Brown is now farming the homestead. Mae came to the reunion by aircraft and visited old and new friends. Gus Hanson homesteaded north of Atlee in 1912.

Rex Bunn had a homestead in 1914. He grew wheat and sold lumber to the homesteaders from Redcliff to Alsask, from Chinook to Empress. He also rafted lumber down the Saskatchewan River to Sandy Point, where the new bridge is near completion on Highway No. 41.

John (Whiskey) Johnson homesteaded in 1912. He is 84 this year (1961). He had the first steam engine an Advance-Rumely threshing machine in Atlee. He plowed many an acre for the homesteaders with the steamer. He came from North Dakota. He'd like to know how he got the name "Whiskey". They're people who have and who are believed to drink more of the stuff than he ever did. John tells that in 1917 Atlee had two General Stores, two lumberyards, one machine agency, a Chinese cafe and a poolroom all doing a good business.

Lewis and Morris Thomas homesteaded north of Atlee in 1911. Lewis tells that they hauled wheat to the two grain elevators in 1915-'16 fording the Red Deer before the ferry was installed. Morris returned to Wales in 1924 to farm their Uncle's farm.

Lewis was well known around the Atlee district. He provided entertainment (of a sort) at the old schoolhouse dances. His wife was a schoolteacher. The following is a story told by Lewis.

A man by the name of Mike Scheer homesteading at Atlee, had been away and came home unexpectedly one dark night. He woke up to find his shack moving. He thought he was dreaming or still seasick from his voyage from Europe. He opened the door to find hi-jackers with a four-horse team stealing his shack.

Minnie Parker flew from London. Her first visit since 1930. Minnie's father was a homesteader. He found he could make a dollar in the poolroom and post office. Minnie was born at Atlee. Len Stegen is now farming there. Len married Alice Holt whose parents also homesteaded at Atlee. Len came from Livingston, Montana and learned to ride at an early age. He rode with Jim Spratt of the Mike Stapleton outfit.

Now Atlee, like other towns, also had people who served refreshments and one Melvill Barret, Atlee homesteader had the reputation of serving the best. Melvill now lives in Vancouver, B.C. He was at the reunion.

Dave Sneddon did not know when he came to Atlee in 1918, to cowboy for John R. Gordon, Stapleton, Hannaford and others, that the good-looking blonde, Grace Bjork, would say, "Yes, I will be your wife". Dave tells this story about the time when he and Bob Howe were working for John R. Gordon. They were out looking for some horses in what was then the Earl Hayes' lease; they decided to have a rest. The day was hot and they turned their horses loose to graze. One of them bet the other he could turn somersaults down hill faster than the other. Forgetting about the loose horses, they frightened their mounts and had to walk home about nine miles, packing their saddles.

Lincoln Howe said he learned to ride and not trust any bronc when he was the youngest of the roundup outfit (just about 16) while with the Shannon and Kennedy horse roundup wagon, around Suffield he was bucked off and had to walk several miles to camp. After a couple of weeks, Frank Kennedy, the boss and owner of the "A Heart" outfit, said, "I'll bet you fifty cents you can't ride this horse." Just for entertainment Lincoln rode the horse and collected the money. He says there was nothing between the two rivers (Red Deer and South Saskatchewan) he couldn't ride at the time.

George Howe, son of C. B. Howe, resides on the Joe Sylvester homestead where the Pound reunion was held on July 8th, 1961, and which we understand is held every second year.

Mrs. George Howe (Lorrie) is indirectly a Pound, that being her mother's maiden name. (See George Brassard Story)

Ernie Aebly now operates the August Price homestead and others as well. He was born at Jenner and his wife is from Redcliff. They have five "cowboys" to help them ride herd and farm. Ernie's wife, Babe, is active in the Atlee Ladies' Good Will Club. She takes the boys to and from school when Ernie is busy.

Alex McLachlan, the handsome young bachelor, is farming the original Clyde Lynn homestead. Lynn filed about 1910, sold to Harry Truman who in turn sold to Alex in 1944.

Ben Squirrel is another handsome rancher of the Atlee district, and lives on the former Lyle Buxton homestead. Ben was born in England, came to Estevan, Saskatchewan with his parents in 1907, to Jenner in 1912 and attended school at High Valley, south and east of Jenner. He began ranching and now has a good herd of cattle and Arabian saddle horses.

Ben and Len Stegen caught quite a number of coyotes via a Model A Ford and fast, well-trained hound dogs in the dirty thirties. These two also used a sawed-off shotgun at times on coyotes.

With Ben is Frank Peterson, born at Parry Sound, Ontario, who has travelled around some. Says he saw the victory march in New York City after World War I (1919). He came to Iddesleigh, then to Jenner and finally to Atlee. He has been away from time to time, but has been with Ben since 1941.

George White came a year after his brothers, to file on a homestead a half mile north of where he now lives. His brothers, Fred and Edward, filed in 1913, Ed on where George now lives (sold to George for $300 after he had title). The George Whites have two sons and four daughters, the youngest son, Dave, farming with his parents. The older son, Cecil, farms at Jenner; the girls have left home.

Phil Dufort Sr., homesteaded here in 1911, we are told, and lived to be nearly 100 years of age. He had a family of ten children. Phil (Jr.) had one of the threshing machines in their part of the Atlee district.

Joe Jorgenson, who homesteaded south of Atlee, and Mrs. Jorgenson now lives at Kelowna, B.C., and did not attend the reunion. Their daughter Ruth (now Mrs. Elmer Johnson of Calgary) was an accomplished pianist and played in the Atlee orchestra. Other members, in addition to Joe Jorgenson, were Cecil Hyde, Del Pound, Don Pound, Gordon O'Brien, Mrs. Ellis Diggin and Alfred Johnson.

I would like to tell a short story that Elmer Johnson tells on himself. Elmer fancied the split ear riding bridles and used it while breaking and helping Lincoln Howe to break a string of saddle broncs for the Mike Stapleton ranch. Lincoln advised Elmer that sometime or other a horse would rub off those split ear bridles because of no throat latch. Elmer didn't think so and kept on using it. So came the day when Elmer's bridle rubbed off, at a time when he was courting Ruth Jorgensen. The only way Elmer had to get to Jenner was ride a half-broke bronc. Lincoln Howe went with him, and when they were out in the farm settlements travelling a road allowance, Lincoln edged his horse close to Elmer's and brushed the split ear bridle off the horse's ears. The horse was only too willing to drop the bit from his mouth. Lincoln then slowed a bit and kicked Elmer's horse in the flank — and Elmer was off for Jenner in high gear, pulling leather, hooking his spurs and shouting to Lincoln to rope his mount and find the bridle. Neither stopped and when they got to Jenner, Lincoln dropped a loop around Elmer's horse and asked, "How much for the split ear bridle?"

The following Atlee homesteaders did not attend this reunion

A. W. Wozeske and Mary Horne, young lad not named.

Mr. and Mrs. J. L. Groves 40th Anniversary Family Reunion. Groves family — F. Baldwin, LeRee Groves, holding son Leslie, Bud Groves holding son, Leon. Max Groves, Mrs. Max Groves, Gerald Groves, Mrs. Gerald Groves, Walter Heiland, Jean Baldwin holding son Gerry, JoLee Groves, Brian, Guy, Carol, Rob, Cheryl and Wade.

Edna and Mrs. Johnson.

Mrs. McKay, Mrs. Mary Silverthorne, Edna Silverthorne, Marion Silverthorne and Rena Monkman.

Sam Hillstead and Martin Gronmere on the W. D. McLennan ranch.

C. B. Howe, unknown, Laurence Howe, Len Stegen, Herb Miller, Bruce Dawson, Jim Walsh, Bob Stewart, George Howe Jr., unknown, Magnus Bjork, Ernie Abbey in Howe's kitchen, 1955.

Mr. and Mrs. Simpson, Bob and Ken, Mr. Smith, Dolly Smith, Mrs. McKay, Mr. and Mrs. Lute Edgington, Jimmy Scanes, Guy Dart, Allen Gatinbee, Mr. and Mrs. Ed Johnson, Ruth Edgington.

Russel Kulyk's first year at school 1955: Joan Anderson, Lily Ertmoed (teacher), Bob Seibert, Jim Stone, Norman Rubbelke, Wing Woo, Marjorie Stone, Sharon Jeske, Sang Woo, Bob Monkman, Gail Rubbelke, Bob Thompson, Duane Beglaw, Leona Stone, Garry Brown, Valerie Ertmoed, Dawne Biglaw, Lynda Stone, Russel Kulyk, Ray Brown, Melvin Brown.

Arethusa School year 1930: Bill Daniels, Harry Muzyka, Rudolf Kulyk, Olive Kulyk, Annie Kulyk, Dorothy Daniel, Stanley Jenks, Lily Dziatkewich, Marj Daniel, Mary Kulyk, Alex Duncanson, Annie Kulyk, Mary Dziatkewich.

Rachel, Ruth, Rena, Olaf, Ragna, Buster, Ada Skjenna, Mr. and Mrs. Olaf Skjenna Sr., George and Doris Mercer.

Chester Howe on his first ride, 1918.

Mrs. C. B. Howe (Eileen Elliott) at the tender age of four.

Four generations — Mrs. Dick Elliott with great-grandson, George Meyer, Edna (Howe) Meyer in doorway and Mrs. Eileen (Elliott) Howe in 1943.

Pals.

Bill Hendry and Slim Tillier at Cavendish.

Mac Meyer, C. B. Howe, young George Meyer in 1946.

This is Bill Mercer and son George 3 years old. Mr. LaFave and boys at Slim Tilliers place at Cavendish, 1935.

Herchel Gravette, Clarence Bjork, Clyde Jarboe, Chester Howe, 1971.

C. B. Howe, Josephine Mitton, Alfred Mitton, Charlotte Mitton, Abigail Mitton at the Mitton Ranch, Kalispell, Montana, March, 1957.

Mac Meyer, Edna Howe, Shirley Howe, Annie Dolback, Laurence Howe, about 1941.

C. B. Howe and daughters, Shirley, Donovan, Dorothy Cicon and Edna Meyer, 1966.

346

Laurence Howe with work horses, "Babe and Peg".

Right to left — Dick Steel, Carl Dziatkewich, Bill Muzyk, Mike Kulyk (Anton's son) lunching at harvest. 1928 model car.

Tom McCarthy left and Byron Nelson, two Red Deer River residents of the past.

Two whitetail bucks found on ice of the Red Deer River in front of Crooked Tree Ranch, December 31, 1970. The deer were very tired, enabling Stan and Lorne Krause to rope and throw them so they could saw off an antler from the smaller one, on the right, thus separating them. The larger buck was so badly injured that Stan, with permission from the Game Officer had to destroy him. The other one staggered off into the bush.

Iris Findlay, Grace McCarthy, Leroy Callaghan and Maxine (Callaghan) Nugent.

Rex Coltman at Victoria.

Chester C. Howe, World War II.

Pumping flood waters out of C. B. Howe's basement in 1965.

Peter Steen, Gus Hanson, Olaf Steen, 1912.

— A. Rodset, Bert Pousland, Ben Maime, Lloyd Hurst, Charlie and Grant Hough, Chris Christianson, Comet brothers, Irvin Dodds, a Mr. Ball who was a well driller in homestead days. Jack and Frank Dobinson (deceased) who were born in England. Frank, after being a street car conductor in Winnipeg, spent some time on a homestead here, then moved to Clive, Alberta.

Also Vincent and Richard (Dick) Ripley. Dick just sold out to George Howe and E. F. Brown a few years ago; he had a 70-cow spread.

And Anton Bunn, now at Verdant Valley, Alberta, and still farming. Ed Hogeson, also a man known only as Captain Seal, a former U.S. naval man and captain of a ship in World War I, who sold out to George White and moved back to Washington in 1925.

And there were the Hovacks and Steward (first names not known); Pete Smith; Mr. Little, who had a hardware store in Atlee and a rooming house above the store. Also Mr. Ahern, who had a lumberyard here, and Mrs. Ahern had a lunch counter. Mr. Hallam, homesteaded north of the Red Deer, a little downstream from the present site of the Vee Bar Vee. There was a post office for a time on the Hallam ranch which also was the site of a Royal Canadian Mounted Police barracks for a number of years.

Stories by CLARENCE (SPOT) BJORK

The Metis lived along the Red Deer River in the early days. They were the descendants of those who fought in the Riel Rebellion. Among those living there were Dick Larock, Joe Dumont (Joe and his father were killed at Duck Lake), Ed Cunningham, Alex LaFramboies, and Ward, I can't remember his first name. Some of them lived on the place now known as "The Crooked Tree Ranch". They built a log cabin which are the two rooms they now use as front room and dining room. Sam McKay lived just across the river from the Crooked Tree. These people used to have their dances in these cabins, some of them were pretty wild affairs. They used to make up a batch of brew, from buffalo berries and corn meal about a week before a dance, sugar and yeast were added to make it ferment. It tasted sour, but sure had the kick to it. Dick Larock was the fiddle player and when he played he sat on a chair and had both feet doing a jig. I can see him yet, in my mind's eye, as he played the Red River Jig. They were very good people to get along with. There were others who moved in, in later years, but they all left in the twenties as game got so scarce they were unable to make a living. The first few years the only white women along the Red Deer River, were Mother, Mrs. George Howe (Cud's mother), Mrs. Andy Gordon, Mrs. Hallam and Mrs. Clint Jarboe.

Another old-timer who used to live just a half mile north of where the bridge is now, was Henry Edger. He walked with a limp from a shot in the hip received while he and some others held up a bank in the Dakotas, when he was just a boy. He was the only one that got away the rest were hanged. Henry died many years ago in Calgary.

There were a few tragedies along the river in those days, too. A man was drowned in that little creek west of the Crooked Tree ranch. He was buried at the Gordon ranch, but a few years later his father had him moved to North Battleford. Clim Frogman was drowned in the Red Deer in front of this ranch. A fellow by the name of Alward was killed when he fell off a wagon on the same ranch. Another fellow named Scoffield was found dead west of Cicon's by a spring. He had unsaddled his horse for some reason. He was found with his saddle in the spring. This would be about 1908.

Some homesteaders were cutting hay in a slough and they found a pair of riding boots with the legs still in them. That man died with his boots on for sure. He was never identified. In later years, my brother Norwood and Clayton Nelson found a gun, sword and a muzzle-loading pistol all together in a coulee. The pistol is still at my brother, Magnus' home.

Jim Spratt and Happy Jack (Jackson) were well known up and down the Red Deer River for their pranks, as were the Howe boys. Jim and Happy Jack came to the Red Deer with Nigger John (Ware). Happy was a nephew of Andrew Jackson, a general in the Civil War in the States. One time Jim Spratt was going to Empress and had just got a new Model "A" Ford, he stopped and picked up Danny Hawkins on the road. Jim got going pretty fast and Danny was scared so he said to Jim, "They say the brakes on these things are not too good." Old Jim says, "Aren't they?", in his Texan drawl and stepped down hard on the brakes putting Danny into the windshield. Danny had enough of that foolishness and decided walking would be safer. Another time, Jim Spratt and Tommy McAlpine went down to a stampede at Bindloss. They both got tight and decided to knock over all the outdoor toilets. The R.C.M.P. locked them up in a cattle car on the railroad track until the next morning. Both Happy Jack and Jim Spratt used to carry forty-fives in the early days. One day Jack was up at the Jenner ferry and the ferryman looked like a monkey, or at least Jack thought he did, so he hauls out his 45 and drives a slug into the door jam along side of the ferryman's head. Another time Fred Nelson was coming from Brooks and was going to stay at Happy Jack for the night. Jim Spratt was there and both Jim and Jack were "high" and they were making hotcakes and when the hotcakes were ready for flipping the two were shooting them over. After a couple of tries by these men, Nelson decided it was no place for him and rode the forty miles home.

Stories by MAGNUS BJORK

In 1914 William McKay was arrested, by the Royal Canadian Mounted Police, for stealing horses. While riding on the train en route to where Bill was to serve his time, he told the Mountie he had to go to the washroom. The Mountie allowed him to go and Bill broke the window in the washroom and jumped from the moving train and made his way home. In those days several homes had doubled cellars. Such was the case in Bill's home and for two years he hid in his own basement. About this time the Mounties were looking for some men who had robbed a bank. When they met up with Bill, they questioned him as to who he was. They remembered his name as one who was wanted by the law. Bill appeared before a judge in Calgary. This was during the First World War, with the Hungarians as enemies of Canada. When the judge asked him who he stole the horses from, Bill said, "From some dirty old Hungarian." The judge quickly replied, "Why man you should get a medal. Case dismissed." It was after this that Bill showed me how he could hide in his own cellar without the Mounties finding him. In one corner of the basement there were some two by four's so arranged that one would think that some one was in the process of building a clothes closet complete with wooden pegs for hanging clothes on. But Bill showed me that by pulling out one of the wooden pegs there was a rope and by pulling this rope the trap door in the floor would open, giving access to another cellar and behind another wooden peg was another rope to close the trapdoor. The two by fours covered the cracks around the trapdoor.

Another such doubled cellar hid a home brew still of Pete Sulley's. This was very ingeniously hidden. It seems that Pete had a "privy" in his home from which a pipe extended up through the roof. By connecting the pipe which carried the fumes from the "still" to the pipe from the privy, he could get rid of the fumes so that the keenest nose could not detect it. One day following a "spree" in Oyen where Pete had gone with a keg of this brew and proceeded to get all the men in the district "well tanked up", for which all the women were after Pete's scalp and reported the episode to the Mounties. An officer had called at Pete's home many times before trying to locate his "still", but to no avail. But this time while he was searching for it, this officer noticed an identification

351

in the ground, this was where the pipe from the still joined up with the privy pipe. When he spotted this the officer immediately started shovelling and thus ended Pete's bootlegging days.

In 1907 a band of Indians of the Blackfoot tribe camped on the south side of the Red Deer River. There were 100 men, women and children, 25 teams and wagons, extra horses, teepees and tents. One morning my father missed his axe which he always kept on the north bank for opening a water hole for the stock to drink in. When he told my mother he was going across to ask the Indians if they had it, she told him to be careful or those Redskins would scalp him. As a youngster of five or six years of age, I was very anxious to go with him, but mother forbade me to go. Dad crossed the river, approached an Indian whom he thought was the Chief. He inquired about the axe and after a few minutes of conversing in their own tongue, a young brave told him they had returned his axe. It was behind a bush in the area where they had taken it from. No doubt if my father hadn't gone and asked about it they would have gone back and taken the axe from where they had left and from then on considered it their property. In a few days the ice was hard enough for them to lead their horses across single file and the men pushed the wagons over by hand. Every year the Indians would make a six-week visit to Fort Macleod from Prince Albert. This was the last year I can recall they made this trip.

MY IMPRESSIONS OF BUFFALO AND THE PEOPLE WHO LIVE THERE by Linda (Calhoun) Kneebone

I only spent a few months in this area, but I was fortunate that these were during the summer and it afforded me the opportunity to meet many of the people living there, as I attended several brandings and was there when the third "Old-timers Picnic" was held, hosted by Mr. and Mrs. Magnus Bjork.

I was very impressed by the people. They were the friendliest, most down-to-earth human beings that it has been my pleasure to meet. If you are a stranger, as I was, they do their best to welcome you and make you feel like one of them.

The people of eastern Canada, where I was born and brought up, tend to be more clanish and distant concerning strangers. They are friendly enough, but it's not the same as the friendliness of the western people, especially those on the ranches who are always ready to lend a hand where needed, and helping hands are often needed by the ranchers during the branding and haying times. I feel that I benefitted greatly as a person from meeting and living among these people.

352

While on the ranch, with my uncle and aunt, Chester and Helen Howe, one got the feeling of well-being as the slower pace of living afforded one the opportunity to just "look around" and enjoy the sights and sounds of that beautiful country along the banks of the Red Deer River.

I can fully understand why Aunt Helen loves that country as she does and why she felt that such a book as this should be written. I am looking forward to receiving my copy and reading about these people, especially about those whom I got to know so well. Such a person is C. B. Howe, whom I was allowed the honor of calling "Grandpa".

I recall one day I drove with him to the post office and as we crossed the bridge and was about to go up the hill on the south side of the river, we spotted a rattler, the first I'd ever seen. Grandpa stopped the car and got out and fooled around with the snake, using a stick, while I sat petrified in the car until he eventually killed it.

Linda Calhoun and Melvill Barret at Old-Timer's Picnic, 1966.

He removed the rattles and I sent them, by mail, to my mother. They made a very interesting conversational piece at her next W.I. meeting.

While there I became very good friends with the Stone Twins, Leona and Lynda. Little we thought then (1966) that Leona would marry my first cousin, Tom Calhoun, in 1969.

Speaking of snakes as I have and also of my cousin, I feel I must tell this story which, of course, I received secondhand, as I returned to New Brunswick before Tom went west.

It seems that when Tom first arrived at Aunt Helen's he was walking very gingerly around the yard and when she asked him if there was something wrong with his foot he replied, "No, but I sure don't want to step on any of those rattlers which Linda told me about." Grandpa Howe was there and heard this and being one to never allow the opportunity to pass without "helping" a greenhorn to become "climatized" said, "Don't worry about those rattlers, it's the hoop snakes you want to worry about". Tom, who had never heard of those kind of snakes, (who has?) wanted to know more about them. "Oh" Grandpa Howe said, "they're the ones which grabs their tail in their mouth and when they see a man coming they wait until he reaches the brow of a hill and then they come over the top and loop themselves around their victim." Apparently this satisfied Tom as he asked no more questions, but a few evenings later he complained about a sore neck, Aunt Helen remembering the story told by Grandpa and knowing that Tom had no reason to doubt the story asked, "You haven't been looking for those hoop snakes have you?" "Well I certainly am not going to allow them to catch me on the downside of the hill, I can tell you."

As I have said I got to know some of the people there very well and as I lived right in their home, I got to know my Aunt Helen very well. Oh I knew her before, but only as one would get to know an aunt who came east during the summer, when one is still just a kid, and then this would only be for a few weeks. Uncle Chester I had only met for a few minutes when he and Aunt Helen spent a week in New Brunswick, while on their honeymoon in 1964. But I did know my Dad, Aunt Helen's brother, and had heard they were very much alike, so I was more or less prepared.

But as I got to know Uncle Chester I found him to be a very mild, quiet-spoken man, whereas Aunt Helen was just the opposite. Granted she had been responsible for the raising, alone, of her five children, since 1952, and perhaps this added to her aggressiveness and when she wanted anything done, she never stopped to ask anyone to do it she would do it herself. One day she had been working all day in her garden and she was no doubt tired, as she was always proned to do more work than she should and as though there was no tomorrow. When Chester came in for supper she told him in detail all that she had done that day, ending with the fact that she had "set" three hens. Uncle Chester nearly lost his head when he asked her very queitly if she had got some eggs from one of her neighbors. "No," she said very annoyed, "I have eggs of my own." Her tone indicated she could certainly supply enough eggs to set a hen. "I know," said Uncle Chester, still keeping his "cool", "but you have no rooster." Poor Aunt Helen stopped in her tracks, with her mouth open, like a fish gasping for air, then suddenly turned and went to the hen-house in an attempt to retrieve her unfertilized eggs.

354

STORIES BY THE LATE JAMES R. HANNAFORD
DIARY OF A BIG-4 TRACTOR

I was shipped to Brooks, Alberta in the spring of 1913 and was sold to Jim Hannaford of Howie for the price of $3,800 — $800 cash and three $1,000 yearly notes bearing interest at eight percent till due and ten percent after due. I was a big, robust engine, my rear wheels being eight feet high and thirty inches wide and I weighed ten tons. My fastest speed was two miles per hour.

After being filled with gas, oil and water I started out for the Hannaford farm at Howie, sixty miles away. When I arrived at the Red Deer River at Steveville there was another tractor, a Rumely, that had crossed on the ice in the winter and was waiting on the far side for the water level to go down as it was going to Brooks to do spring plowing. It weighed seven tons and when it got on the ferry it tipped it up on end so the tractor backed off and gave up the idea of crossing the river that way. The ferries of those times were built to carry only teams and wagons and I was built for land and not for water. So I got cold feet and went back to Brooks and did the Rumely's plowing, completing 1,000 acres before May 15. I was hitched to a ten bottom plow and worked from daylight to dark, having no lights for night work.

After May 15, I went to breaking sod, pulling six plows and covering 325 acres. This was all custom work at $3 an acre for breaking and $1.50 an acre for stubble plowing. But my owner had bought me to break his land so back to that river I went after they reinforced the ferry with ten empty steel drums to carry my extra weight. My owner had to sign a paper to accept all risks. I was slowly run up on to the ferry and I must say the other bank looked a long way off, and there the deepest and swiftest water ran. The ferry pushed off, and glided smoothly for about 200 feet and then I felt it began to quiver under me. Looking back I saw my owner's wife and two little boys, two and four years old, kneeling on the bank. I then felt a steadying force that sent the ferry swiftly to the other shore. When we reached the landing and I went up the bank like a conquering hero a shout of praise went up from a dozen men who had watched the perilous trip. I hoped never to go on the water again!

We were soon on our way to the farm at Howie thirty miles away. The first job I did there was to plow a foot deep five acres for a shelter belt and garden. I could only pull two plows that deep, but the way those trees and flowers grew the experiment worked wonders. I then settled down to regular farm work, plowing and threshing, some years good some bad, but I never got tired and always willing to work. Then came 1937 when I was plowing a fireguard and going uphill, straining every bit of steel I had in me, when a connecting rod broke which really put me out of business. After Jim saw what I had done he sat down on the tool box and felt sorry for me. A neighbor came along and asked what the trouble was, and Jim said "I have lost my best friend!" The neighbor who was good at figures said it was time the old thing was pensioned off as it must have plowed 25,000 acres and threshed over a million bushels of grain. "Forget it," he said, and they went off and left me sitting there alone.

I sat there for about two weeks and then I saw a green, shiny pup come along. When it got close I saw it was a John Deere, jumping and prancing all over, not firing regular and not half as big as me. They hitched it to my front but I would not budge. Then they hitched it to the back of me and with a down-hill pull, I had to follow but it sure hurt my feelings to have that youngster pull me around the farmyard where they left me. Occasionally, they came around to pull out some of my bolts to fix other machines.

Then one day Jim and the two boys, who with their mother had saved my life when crossing the river 25 years earlier, (they were grown men now), came along and took me apart. My radiator was used for a soft water tank, my gas tank was put in the house for a pressure water tank, my pipes and oil tank were for a hot water system and my water pump was put down at a dugout.

There it pumped water over gardens which grew lovely flowers and shrubs. My big wheels, of which I was very proud, were made into stock water tanks. They were laid on their sides, six inches of concrete set on the bottom, and the bolt holes plugged with lead. It made me happy to see the satisfied looks on the faces of horses and cattle after they had quenched their thirst on a hot summer day. Also I was pleased to know that a Big Four tractor can still be useful after over a quarter century of service to a man like Jim Hannaford.

HOMESTEADING ON THE RED DEER

Just fifty years ago, in 1909, there were placed in U.S. and Canadian papers, ads for the homestead and pre-emption of lands in the last Great West or the Dry Area of the Palliser Triangle.

We had been farming in the Moosomin district for seven years with frozen crops and low quality grain. This dry area interested me and another homesteader neighbor. We decided to go west and we landed in Brooks which was the Land Office for the district. After getting maps and plans of land open for homestead we bought a horse and buggy for $50. We stocked up with supplies of food to do us for two weeks and started off for Steveville where we had to cross the Red Deer River.

At Steveville we met many homeseekers, some coming back and some going. There were all kinds of reports — some good and some bad. All were advising to stay close to the creeks as there was not a drop of water to be found, except along the creek bottoms.

So we went north on Berry Creek as far as Township 30 which was as far as the Brooks Land Office had plans for. Then we went along the correction line east till we found the Blood Indian Creek in Range 9. There we met two from Montana who had come up from the Red Deer River. They told us they had seen some good land down in Township 23 but it was in the Medicine Hat district and they had no plans for it. So we decided to go see it and went south on the line between 9 and 10. After two days we found the northwest corner of Township 23, Range 9. To help us in finding stakes we counted the revolutions of the buggy wheel which took just 600 for a miles.

We took two days and mapped the whole Township because we did not know what was open for homestead. That night a thunderstorm came up with a good rain and next morning the district looked better or the best we had seen. So we struck off west to cross the river again at Steveville. It took three days to make Brooks as our horse was feeling the hard trip on only grass. We sold him and the buggy for $25 as we were anxious to get to Medicine Hat. We got to the Hat about six in the morning and after breakfast we sat on the steps till the office opened at eight. We were lucky. The whole Township was open, and I filed on a ½ section. I also had a South African Script for 320 acres.

We were busy that winter getting ready to move in the spring. On the first of May we had three cars loaded on the C.P.R. and pulled out for Brooks, Alberta. Brooks was full of settlers from all parts of the continent all going to the new found land across the Red Deer River. We moved all our stuff to a vacant spot just north of town and put up a shack for my wife and two little boys.

We loaded two wagons and started out for the new country with hundreds of others. It was quite a sight in the early morning to see a stream of horses and wagons miles long moving along the trail. We had to camp at the river and wait our turn to get across, which some days took hours. On the fourth day we landed on the promised land just as we had found it the summer before, just bare prairie.

A site was selected beside a small slough of water which had accumulated from the winter snow. When we got back to Brooks,

357

expecting my wife to be lonesome, she was happy, having made friends with other women from Kansas and Manitoba. It took nine trips to the farm to get everything hauled. We had 15 acres broke and a two-room shack and a barn built as winter was fast approaching. We made a covered wagon and took the family out.

As we had a section of land we had to put in full-time — six months — on each half section, although most of the settlers were there only through the summer. My wife never saw another woman till the next April. It must have been a lonesome winter for her, but she never complained. The two little boys kept her busy. We got our mail every two weeks, which was the only connection with the outside world.

By the fall of 1912 we had quite a few stacks of grain, but there was no threshing machine in the entire district. So we built a hand machine to get enough seed for 100 acres to be sown in 1913. It was a good crop; so I bought a gas engine and separator to thresh it and the crop of a couple neighbors. The news soon spread and we had all kinds of job offered. So we decided to rig up an outfit, a cook car and bunk car. We started off for our first job at Dominion where J. Jacobson assembled eleven 5-acre plots at his place (5 acres was a homestead regulation). When the last sheaf was done the tally was 630 bushels, which was stored in all kinds of containers from washtubs to a piano box and sacks of all kinds.

Our next move was Collholme where jobs were larger, but we had lots of moves. I wonder how my wife did the cooking for ten men with so much moving and baked all the bread too. We threshed all around Chinook and finished up around Dobson.

1914-15-16. The country developed by leaps and bounds. Some farmers refused $30 to $40 an acre for their land. Then in 1917-18-19 the dry years came. The Government supplied the seed grain and feed and food (apples, cheese and fish) for relief. So many, broken financially and in spirit, moved out by the hundreds, leaving those who had taken root so deep that they could not go, to pick up the pieces.

Then a noted engineer, William Pearce from Calgary, saw our plight and suggested a remedy by irrigation. But as some other irrigation projects in the province were not doing so well, we could not get the government to favour it. The government made a mistake when it coaxed in the settlers who had come from all parts of the world — some with money and some without — but the best class of people that ever went into a new land to settle. The government made another mistake when they paid the cost of moving them out instead of helping to develop the land with irrigation. The soil is excellent. All that it needed in some years was water, for it will grow anything from corn to cotton. I have seen wheat grown here that weighed 68 pounds to the bushel, and two-year old steers come off this Gama grass in the fall weighing 1,200 pounds, ready for the butcher without a handful of grain. I also have a record in the Wheat pool office of shipping to them in 1926 five cars of wheat which graded One Northern with no dockage.

It's a great country — only needs developing — and those few settlers who have stayed will sometime hear "well done my good and faithful servants."

HOW AN ENGLISH CITY GIRL MADE GOOD ON A WESTERN CANADIAN FARM

She went to school until she was eleven, then she worked in a factory half time (that is, a half day in school and a half day at work) until she was thirteen, then worked in a shoe factory until she was nineteen. After losing her mother she decided to go to Canada, arriving at Fleming, Saskatchewan, in June, 1904, to work on a farm and get $10.00 a month doing housework. After harvest and threshing were done she went to Moosomin and got work with a town family doing housework for $10.00 a month. She stayed there till September, 1906, when she married a young farmer who had a homestead just south of town. She liked the farm and kept her end up by milking cows and raising chickens, for which she only got five cents a pound dressed and ready for cooking.

She became mother to a baby boy in February, 1909, the start of a happy family life when he was joined by a baby brother in 1911. The question then was two boys and only a quarter section farm, and they decided to go further west and get more land and a section was selected in the Pre-emption Area, 60 miles northeast of Brooks, Alberta, north of the Red Deer River. She stayed in Brooks the first summer in a small shack and made many friends with other homesteaders' wives from all parts of the U.S.A. and Canada while their husbands moved stock and equipment out across the Red Deer River, which trips took from ten days to two weeks to make with team and wagon. By the end of October a shack and barn was ready and a covered wagon fixed up to take her and the two children to their new home 60 miles from any town. It took just five days and just in time to settle down when a snowstorm came down from the north and with it came large flocks of ducks and geese heading south. The first winter was very lonesome for her, for she never saw another woman till the next May, but she never complained but was interested in her family and the great future of this new and good land.

359

The first summer passed very quickly as she had a good garden and helped with other farm work and by fall the foundation of a large house was started and a mail route was started to get mail once a week. By Christmas the house was nearing completion with three bachelor neighbors' help, and all were invited to have Christmas dinner with us. As this was the first Christmas away from home for one young man he broke into tears when she opened the oven and stood with a little suckling pig on a platter and he said that reminded him of his dear mother with the very same dish on her last Christmas before she passed away.

She moved into her new home in the spring of 1913 and she was busy unpacking things from trunks and boxes — things that made a house a home.

The crop was good this year and we had to buy a threshing outfit to thresh the accumulated stacks as the homemade hand outfit was very slow. The news soon spread that there was a threshing outfit in the country and farmers came from as far as forty miles wanting to get their crops threshed and we built a cook car 8' x16' and fitted it with a wood cookstove, table, benches, dishes, pots and pans and she went along with a horse and buggy to do the cooking as most of the farmers were bachelors and had no way of feeding a crew of around ten men.

The first stop was twelve miles north where a farmer had gathered the bundles of eleven other farms at his place. After the last bundle was done the tally said 560 bushels and stored in all kinds of containers from a piano box to washtubs and all kind of sacks. Our next move was eight miles north where one man had forty acres, then on to Collholme where the fields were larger as we moved closer to the railroad at Chinook.

After two months and the weather getting colder we were all ready to go south again, especially the cook as she had done a wonderful job of feeding the crew with so much moving and baking all the bread and cooking with wood and looking after two little boys, 4 and 2 years old.

The winter of 1913-14 was short. There was no snow till the 10th of January and as the area was getting more permanent with more neighbors, and the spring of 1914 came early with work on the land in March and to make the spring more lovely a daughter was born on May 1st. The two boys were delighted to have a baby sister as there were no other children in the district.

In the years that followed the land produced good crops and the house was fitted up with hot and cold water and electric lights. The C.P.R. built through Jenner south of the river which cut the market haul from 50 to 16 miles and made the outside world a little closer.

By 1919 she had added two more boys to the family which kept her busy, and as she liked to sew she made most of their clothes till they grew up and finished schooling.

The road this far had been hard and rough
And some of the days seemed very long
But her heart was good and tough
And the will to do was very strong.

And the years slipped by, forty of them, and we were back to where we started all the children married and making homes of their own. Then we decided to retire and follow the geese south.

We built a small trailer and headed south till we got near Mexico. We camped on the Colorado River just north of Yuma, Arizona, a beautiful warm dry climate and a good fishing spot, but my wife does not like to catch fish, only to cook and eat them, so she took along a sack of cold clothes which she tore into strips and made a lovely mat which she got a First Prize for in the Calgary Exhibition. We made five more trips and each time she got the First Prize. As 1956 approached we decided to celebrate our Golden Years, with family and friends and to thank the One who brought us together to enjoy each other these many years.

Yes we have had our joys and sorrows
Shared them all as well as tears,
Poor we have been, but not forsaken,
Grief we have known but never shame.
Father for Thy endless mercies
Still we bless Thy Holy Name.

A FAMOUS WAGON RACE

It happened back in 1915, the year that the country south of Hanna, Alberta, to the Red Deer River had a wonderful crop — 50 bushels of wheat to the acre was common. We had just finished stook threshing over 80,000 bushels in the Steveville and Cravath Corners districts, and had pulled the outfit back to the Howie district to do some stack threshing. We had set the machine in the center of four big stacks, which were a work of art, each one an exact replica of the dome of St. Pauls. The four pitchers who had climbed to the top of the stacks looked like statues in the bright early morning December sunshine.

Five teams and wagons were lined up around the long grain spout waiting for the golden grain, when for some unaccountable reason the engine stopped. I checked the spark plugs, and the magneto and could find nothing out of order, so started to crank and to crank this "Big Four" was a man-sized job — but no go. The five teamsters gathered at the engine to give advice and compare this year's crop to those they had in Kansas, Iowa and North Dakota. The more I cranked, the madder I got, and I must have called the brute something it was not. "Mr. Turner", our Sunday school teacher scolded me, and I told him to go fly a kite or something. I then gave the crank an extra quick pull. Then Bang! Bang! Bang! It started with a roar, so did five teams and wagons with no drivers, who were still standing at the back of the engine, all watching the best start of a race I had ever seen. Three outfits were neck and neck for the first 500 yards and kept on to the end of the half-mile strip of sod. The other two teams did not go far and were soon rounded up and brought back. We all got to work and by noon all four stacks were cleaned up, and ten wagons were loaded and on the way to the nearest elevator at Iddesleigh, 36 miles away. As we were walking to the house for dinner two women came towards us and Mrs. Yuill said, "That was our team in the lead, wasn't it?" and we confirmed it. Then she turned to Mrs. Wilson and said, "You owe me a quarter." After doing justice to a good dinner, Mr. Howie, whom the district was named after, said, "By jove! if that race had have been run on 'Epsom Downs' it would have caused quite a sensation, don't you know." Mrs. Turner was more interested in the number of bushels as this was their first crop in Canada, and when told the tally was 620 bushels from the twelve acres she said, "The Lord is sure good to this country." It was only a few years later that the Calgary Stampede ran its now famous chuck wagon races. Great ideas have come out of that homestead country. Its settlers came from all parts of the world, only to leave it again when the dry years came, but they took with them experiences of joys and sorrows which could only be gotten in a homestead country.

EXPERIENCES OF A RETIRED FARMER

In 1903 I took up a homestead in the Moosomin district, which was then in the North West Territories, and I bet the Canadian government $10 I would prove it up. Which I did, for in 1906 I coaxed an English city girl to help me make a home of it with me.

The first year she raised a lot of chickens. With the grain crop all frozen that year, 1907, we were depending on them, so we fattened and killed and dressed them all ready for the oven. They weighed over five pounds, so I took them to town but the storekeeper would only offer us 25 cents each for them. I said, "Nothing doing; we will live on chickens this winter." With milking six cows and getting 30 cents a pound for butterfat we got through. But with

362

frozen crops and then the rust in 1911, we decided to move to Alberta for a drier climate and it sure was. There were some good years and some bad. We have had fifty bushels of wheat to the acre, and have had only one; have sold wheat for 25 cents a bushel and for $2.30 in the first war years. Cattle prices have been just as crazy, sold for 1 cent a pound in 1930, and 14 cents in 1942. Taking the bad with the good, we have always been able to work out.

After 40 years we decided to retire and enjoy the fruits of our labor. I have always said a man should retire at 60, so as to give the younger people a chance. From personal experience after you have reached that allotted "three score and ten", you will find the mounds have turned into mountains. So enjoy the golden years from 60 to 70.

In 1946 we were back to where we started. Our family of three boys and a girl were all married and making homes of their own.

I had watched every fall the geese and ducks heading south with the approach of winter, but I had not realized what their call was till it sounded like "Come on! Come on!" The winters seemed to be getting colder and longer here, so we decided to follow the geese.

On the 2nd of December, 1946, we started off with a little house trailer I had built myself from many parts found on the farm. We drove straight south through Montana, Idaho and down to Utah till we got to Salt Lake City. We stayed a few days and saw the Mormon Temple and the large tabernacle which has that wonderful organ in it that we had heard and enjoyed over the radio. It is a large building and built without nails, all wooden pins, and you can hear a pin drop from the front to the back, 200 feet.

We headed south again for Nevada which was all desert but fair and warm and dry, and all down hill, till we reached Las Vegas. We visited the casinos where gambling is the main business. I did not know there were so many silver dollars in the U.S.A. as we saw there, and everyone trying to hit the jackpot, but by the looks on many faces I think they must have lost their shirts. Just as I was getting interested, for it looked so easy, my "better half" said "Come let us get out of here, it looks too much like hell to me."

Our next visit was at Boulder Dam, now called Hoover Dam. We went down below and saw the large dynamos, fifteen of them producing over two million horsepower of electricity, a wonderful piece of man's ingenuity, and supplying millions of people miles away with light, heat and power. The dam is 725 feet high and 1,240 feet wide, and it makes Lake Mead to a size of 145 thousand acres. It took 4,000 men five years to build and it's well done, a glory to man's brain and muscle.

We drove across the top of the dam and on east for about 200 miles, heading for the Grand Canyon. When we got to the park gate the ranger said you folks are kinda late, but seeing we were from Alberta, he said I guess you are used to all kinds of weather. After registering, he said, "You will have the camp by yourselves tonight, but be sure to see the sunrise tomorrow, 8 miles east of the camp, it will be good after a cold night." It went down close to zero that night. We were at Look Out Point before sunrise and the chart on the wall said it would be 7:30 that morning, and right on the dot we saw the world's wonder. Just as the sun came over the horizon and shone on the west rim of the Canyon it made us think of the "Heaven above and the earth beneath." Then every few minutes the scene changed in all colors and shapes as the walls of rock and soil are all colors, and finally as the vapour was coming off the river in colored clouds like huge rainbows dancing in the bright sunlight a sight never to be forgot, and we thought again, "What is man!"

Then we went to look at the far distant front, a visit to the cliff dwellers of long ago, a people no one knows where they came from or where they went. They built their places of abode in the sides of steep cliffs about 20 feet from the ground level, what for no one knows. They never left any records behind. They built their mud abodes with their bare hands. The marks are still on the walls. How they lived is a mystery because now there is no water for 10 miles, unless it was before the water went after the flood. There is not even any trace of any fire. They were of average size and skeletons found buried sitting up under the floors of caves. The walls are upright and still in good shape.

We went on to Indio where we saw our first palm tree with large bunches of dates on them and our first orange groves with flowers and ripe oranges on the same branch. The sweet perfume from these groves will long be remembered. We drove south along the west side of the Salton Sea which is 240 feet below sea level and gets only the waste water from the irrigation of the Imperial Valley which was one time a part of the Pacific Ocean till it dried up and is now the vegetable garden of the U.S.A.

This was our first real hot day and when we got to Kane Springs and stopped for gas my wife asked the attendant how hot it was. He said, "Lady, it was only just a cool 90." I said, "If it's 90 in December, what is it in July?" "Around 130," he said. I said, "How do you stand it?" He said, "You see that big salt bush over there, I goes under that and I thinks I am in the Arctic Circle."

We camped that night on the south end of the Salton Sea, another mystery area where there are large boiling mud spots, and as cold

364

as ice. The gas coming up is made into dry ice, and there are large mounds of what looks like molten glass. The rocks are all pumice and float around in the water. There must have been a volcano there at one time.

Next morning before sunrise we heard such a noise of thousands of geese all around us and we finally caught up with them. All the south end of the sea is a national bird refuge, and the geese were making good use of it and enjoying themselves and they have to be careful whose lettuce field they feed in because the shooting season does not end there till January 15th.

We got to El Centro in the afternoon, and it was all dressed up for Christmas then only two days away. The church bells were ringing and loud speakers were playing Christmas carols from the top of buildings, and everywhere the joy of Christmas was being proclaimed. We thought here was a little bit of heaven so we decided to stop and got in a nice trailer court just east of town.

Christmas Eve we drove around and saw all the lovely tableaux depicting the Nativity. One stable had a real donkey and the Christmas scene of Santa and his reindeer with artificial snow that looked real enough to remind us of Christmas' past with our children, but thankful to think they were now enjoying their children in their own homes.

We visited many parks and gardens in and around El Centro where all flowers were in full bloom. One place stands out, the Desert Seed Farm, with its acres of flowers of all colors being grown for seed and cut flowers for the eastern markets. We liked El Centro and its people so well we have spent nine winters there and on the same ranch. There is a large sign on the edge of town which reads El Centro, where the sun spends its winter. It is very dry here; some years they get no rain, and must depend on irrigation. The ten-year winter temperature average is 60. It is also 60 feet below sea level.

Their grain harvest is in April, so in March we thought about home. We went out to the Pacific coast at San Diego and north to Long Beach and Hollywood where we got on a radio programme, getting a mixmaster as a prize. Then on up to San Francisco where we visited the Golden Gate Park and across the wonderful Golden Gate bridge and on to Santa Rosa and saw the famous Burbank gardens. Then through the redwoods with trees 300 feet high and 15 feet across. What a change from the desert. We followed the Columbia River northeast through the Big Bend wheat country through Spokane, the Crowsnest Pass and Macleod and home in the middle of April, along with the returning geese and found it still winter.

365

THE TRAIL TO THE GOLDEN YEARS

The following wedding notice appeared in a Moosomin, Saskatchewan, newspaper in September, 1906: "Miss Emma Bromage, of Rushden, England, became the wife of James Hannaford, of Fairlight, Sask., at the home of her sister, Mrs. W. Flawn. Rev. J. A. Haw, minister of the Methodist church, officiated."

Arriving home by team and wagon next morning all was quiet and I thought the neighbors got tired of waiting and had left. I put the team in the stable and we went into the shack. But this seemed to be the signal for the shivaree and the neighbors cut loose with wash tubs, pails and bells and bedlam broke out.

My wife looked more like a scared rabbit than blushing bride, but I knew what was up as I had participated in similar affairs when two neighboring weddings occurred. The folks came in with cakes, cookies and lemonade and we all had a good time.

Over the years the district had frozen crops and then rust appeared. We had only 160 acres and two boys came along and we had to look ahead so we moved to what was then known as "the last great west", the pre-emption area of Southern Alberta. We settled on a section of land in the Red Deer River country, 80 miles southeast of where Hanna is now and 60 miles from the railway at Brooks. When I look back, I think we must have had a lot of courage. My wife never saw another woman from October through our first winter, until next spring. The homesteaders only stayed in the summer to do their six month duties. We had a section of South African scrip so it took all our time to fulfill the residence requirements.

When putting up hay in the autumn of 1912 my wife and two boys went along for a load. Coming home we saw the cow tethered in the yard and my wife said, "give old bossie a forkful." I took the fork and drove it into the hay and when I felt it go through something and the little boy yelled, I said, "My God, what have I done!" We examined him and found the tines had gone on each side of his left arm and through his shirt, only one inch from his heart. I put the team in the barn and we went into the house and my wife and I thanked God for His mercy.

In 1913 I was getting quite a few stacks of wheat and no threshing machine in the district. I bought an outfit and went as far as the village of Chinook doing threshing. The jobs were small as most farmers had but ten acres in crop. At Bigstone we threshed for ten different farmers in one day.

We had eight stook teams, a cook car and a cow, and my wife did the cooking. The cow was the main attraction and she went all the way up and back without a rope on her. The secret was that she had lost her calf in the spring and I had skinned it and stuffed the skin with hay and kept it in the back of the buggy and she followed it faithfully.

The next few years were bonanza ones with good crops. Fifty bushels to the acre was common with prices up to $2.00 a bushel. Land became valuable, many good houses were built, and also a school house. Lots of machinery was bought and the whole district was prosperous. Then the dry years came — 1918, 1919 and 1920, and the depression and the whole area went broke. Relief was provided in the form of dried fish, beans and apples and cheese. The federal government provided seed grain and feed, but 1919 was so dry that not a bushel was threshed in the entire area. Then in 1921 settlers were given free freight to move out and hundreds left, leaving buildings, schools, fences and unpaid taxes.

The job of establishing the few that were left was quite a problem and schooling was a major one and we then had five children, and no school. There were 16 children of school age living in what was four regular school sized districts. My idea was to build a school in the centre so that all had to go four miles. We put it up to Edmonton and they sent out the late Mr. Gorman who found that the parents were all willing to send their children to the central point. He thought the plan was all right but there was no provision in the act to carry it out. But we all went together and put up a building and asked the department to supply a teacher. So four school districts were formed with School Inspector Boyce as trustee and myself as secretary, and on June 1, 1920, we opened school. We carried on for four years and when a family in the southwest corner left we moved the school two miles north to be in the centre. We operated there for five years and had 26 pupils attending at one time. Then a family in the northwest moved out and we moved the school two miles east so as to be again in the centre. In the summer of 1929 a cyclone came along and ripped our old building to pieces and the department gave us a new one. It had been in operation for only one year when all the neighbors left and with three tractors and four teams we moved it to our centre and called it Vetford School. It served for many years as school, church and community hall.

In 1925, when Premier Aberhart was minister of education, he came out to investigate the school problem in the deserted districts. He placed the whole area in one big district under Mr. Thurber. This proved too much for one man and in 1926 the Berry Creek School division was formed with five selected trustees. At the first meeting I was chosen as chairman to gather up the pieces, for out of 70 schools only 14 were operating. I stayed with the job ten years, retiring in 1946, and we made a great improvement in education in that area.

In the autumn of 1927 we were 37 head of cattle short and we rode everywhere in search of them, even suspecting rustlers. Then a neighbor came along and said he had seen a cow frozen in the river, under the snow. We went down with ice saws and scoop shovels to clear off a foot of snow and there were our cattle underneath in the ice.

The years that followed this loss saw improvement in the cattle business. Prices rose to an extent that enabled us to retire to Calgary in 1946. Having reached the "golden years" we built a home and developed a good garden and one year were awarded a first prize for it. The best of all we were able to celebrate our fiftieth anniversary with our family and friends — fifty years of happiness, well spent for God and our country!

> Here's to the man who is wisest and best,
> Here's to the man who with judgment is blest.
> Here's to the man who is as smart as can be —
> I mean the man who agrees with me.

REMEMBER . . .

Since 1943, Magnus Bjork has kept a diary for each year and the following are some items of interest. DO YOU REMEMBER . . .

— in 1941 the first rattlesnake to be killed on the north side of the Red Deer River.

— in 1947 the first rattlesnake was in Magnus Bjork's yard and in 1948 the first bullsnake was seen there.

— in 1945 cattle prices were 7 cents to 10 cents per pound.

— the open winter of 1946.

— the very bad winter of 1948 with the most snow in eight years.

— in 1950 when the garden vegetables froze in August.

— in 1952 the ferry at Atlee was sunk while it was being taken out of the river.

— 1952, the hoof and mouth disease in cattle, or the cattle rustlers were active? Magnus Bjork lost 70 head of cattle during a three year period to rustlers.

— in 1953 road gravelled from Atlee to Buffalo in September and the Cereal road done in October.

— 1953 when baled alfalfa sold for $5.00 to $7.00 per ton.

— in 1954, the ranchers petitioned for poison to control the coyote population, which were killing the cattle and wild life.

— in 1956 the re-flooring of the Buffalo Bridge. The first "Old-Timers"

— picnic hosted by Magnus Bjork.
— 1957 Hutterites tried to buy the Vee Bar Vee. Bjork's bunkhouse blew up because of a gas leak under the floor.
— 1958 the big gas well at Johnnie Smith's blew out through the ground 300 feet from where it had been capped, the well water was contaminated.
— 1958 the hydro power was turned on. A plane crashed on the way to Calgary, three miles south of Majestic in a storm and three men were killed.
— 1959 Buffalo lost out to Empress on the paved road, when No. 41 Highway went by Sandy Point Bridge.
Chester Howe's hired man burned to death beneath an overturned tractor and the same day Micheal Kulyk Jr., was run over by a tractor and was seriously hurt.
Lynda Bjork was rushed to Empress Hospital with ruptured appendix, received transfusion from a Saskatchewan Hutterite.
— 1960 the Atlee ferry service was discontinued.
— 1960 when the Government increased the prices on Lease Land from 8¼ cents to 16¾ cents per acre.
A snow storm in April caused 15 inch drifts.
— 1961 the Empress Auction Market opened.
— 1962 the first school van took children from north side of the river to Buffalo School. Leroy Callaghan was the driver.
— 1963 the Atlee Post Office was closed. No one living there now.
— 1964 when the Wardlow road was gravelled.
— in 1965 the ice jammed at the Buffalo Bridge, ice cakes 30" thick and water six to eight inches in C.B. Howe's home. The same year there was snow in September.
— 1966 about 250 people honoured Mr. and Mrs. George Brassard's 50th wedding anniversary at the picnic at Jenner Ferry.
Lightning killed 14 of C. B. Howe's cattle.
Louis Cicon received bad burns to face and hands in a gas well explosion.
— 1967 Melvin Skjenna shot in stomach with a .22 rifle while playing with children at the Vee Bar Vee.
— Alberta Government Telephone crew laid underground cable for telephones.
— 1968 the temperature ranges:
>   January 20 - 52 degrees above,
>   February 4 - 50 degrees above.
>   February 10 - 46 degrees above.

Nicest weather on record for the month of February.

— 1968 telephones connected between neighbors on April 23 and to the outside world on May 5.
Community bought the post office building from Arnold Beglaw.
— 1969 the Pound reunion held at George Howe's in July.
Heavy frost in June killed new growth on evergreens.
Graves were discovered at the Blood Indian Creek of those slaughtered in the famous battle between the Bloods and Blackfoot tribes.
— 1970 dead fish were found in the Red Deer River, no doubt pollution. Chester Howe got .40 for yearling steers and .37½ for heifers.

FIRES TO BE REMEMBERED

In August 1943, a prairie fire started in the bombing area, approximately sixty miles south of Buffalo and burning north to, and destroyed the grazing of both the Atlee and Buffalo community pastures. Students from the local high school were given a holiday to help in fighting fire. Iris Anderson recalls that Mrs. Helen McGuckin gave the girls white tea towels to protect their hair. The bombing area had another fire in 1948, this time it burned for over a week.

In April 1949, George White had a fire get away on him and it burned from the railroad track to the river, a distance of approximately ten miles.

In August 1953, lightning started a fire on Chester Howe's flat which burned half of his lease and the corner of Magnus Bjork's, there were two other fires burning at the same time, one across the river and one at Cavendish. Later in the day a second thunderstorm struck with winds up to 85 miles per hour and heavy rains. This was the worst summer storm in Alberta's history.

In July 1957, there were three fires, two were started by lightning, one of these was on the 26th when Carter's barn, west of Cicon's was destroyed.

In 1958, there were four fires, one destroyed Bruce Dawson's garage and yet another, which was caused by a natural gas explosion, badly burned Alfred Campbell and his son, Allison.

In 1963 in March, the Atlee store and hall were destroyed during the night. The Garrick family living there at the time, barely escaped with their lives.

In 1969, Eugene Anderson lost his haystack to fire. On August 24, with temperatures around the 100 mark, the Cicon Ranch buildings were threatened when a fire started just one-quarter mile away, a creek between the fire and buildings is credited with preventing the fire from reaching the buildings.

The Empress Hotel was destroyed by fire the same day, and there were six fires around the Sunny Nook area, one south of Jenner and still another on the south edge of the bombing area.

In October 1970, goose hunters were thought responsible for the fire which destroyed 300 acres of grazing lease on the flat of Chester Howe's and Magnus Bjork's, before some 50 to 60 people brought it under control.

Old-timers all say there is only one way to fight fires in this country — that's with good neighbors.

BLIZZARDS TO BE REMEMBERED

In March 1951, it stormed so bad that Magnus Bjork had to make a tunnel to get to the root cellar. In April the same year, Lloyd Williamson, lost his life in a blizzard, south of Brooks, within just a few feet of his camp. He and a fellow from Special Areas were out checking the Community Pasture, when a sudden storm came up. The fellow from special areas gave up long before Williamson did.

In December 1964, the temperature dropped to 29 below with winds up to 40 miles per hour, fifty head of cattle died in the ditch along No. 36 Highway. Radio reported all roads blocked and that cattle were dying everywhere. In January and February, ranchers were forced to sell their cattle for as little as 1 cent per pound for dog food. Others lost many head. Bulls froze so badly they became sterile. Antelope and deer were starving. Deer would even eat from stacks despite the fact a dog was on top of the stack. Tunnels were dug through the snow from one building to another.

PROPERTIES BOUGHT AND SOLD

December 1957, Dick Ripley sold out to George Howe and Shorty Brown.

In August 1962, George Howe sold his place to Pete Kornelson and Albert Johnson, while Shorty Brown sold his to Ben Squirrel and Frank Peterson.

In 1969, Pete Kornelson sold to Mr. E. Burrus, who named it Majestic Ranch.

In 1919, John Foster bought the McFarland ranch and later bought the Jarboe and Fisher ranches from W. D. McLennan and in 1922, Foster sold the Jarboe ranch back to McLennan and the Fisher and McFarland ranch to Thomas Campbell, who in turn sold to William Campbell and his two sons, Alfred and George. Then in 1960 Alfred Campbell sold to Ray Egar, who sold to George Howe in 1962.

While the Jarboe ranch is now owned by Perry Minor and his sons.

In 1938, Bruce Dawson bought the Fred Nelson ranch and sold it to Stanley and Lorne Krause in 1968, and is now known as the Crooked Tree ranch.

In the late fifties, the Domelewski Bros., bought the Bushling homestead and in 1965 they sold it to Jack Thompson who sold it to Dr. Lipp in 1970. Jack still owns the place at the river which his parents William and Boo bought from George and/or Alfred Campbell, who had bought from Tom McCarthy. This place was owned one time by Henry Edgar and is now rented to Mr. and Mrs. Billie Campbell.

In 1961 George White bought out the Stewart Brothers.

Johnnie Smith bought the Howard McCullough place and when Mr. and Mrs. Smith moved to Brooks in 1969 they rented their place to Mr. and Mrs. Harry Dirk.

The Vee Bar Vee which is comprised of many of the original homesteads and ranches has changed many times over the years; some of the owners were, in 1959 sold to a Mr. Rider from Arizona, in the sixties was owned by Wm. Loose, in 1969 Lou Carey from Denver, U.S.A., and in 1970 it was bought by Ben Gay from California.

In 1960, Archie Garrick bought Jim Walsh's store at Atlee. It was destroyed by fire in 1963.

In 1969, Walter and Dorothy Heiland bought Woo Sam's General Store. April 1963, the Empress Auction Market was bought by Magnus Bjork, Bruce Dawson, Alex McLachlin, Pete Kornelson, Howard Jones, Bradley Crocker, Jack Longmier, Johnnie Ferguson, Frank Fowlie and Joe Dziatkewich.

FAREWELL PARTIES

April 23, 1957 for Mr. and Mrs. Fred DeWahl.
July 31, 1960 for Mr. and Mrs. Alfred Campbell.
June 22, 1968 for Mr. and Mrs. Elmer Nunweiller.
August 24, 1968 for Mr. and Mrs. Bruce Dawson.
August 31, 1969 for Mr. and Mrs. Arnold Beglaw.
June   , 1969 for Mr. and Mrs. Pete Kornelson.
August   , 1969 for Mr. and Mrs. Johnnie Smith.

EDITOR'S NOTE

In the preceding pages of this book, one can see how the early settlers and ranchers, came to this part of the country, with faith that they would find a better life and in most cases this faith was justified. Mostly because they were not looking for something just for themselves, but rather they were looking and planning ahead for the benefit of those of us to come after.

We owe these people much; more than we can ever hope to repay, for the sacrifices they made and the hardships they endured. But they, like He who made the supreme sacrifice, ask for no payment nor reward, but that we carry on, honoring and respecting their memory, ever mindful of our inheritance and by taking our place in the community, extending a helping hand to our neighbors and by living in harmony with our fellowman.

It is a good thing to give thanks unto the Lord, and to sing praises unto thy name, O most High. Psalm 92:1

As farmers and ranchers we realize that we cannot expect to grow good crops from the soil, year after year, without replenishing or replacing the growing power, such as fertilizer, nor produce good beef without feeding the cattle during the winter months. In other words we have to **do** or **give** in order to receive. Someone has told us this is what we should do. So by faith we do these things and would think it very unwise and foolish not to.

By the same token we should not expect the rain to fall, at the proper time, nor the sun to shine, both free gifts from above and both very essential for the growth of our crops, without our **giving** something in return.

He causeth the grass to grow for the cattle, and herb for the service of man: that he may bring forth food out of the earth. Psalm 104:14

One-tenth of all we have belongs to God and He has promised us prosperity if we will give Him that one-tenth, but for some reason we are prone to shy away from God's way, and stumble selfishly along as paupers when our faith and obedience to God could make us God's children and joint-heirs with Christ. Romans 8:16, 17.

Helen McHome.

INDEX